"You hold in your hands a smorgasbord of theological delights. *Daily Doctrine* is at once a daily devotional, a mini systematic theology, and a reference tool. It is deep but delightful, profound but practical, comprehensive but concise, and accurate but accessible. May the Lord use this manual to raise up more systematic theologians in our pews!"

Joel R. Beeke, Chancellor and Professor of Homiletics and Systematic Theology, Puritan Reformed Theological Seminary; Pastor, Heritage Reformed Congregation, Grand Rapids, Michigan

"A few years after I broke my neck, I wanted to know everything about God. That prompted someone to give me a thick theology textbook, which I read but had a hard time grasping. Oh, if only this fine book had been around back then! Kevin DeYoung has packaged the fundamentals of our faith in a work that is thorough, uncomplicated, and a lot lighter than your average theology book. In all my suffering, the bedrock of great doctrine has always been a comfort, and it is why I heartily recommend this one-of-a-kind work!"

Joni Eareckson Tada, Founder and CEO, Joni and Friends International Disability Center

"In a fragmented age, connecting the dots—between the biblical text and Christian doctrine, between different Christian doctrines, and between Christian doctrines and daily life—is imperative for all Christians, and yet many simply do not have time to read and digest the great classic tomes of systematic theology. This is where this book is so helpful. Using the time-honored genre of a daily devotional, Kevin DeYoung has produced a book that looks at the great doctrines that the Bible teaches. And in doing so, he enables us to grasp more fully the beauty and significance of Christian doctrine both for Bible reading and for how we live our lives."

Carl R. Trueman, Professor of Biblical and Religious Studies, Grove City College; author, *The Rise and Triumph of the Modern Self*

"What a great idea! Who wouldn't want to work through the major issues in systematic theology under the faithful teaching of Kevin DeYoung and structured as *Daily Doctrine*? This book will be so helpful to Christians, day by day, doctrine by doctrine, truth after truth. I am so thankful for DeYoung as a great gift to Christ's church. You will also be thankful for this book as a conduit for truth, doctrine, and spiritual health."

R. Albert Mohler Jr., President, The Southern Baptist Theological Seminary

"Those who care about their spiritual health would do well to read Kevin DeYoung's daily diet of doctrine. Theology at its best ministers understanding of God and the gospel, helping people of faith grow in their faith toward maturity in Christ. This is a one-of-a-kind systematic textbook, the daily doses of which are small yet potent vitamins for the heart and mind."

Kevin J. Vanhoozer, Research Professor of Systematic Theology, Trinity Evangelical Divinity School

"God's command to 'remain steadfast' and 'grow in the grace and knowledge of our Lord and Savior' comes with a warning: those who backslide fall prey to false teachers and heresies. But how does the layperson obey this command to grow in knowledge without seminary training? This book is the answer. Kevin DeYoung masterfully translates complex and necessary systematic theology into 'daily doctrine.' There is no more important time for lay Christians to be firmly rooted in systematic theology, and this accessible and trustworthy book will surely become a classic. I read *Daily Doctrine* devotionally and left each reading in awe of the majesty of God and the richness of the Reformed church's teachings throughout the ages."

Rosaria Butterfield, former Professor of English and Women's Studies, Syracuse University; author, *The Gospel Comes with a House Key* and *Five Lies of Our Anti-Christian Age*

"I cannot remember the last time I kept turning the pages of a book with so much curiosity, eager to find out what difficult question the next chapter would answer. The beauty of this book is Kevin DeYoung's ability to navigate the sophisticated scholastic distinctions that hold our theology together while making them sing with fervency for life in the church. This book is no mere manual but an adventure that charters that ancient course of classical Reformed theology. May this book kill doctrinal indifference wherever it lives and summon a new generation to revel in the deep things of God once more."

Matthew Barrett, Professor of Christian Theology, Midwestern Baptist Theological Seminary; author, *Simply Trinity* and *None Greater*

"*Daily Doctrine* is an extraordinary gift to anyone who yearns to grow significantly in the knowledge of God but will never enjoy the benefit of a seminary education. It brings the brilliance of a Kevin DeYoung systematic theology class to your favorite chair with a kindly blend of readability and rigor. An excellent companion with the daily reading of Scripture, this remarkably organized work will also be among the handiest of theology reference books long after it has been devoured cover to cover."

Paul McNulty, President, Grove City College; former US Deputy Attorney General

"This book is about systematic, doctrinal theology. If those three words make your eyes glaze over, fear not, my friend. This isn't Big Scary Theology for brainy people droning on and on with long-winded, obscure sentences. Quite the opposite, this is theology as it was meant to be. Not suffocating but lifegiving, not esoteric but doxological—ideal for believers wanting to deepen their knowledge of God in brisk installments. Here you'll find daily encouragement to know and love God forever and ever. Highly recommended!"

Hans Madueme, Professor of Theological Studies, Covenant College

"What a great way of reflecting daily on the triune God! This daily devotional inspires as it educates."

Michael Horton, J. Gresham Machen Professor of Systematic Theology and Apologetics, Westminster Seminary California

"Kevin DeYoung has been especially gifted by the Lord to translate complex ideas into simple truths. He has the mind of a scholar and the heart of a pastor, employing his academic gifts to serve the people of God with what Calvin called 'lucid brevity.' In this volume, DeYoung applies those gifts to the task of systematic theology, and the result is a clear, simple, and accessible articulation of Christian doctrine—helpful for busy pastors, overwhelmed seminary students, and interested laypeople alike. Even those of differing theological traditions will be well served by this faithful and spiritually enriching work."

Michael Riccardi, Assistant Professor of Theology, The Master's Seminary; author, *To Save Sinners*

"Your family and church will be strengthened and encouraged by reading and sharing these theologically enriching, spiritually uplifting, daily doses of Kevin DeYoung's accessible summaries of the great truths of Scripture."

Peter A. Lillback, President, Westminster Theological Seminary

Other Crossway Books by Kevin DeYoung

The Biggest Story: How the Snake Crusher Brings Us Back to the Garden (2015)

The Biggest Story ABC (2017)

Crazy Busy: A (Mercifully) Short Book about a (Really) Big Problem (2013)

Don't Call It a Comeback: The Old Faith for a New Day (2011)

Grace Defined and Defended: What a 400-Year-Old Confession Teaches Us about Sin, Salvation, and the Sovereignty of God (2019)

The Hole in Our Holiness: Filling the Gap between Gospel Passion and the Pursuit of Godliness (2012)

Impossible Christianity: Why Following Jesus Does Not Mean You Have to Change the World, Be an Expert in Everything, Accept Spiritual Failure, and Feel Miserable Pretty Much All the Time (2023)

The Lord's Prayer: Learning from Jesus on What, Why, and How to Pray (2022)

Men and Women in the Church: A Short, Biblical, Practical Introduction (2021)

Taking God at His Word: Why the Bible Is Knowable, Necessary, and Enough, and What That Means for You and Me (2014)

The Ten Commandments: What They Mean, Why They Matter, and Why We Should Obey Them (2018)

What Does the Bible Really Teach about Homosexuality? (2015)

What Is the Mission of the Church?: Making Sense of Social Justice, Shalom, and the Great Commission (coauthor; 2011)

DAILY DOCTRINE

A One-Year Guide to Systematic Theology

Kevin DeYoung

WHEATON, ILLINOIS

Daily Doctrine: A One-Year Guide to Systematic Theology
© 2024 by Kevin DeYoung
Published by Crossway
  1300 Crescent Street
  Wheaton, Illinois 60187

Published in association with the literary agency of Wolgemuth & Associates.

Portions of Day 52 are taken from "Discerning God's Will for My Life" by Kevin DeYoung in the *ESV Teen Study Bible*, © 2023, pp. 2054–56. Used by permission of Crossway, a publishing ministry of Good News Publishers, Wheaton, IL 60187, www.crossway.org.

Portions of Day 143 are taken from *The Lord's Prayer* by Kevin DeYoung, © 2022, pp. 40 and 41. Used by permission of Crossway, a publishing ministry of Good News Publishers, Wheaton, IL 60187, www.crossway.org.

Portions of Days 158, 159, 167, and 188 are taken from *Grace Defined and Defended* by Kevin DeYoung, © 2019, pp. 50, 56–57, 73–75, and 78–79. Used by permission of Crossway, a publishing ministry of Good News Publishers, Wheaton, IL 60187, www.crossway.org.

Portions of Days 164 and 184 are taken from *The Hole in Our Holiness* by Kevin DeYoung, © 2012, pp. 88–91, and 94–96. Used by permission of Crossway, a publishing ministry of Good News Publishers, Wheaton, IL 60187, www.crossway.org.

Cover design: Jordan Singer
First printing 2024
Printed in China

Hardcover ISBN: 978-1-4335-7285-2
ePub ISBN: 978-1-4335-7288-3
PDF ISBN: 978-1-4335-7286-9

Library of Congress Cataloging-in-Publication Data
Names: DeYoung, Kevin, author.
Title: Daily doctrine : a one-year guide to systematic theology / Kevin DeYoung.
Description: Wheaton, Illinois : Crossway, 2024. | Includes bibliographical references and index.
Identifiers: LCCN 2023056038 (print) | LCCN 2023056039 (ebook) | ISBN 9781433572852 (hardcover) | ISBN 9781433572869 (pdf) | ISBN 9781433572883 (epub)
Subjects: LCSH: Devotional calendars. | Theology, Practical. | Protestant churches—Doctrines.
Classification: LCC BV4811 .D49 2024 (print) | LCC BV4811 (ebook) | DDC 242/.2—dc23/eng/20240331
LC record available at https://lccn.loc.gov/2023056038
LC ebook record available at https://lccn.loc.gov/2023056039

Crossway is a publishing ministry of Good News Publishers.

RRD   33 32 31 30 29 28 27 26 25 24
15 14 13 12 11 10 9 8 7 6 5 4 3 2 1

To
David F. Wells

Who taught me systematic theology at Gordon-Conwell Theological Seminary

and who taught many of us—through his books and his example—
about the importance of theology in the church and in our world

Contents

THEOLOGY PROPER: THE BEING OF GOD AND THE WORKS OF GOD

ANTHROPOLOGY: MAN AS CREATED AND FALLEN

COVENANT THEOLOGY: HOW GOD RELATES TO HIS CREATURES

CHRISTOLOGY 1: THE PERSON OF CHRIST

SOTERIOLOGY: SALVATION IN CHRIST

ECCLESIOLOGY: THE NATURE, MISSION, AND ORDERING OF THE CHURCH

ESCHATOLOGY: LAST THINGS

Introduction

THIS IS GOING TO SOUND over the top but writing this book has been a dream come true.

I hesitate to share this personal anecdote, lest it sound like a humblebrag or just hopelessly nerdy, but here goes: ever since I was a freshman in college, I have wanted to write a systematic theology textbook. Granted, this is not a textbook per se, and it is certainly not as long or as learned or as sophisticated as the classic systematic works out there. It is also not as in-depth and intellectually conversant as the many fine doctrinal magnum opuses still being written. But for me, this is just the book I wanted to write (at least for now).

I believe my niche as a writer is translation—not from one language to another, but from one register to another. That is to say, I think I can best serve the church by reading the old, dead guys (and some living people too), digesting their technical arguments and terminology, taking the best of their insights, and then writing with clarity and concision for busy pastors, students, leaders, and laypeople.

In the spirit of John the Baptist, I confess and do not deny, but freely confess, that this is not a groundbreaking work of systematic theology. I do not press for any new doctrinal innovation or synthesis. I do not interact with the latest monographs and scholarly articles. I do not attempt to be comprehensive. And I make no attempt to survey all the theological options from the different traditions (e.g., Roman Catholic, Lutheran, Anglican, Anabaptist, Wesleyan, Pentecostal, liberal).

I am a Presbyterian minister, and while I am confident this book can be helpful for all Christians, you will readily see that my understanding of theology has been shaped by the confessions and catechisms of the Reformed tradition and by Reformed theologians like John Calvin (1509–1564), Francis Turretin (1623–1687), Charles Hodge (1797–1878), James Bannerman (1807–1868), William G. T. Shedd (1820–1894), Herman Bavinck (1854–1921), and Louis Berkhof (1873–1957).

Most importantly, of course, I endeavor on every page to be biblical. A big part of systematic theology is learning the proper terms and debates and distinctions. I make no apology for teaching these things. But the overarching goal in all this learning is to understand what the Bible teaches, defend what the Bible teaches, and enjoy the God whom the Bible reveals.

Choose Your Own Adventure

There is an old comedy skit that came out before I was born about Shimmer, the amazing product that is both a floor wax *and* a dessert topping. I've thought of that comedy skit more than once while working on this project. *Daily Doctrine* is not just one thing; it's at least three things.

1. You can read *Daily Doctrine* as a year-long devotional. Each day is around five hundred words and can be read first thing in the morning, at the dinner table, or just before bed as part of a daily routine. Instead of organizing the entries by months, I thought it would be more useful (and more doable) to include five entries for each week. Most of us, when attempting a yearlong discipline, need small breaks and catch-up days. Five entries per week instead of seven allows for that wiggle room. The days themselves will be numbered consecutively, totaling 260 (52 x 5), so you can read the daily devotionals taking breaks when you need them, or (as they are organized) you can read five entries per week each week of the year.

2. You can use *Daily Doctrine* as a reference tool. All the topics are listed in the contents page, so you can easily look up "original sin," or "impeccability," or "*perichoresis*" and get a five-hundred-word synopsis of the term or idea.

3. You can read *Daily Doctrine* straight through as a mini systematic theology. The topics are organized around the traditional systematic categories (often called *loci*). I've grouped the chapters under eight *loci*: prolegomena, theology proper, anthropology, covenant theology, Christology (in two parts), soteriology, ecclesiology, and eschatology. If it suits you better, feel free to ignore the weekly rhythms and move through the material as if it were a Tiny Turretin or a Baby Berkhof.

The pessimist could argue that this book is too many things—too deep to be a devotional, too small to be a reference work, and too streamlined to be a systematic theology. "Just pick a lane, DeYoung!" I hear you. But the optimist in me thinks the book can be stronger by being more than one thing at the same time. It's a floor wax and a dessert topping!

Bits and Bobs

Two quick notes about sources and citations and then some gratitude.

Sources. Because economy of words is critical in a book like this, I will refer to theologians without giving any biographical comment. If the names are unfamiliar to you, that's fine. You can consult the appendix where I give a few sentences about the people and resources I cite most often.

Citations. I reference Bible verses (e.g., John 3:16) and confessional documents (e.g., WCF 1.1) in parentheses in the text. The footnotes are organized by day for handy reference. Shortened citations are used throughout. You'll find full bibliographic information in the Works Cited section beginning on page 379.

It's been great working with my friend Justin Taylor and with all the talented men and women at Crossway. Thank you for taking a risk on a daily devotional loaded with Latin words and scholastic disputations.

This book would not be possible without the support, encouragement, and time provided by Christ Covenant Church. It's a blessing to serve such a theologically minded congregation.

Along with my full-time job as senior pastor, I also have the privilege of teaching systematic theology at Reformed Theological Seminary in Charlotte. Not surprisingly, much of this content began as course lectures at RTS. I'm grateful to my students and my colleagues for giving me the opportunity to teach and for refining my articulation of Reformed theology. In particular, I owe an immense debt to several of my colleagues in the systematic theology department (across the RTS system) who read portions of the book and provided extremely valuable feedback. Their comments improved the book in dozens of ways.

I am thankful for Barry Peterson's and Andrew Wolgemuth's support as well.

Most of all, I'm grateful for the love and grace from my children—Ian, Jacob, Elsie, Paul, Mary, Benjamin, Tabitha, Andrew, and Susannah—and, especially from my wife, Trisha.

The only one to whom I owe more than my wife is God himself. What a joy it has been to think deeply about Father, Son, and Holy Spirit during the years it took to complete this project. It's been a long road, but a good one.

PROLEGOMENA

*Preliminary Considerations
and Doctrine of Scripture*

DAY 1

Theology

The aim of Christian theology is to know, enjoy, and walk in the light of the knowledge of the glory of God in the face of Jesus Christ.

The word *theology* comes from two Greek words: *theos* meaning "God" and *logos* meaning "word," "speech," or "statement." Most simply then, theology is the study of God.

But surely we need to say more than that about theology. The problem with a basic etymological definition is that it makes God sound like another object we analyze and dissect, when theology for the Christian must always aim at more than bare facts and observations. That's why William Perkins defined *theology* as "the science of living blessedly forever,"[1] and Petrus van Mastricht called *theology* "the doctrine of living unto God through Christ."[2]

The goal of theology must never be reduced to merely getting right ideas into our head. The reason we care about theology, the reason we write about theology, the reason you are reading a book about theology is so we can *know* God more deeply, *enjoy* him more fully, and *walk* with him more obediently. We do the hard work of careful, precise, intellectually demanding theology that we might see and savor the glory of God in the face of Christ.

How then should we undertake the task of theological study? In four ways.

Biblically. We must test every theological conviction and conclusion against the Bible. While church tradition is important and human experience cannot be ignored, theology is ultimately not an exercise in explaining what the church has taught or what we feel in our consciousness. We must always search the Scriptures to see if these things are so (Acts 17:11).

Rationally. Reason is not the foundation of faith, but it is the instrument of faith. For two years, Paul reasoned daily in the lecture hall of Tyrannus (Acts 19:9). He reasoned with Felix and Drusilla (Acts 24:24). And he pleaded with Festus, "I am speaking true and rational words" (Acts 26:25). The truth of the Bible may be beyond reason's comprehension, but it is never nonsensical and irrational.

Humbly. We approach the task of theology utterly dependent upon God and eager to learn from those who have gone before us. Mindful of our finitude and our fallenness, our posture is not proud and puffed up, but prayerful and grateful. There is no room for big heads when learning about such a big God.

Doxologically. We learn that we might love. We grow as we behold glory. We dig deeper in doctrine that we might soar higher in worship. God is not just the object of our study. He is the one who reveals all there is to know about himself and the one in himself who is worthy of all our devotion.

1 Perkins, *A Golden Chain*, 14.
2 Van Mastricht, *Theoretical-Practical Theology*, 98.

🏛

DAY 2

Systematic Theology

In doing systematic theology, we are trying to answer the question, "What does the whole Bible say about this?" The "this" could be angels, sin, faith, works, law, grace, the death of Christ, the work of the Holy Spirit, or a hundred other things.

Many prefer the title *Dogmatics* to *Systematic Theology*. While *dogmatics* may sound pretentious and stuffy, it is in some ways a richer term. *Dogma* refers to an accepted doctrine of the church—the mature fruit of the church's reflection on Scripture—while *systematic* speaks to the way in which doctrine is studied. Both terms have their place, and Christians often use the terms interchangeably.

Systematic theology is a specific type of theology, having its own method and structure. If historical theology looks at how doctrine has developed over the centuries, and natural theology examines what can be known about God by reason and observation, and biblical theology traces big themes across the redemptive storyline of Scripture, systematic theology organizes doctrine logically around topics and questions. These topics are sometimes called *loci* (Latin for "places," the plural of *locus*). Systematic theology as we know it is only a few hundred years old, but many trace the discipline back to Origen's *Peri Archon* (c. 220). Philip Melancthon's *Loci Communes* (1521)—which organized biblical teaching around common topics— is often considered the beginning of the Protestant tradition of systematic theology.

There are many ways to organize systematic theology. Some use a key theme, be it love, or covenant, or Christ, or lordship, or the Trinity. None of these approaches is wrong. Traditionally, however, systematic theology has been comprised of seven main topics: *prolegomena* (literally "first words," where ground rules and the doctrine of Scripture are usually covered); *theology proper* (covering the doctrine of God, the Trinity, the decrees, creation, and providence); *anthropology* (the doctrine of man's creation and fall); *Christology* (the person and work of Christ); *soteriology* (how we are saved and how saved people live by the Spirit); *ecclesiology* (the doctrine of the church); and *eschatology* (the doctrine of last things, both personally and cosmically). Others make pneumatology (the doctrine of the Holy Spirit) a separate category. I've included *covenant* as a separate category for ease of reference, but it often forms the last part of anthropology.

Systematic theology is not the only way Christians can learn about God's word, but it is one invaluable way. It builds on the insights of church history and seeks to defend the historic doctrines of the church. Systematic theology helps us put together the whole counsel of God. Even more importantly, it helps us see more of God. Our goal must never be the bare minimum amount of knowledge necessary to get us into heaven. We want to move from platitudes to particulars, from generalities to technical terms and concepts, from seeing the hills of God's glory to seeing the mountains of God's glory. That's why we study, why we learn, and why we need systematic theology.

DAY 3

Divisions of Theology

Most of us think of theology as basically one thing: the study of God. But Reformed theologians have long understood theology to be comprised of various divisions and distinctions. The most influential approach comes to us from Franciscus Junius (1545–1602). His *Treatise on True Theology* (1594) established many of the categories, and set in place the basic outline, that later systematicians would use in defining and delineating the nature of theology. Junius's scheme is too complicated to examine in exhaustive detail, but the main divisions he employs are relatively straightforward and (once we get used to the vocabulary) extremely useful.

According to Junius, theology can be categorized as *true or false*. Technically, false theology is not really theology at all since it is based on human opinion alone. But insofar as we call it "theology," false theology can either be *common*, which is not disciplined by reason, or *philosophical*, which is aided by reason. Philosophical theology flourished among the Greeks and Romans in the time before Christ.

Not surprisingly, Junius spends most of his time discussing true theology. Using a distinction that would be foundational for the entire Reformed tradition, Junius taught that true theology is either *archetypal* or *ectypal*. Archetypal refers to God's knowledge of himself. This is the theology only available to God. Ectypal theology, on the other hand, is that knowledge fashioned by God from the archetype of himself and then communicated by grace to his creatures. This is a key point: only God makes true theology possible.

Ectypal theology can be communicated in three ways: by *union*, by *vision*, or by *revelation*. The first is the theology of Christ as the God-man. The second is the theology of spiritual beings and glorified saints in heaven. The third is the theology of human beings on earth. This last category is what we might call "our theology." It is the theology of pilgrims.

Continuing with his careful distinctions, Junius explains that God communicates this revealed theology in two ways: by *nature* and by *grace*. God is the author of both natural theology and supernatural theology. Natural theology is a type of true theology and a species of divine revelation. The knowledge from natural theology can be either innate (known internally by the book of conscience) or acquired (observed externally in the book of creatures). We can know true things about the Creator and his creation from natural theology.

But natural theology, especially on this side of the fall, is imperfect, uncertain, and unable to save. We need supernatural theology and the saving grace that comes only through the perfect revelation found in God's word.

Theology is not just one thing. There is true theology and false; the theology that only God knows and the theology he gives to us; the theology he reveals in Christ, in heaven, and on earth; the imperfect theology made known in us and around us and the infallible theology made known by the miracle of our speaking God. It is this last type of theology that we (mainly) study in systematic theology, and it is the only kind of theology that can save wayward sinners.

DAY 4

Religion

The etymology of the word *religion* is unclear. Over the years, many have agreed with Cicero (106–43 BC), who derived *religio* from *relegere*, a Latin word meaning "to gather together" or "to reread." On this account, religion is the diligent study of the things pertaining to God. Others have preferred the explanation given by the church father Lactantius (c. 250–325), which Augustine (354–430) adopted, that *religio* comes from *religare*, meaning "to fasten" or "to bind." With this etymology, religion is the binding or reattachment of man to God.

In contemporary parlance religion is often construed in entirely derogatory terms. Even by Christians, religion is supposed to be the opposite of a relationship with God. Or religion is about trying to earn God's favor. Or religion is about a stultifying system of rituals, dogmas, and structures. The problem with this disparaging understanding of religion is threefold.

1. This is a relatively new way for Christians to speak. John Calvin wrote the *Institutes of the Christian Religion*. Jonathan Edwards wrote on *Religious Affections*. Pastors and theologians, especially in the age of awakenings, often wrote about "religion" or "true religion" or "real religion." Our forefathers were well aware of religious hypocrisy and false religious systems, but they did not equate religion with works righteousness.

2. The word *religion* occurs five times in the Bible (ESV) and is, by itself, a neutral word, translating either *deisidaimonia* (reverence for the gods) or *threskeia* (religious worship). Religion can refer to Judaism (Acts 26:5) or the Jewish-Christian faith (Acts 25:19). Religion can be bad when it is self-made (Col. 2:23) or fails to tame the tongue (James 1:26). But religion can also be good when it cares for widows and orphans and practices moral purity (James 1:27). There is no biblical ground for making the practice of religion a uniformly negative phenomenon.

3. In castigating religion, we may be unloading more baggage than we realize. People tend to equate commands, doctrines, structures, and rituals with religion. That's why people want to be "spiritual but not religious." And yet Christianity is a religion that believes in commands, doctrines, structures, and rituals. As a Jew, so did Jesus. Jesus did not hate religion. On the contrary, Jesus went to services at the synagogue and operated within the Jewish system of ritual purity (Mark 1:21, 40–45). He founded the church (Matt. 16:18) and established church discipline (Matt. 18:15–20). He instituted a ritual meal and called for its perpetual observance (Matt. 26:26–28). He told his disciples to baptize people and teach them to obey everything he commanded (Matt. 28:19–20). He insisted that people believe in him and believe certain things about him (John 3:16–18; 8:24).

It's true: for some people *religion* means ritual instead of relationship and earning favor instead of receiving grace. But that's not what the word has to mean or has normally meant. In today's usage, being against "religion" usually means someone is against much that is important to Christian discipleship. We can easily give people the wrong impression about Jesus and affirm unbiblical instincts about true spirituality when we quickly dismiss religion as antithetical to the gospel and at odds with God-honoring piety.

DAY 5

Science

In some circles, Charles Hodge is most famous for this (supposedly) cringeworthy statement:

> The Bible is to the theologian what nature is to the man of science. It is his store-house of facts; and his method of ascertaining what the Bible teaches, is the same as that which the natural philosopher adopts to ascertain what nature teaches.[1]

Critics caricature Hodge as a naïve rationalist who approached his Bible as if he were on a treasure hunt for wooden and timeless principles. Those Christians who stand in the tradition of Hodge, it is said, treat the Bible like a dead insect to be examined or a cold collection of lifeless propositions.

But is that what Hodge really believed? For Hodge, theology was like a scientific discipline because in theological reflection the Christian must arrange the facts of Scripture in their proper order and relation.[2] Hodge never thought of systematic theology as the recitation of barren propositions. But he likened theology to science because he believed the work of the systematician was to show how all the parts of the Bible relate to each other with logical consistency and harmony. The question of whether theology is a science did not start with Hodge. Medieval theologians, employing traditional categories from Aristotle, talked about five types of intellectual dispositions: *intelligentia* (understanding), *scientia* (science), *sapientia* (wisdom), *prudentia* (discretion), and *ars* (technique).[3] Protestant scholastics agreed that theology was not *intelligentia*, which dealt with principles but not conclusions; was not *prudentia*, which was unconcerned with things to be believed; and was not *ars*, which was directed toward practical results but not to virtuous action. Some Reformed theologians like Francis Turretin and John Owen rejected the label "science," arguing that *scientia*—meaning a type of knowledge more than a distinct academic discipline—involved only self-evident principles to the exclusion of revealed principles. Other Reformed theologians, like William Perkins, had no problem calling theology a science.

By the time we get to the end of the nineteenth century, on the other side of Darwin, Reformed theologians were more uniform in their acceptance of theology as a science, and Bavinck is typical in asserting that dogmatics can rightly claim to be a science because it deals with true and trustworthy knowledge of God.[4] Likewise, Shedd maintains, "Theology, then, as a science of God aims to obtain a knowledge of him free from contradictions and is as profound as is possible, considering the nature of the subject and the limitations of the human mind."[5] Theology is a science insofar as it deals with true knowledge, entails inductive analysis, and seeks to gather biblical facts and conclusions into a unified whole.

1   Hodge, *Systematic Theology*, 1:10.
2   Hodge, *Systematic Theology*, 1:19.
3   Muller, *Post-Reformation Reformed Dogmatics*, 1:324–40.
4   Bavinck, *Reformed Dogmatics*, 1:42–43.
5   Shedd, *Dogmatic Theology*, 56.

WEEK 2

DAY 6

Speculative or Practical?

The question is an old one but surprisingly relevant: Is theology chiefly speculative or practical?

From our vantage point, the answer seems obvious. Surely theology must be practical. It must result in faith and obedience. It must bear fruit. The great danger, we are apt to think, is that too much of our theological discourse has become hopelessly theoretical and needlessly esoteric, good for nothing but puffing up small-hearted people with big brains.

And yet the question is not as simple as it sounds. Thomas Aquinas argued that sacred doctrine is more of a speculative science because practical science is concerned with human operations, while Christian theology is chiefly concerned with God. The goal of theology, he maintained, is "the perfect knowledge of God, in which consists eternal bliss."[1] I appreciate Aquinas's emphasis on the knowledge of God for its own sake, but we can still say with Francis Turretin that true theology is "mixed," partly theoretical and partly practical.[2]

We can understand the practical side of the equation. The mysteries of the faith "are impulsive to operation." That is, they are meant to incite us to love and worship. "A practical system is that which does not consist in the knowledge of a thing alone, but in its very nature and by itself goes forth into practice and has operation for its object." Right doctrine counts for nothing if it does not sink into our hearts and find expression in our lives. We want a knowledge of the truth that leads to godliness (Titus 1:1).

But theology is also theoretical. This is not a pejorative term for Turretin. Rather, "a theoretical system is that which is occupied in contemplation alone and has no other object than knowledge." Here Turretin is affirming that we have something to learn from the Thomist emphasis on the beatific vision (i.e., beholding God face-to-face). Knowing the truth and reveling in the truth are worthwhile in themselves (Jer. 31:34; John 17:13). A sermon without any application can still be a life-changing sermon if it causes us to see the glory of God in the face of Christ.

Turretin feared that heretical groups in his day were keen to make theology exclusively practical so as to minimize the doctrines of the Trinity and the incarnation and to pave the way for a universalist religion of good deeds. By contrast, Turretin insisted that knowing what is right and doing what is right must never be separated. The Christian faith unites theory and practice. Theology is theoretical insofar as it points us to God as the chief end in all our knowing and delighting, but we also insist that this *beholding* should result in us *becoming* more like Christ.

1 Aquinas, *Summa Theologica*, 1.1.4.
2 Turretin, *Elenctic Theology*, 1:20–23. These pages include all the Turretin quotations in this week.

Ad Fontes

Ad fontes is a Latin phrase meaning "to the sources," or literally "to the fountains." It comes from the Vulgate version of Psalm 42:1. The Vulgate was the Latin Bible used almost exclusively in the church for a thousand years, until men like William Tyndale and Martin Luther began to translate the Bible in the common language of the people. During the Reformation this little phrase, *ad fontes*, became a rallying cry for those who wanted Christian learning to go back to the sources, back to the original fountains, which meant back to the Greeks and the ancient writers and ultimately back to the Scriptures themselves.

This impulse came from the humanist movement that grew out of the Renaissance in Italy in the fourteenth and fifteenth centuries. This form of humanism—as opposed to today's secular humanism—was a reaction against the scholasticism that was dominant in the twelfth and thirteenth centuries. Scholasticism and humanism were diverse and overlapped in some ways. But in broad terms, the two movements differed in their approach to education and in what they saw as the goals of education.

The scholastics approached their subject by comparing the views of past authorities. The task was to sift through the tradition and learn to harmonize divergent viewpoints. The result was often dense intellectual inquiry and speculation. It was a method of education suited for professional lawyers, doctors, and theologians. The humanists, by contrast, wanted to be practical, edifying, and useful. They had little patience for speculation. They read classical authors in the original languages and urged the study of ancient authors, not just commentaries on those authors.

Humanism was not a set of philosophical beliefs, but a set of intellectual interests, specifically about the value of classical antiquity. It gets this name partly because of a renewed emphasis on the human person, but mostly because of its insistence on studying the humanities, which was the general term for the study of history, grammar, rhetoric, poetry, and moral philosophy. In each of these subjects the humanists wanted to revive the legacy of classical antiquity, skip over the scholastic commentaries, and go back to the original fountains (*ad fontes*).

The humanist movement was not without its weaknesses. At its worst, leading humanists were concerned about what was helpful over what was true and could give priority to good living and civic usefulness over doctrinal defense. And yet humanism laid the groundwork for some of the most important advances of the Reformation. Influenced by humanists like Erasmus of Rotterdam (1466–1536) and Jacques Lefèvre d'Etaples (1455–1536), the Reformers emphasized close attention to texts (the older the better), prioritized education for the laity, and sought a practical combination of head and heart. Humanist-inspired Reformers like John Calvin devoted their lives to the text of Scripture and cultivated an educational and ecclesiastical environment where such word-centered devotion would flourish for centuries to come.

DAY 8

Principia

In philosophy, a *principium* is a fundamental or foundational principle. The plural *principia* has often been used to describe truths that are self-evident and from which other truths can be known or derived. The corresponding Greek term *arche*, when used philosophically, refers to the same thing—a first principle or a primary source.[1]

We can distinguish between two kinds of *principia*. First, there are principles of being (*principia essendi*). These principles form the ground or basis by which something is. Second, there are principles of knowledge (*principia cognoscendi*). These are the principles by which something is known. The first type of *principia* has to do with essence (how things exist), and the second has to do with cognition (how we understand the things that exist). The principles of knowledge can be further divided into the *principium cognoscendi externum* (the external source of knowledge outside ourselves) and the *principium cognoscendi internum* (the way in which knowledge is internally apprehended).

According to the Reformed scholastic tradition, these three categories—*essendi*, *externum*, *internum*—help us understand how to approach every kind of science.

For nontheological sciences, the *principium essendi* is God. He is the ultimate source and fountain of all our knowledge. He is also the reason for the existence of the created world. Everything that is, is because God is. The *principium cognoscendi externum* in the nontheological sciences is God's creation (whether in nature or in man). The *principium cognoscendi internum* is human reason. That is to say, we apprehend the knowledge available to us in God's creation by the intellectual activity of the human mind.

In theology, God is once again the *principium essendi*. All our knowledge of God is rooted in God himself. Only God knows God fully. Everything we know about God is because the one with archetypal knowledge has chosen to make himself known in ectypal fashion.

For the task of theology, special revelation is our *principium cognoscendi externum*. Our authoritative textbook is not the world, our thoughts, or our experiences, but the Bible. Whatever we know by general revelation must be clarified, confirmed, or critiqued by the clearer knowledge we gain through special revelation. Natural theology is a species of true theology, but special revelation is required to interpret it fully and adequately employ it.

Finally, when it comes to theology, faith is the *principium cognoscendi internum*. By faith we accept God's revelation as true, we embrace it as having authority in every area on which it speaks, and we respond in obedience and worship. We receive God's word about himself not by empirical observation, or speculative reason, or by personal experience or religious consciousness. Faith is the organ by which God's special revelation can, and must, be received. We know God because God chooses to be known, and what he has chosen to be known must be believed in order to be truly understood.

---

1 My discussion of *principia* summarizes many of the definitions and categories found in Berkhof, *Introductory Volume*, 93–186. Berkhof's exploration is a distillation of Bavinck, *Reformed Dogmatics*, 207–621.

DAY 9

Faith and Reason

Over the years, many people—both friends and foes of Christianity—have talked about faith and reason as if the two were mutually exclusive opposites in perpetual war with one another. And yet the best theologians of the church have always insisted that faith and reason, though operative in Christianity in different ways, are ultimately not in conflict. This is not a modern idea or an Enlightenment conviction. Rather, it has been the witness of the historic Christian tradition that when used properly, reason is a support, and not a threat, to genuine faith.

Here, then, are six propositions about faith and reason. All quotations below come from Francis Turretin, who modeled as well as any Reformed theologian a rational faith that never gave way to rationalism.

1. Human reason is not the rule by which the doctrines of Christianity are to be judged. "The proper rule of things to be believed and disbelieved is not the apprehension of their possibility or impossibility, but the word of God."[1]

2. Reason does not have a principal office in matters of faith, but an instrumental one. Reason does not tell us whether something is to be believed, but it is the instrument we use in understanding and explaining what ought to be believed.

3. Because reason is properly used in an instrumental sense, we are right to draw necessary consequences from the teaching of Scripture. Jesus and the apostles did this all the time (e.g., when Christ proved against the Sadducees the resurrection because God is the God of the living and not the dead). Likewise, the judgment of noncontradiction can be properly brought to bear on matters of Christian faith.

4. Reason does not carry a primary force in religious debate, but it can be used in a secondary or auxiliary sense. Christian truths are received in faith, but not a blind faith. Our beliefs are supported and defended by reason.

5. "Reason is perfected by faith and faith supposes reason, upon which to found the mysteries of faith."[2] This is another way of saying that we do not build Christianity upon reason, but we cannot comprehend the faith or explain it without using reason. We must distinguish between an incomprehensible thing (which cannot be grasped) and an impossible thing (which cannot be conceived). "Although every truth cannot be demonstrated by reason . . . yet no lie against the truth can be sheltered under the protection of true reason."[3]

6. Philosophical reasoning can be used in theology. Although false dogmas from philosophy can creep in, and philosophy runs the risk of introducing esoteric and unnecessary terms, philosophy (properly conceived) can be a valuable handmaiden to theology in providing categories of thought, in convicting the unbeliever of inconsistency, and in preparing the mind for the greater truths of faith.

1 Turretin, *Elenctic Theology*, 1:28.
2 Turretin, *Elenctic Theology*, 1:30.
3 Turretin, *Elenctic Theology*, 1:44.

DAY 10

Inner Testimony of the Holy Spirit

Why should we accept the authority of the Bible? Do we start with a blank slate and reason our way into accepting the Scriptures? Should we base the Bible's trustworthiness on historical proofs? Do we rely on archaeological evidence and textual consistency? In short, what is the surest and best reason for believing and obeying the word of God?

While historical evidence and rational deduction have their place, the final authority for the word of God must always be God himself. We accept the authority of the Bible because through the Bible God speaks to us. Our confidence in the Scriptures is that in them we hear the very voice of God. As Calvin put it, those "who strive to build up firm faith in Scripture through disputation are doing things backward." We have a better foundation for our faith than human proofs and arguments. "The testimony of the Spirit is more excellent than all reason," Calvin observed. "For as God alone is a fit witness of himself in his Word, so also the Word will not find acceptance in men's hearts before it is sealed by the inward testimony of the Spirit. The same Spirit, therefore, who has spoken through the mouths of the prophets must penetrate into our hearts to persuade us that they faithfully proclaim what had been divinely commanded."[1] This doctrine of the *testimonium spiritus sancti* is critical if we are to believe the Bible on its own terms and for its own sake.

At the same time, we must be clear what the doctrine is *not* teaching. By insisting upon the inner testimony of the Holy Spirit, we are not suggesting that there are no other reasons for trusting the Bible. We *should* talk about the many historical, archaeological, and textual reasons for confidence in the Scriptures.

The *testimonium spiritus sancti* is the most convincing and most important reason for believing the Bible, but not the only one.

Moreover, we should not confuse this doctrine with new revelation or an argument from experience. The Spirit speaking to our hearts is not motivation for faith but the efficient cause of faith, not a feeling upon which our faith rests but the sight whereby our faith sees. As Berkhof puts it, "We believe Scripture, not because of, but through the testimony of the Holy Spirit."[2]

We must be careful to place our faith in Christ, not in our experience of Christ. Likewise, we must understand that the testimony of the Spirit in our hearts is the means *by which* we believe, not the grounds for believing. God must shine in our hearts to give the light of the knowledge of the glory of God in the face of Jesus Christ (2 Cor. 4:6). The *testimonium spiritus sancti* is the work of the Spirit in the heart of the believer granting us eyes to see the infallible truth of the divine word, ears to hear what God has to say, and lips to taste that the Lord is good.

1 Calvin, *Institutes*, 1.7.4.
2 Berkhof, *Introductory Volume*, 185.

WEEK 3

DAY 11

Fundamental Articles

"In essentials, unity. In nonessentials, liberty. In all things, charity."

Sounds great, but which are which?

Some Christians have a list of essentials that reads like a three-volume systematic theology. Other Christians can list their core doctrines on the backside of a business card. Some Christians never met a hill worth dying on. Other Christians charge every grassy knoll with bayonets fixed, ready to kill or be killed. Determining the fundamental articles of the faith is not easy.

But that doesn't mean we shouldn't try to sort out primary, secondary, and tertiary doctrines. As Calvin reminds us, "not all the articles of true doctrine are of the same sort." Some allow for differences of opinion, while "some are so necessary to know that they should be certain and unquestioned by all men as the proper principles of religion."[1] The question of fundamental articles became a major issue following the Reformation as Roman Catholics insisted that true Christians must agree on almost everything, Socinians insisted that Christians only needed a shared morality, and Reformed and Lutheran Christians tried to find a way to work together. The topic was a standard in theological textbooks during the period of Reformed and Lutheran orthodoxy.

While there is no simple and agreed-upon formula for making these determinations, we can make progress by making the right distinctions. Some doctrines are necessary for the existence of faith, others for the perfection of faith. Some errors are about the way we say things; others are about the beliefs themselves. Some truths must be known to be saved, while others must not be denied. Some doctrines are essential for entrance into heaven; others help us on the way to heaven. We are also helped to look at what the church has believed at all times and in all places. The Nicene Creed, for example, while not a sufficient statement of "mere Christianity" (whereas it developed in response to specific controversies), is at least a starting point. A doctrinal floor, not a ceiling.

Of course, when it comes to determining the fundamental articles, the most important place to look is in the Bible. The Pastoral Epistles are particularly helpful because in these three letters Paul deals explicitly with false teaching (1 Tim. 1:3; 4:1; 2 Tim. 3:8) and the need to guard the good deposit of faith (1 Tim. 6:20; 2 Tim. 1:13, 14; Titus 1:9, 13).

And what did this good deposit look like? The gospel message that Paul preached and expected all Christian to adhere to looked something like this: God is glorious; we are sinners; and Jesus Christ is our Savior and God. Jesus Christ is the Son of David and God in the flesh; he died and rose again; he ascended into heaven; he is coming again. Salvation is by sovereign grace, according to the converting power of the Holy Spirit, through faith, not according to works. Jesus Christ saves us from sin, saves us for eternal life, and saves us unto holiness. Notice that this summary touches on the Trinity, the two natures of Christ, the atonement, faith and repentance, justification, sanctification, and heaven and hell. The fundamental articles of the faith may say more than this, but they must not say less.

---

1 Calvin, *Institutes*, 4.1.12.

DAY 12

Knowing God

The God of the Bible is, from start to finish, the God who makes himself known. Though not fully comprehensible by his creatures, God has given us the ability to know him truly and savingly.

But how? In what way does God make himself known? Before answering that question positively, let's approach things negatively. Broadly speaking, there are two means by which Christians have wrongly sought to know God.

The first wrong way is rationalism. As an epistemological approach, rationalism "rejects any other source of knowledge than that which is found in nature and in the constitution of the human mind."[1] The problem with rationalism is not that it values reason or that it finds truth about God in nature. Christianity is not antireason; it is not irrational. But rationalism is something different. Rationalism admits no higher source of truth than reason. As a result, rationalism often becomes antisupernatural and finds itself tied to the latest whims of science and tossed to and fro by the latest intellectual fads.

The second wrong way to know God is mysticism. While Christianity is "mystical" in that it deals with heavenly realities and spiritual truths than go beyond human comprehension and explanation, this is not the same as mysticism. As an epistemological approach, mysticism "assumes that God by immediate communication with the soul, reveals through feelings and intuitions, divine truth independently of the outward teaching of his Word."[2] Mysticism should not be confused with the Spirit's work of illumination. When we pray for illumination, we are not praying for new information or looking to hear from God apart from his appointed means. We are asking for divine light to see and understand the Spirit-inspired Scriptures. Mysticism directs the Christian toward a subjective, inner light and away from the objective truth of the Bible.

Positively, the Bible teaches that the only proper way to know God is by way of objective revelation. Rationalism and mysticism may seem like opposite errors, but at the heart of both mistakes is an attempt to place the locus of authority in the human person instead of outside of ourselves (*extra nos*). This is also the problem with liberalism. As one of the movement's leading scholars puts it, liberal theology "is the idea that Christian theology can be genuinely Christian without being based upon external authority. Since the eighteenth century, liberal Christian thinkers have argued that religion should be modern and progressive and that the meaning of Christianity should be interpreted from the standpoint of modern knowledge and experience."[3] By contrast, historic Christianity has maintained that only God can adequately reveal God (1 Cor. 2:10–16). Modern knowledge and personal experience must be tested by God's revelation (and not the other way around). We must apprehend God's revelation by reason, and we need the illumination of the Spirit to lead us into truth, but reason is not independent of revelation, and the Spirit's illumination is not independent of the Scriptures. We don't want to be subject to our experiences at the expense of the intellect, and we don't want to follow the intellect at the expense of faith.

1 Hodge, *Systematic Theology*, 1.4.
2 Hodge, *Systematic Theology*, 1.7.
3 Dorrien, *Imagining Progressive Religion*, xii.

DAY 13

Natural Law and Natural Theology

Natural law refers to the rule of right and wrong implanted by God in the minds of all people (Rom. 2:14–15). Sometimes called the law of nature, the law of nations, the divine law, or the eternal law, the important point is that natural law is *God's* law even if this law is ascertained by reason and observation (and conclusions deduced from these principles) rather than from the study of Scripture. The conscience bears witness to the law of nature, and the Ten Commandments are a divinely revealed summary of the law of nature.

Closely related to natural law, but not to be confused with it, is natural theology. Natural theology is the philosophical study of what can be known about God apart from special revelation. The Bible itself teaches that we can naturally know something about God—that he exists, what he is like, and what he requires (Ps. 19:1–4; Acts 14:16–17; 17:26–27; Rom. 1:19–20). All this can be known—imperfectly and insufficiently for salvation—because God reveals such knowledge to his creatures (even the unregenerate) by way of natural revelation.

Natural theology, then, refers to the knowledge of God that can be known by reason and by the light of nature. As Archibald Alexander puts it, natural theology "consists in the knowledge of those truths concerning the being and attributes of God, the principles of human duty, and the expectation of a future state derived from reason alone."[1] Typically, theologians have argued that this natural knowledge of God is both *innate* (i.e., implanted in us by God as a seed of divinity or "eternity written on our hearts") and *acquired* (i.e., deduced by rational observation of the works of creation). Acquired knowledge can be further divided into three parts:

we know something of God and his ways by *investigating creation*, by *studying human nature*, and by *observing the works of providence*.

Although natural theology has been held in suspicion by some Protestants over the past century, most theologians throughout the history of the church have believed in the positive and apologetic purposes of natural theology. From the classical tradition of Augustine, Anselm, and Aquinas, to early Reformed thinkers like John Calvin, Heinrich Bullinger, Franciscus Junius, Wolfgang Musculus, Peter Martyr Vermigli, William Perkins, and Amandus Polanus, to Westminster divines like William Twisse, Samuel Rutherford, Thomas Goodwin, and their contemporary colleague James Ussher, to the line of Old Princeton stretching all the way from Francis Turretin and Benedict Pictet to John Witherspoon, Archibald Alexander, Charles Hodge, A. A. Hodge, and B. B. Warfield, natural theology has been affirmed by the best minds in the church for two thousand years.[2] As a divine image bearer, man has the capacity, even after the fall, to know true things about God apart from supernatural revelation. This is why "the sacred writers in contending with the heathen appeal to the evidence which the works of God bear to his perfections."[3] Thus Hodge concludes that it "cannot, therefore, be reasonably doubted that not only the being of God, but also his eternal power and Godhead, are so revealed in his works, as to lay a stable foundation for natural theology."[4]

1   Alexander, *God, Creation, and Human Rebellion*, 13.
2   See Haines, *Natural Theology*.
3   Hodge, *Systematic Theology*, 1:24.
4   Hodge, *Systematic Theology*, 1:25.

DAY 14

General Revelation and Special Revelation

The only way we can know a transcendent God is for God to make himself known. In *general revelation*, God makes himself known in the works of creation and providence. "The heavens declare the glory of God, and the sky above proclaims his handiwork" (Ps. 19:1). The creation speaks across the entire world, testifying to the power and majesty (and existence) of God (Ps. 19:2–6; Rom. 1:19–20). Strictly speaking, general (or natural) revelation refers to God's communication to his creatures, while natural theology refers to the human appropriation of that revelation. Natural theology, rightly conceived, is not man's attempt to work his way up from bare reason to a knowledge of God. Natural theology is what man derives from God's initiative to be known through general revelation.

General revelation is a gracious act of divine condescension, but it does not make known the way of grace. "Although the light of nature, and the works of creation and providence do so far manifest the goodness, wisdom, and power of God, as to leave men inexcusable; yet they are not sufficient to give that knowledge of God, and of his will, which is necessary until salvation" (WCF 1.1). In order to be saved, we need *special revelation*—a declaration of God's will to his people, communicated in former days in manifold ways, and now committed unto writing in the Holy Scriptures (WCF 1:1).

The phrase "light of nature" occurs five times in the Westminster Confession of Faith (1.1, 1.6, 10.4, 20.4, 21.1) and three times in the Westminster Larger Catechism (Questions 2, 60, 151). The phrase, used in contrast to the light of the word, is shorthand for that sense of God all humans are born with. According to general revelation, man can know of God's existence, his power, his judgment, and a general sense of his commands. Supernatural theology, however, is necessary for man to know how to be justified before God and how to be reconciled to him. In other words, our knowledge of God is twofold (*duplex cognition Dei*): we can know God as Creator by natural theology, but we can know him as Redeemer only by special revelation.[1] The heavens may declare the glory of God, but the law of the Lord is perfect, the testimony of the Lord is sure, and the word of the Lord is more to be desired than gold (Ps. 19:7–11).

A Christian understanding of revelation provides a basis for science, and it limits science at the same time. Because the world reveals God and something of his creativity and order, it can be studied and analyzed. There is an objective universe that can be the subject of evaluation and investigation. There are spiritual truths for us to see in the farthest galaxies and in the smallest quarks. But because of our own blindness and ignorance we should not think that science answers all our questions. There are some truths—truths about God's will for us and the means of salvation—that require God to speak more clearly. Science is good and necessary, but it is not final or absolute. To know God and his ways, we need the Bible, the surest and clearest word and the last word concerning every subject on which it means to speak.

---

1   See Fesko and Richard, "Natural Theology and the Westminster Confession of Faith," 3:223–66.

⚎

DAY 15

Inspiration

The doctrine of inspiration is taught in dozens of places throughout the Bible, but two passages are especially important.

The first passage is 2 Timothy 3:16–17: "All Scripture is breathed out by God and profitable for teaching, for reproof, for correction, and for training in righteousness, that the man of God may be complete, equipped for every good work." The English phrase "breathed out by God" translates a single Greek word: *theopneustos*. The Latin term *afflatus* (a breathing on someone or something) gets at the same idea. When we speak of the doctrine of inspiration, we don't mean that the Bible is inspir*ing*, in an active sense (though that is also true). We mean the Bible is inspir*ed*, in a passive sense. The inspiration of Scripture is a past established fact, not a future hoped-for occurrence. Scripture is absolutely, authoritatively, and completely trustworthy because it is nothing less than divine exhalation.

We don't believe that only part of the Bible is inspired. *All* Scripture is the breathed-out word of God. Not just the obviously theological parts. Not just the memorable passages. Not just the verses that resonate with us. History, chronology, anthropology—every word in the Bible is there because God wanted it there. We should listen to the Bible and submit ourselves to its teaching as if we were hearing from God himself (which we are). And if someone objects that Paul's idea of Scripture only included what we call the Old Testament, recall that Paul considered his apostolic preaching to be the very word of God (1 Thess. 2:13) and that Peter considered Paul's writings to be holy Scripture (2 Pet. 3:15–16).

The second key text is 2 Peter 1:19–21: "And we have the prophetic word more fully confirmed, to which you will do well to pay attention as to a lamp shining in a dark place, until the day dawns and the morning star rises in your hearts, knowing this first of all, that no prophecy of Scripture comes from someone's own interpretation. For no prophecy was ever produced by the will of man, but men spoke from God as they were carried along the by the Holy Spirit." There is a lot to say about these verses but notice two things in brief.

1. When Peter says "no prophecy of Scripture," he has in mind written texts. That's what the Greek word *graphe* (scripture) means. This is significant because neo-orthodox theologians like Karl Barth argued that the Bible *contains* the word of God or that in the *event* in which God speaks to us through the Bible, we encounter that as the word of God. Some Christians will gladly speak of inspiration, but then they will quickly distance the concept from the written words of

Scripture. But the Bible knows of no such distinction. The inspiration of Scripture is an objective reality outside of us and our experience of God. The Bible does not become the word of God; it *is* the word of God.

2. The goal of inscripturated revelation is not merely information, but worship. We are told to pay attention to the word until the day dawns and the morning star rises in our hearts. This is likely a reference to Christ being exalted in us on the day of his return (Num. 24:17–19). The point of inspiration is never orthodoxy by itself, or even orthopraxy, but ultimately doxology.

WEEK 4

DAY 16

Concursive Operation

Having established the fact of inspiration, we still have to consider the *how* of inspiration. Generally speaking, there are three views concerning the nature of inspiration.

Some hold to a *dynamic view of inspiration*. This was the view of Friedrich Schleiermacher (1768–1834) and is often taught (usually implicitly rather than explicitly) by theological liberals. According to this view, the biblical authors came under divine influence to write down exalted works of religious insight and life-giving spirituality. This theory does not argue for God's direct influence upon the biblical authors, but rather insists on a generic illumination enlightening the consciousness of men. Biblical inspiration differs in degree from the Spirit's work in our lives but does not fundamentally differ in kind. A dynamic view of inspiration does not deny that the Bible is a special book, but it does not require the individual words of Scripture to be divine, let alone infallible or inerrant.

At the other extreme is the *mechanical dictation view of inspiration*. According to this view, the words of Scripture were taken down by the biblical authors as one would write down dictation. While many fine theologians have remarked that the Bible is so trustworthy that it's *as if* the biblical authors simply transcribed what they heard from God, verbal plenary inspiration does not require or insist upon mechanical dictation. Indeed, those holding to verbal plenary inspiration have almost always argued against such a view. The mechanical dictation theory has more in common with Muslim and Mormon views of revelation than with historic Christian teaching.

In contrast to the two views mentioned above, the Bible teaches that the word of God was spoken and written down by means of *concursive operation*. According to this view, God did not use the biblical authors in a mechanical way (e.g., moving their pens like typing on a keyboard). He did not whisper in their ears what words to write down. Instead, he "acted upon them in an organic way, in harmony with the laws of their own inner beings."[1] God used the intellect, skills, and personality of fallible men to speak and write down what was entirely infallible. We can say the Bible is human and divine, so long as we understand that "human" means the Bible uses human language and employed human authors, not that the Bible contains human errors.

Again, the passage from 2 Peter 1 is key. Verse 21 tell us that "men spoke from God as they were carried along by the Holy Spirit." The verb "carried along" is the Greek word *phero*, translated earlier in the verse as "produced." It's the same word translated as "borne" in verse 17 and in verse 18. The words from heaven (on the Mount of Transfiguration) and the words from the prophets (written down in Scripture) came from the same place: they were borne from God. Though spoken and written down through the instrumentality of men, the words of Scripture are at the same time, by virtue of being carried along by the Holy Spirit, nothing less than God's own words.

1 Berkhof, *Introductory Volume*, 153.

DAY 17

Perfections of Scripture

Just as God has attributes, so does the Bible. The classic perfections of Scripture can be remembered (in English) using the acronym SCAN: sufficiency, clarity, authority, and necessity.

Sufficiency. Scripture does not tell us everything about everything, but it tells us all we need to know to make us wise unto salvation (2 Tim. 3:15). In Christ we have the fullness and the finality of God's redemption and revelation (Heb. 1:1–4). We must never separate fullness and finality, nor must we separate redemption and revelation. Both pairs stand or fall together. In these last days, God speaks to us not by many and various ways, but in one way, through his Son, those former ways of revealing God's will having ceased (WCF 1.1). And how does God speak through his Son? By the revelation of the Son's redeeming work—the saving work announced in the Gospels and then interpreted by the Spirit through the apostles in the rest of the New Testament (John 16:12–15). The Son's redemption and the Son's revelation must both be sufficient. As such, there is nothing more to be done and nothing more to be known for our salvation and for our Christian walk than what we see and know about Christ in the Bible. Scripture is enough because the work of Christ is enough.

Clarity. The clarity, or perspicuity, of Scripture does not mean that everything in the Bible is easy to understand (just like sufficiency does not mean the Bible tells us everything about everything). Rather, perspicuity means that even the unlearned, if they are willing to think and study and pray, can understand the Bible in such a way that they can be saved and live a life pleasing to God (WCF 1:7). God's word is not beyond us (Deut. 30:11–14). That's why the Bible frequently compares the word of God to a lamp (Ps. 119:105, 130) or to light (Ps. 19:7, 8). When the book of the law was rediscovered in Josiah's day, the people read it and knew what to do in response (2 Kings 22). Likewise, when Ezra read the law to the returned exiles in Jerusalem they were able to understand the reading (Neh. 8:5–8, 12). Jesus often referenced the Scriptures to the effect that his opponents should have understood the meaning of the text (Matt. 21:13, 42–44; Mark 7:6–7, 10; 10:4–9; John 3:10; 10:34–35).

Authority. Every Christian and every church will affirm that our theology must accord with Scripture. But what is our *ultimate* authority? How do we make our closing arguments? Do we give the final word to reason and experience? To science? To tradition? To our confessions? For Christians, our final authority must be the Holy Spirit speaking in the Scripture (WCF. 1:10). That's what we mean by *sola Scriptura*, not that we only study the Bible but that when it comes to our final authority, we rely on the Bible alone. Like the Bereans, we are eager to let the Scriptures have the last word (Acts 17:11).

Necessity. The only being knowledgeable enough, wise enough, and skillful enough to reveal God is God himself (1 Cor. 2:6–13). As long as the apostles were alive, the spoken word and the written word existed side by side. Tradition and Scripture could be equally authoritative for a time. But with the close of the apostolic age, the writings of the apostles became absolutely necessary. We need God's book if we are to know God and his ways. The church is built not upon impressions and ecstatic revelations but upon the words of the apostles and prophets (Eph. 2:20).

⛫

DAY 18

Inerrancy

There are many texts we could use to show that the Bible is without error, but here's the simplest argument: no word of Scripture came from the will of man, but from God (2 Pet. 1:21). And if the Bible is truly God's word, then it must all be true. As Romans 3:4 says, "Let God be true though every one were a liar."

Some prefer the term *infallibility* to *inerrancy*, but the words by themselves hardly mean anything different. *Infallibility* refers to the inability to be wrong. *Inerrancy* means without error. I fear that oftentimes *infallibility* is used to signify: "I don't want to be associated with inerrancy." At any rate, the word we use is not as important as the conviction that the Bible is unfailingly true in all that it affirms. After all, it was Jesus who—in emphasizing one word in an obscure psalm—maintained that the Scriptures cannot be broken (John 10:35). It was Jesus who said he did not come to abolish one jot or tittle of the Law or the Prophets (Matt. 5:17–19). It was Jesus who assumed a straightforward reading of the chronology and the miracles of the Old Testament (Matt. 12:38–42). And it was Jesus who cited the Scripture as coming from the Creator himself (Matt. 19:4–5; cf. 12:36; Rom. 9:17; Gal. 3:8; Heb. 3:7).

The Bible can no more fail, falter, or err than God himself can fail, falter, or err. Calvin claimed that if we follow the Scriptures, we will be "safe from the danger of erring." We ought to embrace "without finding fault, whatever is taught in Sacred Scripture." We "owe to the Scripture the same reverence which we owe to God." In Scripture, God "opens his own most hallowed lips," and the apostles were "sure and genuine scribes of the Holy Spirit."[1] We could easily multiply quotations like this from Calvin, and his view of inspiration was far from novel.

Inerrancy means the word of God always stands over us, and we never stand over the word of God. When we reject inerrancy, we put ourselves in judgment over God's word. We claim the right to determine which parts of God's revelation can be trusted and which cannot. When we deny the complete trustworthiness of the Scriptures, then we are forced to accept one of two conclusions: either the Scripture is not all from God, or God is not always dependable. To make either statement is to affirm what is sub-Christian. These conclusions do not express a proper submission to the Father, do not work for our joy in Christ, and do not bring honor to the Spirit who carried along the men to speak the prophetic word and author God's holy book. As J. I. Packer puts it, "One cannot doubt the Bible without far-reaching loss, both of fullness of truth and of fullness of life. If therefore we have at heart spiritual renewal for society, for churches and for our own lives, we shall make much of the entire trustworthiness—that is, the inerrancy—of Holy Scripture as the inspired and liberating Word of God."[2]

1 These five quotations come from, respectively, Calvin's *Commentaries* (on Matt. 22:29); *Institutes*, 1.18.4; 1.6.1 (cf. 1.8.5); *Institutes* 2.12.1 (see also 1.8.5; 3.22.8; 3.23.5; *Commentaries* [on 1 Pet. 1:25]); *Institutes*, 4.8.9; and *Commentaries*, 3:50.

2 Packer, *Truth and Power*, 55.

DAY 19

The Question of Canon

The Bible is a single book made up of many books. There are thirty-nine books in the Old Testament and twenty-seven books in the New Testament. Together these sixty-six books make up the Christian Scriptures. This collection of authoritative books is called a canon, meaning a fixed rule or standard.

The question of how we got our present canon is complex but not impossible to trace. Let's start with the Old Testament. We know that Jesus and the apostles recognized the inspiration of the Hebrew Scriptures. We also know that their Hebrew Bible consisted of the thirty-nine books—in a different order, and sometimes called by different names—that make up our Old Testament. For a long time it was thought that the Council of Jamnia (AD 90) fixed the Old Testament canon; now scholars believe the canon was already well established and the Council less decisive than we once thought. The assortment of books called the Apocrypha, which Roman Catholics include in their Bible, was not included in the Hebrew Scriptures, though they were found in the Septuagint (the Greek translation of the Hebrew Scriptures). The church father Jerome included the Apocrypha in his Latin Vulgate, but he made clear that the books in the Apocrypha belonged to a different class and were not the same as the canonical books. Over time, as copies were made of the Vulgate, Jerome's original distinctions were overlooked, and the Apocrypha came to be seen as equally authoritative.

Turning to the New Testament, we find that the early church believed in an expanding canon (1 Tim. 5:18; 2 Pet. 3:16). While it may seem strange that Jewish Christians added to their Scriptures, this was in keeping with their understanding that God had initiated a new covenant with his people (2 Cor. 3). Covenants typically included written texts to testify to the terms of the new arrangement. We can trace the development of this new canonical awareness from Papias at the beginning of the second century, to the Muratorian Fragment and Origen's writings in the third century, to the list provided by Eusebius in the first part of the fourth century. Although several books were disputed during this period, we should not exaggerate the level of disagreement. None of the twenty-seven books in our New Testament were ever rejected, and no books besides these twenty-seven were ever clearly accepted. Our present canon was accepted in the East with the publication of Athanasius's *Festal Letter* (367) and in the West at the Synod of Rome (382). In 397 the Synod of Carthage formally recognized the biblical canon for the entire church.

The idea of a fixed list of books is not a foreign imposition on the Bible. The New Testament canon was always tied to apostolic authority. Apostolicity explains why the canon had to grow (the apostles spoke with divine authority) *and* why the canon would eventually be closed (once the apostles died, that level of divine authority also passed way). When we see how deliberately Revelation 22:18–19 (do not add or subtract from this book) echoes Deuteronomy 4:2 and how Revelation concludes like a bookend with rich imagery pulled from Genesis, it's hard not to conclude that John understood his Apocalypse as the closing of canonical revelation. God's inspired word was now tied to this authoritative collection of inspired texts.

DAY 20

Which Books Belong in the Bible?

Once we establish the biblical justification for a canon, a further and more difficult question remains: How do we know which books *belong* in the canon? We need to explore not just who wrote what canonical list when, but how the books in our Bible were determined to be canonical.

One response is to suggest that the canon was *historically determined*. To be sure, the formal recognition of the canon was a historical process, but this is not the same as saying the canon was determined by historical forces. Evidence was important, and texts were scrutinized for apostolicity, catholicity, and orthodoxy, but it wasn't as if the church wrote up a job description for canonical books and then interviewed potential candidates. No church leader or church council determined the criteria for canonicity. The process was much more organic. The church never saw itself as picking new Bible books from a list of competitors.

A second response argues that the canon was *community determined*. Roman Catholics often criticize Protestants for having inspired books without having an inspired table of contents. In Catholic theology, the creation of the canon demonstrates the need for an infallible magisterium. The reason we can trust the canon, they insist, is that the church was given supernatural and unerring authority to determine which books belong in the canon. The problem with this approach (besides the circularity of arguing for the authority of the church to determine the rule of Scripture when we need the Scriptures to teach us about the authority of the church) is that it runs counter to the examples in redemptive history. The word summoned Abraham, the word constituted Israel as a nation, the word called the disciples. The word of God always forms the people of God, not the other way around.

The third and best approach maintains that the church did not choose the books of the Bible as much as the canonical books were *self-authenticating*.[1] There is no reason to think that Israel had an infallible revelation from God to help them select their Scriptures. And yet Jesus accepted them as divine and authoritative. Why? Because the writings themselves proved to be inspired. The church did not give us the canon any more than Isaac Newton gave us gravity. There's a reason Eusebius referred to the canonical books as "recognized," not as "chosen" or "selected." Within a generation of John's death as the last apostle, the four Gospels and thirteen Pauline epistles were already widely accepted as canonical revelation. The church did not pick canonical winners and losers. Just as a child making her way through a mass of people does not choose her parents from the crowd but finds them and recognizes them, so the church did not create the canon. The church accepted the authority that the canonical books already possessed.

1   Kruger, *Canon Revisited.*

THEOLOGY PROPER

The Being of God and the Works of God

DAY 21

The Existence of God

The existence of God is not a conclusion to be reached so much as a given to be assumed. "In the beginning, God" is, after all, how the Bible begins (Gen. 1:1). We all have an innate idea of God, a sense of the divine that leaves us without excuse (Eccl. 3:11; Acts 17:24–28; Rom. 1:19–20). Only the fool says in his heart that there is no God (Ps. 14:1). God's existence is the starting place for human knowledge, not the end point of human deduction.

This does not mean, however, that arguments for the existence of God are necessarily misguided. One can argue for the existence of God in a way that is subservient to human reason or in a way that supports divine revelation. Aquinas, for example, begins his discussion with Scripture, establishing God's existence from Exodus 3:14 ("I AM WHO I AM"). Only after this does he argue that the existence of God can be proven "in five ways."[1]

- Argument from motion: There cannot be an infinite regression of motion. Someone or something must have absolute actuality, an unmoved mover.
- Argument from the nature of efficient causation: Cause and effect must have begun with some first cause.
- Argument from possibility and necessity: Existence cannot come from nonexistence. Something must exist of its own necessity, not as a mere possibility.
- Argument from gradation: Something must be most good, most perfect, and most true—a supreme being from which all degrees of lesser perfection are determined.
- Argument from the governance of the world: Some intelligent being must exist by whom all natural things are directed to their appointed ends.

Protestant theologians often built upon Aquinas's five ways. Turretin, for example, posited four proofs for the existence of God: the voice of universal nature (which encapsulated most of Aquinas's arguments), the intricate design of human beings, the testimony of conscience, and the religious nature of all peoples throughout history.[2]

Similarly, Shedd mentioned five principal arguments: ontological (a perfect being greater than which nothing can be conceived must by necessity possess existence), cosmological (motion implies a prime mover), teleological (the world is marked by design), moral (the testimony of conscience), and historical (all peoples believe in some kind of supreme being).[3]

To be sure, we should not try to argue people into the kingdom of God, much less build a theological system on a rationalistic foundation. We know from the Bible that belief in the existence of God is ultimately an article of faith (Heb. 11:6). For the Christian, arguments for God's existence are better thought of as witnesses than as proofs. Nevertheless, there is a place for showing that the existence of God is rational and makes better sense of the world than does atheistic unbelief. Philosophy and human reason must not be the starting point for faith, but they can be used to defend, clarify, and confirm the faith.

1   Aquinas, *Summa Theologica*, 1.2.3.
2   Turretin, *Elenctic Theology*, 3.1.1–27.
3   Shedd, *Dogmatic Theology*, 201–16.

DAY 22

The Knowability of God

In studying the doctrine of God (theology proper) we need to ask two foundational questions: (1) What is God like? and (2) Who is God? The first question leads us to investigate the *nature* of God, while the second question leads us into an exploration of the *persons* of God. We can answer the question "What is God like?" by looking at the attributes of God, while we answer the question "Who is God?" by understanding the doctrine of the Trinity.

In approaching the question "What is God like?" we first must establish whether it is possible to know what God is like. There is a long history in the tradition of the church of speaking of God as the incomprehensible one. And with good reason. Isaiah 40:18 asks, "To whom will you liken God, or what likeness compare with him?" In Job 38–41, the Lord answers Job out of the whirlwind with a barrage of questions. Job wanted to know why God was the way he was and why he had done what he has done. God responded by reminding Job that he was God and Job was not.

Although systematic theology deals with many careful definitions and distinctions about God and his ways, we must never forget that we cannot know God as God knows God. Luther referred to God as *Deus absconditus*, the hidden God. Calvin believed God's essence was wholly beyond our human senses and beyond human understanding. Especially on this side of heaven, we must confess that we see through a glass dimly (1 Cor. 13:12). Our knowledge of God is never exhaustive and never perfect. We know only in part. Our God is incomprehensible.

But incomprehensible is not the same as unknowable. The entire Bible is predicated upon the idea that the God beyond human comprehension can be known by his human creatures. While we cannot penetrate into the deep things of God, God can be known insofar as he makes himself known. "The secret things belong to the LORD our God, but the things that are revealed belong to us and to our children forever" (Deut. 29:29). The whole Bible is about the God who makes himself known. "This is eternal life," Jesus said, "that they know you, the only true God, and Jesus Christ whom you have sent" (John 17:3).

Affirming that God is both incomprehensible and knowable has practical ramifications for the Christian life. On the one hand, God's incomprehensibility means we must never treat God as a specimen to be examined under the microscope of our human minds. We must allow—indeed, rejoice in the fact—that God is metaphysically sublime and his ways are beyond tracing out. At the same time, we must not confuse ignorance about God with humility. If God has made himself known, we should not castigate systematic theology as "putting God in a box" or treating him as "freeze-dried" or "shrink-wrapped." Surely the God who speaks wants to be heard—if only we have ears to hear.

DAY 23

Words for God

Our words for God can be thought of in one of three ways: univocal, equivocal, or analogical.

Language is *univocal* when it has only one meaning (uni-vocal). In theology, this means that whatever is predicated of various things under the same word carries the same meaning. So if we say "God is good," the word "good" carries the same meaning as when we say, "Sam is good" or "Those flowers are good" or

"That pizza is good." Right away we should be able to see that the language we use for God and the language we use for other things cannot be univocal. This is so for at least two reasons.

1. Attributes like "goodness" relate to things differently than they relate to God. God is good in his essence. You cannot remove goodness and still have God. By contrast, even if Sam is not good, or the flowers are not good, or the pizza is not good, Sam is still Sam, the flowers are still flowers, and the pizza is still pizza.

2. God does not belong to the same genus as his creation. He is not in the same class of things as any other thing. Strictly speaking, God does not even belong to a class or genus, because these terms suggest the possibility of more than one member. This means our language for God cannot be univocal. If we say, "The dog is happy," we do not mean the exact same thing as saying, "The man is happy," because dogs and men are different kinds of creatures and because, as human beings, we cannot truly know what dogs experience when they are happy. If the ontological gap between dogs and men disallows for univocal language, how much more when we are using human language to speak about God.

Language is *equivocal* when the same word means two different things. If I say, "Row your boat to the south bank and deposit the check in the bank at the top of the hill," the word *bank* is used in that sentence in two different ways. The word equivocates; "bank" has an equal voice (equi-vocal) in both halves of the sentence, but it does not mean the same thing. In theology, this means that when the same word is predicated of God and man, there is no correspondence between the two uses of the word. Right away we should be able to see that our theological language cannot be purely equivocal. If "God is good" means nothing like "Sam is good," how can we say anything meaningful about God with human language?

The answer to that question is to insist that our words about God are *analogical*. The great ontological distance between God and man means that our words for God can never mean exactly the same thing as when we use those words for man. And yet there is a similitude between God and human beings—the latter being creatures made in the image of the former—so there must be some relationship between the words we use for human beings and the words we use for God. If God's eternal power and divine nature can be clearly perceived in the created world (Rom. 1:20), how much more can human language—a gift from the Word himself—say something meaningful and discernible about God? Human words cannot capture God, but they can communicate the truth about God, even if the infinite God himself is beyond our finite comprehension.

The Unity of God

Other truths may be equally important, but nothing is more basic about God than his unity. "Hear, O Israel: The Lord our God, the Lord is one" (Deut. 6:4). As God says in the first of the Ten Commandments: "I am the Lord your God. . . . You shall have no other gods before me" (Ex. 20:2–3).

When we speak of God being numerically one, we are using *one* in two different senses. In the first sense we mean that God is indivisible. God cannot be split into parts, either physically (as if he had literal arms and legs) or spiritually (as if he were the sum of his attributes). God is numerically one in his essence, though this does not demand a personal numerical unity. The unity of God does not preclude this unity being a triunity, so long as we do not conceive of this triunity as dividing God into parts and pieces.

In the second sense of *one* we mean that God is one to the exclusion of all others. The issue is not whether there are many so-called gods believed upon in the world (1 Cor. 8:5) or whether angels or magistrates might be called "gods" in a metaphorical sense (Ps. 82:6; John 10:34). The question is whether there is, properly speaking, more than one supreme, perfect, infinite, eternal being.

Besides being logically impossible—how can multiple beings be infinite and supreme?—the Bible is adamant that the Lord is God and God alone. This is the testimony of the Pentateuch: "Know therefore today, and lay it to your heart, that the Lord is God in heaven above and on the earth beneath; there is no other" (Deut. 4:39). And the Psalms: "For you are great and do wondrous things; you alone are God" (Ps. 86:10). And the major prophets: "Thus says the Lord, the King of Israel and his Redeemer, the Lord of hosts: 'I am the first and I am the last; besides me there is no god'" (Isa. 44:6). And the minor prophets: "You shall know that I am in the midst of Israel, and that I am the Lord your God and there is none else" (Joel 2:27). And the Gospels: "The scribe said to him, 'You are right, Teacher. You have truly said that he is one, and there is no other besides him'" (Mark 12:32). And the Epistles: "For there is one God, and there is one mediator between God and men, the man Christ Jesus" (1 Tim. 2:5). In the Bible even great men from other nations often confess that Israel's God is the only God: "Then [Naaman] returned to the man of God, he and all his company, and he came and stood before him. And he said, 'Behold, I know that there is no God in all the earth but in Israel'" (2 Kings 5:15).

God is one in his essence and one of a kind. The world is not an anarchy (rule by no supreme being) as atheists maintain, nor a polyarchy (rule by many supreme beings) as ancient pagans and many Eastern religions maintain, but a monarchy (rule by one supreme being). The Lord is a great God, and a great king above all gods (Ps. 95:3).

DAY 25

The Spirituality of God

One of the shortest definitions of God in the Bible is the one Jesus gave to the Samaritan woman at the well: "God is spirit" (John 4:24).

Most people understand the spirituality of God by thinking of "spirit" as the opposite of "material." And that's certainly part of what Jesus is getting at. God is a spiritual being rather than a material being. He has no form and cannot be seen (Deut. 4:15). Isaiah 31:3 says, "The Egyptians are man, and not God, and their horses are flesh, and not spirit." To be God is to be spirit instead of flesh. Proper worship of God, therefore, is a matter of the spirit rather than determined by physical location, as the Samaritan woman (and most of her contemporaries) thought. The spirituality of God is another way of speaking of the immateriality of God.

But it's more than that. God is not just a spirit or spiritual. God is spirit itself, spirit absolutely. There is a reason that 1 Timothy 1:17 puts eternal, immortal, and invisible together as attributes of the one God. That God cannot be seen suggests that he is also free from the limitations of time and space. He has immortality and eternity because he alone has absolute spirituality. God is a "most pure spirit" (WCF 2:1).

If we only think of God's spirituality as his nonphysicality we are liable to misunderstand the doctrine. William Shedd argues that two predicates are fundamentally important in comprehending the idea of God as spirit: substantiality and personality.[1]

By *substantiality* we mean that God is an essence or a substance. This is a crucial point because it means that God is not a mere idea or construction of the mind. He cannot be reduced to a mere power or influence or energy. God is not a property or quality. He is *ens* (Latin, from the verb *esse*, to be). As a spiritual substance, God does not occupy space, but he is still a real being. In fact, as independent and uncaused in his existence, God is being in the most absolute sense.

By *personality* we mean that God is a personal being. In talking about the personality of the one true God, we are talking about two characteristics in particular: his self-consciousness and his self-determination.[2] If self-consciousness sounds too abstract, think of God as self-knowing and self-contemplating. God is a personal being in that he is a knowing subject and an object to be known. God is aware of himself and aware of others. He is not an impersonal force. Self-determination is easier to understand. It means that God has agency. His decisions are freely chosen and self-directed.

Finally, the word *personality* in this context should not be confused with *persons* in the Trinity, though the two concepts are related. God is one personal being who eternally exists as three distinct divine persons. There is a single consciousness in God and a single self-determined will. But there are, nevertheless, three subsistences within the Godhead. This allows the one God to be fully personal in himself and by himself. By reason of the three persons, the divine essence "is self-contemplative, self-cognitive, and self-communing."[3]

1   Shedd, *Dogmatic Theology*, 156.
2   Shedd, *Dogmatic Theology*, 169.
3   Shedd, *Dogmatic Theology*, 178.

DAY 26

The Names of God

In the world of the Bible, names are not just ways of identifying one person from another. Names speak to the character of a person. This is true for human beings as well as for God. The way the Bible names God reveals something about the nature of God.

Theologians often distinguish among three different kinds of names for God: proper names, essential names, and personal names. The last two categories concern the attributes of God (essential names) and the triunity of God (the personal names of Father, Son, and Holy Spirit). These topics will be covered elsewhere; our concern here is with the proper names of God.

While the Bible contains many variations on the names of God, in general we can highlight seven. (1) The simplest name by which God is called in the Old

Testament is *El* or *Elohim* or *Elyon*, all of which are usually translated "God." These words are not unique to the one true God. The terms are also used of idols, false gods, and rulers. The word *El* is sometimes partnered with other words to name the God of the Bible, as in *El Ro'i* (the God who sees me) in Genesis 16:3. (2) The word *Adonai*, usually translated Lord, speaks to God as high and lifted up and as an exalted ruler. (3) The name *Shaddai* or *El-Shaddai* is notoriously difficult to translate but is usually rendered "God Almighty" (Gen. 17:1; 28:3; 35:11; Ex. 6:2–3).

Turning to the New Testament, we find frequent use of (4) *theos* (God) and (5) *kyrios* (Lord). God is also (6) *pater* (Father). God is often called Father in both Testaments (Deut. 32:6; Ps. 103:13; Isa. 63:16; 64:8; 1 Cor. 8:6; Eph. 3:15; Heb. 12:9; James 1:18). Importantly, although God is sometimes described using feminine imagery—as being *like* a mother hen, for example—God is only named with masculine names. Thus, God is king (not queen), husband (not wife), and father (not mother). (7) The last name to consider is the special covenant name Yahweh (or Jehovah). The word Yahweh comes from the tetragrammaton YHWH, which occurs nearly seven thousand times in the Bible and is rendered in most English translations as "LORD" (in small capital letters).

Although the name Yahweh was not unknown in the days of the patriarchs, we might say the official revelation of the name didn't take place until the burning bush in Exodus 3:13–15. Moses asks God for his name in verse 13, and God responds in verse 14 by linking "the God of your fathers" with the name I Am Who I Am (*ehyeh asher ehyeh*). This name, in turn, is connected to the covenant name, the LORD (*yhwh*), given in verse 15. Yahweh comes from the Hebrew verbal root *hayah*, meaning "to be," the same word used in the previous verse (*ehyeh asher ehyeh*). Yahweh is the most important name for God in the Old Testament because it was God's way of reminding his people, "I am your God. I have been your God. I will be your God. And I am the only God. This is what it means for me to be God. I am the self-existent, transcendent, independent Great I Am. I am the Lord." Truly, God has exalted above all things his name and his word (Ps. 138:2).

DAY 27

The Attributes of God

Divine attributes are qualities or characteristics that can be predicated of God. Some people prefer to speak of God's perfections or virtues or excellencies (1 Pet. 2:9). Others use the word *property* because it speaks to what is proper to God. Eastern Orthodox theologians often speak of God's essence and God's energies;

just as we cannot land on the sun (essence) but can experience the rays of the sun (energies), so we are capable of knowing true things about God even if we cannot plumb the depths of the very God-ness of God.

These terms have their place, but *attribute* is the common designation and can be used appropriately so long as we put some safeguards around the term. We should not imagine that in attributing qualities to God, we are assigning something outside of God to God or adding something to his essence. God's attributes are not things that exist apart from God himself, neither are God's attributes things that come together to form God. We must also admit that in an absolute sense the divine attributes cannot be distinguished from the divine essence. What God *is* cannot be separated from what God *has*, and vice versa.

While there is no authoritative list of the divine attributes, a number of excellent summaries have been offered in the history of the church. The Belgic Confession describes God as a "single and simple spiritual being . . . eternal, incomprehensible, invisible, unchangeable, infinite, almighty; completely wise, just, and good, and the overflowing source of all God" (BC Art. 1). The Westminster Confession of Faith is more exhaustive, describing our infinite and perfect God as "a most pure spirit, invisible, without body, parts, or passions; immutable, immense, eternal, incomprehensible, almighty, most wise, most holy, most free, most absolute, working all things according to the counsel of His own immutable and most righteous will, for His own glory; most loving, gracious, merciful, long-suffering, abundant in goodness and truth" (WCF 2:1).

One of the best single statements on the attributes of God comes from John of Damascus (675–749) whose apophatic theology describes God mainly by what he is not:

> So then, we both know and confess that God is without beginning, without end, eternal and everlasting, uncreated, immutable, unchangeable, simple, non-composite, incorporeal, invisible, impalpable, uncircumscribed, limitless, ungraspable, incognizable, unfathomable, good, just, almighty, the creator of all created things, sovereign over all, overseeing all, exercising foresight over all, having supreme power over all, and judge of all.[1]

Some may criticize these statements as reducing the God we meet in biblical stories to a God of lists and Latinate words. But the precise language of systematic theology helps to protect and propagate what is precious about the God of the Bible. The divine attributes are not the only way to think about God, but they are invaluable for thinking about his nature carefully and, dare we say, gloriously.

---

1 John of Damascus, *On the Orthodox Faith*, 61.

Incommunicable and Communicable Attributes

There are many ways to categorize the attributes of God.

- Some speak of *absolute attributes* (those properties God has in himself apart from anything else) and *relative attributes* (the properties he expresses in relation to his creation and his creatures).

- Some use the language of *constitutional attributes* and *attributes of personality*; that is, those attributes that are natural to God and those that are moral and personal.

- Others prefer the categories *attributes of greatness* (those qualities that highlight the grandeur of who God is) and *attributes of goodness* (those qualities that highlight the excellency of what God does).

We can see in each of the formulas the same impulse to distinguish between attributes that God would have on a desert island (so to speak) and those attributes that manifest themselves toward others. This sort of distinction can be useful but also potentially misleading. We don't want to think that some attributes are more essential to God or that God needs other creatures in order for certain attributes to be actualized. All of the divine attributes are predicated of the divine nature, and all of them belong to God eternally and absolutely.

The most common approach is to distinguish between God's incommunicable attributes and his communicable attributes. The incommunicable attributes are those that cannot be "communicated" to us. Immensity, eternity, and infinity, for example, are classified as incommunicable because nothing analogous to these attributes can be found in God's creatures. Likewise, love, mercy, and goodness are deemed communicable because we can also be loving, merciful, and good. When we speak of a communicable disease, we mean the disease can be caught. That's one way to think of the communicable attributes—they can be "caught" by God's creatures in a way that the incommunicable attributes cannot.

Of course, this distinction is not perfect either. Even the incommunicable attributes—though not strictly communicable—are analogous to human qualities.

We may not be immutable, but we can possess a degree of constancy. At the same time, in another sense, none of God's attributes are communicable *as God has them*. When we speak of God as love and mankind as loving, we are using the language of love analogically, not univocally. Only God possesses the attributes infinitely and perfectly. This is why Jesus can say that only God is good (Matt. 9:17). Obviously, the Bible is full of positive descriptions of all sorts of human beings, but man's goodness is dependent, secondary, and accidental (in the philosophical sense). Only God's goodness is independent, original, and essential.

Despite these reservations, the language of "incommunicable" and "communicable" is too common to be discarded. Besides that, the categories hit upon an important distinction. The incommunicable attributes help us to glory in the bigness and otherness of God, while the communicable attributes shine with more splendor when we consider what sort of God it is who deals with us so kindly and so graciously.

DAY 29

Substance and Accidents

Before turning to the divine attributes themselves we need to understand the scholastic distinction between substance and accidents.

According to Aristotle's logic, there is a basic distinction between the thing itself (substance) and what may be said about the thing (accidents). Substance is whatever exists in and of itself, whereas accidents are what modify substances. As a philosophical category, *accident* does not mean a crash or an "oops" or a mistake. The word *incidental* gets closer to the philosophical meaning of the term.

In a previous chapter, we saw that God's attributes are not to be thought of as separate from his essence. Theologians make this point because they want to safeguard that attributes are not the same as accidents. An accident adds a quality to the substance of a thing, although without changing the kind of thing the substance is. Take a dog, for example. A dog has doggy-ness; that's its substance. But a dog can be brown and fluffy or spotted and small or a host of other qualities; those are the accidents (and don't think here about the more familiar sort of doggy accidents!). A dog is a dog no matter its color or size. Take away the specific accidents, and the dog is still a dog. The accidents, though, change what sort of dog we are talking about. In simplest terms, we can think of accidents as giving to a substance its quality or quantity.

Although Protestant theologians reject the distinction as Roman Catholics apply it to the doctrine of transubstantiation, most Reformation and post-Reformation theologians embraced substance and accidents as integral to a proper understanding of God's nature. As a simple being, God is not a compound or made up of parts. God is not like a dog that can exist in many different forms. The color brown is incidental to the nature of a dog because the dog could just as well be black and still be a dog. But nothing true about the essence of God can be taken away from God if we are to still have God.

As is often the case, Turretin parses the matter with precision. He argues that "no accident can be granted in God" because of God's simplicity (accidents imply that God is composed of parts), God's infinity (accidents would add to the substance some new quality), and God's immutability (accidents always allow for change). God is the Great I Am, the one who is that he is, the one whose essence and existence cannot be augmented by any further properties.[1]

In other words, if God is whatever God has—that is, if every attribute of God is identical with his essence—then it does not make sense to say that God can undergo a change of any kind (atemporal or temporal, essential or nonessential). God possesses all of his attributes to the uttermost in such a way that they can be identified with God himself. Consequently, God is only substance. Divinity, by definition, is that true being that can admit no accidents.

The bottom line: everything about God is essential to God; nothing is incidental.

1 Turretin, *Elenctic Theology*, 4.1.4.

DAY 30

Christian Theology and Greco-Roman Philosophy

An important question might be raised at this point: Should Christian theology rely so heavily on the categories and terminology of the Greek philosophical tradition and Aristotle in particular? That's a fair question. We should always be Bible people first and foremost. We don't want to let any system—Aristotelian or otherwise—determine what the Bible means. We never want to dilute Scripture or alter the truth of Scripture so that we end up with a syncretistic blending of God's word and Greek philosophy. Nevertheless, there is warrant for systematic theology to judiciously employ the concepts and language of metaphysics.

Five points to consider.

1. For starters, the influence of the Greek philosophical tradition is so ubiquitous in Western thought that it's doubtful we could get rid of Aristotle even if we tried. To talk about the soul, or the logos, or telos, or form and matter, or substance and accidents, or genus and species, or potential and actual, or the difference between efficient, material, formal, and final causes—to write (or even to think) in these terms is to betray a debt to Aristotle.

2. Along the same lines, it is impossible to be conversant with, and make an informed contribution within, the long history of Christian theology apart from many of the categories of metaphysics. It's not just one or two theologians, for example, who speak of God as Pure Act. Scores of theologians across continents, eras, and languages have used this terminology.

3. We need finely tuned philosophical distinctions in order to show that two or more biblical truths can be affirmed at the same time. There is one God; and the Father, the Son, and the Spirit are each God. How do we explain this biblical truth? The language of essence and persons helps. We might also say that the incarnate Son is *homoousion* (of the same substance) with the Father, not a lesser God who was created by the Father. The concept of essence, so central to Nicene orthodoxy, was not employed to undermine biblical truth, but to safeguard it.

4. More than we often realize, the New Testament already employs concepts from metaphysics and anticipates their further development. Philippians 2:6 speaks of Christ being in the form (*morphe*) of God, and Hebrews 1:3 says the Son is the exact imprint of God's nature (*hypostasis*). Elsewhere we read of the "divine nature" (Rom. 1:20), the fullness of deity (Col. 2:9), and "those that by nature are not gods" (Gal. 4:8). First Timothy 1:17 praises the King of glory as "immortal, invisible," and "the only God." It's not as if the New Testament never uses the concepts familiar to Greek philosophy.

5. We might even say that the concepts of pagan philosophy are subversively fulfilled in the New Testament. Paul was not just making connections with Greek culture in Acts 17 by quoting from their poets or by noting the statue to "an unknown God." He was explaining how some of the ideas and ideals they were groping after in the dark could now be known in the light of Christ and his word. This is often how the Reformers viewed pagan philosophy: it was not true revelation, but it could be insightful and preparatory for the truth that would be revealed in the fullness of time.

DAY 31

The Simplicity of God

Some theologians list as many as nine or ten incommunicable divine attributes. My list has five: simplicity, aseity, infinity, immutability, and impassibility.

The Belgic Confession begins with the declaration "that there is a single and simple spiritual being, whom we call God" (Art. 1). Notice those three words. God is a *single* being, meaning there is only one God. He is a *spiritual* being, meaning he is immaterial. And God is a *simple* being.

The simplicity of God is an important truth few Christians think about. By "simple" we do not mean that God is slow or dim-witted. Nor do we mean that God is easy to understand. Simple, as a divine attribute, is the opposite of compound. Simplicity means God is not made up of things. He doesn't have parts, like a tower of building blocks. He isn't a kitchen recipe with lots of ingredients.

Simplicity means we should not think of God as what you get when you combine goodness and mercy and justice and power and infinity and immutability and roll them all together into one divine being. This would make God the sum of his attributes, and it would make each of his attributes a certain percentage of God. And that would lead us to rank some attributes higher and more essential than others.

Consequently, we ought not suggest, for example, that the love of God is the true nature of God while omnipotence (or holiness or sovereignty or whatever) is only an attribute of God. We often hear people say, "God may have justice or wrath, but he *is* love." The implication is that love is more central to the nature of God, truer to his real identity, than other less essential attributes. But this is to imagine God as a composite being instead of a simple being.

It is perfectly appropriate to highlight the love of God when Scripture makes it such a central theme. But the declaration "God is love" (1 John 4:8) does not carry more metaphysical weight than "God is light" (1 John 1:5), "God is spirit" (John 4:24), "God is a consuming fire" (Heb. 12:29), or any scriptural statements about God (whether the word *is* is there or not). God does not just *have* some attributes. There is no attribute that attaches to him like a barnacle on a ship. He's not a jigsaw puzzle of divine properties. He's not a ball of duct tape with lots of attributes stuck to him.

Divine simplicity helps us think about God in the right way. We should not first conceive of a class of beings called "God" and then relate certain attributes to this particular God. God is in a class by himself. God is not a *type* of divine being, like a giraffe is a type of mammal. There is only one way to be God. And everything about this one God is absolutely essential to being God. God is whatever he has. Every attribute is identical to his essence. He is not the composite of his attributes, some in greater and some in lesser amounts. God is a simple being without parts or pieces. His attributes do not stick to him; he is what they are.

DAY 32

Aseity

The first attribute of God we encounter in the Bible is his self-existence. Alongside God as Creator we immediately encounter God in his aseity. The word *aseity* comes from Latin—*a* meaning "from" and *se* meaning "self." Divine aseity means God exists in and of himself. He is before all things and on him all things depend. He exists absolutely independent of anything or anyone else.

Think about the first verse of the Bible: "In the beginning, God created the heavens and the earth" (Gen. 1:1). These ten words (seven words in Hebrew) are more than an introduction to a chapter, or an introduction to Genesis, or the Pentateuch, or even an introduction to the Bible. These ten words introduce the entire history of the universe. They lay the first brick in the foundation—actually several bricks—for an entire way of seeing, understanding, and inhabiting our world. They tell us the origin and the telos of all things.

In the beginning, there was God.

Actually, even *before* there was a beginning, there was God. Genesis is about the beginning of everything except for God. He always has been, always is, and always will be. God is God. And there is nothing else and no one else who compares with him. God doesn't get lonely or bored or scared. He doesn't need anything from anyone. He is the Great I Am. The Bible starts with the God who never started.

The Bible's opening sentence is crucially important, not only for what it says but for what it does *not* say. Notice that there is no prefatory material before the first verse, no background material before the action gets started in Genesis. There is nothing about a struggle among the gods and goddesses, like we read about in ancient Near Eastern mythology. There is nothing about God needing something or someone. There is nothing about preexistent matter that God then shaped and formed. God predates the story because the story that has been decreed, that one we read in the Bible, the one that you and I inhabit, is a story that has God as its author and its object and its center. God doesn't *enter into* the story, because he *is* the story.

God's independence and self-existence are assumed throughout the Bible and underscored in several passages. Jesus tells us that the Father has life in himself and has granted the Son also to have life in himself (John 5:26). Likewise Moses prays, "Lord, you have been our dwelling place in all generations. Before the mountains were brought forth, or ever you had formed the earth and the world, from everlasting to everlasting you are God" (Ps. 90:1–2). Aseity means that God is distinct from his creation. We live and move and have our being in God (Acts 17:28), not the other way around. In a world that constantly tells us to "express ourselves" and "find ourselves" and sometimes even to "create ourselves," we must remember that only God has life in himself, only God exists of himself, and only God owes his being to no one and nothing.

Divine Infinity

We can understand divine infinity in three ways.

First, God is infinite in relation to himself. We can call this God's *absolute perfection.* All that God has, he is, and all that God is, he is ad infinitum. He possesses love and grace and sovereignty, not largely or mostly or partially but in infinite measure. His greatness is unsearchable (Ps. 145:3). His power and perfection know no limit. God does whatever he pleases, and no one can thwart his plans or purposes. "O Lord, God of our fathers, are you not God in heaven? You rule over all the kingdoms of the nations. In your hand are power and might, so that none is able to withstand you" (2 Chron. 20:6). The nations are as a drop in the bucket (Isa. 40:15). "Our God is in the heavens; he does all that he pleases" (Ps. 115:3).

Second, God is infinite in relation to time. We can call this God's *eternity.* He is without beginning and without end (Ps. 90:2; 1 Tim. 1:17). Unlike all created things, God has no origin and no starting point. Hence, God does not live in time, if by "time" we mean a sequence of before and after events. There never was when

God was not. God has always been God and has always been, even before there was matter or a universe or time as we understand time.

While God relates to his creatures in their hours and days and years, we must be careful with the word *time*. Following Augustine, Reformed theologians have typically understood time not as a thing but as an attribute of a thing. Time and eternity are two different ways of describing *duration*. God and his creatures both have duration, but God's duration, as eternal, is nonsuccessive. There is no unfolding, no before and after (as we know it) with God. The creature, by contrast, has duration with time, which is another way of saying the creature experiences succession. Eternity, then, is not so much a property of God as it describes how God experiences what we call "time" but should be called "duration." In this way, older theologians meant to protect God from all mutation and every kind of succession that would put God in the category of becoming instead of being.

Third, God is infinite in relation to space. We can call this God's *immensity*. He is not constrained by physicality or geographic location. The God who made everything in heaven and earth does not live in temples made by human hands (Acts 17:24). "Am I a God at hand, declares the Lord, and not a God far away? Can a man hide himself in secret places so that I cannot see him? declares the Lord. Do I not fill heaven and earth?" (Jer. 23:23–24). Even heaven and the highest heaven cannot contain God (1 Kings 8:27). Whereas omnipresence suggests God fills every part of space with his being (Eph. 1:23), the attribute of immensity stresses that God's being is not subject to any limitations. The former emphasizes God's immanence, while the latter emphasizes his transcendence. There is nowhere God is not and no way God can be contained—by imperfection, by time, or by space. He is endless, inexhaustible, and unlimited. Though we are finite, we have the privilege to know and to worship the God who is infinite.

DAY 34

Immutability

Immutability, as a divine attribute, means that God does not change. Immutability by itself could be good or bad. If you are implacably wicked, or in unimaginable pain, or just in line at the DMV, then immutability is not a good thing. But as a divine attribute, the immutability of God is a perfection of the divine nature. And not just a single perfection but rather a glory belonging to *all* the attributes of God. God is whatever he has, and all that he is and all that he has can never change.

Immutability is what it means for God to be God. God cannot increase or grow, neither can he decrease or diminish, for any change in God presupposes room for improvement. As Turretin puts it, "He can neither be changed for the better (because he is the best) nor for the worse (because he would cease to be the most perfect)."[1]

God is not just a being; he is pure being. As God says to Moses, "I AM WHO I AM" (Ex. 3:14). As a matter of ontology, there is no *was* or *will be* in God, only I Am. The very name of God—Yahweh, from the verb *to be*—speaks to his unchangeableness. The difference between being and becoming is the difference between the Creator and the creature.

God is not the sort of being that can ever be other than the truth, nor is he the sort of being that can ever be other than what he now is (Num. 23:19). God always does what he says. He fulfills what he speaks. The heavens and the earth may pass away, but God will not change (Ps. 102:25–28). There is no one like God, for only God declares and decrees the end from the beginning. Only God's plans are immovable (Isa. 46:8–11). Only his purposes are absolutely guaranteed (Heb. 6:17).

Malachi 3:6 is a key verse: "For I the LORD do not change; therefore you, O children of Jacob, are not consumed." This is more than just a way of saying God is ethically constant. For God to be morally constant, he must be constant in his character. And if his character is unchanging, his nature must be unchanging. In other words, the children of Judah can count on God's mercy because there is no possibility that God will ever be other than he now is.

There is a reason God is often called a rock (2 Sam. 22:2–3; Pss. 31:3; 62:2, 6). He is not like shifting sand. He is solid and immovable. We can count on God's good and perfect gifts because it is impossible for God to be something more or less than God. Not only is God incapable of change; there can be no shadow or hint of change (James 1:17). God admits no variation, no alteration, no equivocation.

In summary, we can say that God is immutable in his essence, his knowledge, his will, and his purpose. His nature cannot be altered for better or worse. His knowledge can never increase or diminish. Whatever he purposes comes to pass. He is all being and no becoming. There are no latent possibilities in God. Nothing can be added to or subtracted from God. He learns nothing and needs nothing. He does not grow. He does not improve. God does not change.

---

1 Turretin, *Elenctic Theology*, 3.9.4.

DAY 35

Impassibility

Divine impassibility means that God does not suffer. God cannot be acted upon from without, neither can his inner state change for better or worse. As the Westminster Confession puts it, God is "without body, parts, or passions" (WCF 2.1).

Of all the classic attributes, impassibility is the one most likely to be rejected by contemporary Christians. A number of questions are often raised: Isn't the God of the Bible full of emotion and pathos? Isn't impassibility just a holdover from Greek philosophy and the idea of an unmoved mover? In a world of pain, who wants a God immune from human suffering? Besides, doesn't the crucifixion reveal that God—in his very nature—is a suffering God?

Given these objections, why should Christians still affirm divine impassibility? Four reasons.

First, this has been the position of the Christian church from the beginning. The early church held it as self-evident that God was unchangeable, eternal, and incapable of being acted upon from within or without. This did not mean that God was static and lifeless. The church fathers stated strongly that the impassible God was also entirely active. He is immovable, but not inert. He does not have emotions like us, but he is not motionless. From Anselm to Aquinas to Calvin, almost no theologian believed that God suffered. At the same time, they never thought of God as distant or uncaring.

Second, divine passibility leads to all sorts of problems. If God suffers along with us, then not only must God be miserable all the time; God must be undergoing constant change. This places God on the same ontological level as his creation. He is no longer being; he is becoming. This in turn leads to errors like process theology whereby God is in process with us, hoping to solve the problem of human suffering so that he himself can be free from his own suffering.

Third, God's affections are not identical to our emotions. Just as the Bible is full of anthropomorphisms (describing God as having a human body), so the Bible is full of anthropopathisms (describing God as having human emotions). While we do not want to be afraid to use the language of Scripture, we must not think that God "feels" the way we feel. Emotions sweep over us, but God is not made to feel by forces outside of himself. Nor does he will changes in his inner life. God is so completely full of action that he cannot change. Impassibility does not reject God's vitality; it safeguards it.

Fourth, impassibility maintains the full glory and mystery and condescension of the incarnation. If God as God can suffer, then there was no need for the Son of God to become for a little while lower than the angels so that by the grace of God he might taste death for everyone (Heb. 2:9). Think of the line from Wesley's hymn "And Can It Be": "'Tis mystery all, the Immortal dies." There is nothing remarkable about the mortal dying and nothing amazing about the possible suffering. The wonder is that in the incarnation, God did the most un-Godlike thing possible; he suffered and died. The incarnation is not a revelation of the eternal suffering of God but the deepest expression of God's love whereby God chose freely to suffer as one of us. The good news is not that God feels our pain but that on the cross, the God-man felt human pain, and that by his suffering and death he conquered sin, death, and the devil.

WEEK 8

DAY 36

Theopaschitism and Patripassianism

Over the past century, the doctrine of divine impassibility has come under increasing scrutiny. To suggest that God can suffer—and indeed that he *must* suffer if he is to be truly loving—has become the new orthodoxy. But for most of Christian history theologians understood that God does not and cannot suffer. In fact, divine passibility is at the heart of two ancient heresies: theopaschitism and patripassianism.

True, some theologians teach that God suffers without affirming all the doctrinal implications of these two heresies. That was the position of John Stott, who believed that God suffered in Christ and suffers with his people still, in his otherwise excellent book *The Cross of Christ*.[1] Stott's nuances notwithstanding, it is important to be aware that impassibility has been the majority opinion in the history of the church and that notions of God suffering as God on the cross have been ruled out of bounds. Both theopaschitism and patripassianism were rejected by the church in the sixth century, by the patriarch of Constantinople in the East, and in the West by Pope Hormisdas.

Theopaschitism comes from two Greek words: *theos* meaning "God" and *pascho* meaning "to suffer." Hence, theopaschitism is the belief that God suffered as God on the cross. So that when Jesus died, God suffered. Theopaschitism was a Christological heresy, defended by monophysites like Peter the Fuller of Antioch, who believed that Christ had only one nature (*mono* + *physis*). When Christ died on the cross, then, the divine nature also suffered because there is no strict distinction between the divine and human natures.

Patripassianism, on the other hand, was a Trinitarian heresy. It asserted that the Father (*patri*) suffered (*passian*) along with the Son on the cross. Not only did the Son suffer in his God-forsakenness on the cross; the Father also suffered in his dying Son. Patripassianism was essentially modalistic, believing that the Father and the Son were the same person appearing in different modes of being. Therefore, whatever the Son experienced, the Father also experienced because the persons of the Trinity are not distinct persons. The Son cannot suffer, it is argued, without the Father also suffering, for there is one God, and this one God is the Father.

Long before official rejection in the sixth century, the ideas espoused in theopaschitism and patripassianism were considered dangerous, if not outright heretical. Even if we do not wish to embrace all the implications of these -isms, we cannot assert the suffering of God without running into Trinitarian and Christological problems. The reason the incarnation was necessary—and the reason it is so ineffably glorious—is that only by taking on human flesh could the Son of God suffer. The Council of Rome (382) put it well: "If anyone says, that in the passion of the cross God felt pain, and not the body with the soul which the Son of God Christ had assumed—the form of a servant, which He had taken upon himself [cf. Phil. 2:7], as says the Scripture—he does not think rightly."

1 Stott, *The Cross of Christ*, 155, 326.

DAY 37

Attributes of Intellect

The list of God's communicable attributes can be very long, with most lists counting as many as ten or fifteen or twenty different attributes. I'm going to group eleven communicable attributes under three headings: intellect, will, and power (i.e., God's thinking, God's choosing, and God's doing).

Under the category of intellect, we can mention three attributes: knowledge, wisdom, and truthfulness.

1. Although *knowledge* is considered a communicable attribute insofar as human beings also know things, God's knowledge is different from ours in both nature and extent.

The nature of God's knowledge is archetypal while ours is ectypal. Unlike human knowledge, God's knowledge is innate and immediate. That is, he does not acquire knowledge by observation, learning, or reason. He cannot increase in what he knows. All that God knows, he knows simultaneously, not by successive insights or experiences.

God's knowledge also differs from ours in extent. We know in part. God knows everything. God's knowledge of all things past, present, and future is called omniscience. God knows the heart (Ps. 119:1–4). He knows the ways of men (Deut. 2:7; Pss. 1:6; 119:168). Nothing can be hidden from his sight (Isa. 29:15). God knows the place of our habitation (Ps. 33:13), the hairs on our head (Matt. 10:30), and the days of our lives (Ps. 37:18). God knows all contingent events (1 Sam. 23:10–11; 2 Kings 13:19; Ps. 81:14–15; Isa. 42:9; 48:18; Jer. 2:2–3; Matt. 11:21), and he has certain knowledge of all future events (Acts 2:23; Rom. 9:16; Eph. 1:11; Phil. 2:13). "No creature is hidden from his sight, but all are naked and exposed to the eyes of him to whom we must give account" (Heb. 4:13). "Great is our Lord, and abundant in power; his understanding is beyond measure" (Ps. 147:5).

2. God's *wisdom* is "that perfection of God whereby he applies his knowledge to the attainment of his ends in a way that glorifies him most."[1] Scripture often extols the wisdom of God (Ps. 104:1–34; Prov. 8). When we are tempted to doubt this attribute, we should consider that if human parents know more than their children—even though parental ways do not always make sense to their children—surely, we can trust the manifold wisdom of God even when his ways may not make sense to us (Eph. 3:10). "Oh, the depth of the riches and wisdom and knowledge of God! How unsearchable are his judgments and how inscrutable his ways" (Rom. 11:33).

3. God is *truthful* in all his ways. His veracity is metaphysical in that he is to be distinguished from all false gods (Ps. 115:4–8; Isa. 44:9–20). His veracity is ethical in that he cannot lie (Num. 23:19; Rom. 3:4; Heb. 6:18). And his veracity is promissory in that he is the faithful God who always keeps covenant and steadfast love (Deut. 7:9; 1 Cor. 1:9). God knows all things and all creatures as they really are. He only and always speaks and does what is the truth.

---

1 Berkhof, *Systematic Theology*, 69.

DAY 38

Attributes of Will

Under the heading of "will" are a number of moral attributes (so classified because they give expression to God's revealed will). Let me mention seven of these attributes.

1. God is *holy*. Famously, this is the only divine attribute mentioned in three-fold repetition. "Holy, holy, holy is the LORD of hosts; the whole earth is full of his glory" (Isa. 6:3). Holiness refers to the perfection of God's ethical character (1:16). It also refers to the otherness of his nature. Just as Israel had priests, garments, days, utensils, buildings, places, and artifacts that were set apart, so God is a being set apart. Our holy God is wholly other, the one who was and is and is to come (Rev. 4:8).

2. God is *good*. On an ontological level, no one is truly good except for God (Mark 10:18). God's goodness is the opposite of what is harsh, cruel, severe, exacting, demeaning, or gruff. God only and always does what is good (Acts 14:17). "For the LORD is good; his steadfast love endures forever, and his faithfulness to all generations" (Ps. 100:5).

3. God is *love*. Even though our culture frequently misunderstands this attribute, reducing love to a feeling of unconditional affirmation, the Bible loves to exult in the love of God (1 John 4:7–12). Most poignantly, we see the love of God displayed in the sending and the sacrifice of his Son (John 3:16; 16:27; Rom. 5:8; 1 John 4:10). Although we think of God's love as one thing, earlier theologians helpfully distinguished among three kinds of divine love: the love of benevolence (God's good will toward human beings), the love of beneficence (God's kind actions toward his creatures), and the love of complacency (God's satisfactory delight in himself, in the Son, and in all those who are united to the Son).

4. God is *gracious*. He shows unmerited favor toward sinners (Eph. 1:6–7; 2:7–9; Titus 2:11; 3:4–7).

5. God is *merciful*. He is kind to the weak, the weary, the mournful, and the miserable (Pss. 51:1; 145:9; Hab. 3:2; Eph. 2:4; 1 Pet. 2:10).

6. God is *long-suffering*. He is patient with his wayward people, slow to anger, and eager to forgive (Ex. 34:6; Rom. 2:4; 2 Pet. 3:9).

7. God is *righteous*. The quality of righteousness can be predicated of God himself in reference to God's uprightness and moral excellence. God never fails to do what is right. As expressed toward his creatures, God's righteousness is displayed in giving to each one his due. The attribute of righteousness is closely linked to divine justice. The remunerative justice of God means God rewards what is good, while

retributive justice means God punishes the one who does evil. God is always just. Indeed, righteousness and justice are the foundation of his throne (Ps. 89:14). The cross is how God can be both just and the justifier of the ungodly. Mercy does not triumph by the removal of justice. God's grace and mercy are made evident through the satisfaction of divine justice, such that we are cleansed from all unrighteousness not just because God is loving but because God is faithful and just (1 John 1:9).

DAY 39

Attributes of Power

Many Christians are familiar with the three *omnis* as a shorthand description of God's character. God is omniscient (there is nothing he does not know). God is omnipresent (there is nowhere he cannot be). God is omnipotent (there is nothing he cannot do). It's this last category that concerns God's unrivaled power.

Although we have classified omnipotence as a communicable attribute (because we too can exercise power), the attribute is, in another sense, incommunicable because our exercise of power is not like God's. When God exercises power, no step is necessary between the willing and the doing. We cannot will a book into existence or create a painting by merely deciding that we want the painting to exist. The production of these things may start in the will, but they take considerable time and effort to produce. God, on the other hand, can do by willing whatever he pleases. To be sure, he often uses means to accomplish his purposes, but he does not *need* to use means. And even when God does employ means (i.e., feeding his people by seed and rain and sun and harvest instead of by manna from heaven), there is never the possibility that what God purposes will not come to pass. This is the highest conceivable idea of power.

For God, the mere willing of an outcome guarantees that outcome. God's power is unlimited. He does not struggle to accomplish his purposes. There is nothing too hard for God (Jer. 32:6). With God all things are possible (Matt. 19:26). Our God is in the heavens; he does whatever he pleases (Ps. 115:3). Compared to God, all the inhabitants of the earth are as nothing. None can stay his hand (Dan. 4:35). God's purposes and God's promises never fail because God's power never falters.

Divine sovereignty is related to divine omnipotence. Only a God possessing absolute power can exercise absolute control over all things. God works all things after the counsel of his own will (Eph. 1:11). He determines the number of the stars and gives to all of them their names (Ps. 147:4). The God of heaven rules over all the kingdoms of the nations. Power and might are in his hands, and no one can withstand him (2 Chron. 20:6). Although God is not the doer of all that is done—we believe in proximate causes, human volition, and human responsibility—yet everything that comes to pass has its origin in the sovereignty of God. Nothing escapes his control, and no one operates independent of his will and power.

Coming to terms with divine sovereignty can be hard for many Christians. We will have opportunity to revisit the topic when we look at the decrees of God. But for now it is worth remembering that no attribute of God should be divorced from all the other attributes. God's absolute power, for example, does not exist independent of God's goodness, love, mercy, knowledge, truth, immutability, and wisdom. Unlike our exercise of power, God never wields power capriciously or callously. The good news in God doing whatever he pleases is that God always works for the good of his people and for the glory of his name.

DAY 40

Transcendence and Immanence

At the heart of many theological errors is a failure to pay proper attention to either God's transcendence or God's immanence.

God is infinitely above us and beyond us. That's transcendence. We need a God who is strong, sovereign, all-knowing, all-powerful, independent, unchangeable, holy, and utterly unlike us. At the same time, God draws near to us in Christ—not simply as God in the midst of the camp, but as God in human flesh. That's immanence. We need a God who is caring, compassionate, good, loving, patient, just, and kind.

True doctrine, true devotion, and true religion require us to affirm transcendence and immanence at the same time. False religious systems that undervalue transcendence end up with a weak, sentimental, temperamental, localized deity who looks more like the creature than the Creator. False religious systems that undervalue immanence end up with an impersonal and unknowable God who is to be feared more than he is to be loved.

The prophet's word of comfort to the Babylonian exiles in Isaiah 40 is, among other things, a long meditation on God's transcendence and God's immanence. The God of Isaiah 40 is absolute immensity (v. 12), absolute intelligence (v. 13), and absolute independence (v. 14). He has power over the nations (vv. 15–17). He has power over idols (vv. 18–20). He has power over the people of the earth (vv. 21–24) and over all creation (vv. 25–26).

God's favorite name in Isaiah is "the Holy One." Thirty-five times in Isaiah God is called the "Holy One" or the "Holy One of Jacob" or the "Holy One of Israel." No doubt Isaiah's experience in chapter 6 had a profound effect on him. He saw the Lord high and lifted up. He heard the angels cry out, "Holy, holy, holy is the LORD of hosts; the whole earth is full of his glory!" (6:3). This is no small God.

And that is welcome relief to Judah! When Jerusalem is told to be a gospel herald, it is the God of transcendence that she declares. It is precisely because God is wholly other that drawing near is such good news. God comes to his people in Isaiah 40:28–29 with grace-filled, hope-inspiring theology. The Lord reminds Israel of his power, as if to say, "I am the everlasting God. I am the Creator of everything everywhere. I don't get tired. I don't get weary. That is your comfort. *I* am your good news."

In our suffering and pain, we must not think that God is stumped or that he is baffled by it all, or that he'd like to help but he's too enmeshed in the same mess. God's bigness does not mean he is too great to care, just like his nearness does not mean he is too weak to help. Instead, the right inference to draw in all of life's afflictions is that the God of transcendent glory and personal immanence is too good to forget and too great to fail.

WEEK 9

DAY 41

God as Trinity

As we saw earlier, studying the doctrine of God invites us to ask two foundational questions: "What is God like?" and "Who is God?" The first question leads us to investigate the *nature* of God, while the second question leads us into an exploration of the *persons* of God. We answered the question "What is God like?" by looking at his attributes. We can only answer the second question, "Who is God?" by understanding the Trinity.

If any doctrine makes Christianity Christian, then surely it is the doctrine of the Trinity. Augustine, in his work *On the Trinity*, observed that "in no other subject is error more dangerous, or inquiry more laborious, or the discovery of truth more profitable."[1] More recently, Sinclair Ferguson commented, "I've often reflected on the rather obvious thought that when his disciples were about to have the world collapse in on them, our Lord spent so much time in the Upper Room speaking to them about the mystery of the Trinity. If anything could underline the necessity of Trinitarianism for practical Christianity, that must surely be it!"[2]

Yet when it comes to the doctrine of the Trinity, many Christians are poor in their understanding, poorer in their articulation of the doctrine, and poorest of all in how the doctrine matters in real life. But the doctrine of the Trinity is not meant to demoralize the Christian; it is meant for our devotion and our delight.

The great creeds and confessions of the church are structured around our three-in-one God.

- The Apostles' Creed is divided into three sections based on the Trinity: I believe in God the Father. I believe in Jesus Christ his only Son, our Lord. I believe in the Holy Spirit.

- The Athanasian Creed claims, "This is the catholic faith: That we worship one God in trinity and the trinity in unity, neither blending their persons, nor dividing their essence. For the person of the Father is a distinct person, the person of the Son is another, and that of the Holy Spirit, still another. But the divinity of the Father, Son, and Holy Spirit is one, their glory equal, their majesty coeternal."

- The Belgic Confession states: "In keeping with this truth and Word of God we believe in one God, who is one single essence, in whom there are three persons, really, truly, and eternally distinct according to their incommunicable properties—namely, Father, Son, and Holy Spirit."

If we are to have a historic, robust, thoroughly biblical understanding of God, we must know him as three in one and one in three; we must know him as Trinity. All the talk of essence and persons and co-this and co-that may seem like esoteric theological wrangling reserved for philosophers and scholars, not for moms and mechanics and college students. But, despite all the complicated vocabulary, the doctrine is quite understandable (if not fully comprehensible). We just have to be prepared to think, to learn, and to listen to the voices of those who have gone before us and have done the hard work of safeguarding all that the Bible means to affirm by one God and three divine persons.

1 Augustine, *On the Trinity*, 1.3.5.
2 Quoted in Letham, *The Holy Trinity*, 375.

DAY 42

The Bible and the Trinity

The doctrine of the Trinity can be summarized in seven statements: (1) There is only one God. (2) The Father is God. (3) The Son is God. (4) The Holy Spirit is God. (5) The Father is not the Son. (6) The Son is not the Holy Spirit. (7) The Holy Spirit is not the Father.

All of the creedal formulations and precise theological terms and philosophical apologetics have to do with safeguarding each one of the seven statements and doing so without denying any of the other six. When the ancient creeds employ extrabiblical terminology and demand careful theological nuance, they do so not to clear up what the Bible leaves cloudy, but to defend, define, and delimit essential biblical propositions.

Although the word *Trinity* is famously absent from the Bible, the theology behind the word can be found in a surprising number of verses.

For starters there are verses that speak of God's oneness (Deut. 6:4; Isa. 44:6; 1 Tim. 1:17).

Then there are a myriad of passages which demonstrate that God is Father (e.g., John 6:27; Titus 1:4).

Next, we have scores of texts that prove the deity of Jesus Christ, the Son—passages like John 1:1 ("the Word was God"), John 8:58 ("before Abraham was, I am"), Colossians 2:9 ("in him the whole fullness of deity dwells bodily"), Hebrews 1:3 ("He is the radiance of the glory of God and the exact imprint of his nature"), and Titus 2:13 ("our great God and Savior Jesus Christ"). And this is to say nothing of the worship Christ willingly received from his disciples (Luke 24:52; John 20:28) and the charges of blasphemy leveled against him for making himself equal with God (Mark 2:7).

Then we have similar texts that assume the deity of the Holy Spirit, calling him an "eternal Spirit" (Heb. 9:14) and using "God" interchangeably with the "Holy Spirit" (Acts 5:3–4; 1 Cor. 3:16; 6:19) without any embarrassment or need for explanation.

The shape of Trinitarian orthodoxy is finally rounded off by texts that hint at the plurality of persons in the Godhead (Gen. 1:1–3, 26; Ps. 2:7; Dan. 7:9–14)—texts like 1 Corinthians 8:6 that place Jesus Christ as Lord right in the middle of the Jewish Shema, and dozens of texts that speak of Father, Son, and Holy Spirit in the same breath, equating the three in rank while assuming distinction of personhood (Matt. 28:19; 1 Cor. 12:4–6; 2 Cor. 2:21–22; 13:14; Gal. 4:6; 1 Pet. 1:1–2).

The book of Ephesians, for example, is full of triadic formulas like Christ/Spirit/ God or Spirit/Lord/Father (1:13–14; 2:18, 20–22; 3:14–17; 4:4–6; 5:18–20; 6:10–18), indicating that the persons are deserving of the same honor and that each person can be distinguished from the other two persons.

The doctrine of the Trinity, as summarized in the seven statements above, is not a philosophical concoction by overzealous and overintelligent theologians, but is one of the central planks of orthodoxy that can be demonstrated from a multitude of biblical texts and is meant to be understood, articulated, and celebrated.

DAY 43

Trinitarian Terms

The twentieth-century theologian Bernard Lonergan once quipped, "The Trinity is a matter of five notions or properties, four relations, three persons, two processions, one substance or nature, and no understanding."[1] Although meant to poke fun at the complexity of Aquinas, Lonergan's wry observation provides a good introduction to the world of Trinitarian terminology.

Five notions. A notion is the idea whereby we know a divine person. Aquinas argued that the five notions in God are: innascibility, paternity, filiation, common spiration, and procession.[2] The Father is known by innascibility ("incapable of being born") because he is from no one, and by paternity because he is a Father to the Son. The Son is known by filiation because he is a Son to the Father. The Father and the Son are both known by common spiration because they both breathe out (spirate) the Holy Spirit. Procession belongs to the Holy Spirit because he proceeds from the Father and the Son.

Four properties. In Lonergan's quip he equates a notion with a property, but according to Aquinas the terms are not identical. A property is what is proper to each divine person alone. Since common spiration is an idea associated with the Father and the Son, there are only four properties. Innascibility and paternity are proper to the Father; filiation is proper to the Son; procession is proper to the Holy Spirit.

Four relations. Look again at the five notions. Only four are relations. Innascibility is not a relation because it does not speak of relating to the other persons.

Three persons. The three persons are distinguished by their relations of origin, what Aquinas calls their "personal notions." Innascibility and common spiration are notions of persons (ideas associated with the person), but paternity, filiation, and procession are personal notions because they constitute divine persons. That is to say, we distinguish among the three persons of the Trinity by recognizing that the Father is the Father because he begets the Son, the Son is the Son because he is begotten by the Father, and the Spirit is the Spirit because he proceeds from the Father and the Son. It's important to recognize that notions and properties and processions are not realities in the philosophical sense (which is why, for example, we don't call God a quinary on account of the five notions). Philosophically, the single divine substance is a reality, and the three divine persons are realities.

Two processions. A procession refers to the origin of one thing from another. Although procession is the personal notion of the Spirit (proceeding from the Father and the Son), we can also speak, in general terms, of the Son's procession from the Father. Since the relation is of a Father and a Son, we call this "generation" or "filiation," but those words simply describe how to conceive of the Son proceeding from the Father.

One substance. The three persons of the Trinity share the same substance. They all possess the same essence or "God-ness." One person is not more or less God than another. There is only one God—and Father, Son, and Holy Spirit are each fully God, equal in glory, rank, and power.

Yes, it is confusing, but hopefully we can do better than "no understanding"! The most important thing to remember is one and three. God is one by unity of essence, and three by trinity of persons.

1 Quoted by O'Collins, "The Holy Trinity," 2.
2 Aquinas, *Summa Theologica*, 1.32.3.

DAY 44

One and Three

The Westminster Confession of Faith gives a succinct definition of the doctrine of the Trinity:

> In the unity of the Godhead there be three persons, of one substance, power, and eternity: God the Father, God the Son, and God the Holy Ghost: the Father is of none, neither begotten, nor proceeding; the Son is eternally begotten of the Father; the Holy Ghost eternally proceeding from the Father and the Son. (2.3)

This definition is less complicated than Aquinas's. And yet the same basic outline is present. The three persons of the Trinity are not three existences, as if they were independent beings; they are three *subsistences*, meaning each person (*hypostasis*) shares the same essence and can be identified equally as God. The three persons are distinguished by their personal properties, that is, by how each person relates to the other two. The Father is of none, he is the begetter of the Son; the Son is begotten of the Father; and the Spirit proceeds from the Father and the Son.

Sometimes it's easier to understand what we believe by stating what Christians *don't* believe.

- Orthodox Trinitarianism rejects *adoptionism*, which believes that the power of God came upon Jesus at his baptism, thereby "adopting" him into the Godhead and deifying his humanity.

- Orthodox Trinitarianism rejects *monarchianism*, which believes in only one supreme divine person (*mono*) and maintains that the Son and the Spirit subsist in the divine essence as impersonal attributes, not distinct and divine persons.

- Orthodox Trinitarianism rejects *modalism* (also called Sabellianism, after its most famous proponent) which believes that Father, Son, and Holy Spirit are different names for the same God acting in different roles or manifestations (like the well-intentioned but misguided "water, ice, vapor" analogy).

- Orthodox Trinitarianism rejects *Arianism* and all forms of ontological subordinationism that deny the full deity of Christ. In Arianism, the full divine essence is only to be identified with the Father. The Son and the Spirit are separate entities who do not share the divine nature. They are subordinate in rank, power, glory, and being to the Father. They are created beings and not eternal.

- And finally, orthodox Trinitarianism rejects all forms of tritheism, which teach that the three members of the Godhead are, as in Mormon theology, three distinct beings and three separate Gods.

In orthodox Trinitarian theology, God is one, and the divine essence is held in common by Father, Son, and Holy Spirit. The three divine persons are consubstantial, coinherent, coequal, and coeternal. They are distinguishable with respect to their personal properties, but they do not differ in authority, rank, power, or glory. Gregory of Nazianzus, the fourth-century Cappadocian father, put it memorably:

"No sooner do I conceive of the one than I am illumined by the splendor of the three; no sooner do I distinguish them than I am carried back to the one."[1]

1 Nanzianus, *Theological Orations,* 40.41.

Eternal Generation

Eternal generation refers to the never-beginning and never-ending act whereby God the Father communicates the divine essence to God the Son. To put it another way, eternal generation is how the Son can be every bit as divine as the Father, and yet the Son is still not the same person as the Father.

Although some evangelical scholars have argued that we don't need the doctrine and that it's more speculative than biblical, eternal generation has been a key tenet in Trinitarian theology since the first centuries of the church, through the Reformation, and in most expressions of the Protestant tradition. Five times in the New Testament the Greek word *monogenes*—translated as "only begotten" in the KJV—is used with reference to Jesus (John 1:14, 18; 3:16, 18; 1 John 4:9). While most newer translations render the term "only" or "one of kind," Lee Irons has made a compelling argument that historically, etymologically, and contextually the term normally means "only begotten." If Irons is correct, then the apostle John views Christ as the Father's only proper offspring and as deriving his divinity from the Father.[1]

We should not think, however, that eternal generation depends on *monogenes* alone (indeed, many scholars who think *monogenes* means "only" still affirm eternal generation). Psalm 2:7 speaks of the Messiah as a begotten Son, Proverbs 8 refers to the Lord's Wisdom as the first act of old, and Micah 5:2 says that the child to be born in Bethlehem went forth from of old, from the days of eternity. These verses suggest an eternal act whereby the second person of the Trinity is begotten (but not created) from the first person of the Trinity.

The doctrine is difficult because we must rely on human language to describe a divine mystery.

- Eternal generation is like human generation in that one essence begets the same essence, but unlike human generation in that it does not involve physical reproduction.

- Eternal generation is hyperphysical (not material), infinite (does not take place in time), and ineffable (beyond total comprehension).

- Eternal generation is the communication of the divine essence, but not the creating of a divine being or the act whereby the Son became divine.

- Eternal generation is the unchanging act whereby the Father generates the person (but not the essence) of the Son.

Confusing, isn't it? And yet orthodox theologians have insisted upon the doctrine because it explains how the Godhead can have multiple subsistences without multiplying essences. Eternal generation answers the question: How can the Son be of the same God-ness as the Father and yet not be the Father? The answer, in the words of the Nicene Creed, is that the one Lord Jesus Christ is "the only Son of God, begotten from the Father before all ages, God from God, Light from Light, true God from true God, begotten, not made; of the same essence as the Father." Or consider the Christmas carol: "God of God, Light of Light. Lo, he abhors not the Virgin's womb; Very God, begotten, not created." That's the doctrine of eternal generation. We do well to affirm it, even better to sing it.

1 Irons, "A Lexical Defense."

WEEK 10

DAY 46

The *Filioque* Clause

The doctrinal formulation approved at Nicaea (325)—and the subsequent Nicene Creed (as we know it) adopted at the Council of Constantinople (381)—affirmed that the Holy Spirit "proceeds from the Father." Later, as the Arians continued to reject the full deity of the Son, churches in the West began to confess that the Holy Spirit "proceeds from the Father and the Son." In Latin, the phrase "and the Son" is one word: *filioque*. That new word was added to the Nicene Creed at the Council of Toledo (589) and has been accepted in the Western church—implicitly at first, and over time explicitly—ever since.

In the East, however, the *filioque* clause has always been controversial. For starters, the Eastern church objected to the West adding to the Nicene Creed on its own, apart from an ecumenical council. On theological grounds, the East worried that the *filioque* clause undermined the authority and primacy of the Father, making the Father and the Son two coordinate *arches* or two principles from which the Spirit proceeds. In 1439, the Council of Florence brought some healing to this East-West division by determining that the Spirit proceeds from the Father through the Son. This language allowed for the West's insistence that the Son is consubstantial with the Father, while also dealing with the East's insistence that the Father is the origin of both the Son and the Spirit.

While sympathizing with the East's initial reasons for being wary of the *filioque* clause, there are nevertheless good reasons for affirming that the Spirit proceeds from the Father and the Son. Turretin mentions four reasons.[1]

1. The Holy Spirit is sent from the Father and the Son (John 16:7). Surely, this temporal mission (sending) must reflect something of eternal procession.

2. The Holy Spirit is often called the Spirit of Christ (Rom. 8:9; Gal. 4:6; 1 Pet. 1:11). If he is the Spirit of Christ, shouldn't we also conclude that he is the Spirit *from* Christ?

3. Jesus tells the disciples that the Spirit glorifies him, takes what is his, and will declare it to them. If the Son glorifies the Father and speaks only what the Father gives him—and the Son is generated from the Father—then the Spirit who glorifies the Son and speaks only what the Son gives him must owe his origin, in some respect, to the Son (John 16:13–15).

4. Christ breathed out the Spirit on his disciples in time (John 20:22). He must have, therefore, breathed out the Spirit in eternity.

Although John 15:26 says that the Spirit proceeds from the Father and does not mention procession from the Son, the latter truth is implied by the teaching in John 16 that whatever the Father has, the Son has as well. The Spirit does not proceed from the Father and the Son as if they were two separate principles, nor does the Spirit proceed from both as if the Father breathes into the Son and then the Son breathes again. The breathing power, as Turretin puts it, is numerically one. The language of "through the Son" means that the Father is the fountain of deity from whom the Son is eternally begotten, even though the Spirit proceeds from both.

The double procession of the Spirit, though a complex and controversial doctrine, reminds us that the Holy Spirit is now and always has been the Spirit of Christ and that our theology (according to the Word) and our worship (by the Spirit) are ever connected.

---

1 Turretin, *Elenctic Theology*, 1.309–10.

Perichoresis

It is a recurring theme from the lips of Jesus that the Father dwells in the Son. "I am in the Father and the Father is in me" (John 14:11). All that Jesus asks in the high priestly prayer is rooted in the reality that the Son is in the Father, and the Father is in the Son. The apostle Paul, likewise, testifies that in the incarnate Son "all the fullness of God was pleased to dwell" (Col. 1:19).

We usually understand these verses to be about Christ's deity. And rightly so. But they also speak to the mutual indwelling of the persons of the Trinity. The Father, the Son, and the Holy Spirit are distinct persons—distinguished, as we have seen, by paternity, filiation, and spiration. And yet we must not think of the three persons as three faces in a yearbook. The Father indwells the Son; the Son indwells the Spirit; the Spirit indwells the Father (and you could reverse the order in each pair).

The Greek term used to describe the eternal mutual indwelling of the persons of the Trinity is *perichoresis* (in Latin, *circumincession*). The word *circulatio* is also sometimes used as a way of metaphorically describing the unceasing circulation of the divine essence such that each person is in the other two, while the others are in each one. At the risk of putting things in physical terms, *perichoresis* means that "all three persons occupy the same divine 'space.'"[1] In other words, we cannot "see" God without seeing all three persons at the same time.

The mutual indwelling of *perichoresis* means two things. First, the three persons of the Trinity are all fully in one another. And second, each person of the Trinity is in full possession of the divine essence. To be sure, the Father is not the Son, the Son is not the Spirit, and the Spirit is not the Father. *Perichoresis* does not deny these distinctions. What *perichoresis* maintains is that you cannot have one person of the Trinity without having the other two, and you cannot have any person of the Trinity without having the fullness of God. As Augustine put it: "Each are in each, and all in each, and each in all, and all are one."[2]

Like many aspects of Trinitarian theology, this one can be hard to grasp because we have to rely on careful verbal definitions rather than concrete analogies. We must not think of *perichoresis*—as some have wrongly suggested from the etymology of the word—as a kind of Trinitarian dance. Such an analogy, and its social Trinitarian implications, undermines the truth that *perichoresis* means to protect. In asking the question, "How can three persons simultaneously share the same undivided essence?" the answer is not that Father, Son, and Holy Spirit waltz in step with each other. The answer (insofar as we can understand an ineffable mystery) is that Father, Son, and Holy Spirit coinhere in such a way that the persons are always and forever with and in one another, yet without merging, blending, or confusing. Only by affirming the mutual indwelling of each in each other can we worship our triune God as truly three and truly one.

1   Bray, *The Doctrine of God*, 158.
2   Augustine, *On the Trinity*, 6.10.

DAY 48

Taxis

Taxis is the Greek word for "order." In Trinitarian theology, *taxis* is not meant to suggest a hierarchy of persons, but refers to the order of relations whereby God's inner and outer life is *from the Father through the Son by the Holy Spirit* and never in the reverse order.

In his explanation and defense of the divinity of Christ, Zacharias Ursinus raises and refutes a number of "sophisms of heretics against the eternal Deity of the Son."[1] The eighth sophism is that "the Son has a head and is less than the Father. Therefore he is not one and the same essence with the Father." To this Ursinus replies, "The Son has a head in respect to his human nature, and his office as mediator. These things, however, do not detract any thing from his Divinity." Later, Ursinus argues that "the Father, therefore, is greater than the Son, not as to his essence, in which the Son is equal with the Father, but as to his office and human nature." In other words, we can properly speak of order so long as we understand that we are talking about Christ's mediatorial office and about his earthly mission, not about his person being inferior or subjugated to the Father.

Ursinus maintains that the persons of the Godhead can be distinguished in two ways: (1) by their works *ad intra* (on the inside) and (2) by their mode of operating *ad extra* (on the outside).

The first point has to do with the way in which the three persons relate to one another. The Father is the first person because he is the fountain of divinity. The Son is the second person because the divine essence is communicated to him from the Father. And the Spirit is the third person because the divine essence is communicated to him from the Father and the Son. None of this means that the

Son or the Spirit became God at a moment in time; generation and procession are from eternity.

The second point has to do with how the three persons operate out of themselves toward their creatures. Ursinus argues that while all the works toward their creatures come by the common will and power of Father, Son, and Holy Spirit, yet at the same time there is an order to their work. The Father works through the Son, and the Son works by the Holy Spirit. In their external operations, the Father sends the Son, and the Son saves and sanctifies by the Spirit.

All of this means that we are right to speak of a *taxis* in the Trinity. In this way, in a qualified sense, some have spoken of the Father being greater than the Son, or the Son being subordinate to the Father. This language, however, if used at all, must be carefully guarded so as not to undermine the unity of the persons as having one essence and one will and sharing in all the same perfections. The three persons are not distinguished by roles of authority and submission. The persons are distinguished *ad extra* by their economic modes of operation: in the one work of the triune God, the Father works by the Son, and the Son works, together with the Father, through the Holy Spirit.

1 Ursinus, *Commentary*, 200–201.

Inseparable Operations

The Latin phrase *opera Trinitatis ad extra sunt indivisa* ("the external works of the Trinity are undivided") affirms that the three persons of the Trinity share one principle of operation. There are three agents that act, but these three share one agency by which they act. Since Father, Son, and Holy Spirit are one in essence, in will, and in power, it is not possible that one person of the Trinity would do or decide one thing, while another person would do or decide something different. God is indivisible in being, and so he must be indivisible in his work.

Scripture testifies that creation, redemption, and providence are each the work of the whole Trinity.

In the beginning, God created by the word of his mouth, with the Spirit of God hovering over the face of the waters (Gen. 1:1–5). Likewise, Psalm 33:6 exclaims, "By the word of the LORD the heavens were made, and by the breath of his mouth all their host." The Word was with God in the beginning, and all things were made through him (John 1:2; Col. 1:15; Heb. 1:2).

Redemption is especially linked to the unified work of the Trinity. The incarnation is, in one sense, the work of the Father sending the Son (John 3:16–17), but it is also the work of the Son taking the form of a servant (Phil. 2:7), and the work of the Spirit bringing forth new life (Luke 1:34–35). The three persons of the Trinity are present at Jesus's baptism at the beginning of his earthly ministry (Matt. 3:13–17) and are explicitly referenced again at the end of his earthly ministry (Matt. 28:19–20). On the cross, the Son poured out his blood "through the eternal Spirit" and "offered himself without blemish" to God the Father (Heb. 9:14). The resurrection is described as God's Spirit raising Jesus from the dead (Rom. 8:11). Our redemption is, from start to finish, the work of our triune God (Gal. 4:4–6; Eph. 1:3–14; 3:14–19).

Similarly, the works of providence are executed by God, who holds all things together in Christ (Col. 1:17) and "upholds the universe by the word of his power" (Heb. 1:3). The Spirit also blows where he wishes in order to carry out the purposes of God (John 3:8; cf. Ezek. 36:22–32; 37:1–14).

The doctrine of inseparable operations does not eliminate all distinctions between the persons of the Trinity. The Spirit was not born of Mary; the Father did not die on the cross; the Son was not poured out at Pentecost. The indivisible works of God are not *indiscriminate* works. That is, certain works are appropriated, or attributed, to individual persons of the Trinity. A specific work may conclude on one person as its terminus (i.e., the incarnation terminates on the Son), but the works *ad extra* are still indivisible because they arise from all three persons as their source, they all serve one unified purpose, and they are all expressions of one will. The affirmation *opera Trinitatis ad extra sunt indivisa*—when clarified by the doctrine of distinct appropriations—protects the unity of the Trinity against any notion that one or more divine persons could be inactive in creation, redemption, and providence or that the persons could ever operate independently or in opposition to each other.

DAY 50

Our Triune God and the Christian Life

So why does the doctrine of the Trinity matter? What is the "payoff" for the ordinary Christian who is never going to be an expert in the metaphysics of Aquinas and is never going to throw around Latin and Greek phrases at the dinner table? Let me try to answer that question with seven points.

1. Most importantly, we should joyfully affirm that if God is triune, in one sense, no other justification is necessary for learning the doctrine of the Trinity. When you learn more about your spouse or grow to understand your child more fully, do you need a "payoff"? Isn't it enough simply to know more fully the one you love so deeply? Every true Christian should thrill to know God as he really is.

2. The doctrine matters for creation. Unlike the myths of the ancient Near East, our God did not need to go outside himself to create the universe. Instead, in fashioning the cosmos, the Word and the Spirit were like his own two hands (to use Irenaeus's famous phrase). Creation, like regeneration, is a Trinitarian act, with God working by the agency of the Word and the mysterious movement of the Holy Spirit.

3. The doctrine of the Trinity helps us comprehend a world of unity and diversity. Robert Letham has noted that the two main rivals to Christianity in our day are Islam (which stresses cultural unity at the expense of diversity) and postmodernism (which emphasizes diversity without attempting to see things in a broader meta-unity). If God subsists as three persons sharing the same essence, then the world God made is likely to exhibit stunning variety and individuality while still being part of one larger story directed toward one shared purpose.

4. The doctrine of the Trinity matters for worship. Prayer, worship, and communion are Trinitarian acts. We pray to the Father in the name of the Son by the power of the Spirit. A time is coming, Jesus told the woman at the well, when true worshipers will worship the Father in spirit and truth (John 4:23). No worship can be fully Christian if it is not deeply Trinitarian.

5. The doctrine of the Trinity means that love is eternal. God did not create in order to be loved; he created out of the overflow of the perfect love that has always existed among Father, Son, and Holy Spirit.

6. The doctrine of the Trinity informs how we relate to others. While we must be careful not to think of the Trinity in social terms (as if God is a group of three friends hanging out), the fact that God is three in one does have social implications. The doctrine of the Trinity means communion and communication are inherent in the divine being, and thus we reflect God when we commune and communicate with others. Moreover, the Trinity shows how there can be relational mutuality without indistinguishability. Reflecting this pattern, we can know and be known by another while still retaining our own personhood.

7. Finally, the doctrine matters for how we relate to God. As John Owen insisted, we ought to enjoy distinct communion with each divine person. We know the Father as the fountain and source of all good. We know the Son as our advocate, our intercessor, our sacrifice, and our brother. And we know the Spirit as our sanctifier and comforter. In all three persons we find safety, satisfaction, sweetness, and delight.

DAY 51

The Divine Decrees

A decree, in common parlance, is an official order, edict, or command. Thus, when we speak of the divine decrees, we mean God's "eternal purpose, according to the counsel of his will, whereby for his own glory, he hath foreordained whatsoever comes to pass" (WSC 7).

The divine decrees are both an exercise of God's will and an expression of God's nature. The decrees of God must possess the character of God himself. Here, then, are six attributes of the decrees that mirror God's own attributes.

1. *The decrees are simple.* Although the word is often given in plural, strictly speaking there is only one decree. We speak of many because the human mind cannot help but think of order and sequence. But for God, all that he decrees is founded upon "a single, all-comprehensive, and simultaneous act."[1] God is not composed of parts, and neither is his sovereign ordering of all things.

2. *The decrees are eternal.* While the execution of God's plan takes place in time, the establishment of that plan does not. God's purposes for us in Christ Jesus are eternal (Eph. 3:11). We have been chosen before the foundation of the world (1:4). God saved us and called us "because of his own purpose and grace, which he gave us in Christ Jesus before the ages began" (2 Tim. 1:9).

3. *The decrees are immutable.* Just as God is unchangeable, so are his decrees (Heb. 6:17). He completes whatever he appoints and does whatever he desires (Job 23:13–14). The counsel of the Lord stands forever (Ps. 33:11; Isa. 46:10). All things happen as God has determined (Luke 22:22). God does according to his will, "and none can stay his hand" (Dan. 4:35).

4. *The decrees are absolute.* That is to say, God's decretive will is not based on foreseen faith or foreseen good works. All that God has willed from eternity, he has willed unconditionally, not in any way contingent upon his creatures. He predestines according to the purpose of his own will, not according to any other will (Eph. 1:5).

5. *The decrees are wise.* The absolute nature of the divine decrees does not make God arbitrary or capricious. Everything he does and everything he decrees, he works after the counsel of his will (Eph. 1:11). The language of "counsel"

suggests deliberate planning and prudence. It also suggests intra-Trinitarian deliberation whereby all three persons—possessing one will—are operative in the decrees.

6. *The decrees are good.* God has written all of our days in his book (Ps. 139:16). Nevertheless, God is not the "author of sin," if by this we mean God does the sin or is culpable for sin. Even though God's decrees include wicked events in their purview, the decrees themselves are always good. There is no unrighteousness in God (Ps. 92:15). He "cannot endure iniquity" (Isa. 1:13). "God is light, and in him is no darkness at all" (1 John 1:5). Even when sinful men act in wicked ways, what they mean for evil, God simultaneously means the same act for good (Gen. 50:20).

1 Berkhof, *Systematic Theology*, 102.

The Will of God

The "will of God" can be confusing because the Bible uses the phrase in two different ways. While we don't want to speak of two wills in God (for that would imply more than one essence), theologians have often talked about two aspects of the one divine will.

On the one hand, the will of God can be used to describe "God's will of decree." This refers to what God has ordained, what he has planned from all eternity according to his sovereign purposes. Think of passages like Isaiah 46:10 where God says, "I will accomplish all my purpose," or Matthew 10:29–30 where Jesus says that not even a sparrow falls to the ground apart from the will of the Father, or Ephesians 1:11 where Paul says all things work according to the counsel of God's will. In one sense, everyone everywhere all the time is following the will of God. Whatever God decrees will surely come to pass. No one can turn back the purposes and plans of God (Dan. 4:35).

On the other hand, the Bible also speaks of "the will of God" as something human beings can obey or disobey. This is what theologians sometimes call "God's will of desire." Think of Matthew 7:21 where Jesus says only those who do the will of the Father will enter the kingdom of heaven, or Hebrews 13:20–21 where the author prays that God would equip his people with everything good for doing his will, or 1 John 2:15–17 where John describes the will of God as the opposite of the way of the world. In this sense, we can follow God's will, or we can reject it and go our own way. These two aspects of God's will—his will of decree and his will of desire—are found plainly in Scripture.

There is a third aspect of God's will that we might call "God's will of direction." This is what Christians often mean when they talk about discerning the will of God. We are eager to know which way to turn when we come to a fork in the road. And yet there is no indication in Scripture that God has a will of direction he normally means for us to find out ahead of time. To be sure, God does have a specific plan and purpose for each one of us. All of our days were written in his book before one of them came to pass (Ps. 139:16). But he does not mean for us to see every step of that plan *ahead of time*. We walk by faith, not by sight.

All of this means that understanding the will of God is easier and harder than we think. It's harder in that following God takes a lifetime of growing, repenting, believing, and striving. But it's also easier in that God has already told us what he wants from us. God's will is that we live holy lives, set apart and consecrated to him (1 Thess. 4:3). God's will is that we bear fruit and grow in our knowledge of God and his ways (Col. 1:10). God's will is that we be filled with the Holy Spirit (Eph. 5:18). In short, God's will is that we grow in godliness and be evermore transformed into the image of his Son (Rom. 8:28–29).[1]

---

1   This section has been adapted from my entry on the same topic in the *ESV Teen Study Bible*. Used by permission.

Freedom of the Will

Since at least the time of Augustine, Christian theologians argued about the nature of the fallen human will: is it free or is it bound? In order to make sense of this question, medieval scholastics like Peter Lombard (c. 1096–1160) and Bernard of Clairvaux (1090–1153) made distinctions among different types of necessity, distinctions John Calvin would later use to explain how man could be enslaved to sin and at the same time responsible for his sin.

Our sin, which the fallen will chooses by necessity, is also voluntary because the choice is owing to our own corruption. There is no external coercion, no outside compulsion that makes us sin. Our willing, though bound to wickedness on this side of Eden, is still self-chosen.

Turretin argued to the same effect, postulating six different types of necessity. (1) The *necessity of coaction* arises from an external agent compelling us to do something. (2) *Physical necessity* involves innate appetites and responses, like how fire must burn or a bent leg will straighten when struck under the knee cap. (3) *Necessity of dependence* means we cannot exist or do anything apart from God. (4) *Rational necessity* means we choose what we believe is best (even if our belief is mistaken). (5) *Necessity of event* affirms that future events are fixed and certain according to God's foreknowledge and decree. (6) *Moral necessity* arises from habits and inclinations, either good or bad. Only the first two types of necessity are incompatible with free choice and human responsibility. That is to say, if the intellect has the power of choice (freedom from physical necessity) and the will can be exercised without external compulsion (freedom from the necessity of coaction) then our sins can be called voluntary, and we are culpable for them.

Arminian critics sometimes accuse Calvinists of believing that when people are maimed, murdered, and tortured that it must be their all-determining God who performs these heinous acts. What this criticism misses, however, is the distinction between remote and primary causes. No thoughtful Calvinist would say God abuses innocent people. God is never the doer of evil. Reformed theologians have always made clear that there is a difference between the role of God in ordaining what comes to pass and the role of human agency in actually and voluntarily performing what has been ordained. Herod and Pontius Pilate conspired against Jesus in accordance with divine predestination, but their conspiracy was still wicked and culpable (Acts 4:25–28; cf. Gen. 50:20).

It is sometimes suggested that the human will in Reformed theology is only an illusion. The picture painted is of a God who forces people to do what he wants, whether they will to do so or not. This is not the view of the Reformed confessions or of the Bible. According to Jesus, only those enabled by the Father can come to him, but they still must come (John 6:37, 44).

Reformed theology denies that our choices can be other than God has decreed and that our will is free to choose what is good, but it does not deny human choice and human willing altogether. We are not puppets on a string, because puppets have no will of their own. The Canons of Dort make clear that divine sovereignty "does not act in people as if they were blocks and stones; nor does it abolish the will and its properties or coerce a reluctant will by force" (3/4.16).

In short, there is a divine will prior to all human willing, and the will of the unregenerate man is enslaved by sin. At the same time, our wicked choices are really our choices, and they do have real-world consequences.

DAY 54

God's Permission

If God is completely sovereign—working all things after the counsel of his will (Eph. 1:11)—we might wonder whether God exercises his sovereignty in the same way over all things. Is God sovereign over evil in the exact same way he is sovereign over good? Is there any distinction between, say, God's decree to save humanity and God's decree that humanity would fall?

Many Christians would answer these questions by arguing that God actively wills certain things but only permits other things. There is something to be said for this distinction, but we need to understand it and appropriate it carefully. Consider two different sections from the Westminster Confession of Faith.

> The almighty power, unsearchable wisdom, and infinite goodness of God so far manifest themselves in his providence, that it extendeth itself even to the first fall, and all other sins of angels and men; and that not by a bare permission, but such as hath joined with it a most wise and powerful bounding, and otherwise ordering, and governing of them, in a manifold dispensation, to his own holy ends; yet so, as the sinfulness thereof proceedeth only from the creature, and not from God, who, being most holy and righteous, neither is nor can be the author or approver of sin. (5.4)

Drawn from texts like Genesis 50:20, Isaiah 10:12, John 12:40, and 2 Thessalonians 2:11, this is a strong statement of divine sovereignty. God never does the sin, and he never approves the sin, but his wise ordering of the universe extends to the sins of men and angels, even to the fall—and "not by a bare permission." But that's not all the confession says about the fall.

> Our first parents, being seduced by the subtility and temptation of Satan, sinned, in eating the forbidden fruit. This their sin, God was pleased, according to his wise and holy counsel, to permit, having purposed to order it to his own glory. (6.1)

These two passages seem contradictory—one seems to disavow divine permission while the other affirms it. But notice the language of WCF 5.4 is "*bare* permission." Yes, God has a permissive decree, but it is still a decree. That's why WCF 6.1 speaks of purpose and order. God does not sit back and passively allow the fall to happen. That would be a bare permission. But neither does he ordain the fall by the same positive determination as he does righteous events. God *wills* to *permit* the fall.

Nothing is outside God's sovereignty. Job never once considered that the Lord's hand was not behind all that had befallen him (Job 1:21). And yet we must not take this to mean that God superintends good and evil in the same way. God works in us to will and to do according to his purpose (Phil. 2:12–13). We are not told that God works in us to will and to do what is contrary to his purpose. The most heinous act in the history of the universe—the crucifixion of the Son of God—was clearly and directly decreed by God, but that did not render Herod, Pontius Pilate, and the people of Jerusalem innocent of their sin (Acts 2:23; 4:27–28). The decree to act is not the same as the act itself. Everything happens according to God's will, but he does not will that everything comes to pass in the same way.

DAY 55

Election and Reprobation

The terms *election* and *predestination* are often used interchangeably, both referring to God's gracious decree whereby he chooses some for eternal life. In Romans 8:30 Paul speaks of those whom God has predestined, called, justified, and (in the end) glorified. In 8:33 Paul references the "elect," apparently a synonym for the predestined ones described a few verses earlier.

A sharp distinction between the two words is not warranted from Scripture, but if there is a distinction to be made, predestination is the general term for God's sovereign ordaining, while election is the specific term for God choosing us in Christ before the foundation of the world. For some theologians, election is the divine ordination to the appointed *end* of salvation, while predestination is the divine ordination regarding the *means* of salvation. Calvin defined predestination as "God's eternal decree, by which he compacted with himself what he willed to become of each man. . . . Therefore, as any man has been created to one or the other of these ends, we speak of him as predestined to life or to death."[1] For Calvin, predestination encompasses the entire eternal decree. Election and reprobation, then, represent two different aspects of that decree. The Canons of Dort make this same distinction, expounding on "election and reprobation" as the two elements of "divine predestination" (Art. 1).

This delineation is not without merit. The "elect" is always a positive designation in Scripture (e.g., Matt. 24:31; Titus 1:1), suggesting that election implies eternal life (though Romans 9:11 may be an exception to this rule). Predestination, on the other hand, can be used more broadly. Herod and Pontius Pilate, along with the Gentiles and people of Israel, did to Jesus what God's "plan had predestined to take place" (Acts 4:27–28). Of course, the doctrine of election does not depend upon the word itself. Numerous passages speak of believers being chosen in Christ (Eph. 1:4), chosen by God (2 Thess. 2:13), or prepared as a gift from the Father to the Son (John 6:37).

The opposite of election is reprobation, sometimes called double predestination. This is the belief that God not only predetermines those who will be saved but also predetermines those who will not be saved. Admittedly, this is a hard doctrine. Even Calvin called it a dreadful decree. But reprobation is more than a logical corollary to election. According to the Bible, God has vessels of wrath prepared for destruction (Rom. 9:22). The reprobate have been designated for condemnation (Jude 4), and they disobey the word as they were destined to do (1 Pet. 2:8).

It is important to note that in typical Reformed theology, reprobation has two parts: preterition (the determination to pass by some) and condemnation (the determination to punish those who are passed by). This distinction safeguards that God's decree to punish the reprobate is not arbitrary or without justice. God wills to punish the guilty, not the innocent. While the decrees of God are beyond full human comprehension (Deut. 29:29), we must not shy away from testifying to the God who works "according to the purpose of his will, to the praise of his glorious grace" (Eph. 1:5–6).

1   Calvin, *Institutes*, 3.21.5.

WEEK 12

DAY 56

Is Predestination Fair?

The doctrine of double predestination is not easy. Romans 9 tells us that before Jacob and Esau were born or had done anything good or bad, God had already determined to "love" Jacob and to "hate" Esau (vv. 11–13). That is a hard word, prompting questions about God's fairness and man's responsibility. Thankfully, the apostle Paul anticipates both questions.

1. In Romans 9:14, Paul asks the question: "Is there injustice on God's part?" His answer is a resounding, "By no means!" Notice, Paul does not defend God by appealing to human free will or by suggesting that election is based on God's foreknowledge of our choice. Instead, Paul argues that God is not unjust in election, because election displays the character of God, and election serves the purposes of God. Paul makes both of these points in the same way, by quoting Scripture and then offering a summary statement of what Scripture teaches.

On the first point, Paul quotes from Exodus 33:19 where God reveals himself to Moses by announcing that he will have mercy on whomever he chooses to have mercy. For God to be God, he must be merciful, and he must be sovereign. The freedom of God to dispense his mercy to whomever he pleases, apart from any constraint outside of his own will, is at the heart of what it means to be God. Thus Paul summarizes: the ultimate reason some people believe and others do not depends on God, not on us (Rom. 9:16).

Paul's second point is the other side of the same coin. God not only has mercy on whom he will have mercy. He also hardens whom he wants to harden. If verses 15 and 16 demonstrate God's righteousness in loving Jacob, verses 17 and 18 demonstrate God's righteousness in hating Esau. This is why Paul quotes from Exodus 9:16. God raised Pharaoh up for the explicit purpose of hardening Pharaoh's heart and thereby having occasion to show his (i.e., God's) power.

2. In Romans 9:19, Paul anticipates a second objection: If salvation is up to God, why does he still find fault with us? Paul doesn't back down from this objection, and he doesn't deny that we are responsible for our choices and for our sins. Paul's response is to question whether the question is even appropriate. To this end, Paul makes three points: We have no right to question God (v. 20); God has every right to do what he pleases (v. 21); predestination serves a divine purpose (vv. 22–23).

Election and reprobation are not arbitrary exercises of divine power. They serve a good purpose in revealing the holiness of God, the power of God, and the glory of God. We would be unable to see and experience the full glory of God's mercy apart from the backdrop of powerful wrath. It may seem as if Paul has not really answered the original questions he raised, but he has. His "answer" is to put God in his place and to put us in our place. Paul measures God by the only two things against which God *can* be measured: against Scripture and against himself. Paul defends the righteousness of God by helping us see what righteousness is all about. Righteousness is not about our fallible opinions of fairness or what we wish God were like. It's about God's character and God's purposes as they are revealed in the Bible.

The Order of the Decrees

There are no two words in the theological lexicon quite like supralapsarianism and infralapsarianism. They sound dreadfully esoteric and hopelessly elitist, like words that might be concerned with how many angels can dance on the head of a pin if that pin were resting upon a rock which God made so heavy that he could not lift it. Some seminary students love to throw out the terms as a not so subtle reminder that they are in seminary. Pastors of a certain ilk toss around the words when they want to demonstrate how impractical theology can be. Parishoners hear the words and furrow their brows.

So what are these highfalutin -*isms* all about?

Reformed theologians have often argued about the order in which God decreed certain things to happen. The debate is not over the temporal order of the decrees. After all, we are talking about what God has determined in eternity. Time is not the issue. Instead, the debate is about the *logical* order of the decrees. In the mind of God, which decisions did God make first, second, third, and so on?

Specifically, which is logically prior: the decree of election and reprobation or the decree to create the world and permit the fall? Supralapsarianism—*supra* meaning "above" or "before" and *lapsum* meaning "fall"—is the position which holds that God's decree to save is logically prior to his decree to create the world and permit the fall. Infralapsarianism, on the other hand, insists that God's decree to save is logically after his decrees related to creation and fall (*infra* meaning "below" or "after"). Both positions are well attested in Reformed theology, though infralapsarianism seems to be more common.

The debate is, admittedly, somewhat speculative, but before dismissing the controversy as silly and irrelevant, we should appreciate how our understanding of the order of the decrees may influence (or perhaps reflect) our understanding of God.

The *supra* position underscores the high sovereignty of God. Before the twins had done anything good or bad, the Lord loved Jacob and hated Esau (Rom. 9:11). Therefore, argues the supralapsarian, God must have first purposed to ordain some for life and some for death. After that (in his mind), God purposed to create the world and to ordain a fall so that the glory in election and reprobation might be realized.

By contrast, the *infra* position highlights the mercy of God. The reference in Romans 9:11, infralapsarians argue, is a statement about merit—neither son was more deserving of salvation than the other. Besides, Romans 9:14 describes election as God having mercy on whom he will have mercy. Therefore, the decree to save must follow God's decree to permit the fall, or how else would mercy be mercy?

In the end, I affirm the infralapsarian position taught in the Canons of Dort, that predestination is about God "distinguishing between people equally lost" (1.7) and that election is "God's unchangeable purpose" to choose in Christ a particular people out of the fallen human race (1.7). At the same time, I also agree with those who caution against being overly dogmatic on a matter that is not clearly expounded in Scripture. The debate is not insignificant, but neither is it a hill to die on. In the end, the decrees of God are meant to underscore God's mercy *and* God's glory.

DAY 58

Amyraldianism

Following the Synod of Dort, for much of the seventeenth century, the international Reformed community was divided over the views of Moïse Amyraut (1596–1664). A professor at Saumur in France, Amyraut is remembered today (if remembered at all) for his views on the extent of the atonement. Amyraut believed in the particularity of election, but he also believed that Christ died on the cross for all people. He reconciled these two ideas by positing that Christ died for all people on the *condition* that they believe. For Amyraut, Christ's death wasn't just sufficient for all; it was *intended* for all. For Amyraut, the extent of the atonement was universal. Four-point Calvinists—so-called because they don't accept the doctrine of limited atonement—are sometimes labeled Amyraldians, even if their views are not dependent upon Amyraut or identical with his.

Like Amyraut, the British theologian John Davenant also taught a version of hypothetical universalism (hypothetical meaning "conditional" and universalism referring to the extent of the atonement, not that everyone will be saved). Davenant argued that God willed for Christ to die efficaciously only for the elect. In addition, however, he believed that Christ *also* intended to die for all, with the salvific accomplishment of that death conditionally applied.

Unlike Davenant's version of hypothetical universalism, Amyraut altered the order of the decrees. This may seem like splitting hairs, but it's important to note that in Davenant's view the conditional decree stood alongside the unconditional one. God willed to effectively redeem the elect while at the same time he willed to redeem all people who believe. By contrast, Amyraut argued that God first decreed a universal atonement, and then, seeing that none would be saved by that decree alone, decreed that the elect would be enabled to believe.

Amyraut was not an Arminian. The Arminians taught that God's decree of election was based on foreseen faith. On their account, God, by his eternal decree, chose *believers*. That is, the elect are not chosen so that they might believe; God knows we will believe and therefore we are chosen. Amyraut didn't go this far, but Turretin and others thought his views were dangerously similar. They believed Amyraut's view implied a conditional decree—not just that God willed something with a condition (like a divine promise or divine threat), but that God's will itself was conditional. Amyraut's theology was put outside confessional Reformed boundaries by the (short-lived) Formula Consensus Helvetica (1675).

The controversy over Amyraldianism was about both the extent of the atonement and about the order of the decrees. Amyraut's mistake was to insist upon two decrees in election—a general decree to have mercy upon all and a special decree to effectually bestow faith on some. Amyraldianism called into question the efficacy of Christ's atonement and the immutability of the decrees. Any sort of conditional decree implies that God did not know the future, did not have the power to affect the future, or had determined to leave the future uncertain. None of these possibilities can be ascribed to a sovereign God. Every decree of God is eternal, and as such they cannot be dependent upon a condition that takes place in time. God's decrees are dependent upon nothing except his own good pleasure (Matt. 11:26; Rom. 9:11; Eph. 1:5).

DAY 59

Middle Knowledge

Among the various attempts to reconcile divine sovereignty and free will, the "solution" proposed by Jesuit theologian Luis de Molina (1535–1600) was one of the most innovative, if ultimately unpersuasive. Molina believed he could uphold the efficacy of God's decree with a libertarian account of human free will by a concept he called middle knowledge (also known today as Molinism).

Molina argued that God's knowledge can be logically divided into three types: natural knowledge ("must be" and "could be" truths), free knowledge ("will be" truths), and middle knowledge ("would be" truths).[1]

Natural knowledge is what God knows by his very nature or essence. In this category are necessary truths like "2 + 2 = 4" and "all bachelors are unmarried." These are truths that cannot be otherwise. Along with what must be, God also knows what could be (i.e., all possibilities that God could decree). Importantly, natural knowledge is prevolitional; it refers to what God knows logically prior to his decision to decree what will be or will not be.

Free knowledge is what God knows because God knows his own will. Importantly, this type of knowledge is postvolitional. That means the truths in this category are dependent on God's will. If natural knowledge deals with necessary truths (things that must be), free knowledge deals with contingent truths (things that could have been otherwise).

In between these two types of knowledge is middle knowledge. Middle knowledge refers to God's prevolitional knowledge of all counterfactuals of creaturely freedom. That means the truths in this category, like the truths of natural knowledge, exist independent of and prior to God's will. This is crucial, because Molina does not make human choice dependent on God's decrees. At the same time, Molina insists that God's will is sovereign. This is where middle knowledge comes in. God knows everything that is *and* all the decisions and choices free human beings would make in a particular situation. Knowing all the possible contingencies arising from human freedom, God is then able to will the world he wants and knows what will come to pass.

The debate surrounding middle knowledge is complicated and often highly technical, but from a Reformed view we can note three problems.

1. Middle knowledge assumes a degree of autonomy in human free will that is hard to square with passages like John 6, Romans 9, and Ephesians 1 and many other texts that highlight God's superintendence over the decisions of mankind.

2. Middle knowledge does not answer how the counterfactual truths are grounded in the first place. By definition, the truths are not grounded in God's nature or God's will, but neither can they be grounded in the creation (that doesn't exist). The very existence of counterfactual truths conflicts with libertarian free will.

3. Middle knowledge posits that God's will is based upon his knowledge, and that this knowledge concerns free human choices. This makes God's will dependent on something outside himself. In Molinism, God is not ordering all things solely after the counsel of his will; instead, God's will must seek counsel from the possible decisions of his free creatures. This is not a small change to a traditional understanding of divine knowledge and divine aseity, nor is it a change that befits the sovereign God of the Bible.

---

1 This way of putting things ("must be," "could be," "will be," "would be") comes from my Reformed Theological Seminary colleague James Anderson.

DAY 60

Evangelism and the Sovereignty of God

Of all the objections to the doctrine of election, the most popular objection among ordinary Christians today is that a Reformed view of God's sovereignty undermines evangelism and missions. In some circles, it is considered an undeniable fact that Calvinism implies an indifference to sharing the gospel. "If God is the one who chooses," the argument goes, "and all the elect, and only the elect, will be saved, why bother with the Great Commission?"

On the face of it, this argument may make strictly logical sense, but it is miles away from *biblical* logic. The Bible has no problem joining the absolute sovereignty of God with a zeal for evangelism. For example, in Romans 9, before Paul declares that God "has mercy on whomever he wills, and he hardens whomever he wills" (v. 18), Paul first confesses: "I have great sorrow and unceasing anguish in my heart. For I could wish that I myself were accursed and cut off from Christ for the sake of my brothers, my kinsmen according to the flesh" (vv. 2–3). Paul believed in election and reprobation, *and* his heart broke for the lost, which is why his heart's desire and prayer to God was that his fellow Jews might be saved (10:1).

The doctrine of election is not a hindrance to evangelism and missions. To the contrary, election is a support to these noble tasks. When Paul was ready to leave Corinth for some place more responsive to the gospel, God kept him there with the assurance that he had many people in that city (Acts 18:9–11). A strong belief in God's sovereignty is what can keep a missionary on the field when the opposition is thick and the harvest seems thin. As Paul told Timothy, "I endure everything for the sake of the elect" (2 Tim. 2:10).

Many of the greatest evangelists and missionaries in the modern era have been Calvinists. Theodore Frelinghuysen, William Tennent, Jonathan Edwards, and George Whitefield were all instrumental in the Great Awakening, and all of them believed in God's determinative choice in salvation. John Eliot, David Brainerd, William Carey, Henry Martyn, Adoniram Judson, Robert Moffat, David Livingstone, and Robert Morrison were all pioneers in the modern missionary movement, and they were all Calvinists. Neither the Bible nor the history of the church supports the idea that a high view of God's sovereignty kills missions and evangelism.

God can work without means or contrary to means, but he usually works through means; which means he uses us to share the good news with others. Jesus taught that sinners could not come to him unless the Father drew them

(John 6:44), but this did not prevent Jesus from presenting a genuine offer of the gospel (6:35). Election is the reason people *can* come, never a reason for people to be turned away. All that the Father gives to Christ will come to Christ, and whoever comes will never be cast out (6:37).

Far from a detriment to sharing the gospel, a firm belief in election provides evangelistic hope in a hard-hearted, disobedient world. The Lord has elect sheep in the world, and though they may be far from the fold now, one day they will hear their Master's voice and believe. Our task is to open our mouths and speak on behalf of the Good Shepherd.

WEEK 13

DAY 61

Our Creator God

When considering the creation of the universe, there are three principal questions we can ask: Who? How? and Why? Of those three questions, the first question is the most foundational. It also is the most obvious. According to the Bible, God is Creator of all things visible and invisible.

We cannot overstate the importance the Bible gives to the revelation of God as Creator. "In the beginning, God created the heavens and the earth" (Gen. 1:1). Reading in English, we could say *aseity* is the first thing we encounter about God. In the beginning—before all and independent of all—there was God. In the original Hebrew, however, the verb *bara* ("to create") comes prior to the word *Elohim* ("God"). This is not an unusual grammatical construction for Hebrew, but it does mean that even before we are introduced to the word for God, we know that he is a creator.

Our God is the one through whom all things came into being. He is the maker of heaven and earth. Over and over the Bible reminds us that the God of Israel is no territorial deity. As the people confessed in Nehemiah's day, "You are the LORD, you alone. You have made heaven, the heaven of heavens, with all their host, the earth and all that is on it, the seas and all that is in them; and you preserve all of them; and the host of heaven worships you" (Neh. 9:6). There is only one Creator, and therefore there is only one God. "For thus says the LORD, who created the heavens (he is God!), who formed the earth and made it (he established it; he did not create it empty, he formed it to be inhabited!): 'I am the LORD, and there is no other'" (Isa. 45:18).

When Paul preached to the Gentiles, he emphasized that they should put away their idols and turn to "a living God, who made the heaven and the earth and the sea and all that is in them" (Acts 14:15). As the Creator of all things, God needs nothing from his creatures. Famously, Paul explained to the Athenians that "the God who made the world and everything in it, being Lord of heaven and earth, does not live in temples made by man, nor is he served by human hands, as though he needed anything, since he himself gives to all mankind life and breath and everything" (17:24–25).

God gives us the answer to one of the most enduring questions: Where did the cosmos come from? Is the universe the result of some free personal agent, or did the universe somehow create itself? The biblical account teaches that creation is distinct from God (the two are not the same being) and at the same time that creation is entirely dependent on God. He is before all things and on him all things depend. As we've seen before, there never was when God was not, but there was when matter was not. As the psalmist exclaims, "Lord, you have been our dwelling place in all generations. Before the mountains were brought forth, or ever you had formed the earth and the world, from everlasting to everlasting you are God" (Ps. 90:1–2).

DAY 62

Creation *Ex Nihilo*

The Genesis creation account tells a very different story than the kind found in other ancient Near Eastern texts. For example, in the *Enuma Elish* (the Babylonian creation myth), Apsu, the god of fresh water, and Tiamat, the goddess of saltwater, mingle together and create many other deities. Eventually there is a god named Marduk who vanquishes the army of Tiamat, and the world is formed from her carcass. By contrast, the God of the Bible creates the world by himself, without any primordial conflict and without any preexistent material.

The phrase for that last truth is captured by the Latin phrase *ex nihilo*, meaning God created all things, visible and invisible, out of nothing. Romans 4:17 testifies that God "gives life to the dead and calls into existence the things that do not exist." Likewise, we read in Hebrews, "By faith we understand that the universe was created by the word of God, so that what is seen was not made out of things that are visible" (11:3). While it's true that God created the world by giving shape and order to the formless chaos, we must remember that even this "material" was the result of God's personal creative agency.

The nothingness of creation *ex nihilo* was an absolute nothingness. In some strands of Greek thought, nothingness could be conceived of as a pregnant or positive nothingness, as something that might limit divine activity. The Bible does not understand *ex nihilo* in these terms. The nothingness before creation was a negative nothingness, a "space" without any characteristic and without any quality that would be an obstacle to God's work. There were no rivals to God in creation, no obstacles to overcome, not even the nothingness out of which God created all things.

We should not underestimate the importance of creation *ex nihilo*. According to the Bible, we have a God who relates *to* his creation but is in no way to be identified *with* his creation. Peter Jones has highlighted this truth by speaking of Oneism and Twoism. Oneism means that God and the material world are basically of the same "stuff," whereas Twoism means that God and the material world do not share the same substance. The difference is between one "thing" in the universe or two "things."

The biblical account of creation—a good, personal God personally creating a good world—does not allow for dualism (the spiritual is good, and the material is bad), or deism (God created the world and now stands aloof from it), or pantheism (God and creation are one), or panentheism (God is in creation and beyond creation). Neither can we accept any species of process theology, whereby God is so bound up in creation that he is also in process of growing, changing, and overcoming.

The Christian account of creation is unique, especially when it is coupled with the Christian belief in the incarnation. It is because God is transcendent that we can truly experience his immanence. Only a God distinct from his creation can enter into genuine personal relationship with his creatures as an act of love and self-sacrifice rather than an act of personal liberation and self-actualization.

DAY 63

Creation Days

Of the three questions—Who? How? and Why?—the how question is the one where the most controversy has arisen. At the heart of the how question is the debate surrounding the creation days. Among evangelicals, there are four typical approaches.

(1) The six days of creation are *normal twenty-four-hour days*. This view usually means (but doesn't have to equal) a belief in a young earth (e.g., thousands

of years old instead of billions of years). (2) The *Day-Age view* argues that the creation days represent an unspecified length of time and that a "day" in God's reckoning can refer to a long period of time (Isa. 11:10–11; 2 Pet. 3:8). (3) The *Framework Interpretation* popularized by Meredith Kline maintains that the first three days represent creation kingdoms, ruled over by the creation kings of days four through six. The days, therefore, should be read topically, not sequentially. Based on Genesis 2:5 ("the LORD God had not caused it to rain"), Kline argues that God oversaw creation by means of ordinary providence. (4) The *Analogical approach* understands the days more generally as divine work days. While the events recorded may be broadly consecutive, the length of the time is irrelevant to the purpose of the Genesis account. The days are God-divided days or extraordinary cosmic days. Our human week is copied from this creation week, but "copy" is to be considered analogically not literally.

While there are plausible reasons for each view, and orthodox Reformed representatives can be listed for each of them, I find the twenty-four-hour view most convincing.

First, there are several indications that the Hebrew word *yom* is used in Genesis 1 in the normal sense of a twenty-four-hour day: the references to morning and evening, the cycles of darkness and light, the fact that we still have seven days in our week. Most crucially, the refrain of "days, years, signs, and seasons" suggests we are dealing with normal calendar demarcations.

Second, there are good explanations for the appearance of the sun on day four. For example, the universe might have been illuminated by the special, supernatural presence of God. Alternately, one can argue that the sun was already made (Gen. 1:1), but not separated until the fourth day. Light wasn't created on the fourth day; rather, the greater light and lesser light were separated (1:14).

Third, normal days allow for the world to be relatively young, which means that death in the animal world need not have existed before the fall.

Fourth, God could have created the world with the appearance of age. Just as Adam on his first day did not look like an infant, so the universe, though created in six normal days, may look much older.

Fifth, this view of the creation days was affirmed by early commentators (Basil, Ambrose), by medieval scholastics (Lombard, Aquinas), by the magisterial Reformers (Luther, Calvin, Beza), by the Puritans (Perkins, Owen, Edwards), and was the only known view of the Westminster divines.

Sixth, God did not merely accommodate himself in how he *explained* the work but in how he actually *accomplished* the work. As Calvin put it, Moses didn't speak of six days "for the mere purpose of conveying instruction. Let us rather conclude that God himself took the space of six days, for the purpose of accommodating his works to the capacity of men."[1]

---

1 Calvin, *Commentaries*, 1:78.

Historical Adam

Belief in a historical Adam is essential to the logical coherence of the Bible. There are many good reasons to affirm that Adam was a historical person created by God's direct, immediate, and supernatural agency.

1. The Bible does not put an artificial wedge between history and theology. The biblical story of creation is meant to supplant other ancient creation stories. The Pentateuch is full of warnings against compromise with the pagan world. It would be surprising, then, for Genesis to start with one more mythical account of creation like the rest of the ancient Near East. Moreover, there is a seamless strand of history from Adam in Genesis 2 to Abraham in Genesis 12. We can't set Genesis 1–11 aside as prehistory, if that term means "less true than other kinds of history." Moses deliberately connects Abraham with the history that comes before him, all the way back to Adam and Eve in the garden.

2. Without a historical Adam, we have no basis for affirming a true organic connection between all peoples. Some scholars argue that Adam was chosen from a group of neolithic farmers six thousand to eight thousand years ago. God then imbued this hominid with the image of God and made him spiritually alive. This may be a kind of "historical" Adam, but not one familiar to most Christians and not one without significant problems. If Adam were chosen from a group of hominids, in what way was his sin the first sin, and what changed after that first sin, if death was already in the world? Moreover, what are we to do with the Bible's description that Adam was formed from the dust of the ground and Eve was made from his rib? And finally, if Adam was just one of many neolithic farmers in the world, how do we know we are all descended from the same pair, and consequently that we all share in the same inherent worth and dignity?

3. Without a historical Adam, Paul's doctrine of original sin and guilt does not hold together; neither does his teaching on Christ as the second Adam (Rom. 5:12–21; 1 Cor. 15:21–22, 45–49). Paul does not think of Adam as a mere teaching model or literary character. Adam is a *typos* of Christ (Rom. 5:14), a real person in the unfolding of redemptive history. For Paul, Adam and Christ are both representatives, standing at the head of different categories of humanity. One cannot be historical and the other literary. The historical reality of the resurrection of the second Adam corresponds to the historical reality of the fall of the first Adam.

4. The historicity of Adam is assumed throughout both Testaments (and in Second Temple Judaism for that matter). Adam is mentioned as a historical person

in the genealogies in 1 Chronicles 1 and in Luke 3; Paul treats Adam and Eve as real people in 1 Timothy 2; and Jude's reference to Enoch as the "seventh from Adam" implies a specific distance between two historical persons. The Adam of Genesis was a flesh and blood human being. Until very recently, every Christian has assumed this commonsense reading of the Bible. We ought to do the same.

DAY 65

The End for Which God Created the World

We do not look at the universe rightly unless we see in creation a glorious reason to praise the living God.

"Let all the earth fear the LORD," the psalmist tells us, "let all the inhabitants of the world stand in awe of him!" And why? "For he spoke, and it came to be; he commanded, and it stood firm" (Ps. 33:8–9). Similarly, Psalm 148 calls on the heavens and the heights, the Lord's angels and his hosts, the sun and moon and shining stars, the highest heavens and the waters above the heavens to praise the name of the Lord. The reason? "For he commanded and they were created. And he established them forever and ever; he gave a decree, and it shall not pass away" (Ps. 148:5–6). In short, God formed us and made us; he created us for his glory (Isa. 43:7).

To use the language of Jonathan Edwards's famous treatise, divine glory is "the end for which God created the world." We must never suppose that God created the cosmos out of lack—because he wanted a relationship, or he wanted someone to love. God did not create the world because he was thirsty. Rather, God created the world because it is the nature of a fountain to overflow. Creation is the super-abundance of divine goodness, beauty, mercy, love, wisdom, power, sovereignty, self-sufficiency, self-existence, justice, holiness, faithfulness, and freedom.

Edwards puts the matter wonderfully. We should slow down and read him carefully:

> As there is an infinite fullness of all possible good in God—a fullness of every
> perfection, of all excellency and beauty, and of infinite happiness—and as this
> fullness is capable of communication, or emanation *ad extra*, so it seems a thing
> amiable and valuable in itself that this infinite fountain of good should send forth

abundant streams. . . . Thus it appears reasonable to suppose that it was God's last end that there might be a glorious and abundant emanation of his infinite fulness of good *ad extra*; and that the disposition to communicate himself, or diffuse his own fulness, was what moved him to create the world.[1]

To put the matter much less elegantly, we can say the creation was God's decision to go public with his glory. From the microscopic level to the cosmic level, we have reason to give God praise. Just consider that by some scientific estimates there are more stars in the universe than there are grains of sand on earth. The Milky Way has 150 billion to 200 billion stars, and our galaxy is only one of hundreds of billions of galaxies. Depending on which estimate you follow, there are more than 100 billion trillion stars. Think of the number one followed by twenty-three zeroes. That's about how many stars there are in the universe. The number defies human comprehension. And Psalm 147:4 says, "He determines the number of the stars; he gives to all of them their names."

All good theology begins with the beginning. There is no Christianity without the doctrine of creation. "Worthy are you, our Lord and God, to receive glory and honor and power, for you created all things, and by your will they existed and were created" (Rev. 4:11).

1 Edwards, *Ethical Writings*, 432–34.

DAY 66

Angels

Angels are more important in the Bible than we often realize. By one count, there are seventeen books in the Old Testament that reference angels and seventeen books in the New Testament that reference angels, with 273 total references. Let's look at several things angels *are* and then several things angels *do*.

First, what are angels?

1. Angels are created beings accountable to their Creator. Some angels fell; we call them demons. Those that didn't, we call angels. The present reality of "good" angels and "bad" angels appears to be fixed in that we do not hear of further defections nor of the possibility of redemption.

2. The nature of an angel is spirit. Augustine made the point that "angel" is their office, spirit is their nature. Angels are personal spirits who sometimes appear in bodily forms (cf. Heb. 13:1).

3. Angels are intelligent creatures. They speak and act, although they are not made in the image of God. In fact, angels will be judged by believers (1 Cor. 6:3). They are not superhuman as much as they are suprahuman (beyond human beings).

4. Angels have personal names. We know two of those names: Gabriel and Michael. The Apocrypha mentions five others: Raphael, Sariel, Uriel, Raguel, and Remiel (note: the suffix *el* is short for Elohim, or God).

5. There are different kinds of angels. Michael is called an archangel in Jude 9. He fights against the devil in Revelation 12:7. Gabriel is the other named angel and is traditionally considered another archangel. Cherubim and seraphim are sometimes called "throne room angels" because they are associated with guarding God's presence in the tabernacle and in the temple.

6. Angels are more glorious than human beings in some ways (Ps. 8:5), but their glory should not be exaggerated. Angels are wise and powerful, but they are neither omniscient nor omnipotent.

Second, what do angels do? Here we can also make six points.[1]

(1) Angels are guardians. They guard Eden, the ark, and God's people. (2) Angels are bridges between two worlds. Think of Jacob's ladder or Jesus's word about seeing the angels ascending and descending on the Son of Man. (3) Angels are intermediaries, like at the giving of the law (Gal. 3:19). (4) Angels are messengers. That's what the word means in Hebrew and in Greek. Angels bring messages to Joseph, to Mary, and to Paul. They interpret divine messages for Daniel. (5) Angels are patrol officers. They walk the earth (Zech. 1) and serve as agents of divine justice (2 Sam. 24; Acts 12:2). (6) Angels are servants. They guide God's people (Acts 8:26) and care for God's people (1 Kings 19:5–6). They also ministered to Christ. Angels attended Jesus at every key moment of his life and ministry: they were there at his conception, his birth, his temptation in the wilderness, his trial in the garden, and at the empty tomb.

If one danger is to make angels (role players in the Bible) into the stars of the show, the other danger is that we ignore angels altogether, smiling at their part in the Christmas pageant each year, but other than that hardly thinking about them. This too would be a mistake.

---

1 See Cole, *Against the Darkness*, 52–62. Cole lists twelve tasks, but my six points overlap with many of his.

Demons

If we are to take God at his word and take the Bible seriously, we must not only conclude that there is real evil in the world; there is also a devil and demonic beings hell-bent on promoting evil in the world.

The book of Ephesians uses four different words or phrases to describe evil spiritual beings. Besides a personal devil (6:11), Paul calls these personal demonic intelligences "rulers," "authorities," "cosmic powers over this present darkness," and "spiritual forces of evil in the heavenly places" (6:12). While the terms are not identical, they all hit upon the same idea: there are powerful spiritual beings ruling over the realm of evil (1:21; 3:10).

The darkness in our world is not by accident. It is not the mere product of secularization or the sexual revolution. Behind the manifestation of evil in our day (and every day) lies a devil and his demons. Wherever we turn from the light of the gospel, the light of the glory of God in the face of Christ, whenever we suppress the conscience and prefer darkness over light, we are putting ourselves in the way of the devil's wishes.

We can't be sure how and why the devil fell, but several texts suggest there was an angelic rebellion (prior to man's sin) motivated by pride. First Timothy 3:6 hints that the devil was condemned for being "puffed up with conceit." Likewise, Jude 6 says that "angels who did not stay within their own position of authority, but left their proper dwelling, he has kept in eternal chains under gloomy darkness until the judgment of the great day." And if the exalted description of the king of Tyre in Ezekiel 28:11–19 can be taken as an allusion to the devil ("an anointed guardian cherub"), then we have further evidence that the devil sinned because his heart was proud and vainglorious.

The devil assaults the people of God in two main ways: he is a deceiver and an accuser. Those two words describe his identity and his weapons. The devil lies, and he slanders. Revelation 12 calls him "the deceiver of the whole word" (v. 9) and "the accuser of our brothers" (v. 10). Zechariah 3 presents a striking picture of the Lord rebuking Satan for accusing Joshua the high priest, who, despite his filthy garments, was saved by God as a brand plucked from the fire.

There is much we don't know about the devil and his minions, so we ought to be leery of elaborate constructions of demonic hierarchies and the assigning of territorial spirits and giving names to demons. Recall that when Jesus asked for the name of a demon, he got a number: "Legion" (Mark 5:9). Although we don't know much about demons—and that's probably for our good—we do know that we are at war with them. Surely it is significant that the recurring theme in Ephesians 6:10–18 is not "cast out demons" or "conquer strongholds" but "stand." We do not have to vanquish hell. Jesus did that on the cross. We are called to fight, to resist, and to stand.

DAY 68

Providence

The story of the Bible is nothing if not a story of divine providence. On every page, in every promise, behind every prophecy is the sure hand of God. He sustains all things, directs all things, plans all things, ordains all things, superintends all things, and works all things after the counsel of his will (Matt. 10:29–30; Eph. 1:11).

Theologians have often remarked that providence consists of three elements: preservation, concurrence, and government. In providence, God keeps his creatures (preservation), works by his creatures (concurrence), and directs his creatures (government). As Berkhof puts it, "Providence may be described as that continued exercise of divine energy whereby the Creator preserves all His creatures, is operative in all that comes to pass in the world, and directs all things to their appointed end."[1]

Providence is not a minor theme in the Scriptures. It is not merely an implied truth, deduced from a handful of obscure passages. The doctrine of divine providence is the soundtrack of Scripture. It is everywhere present even when we are not consciously aware of it—like the book of Esther, where God's name is never mentioned, but everything from a beauty contest (2:18) to a king's insomnia (6:1–3) serve to advance God's purposes. God does not merely turn hard situations for our good; he ordains hard situations for our good (Gen. 50:20).

The God of the Bible is a God with absolute power and sovereign sway over all things. "The LORD brings the counsel of the nations to nothing; he frustrates the plans of the peoples" (Ps. 33:10). "He it is who makes the clouds rise at the end of the earth, who makes lightnings for the rain and brings forth the wind from his storehouses" (Ps. 135:7). He shuts the mouths of lions to preserve the righteous (Dan. 6:22) and unleashes lions to judge the wicked (2 Kings 17:25). He hardens hearts (Ex. 14:17; Josh. 11:20).

God cannot sin. He is not the author or enactor of evil. At the same time, nothing happens apart from his good purpose and will. Even the most abominable act in history, the crucifixion of Christ, was according to his preordained plan (Acts 4:27–30). From the big pictures to the tiniest details, God guides all our steps (Prov. 16:33; 20:24; Jer. 10:23). God providentially reigns over evil (Judg. 9:23; 1 Sam. 16:14; Isa. 45:6–7; Amos 3:6). Death too is in the Lord's hands (Deut. 32:39; 1 Sam. 2:6). All our days were written in God's book before one of them came to be (Ps. 139:16). Our God "does according to his will among the host of heaven and among the inhabitants of the earth" (Dan. 4:35). God is God because he has the power to do what he wants, the wisdom to carry it out, and the sovereign authority to immutably appoint whatsoever shall come to pass (Isa. 46:9–10).

If sovereignty is God's power to do whatever he pleases, providence is the wonderful good news that this power is pro-us. "Providence is the almighty and ever present power of God by which he upholds, as with his hand, heaven and earth and all creatures, and so rules them that leaf and blade, rain and drought, fruitful and lean years, food and drink, health and sickness, prosperity and poverty—all things, in fact, come to us not by chance but from his fatherly hand." Therefore, we can be patient when things go against us, thankful when things go well, and have confidence for the future that nothing will separate us from God's love (Heidelberg Catechism Q/A 27, 28).

1 Berkhof, *Systematic Theology*, 166.

DAY 69

Miracles

God's work in the world is not all of one kind. In providence, God works through the ordinary means of the created order. By this definition, the birth of a child is (normally) not a miracle, because a child is (normally) conceived, gestated, and birthed by means of ordinary biological processes. Cancer going into remission after chemotherapy may be an answer to prayer, but it is not, strictly speaking, a miracle. A pilot landing a plane on the Hudson River may be unusual and heroic, but it is not a miracle. Miracles require immediate, supernatural intervention. They do not operate according to the natural order with which God has endued creation. Miracles are examples of extraordinary providence.

The Bible is full of miracles. And yet the presence of those miracles is relatively concentrated. Miracles are intimately connected to God's plan of redemption and are concentrated in epochal moments of salvation history. Thus, we see a proliferation of immediate, supernatural activity during the exodus from Egypt, during the prophetic ministries of Elijah and Elisha, and especially during the ministry of Jesus and the apostles. In a unique way, the events and message of the gospel were validated by signs and wonders and various miracles and by (the miraculous?) gifts of the Holy Spirit (Heb. 2:4).

While there are many methods that Christians can take to defend the miraculous (e.g., highlighting the gaps in our scientific knowledge, pointing to unexplained phenomena in our own day, making a philosophical case for interruptions into the natural order), the best approach is to focus on the most important miracle in the Bible: the resurrection of Jesus.

Note three things from Paul's defense of the resurrection before Festus and King Agrippa in Acts 26:19–29.

1. Festus thought Paul was out of his mind for believing that a man had been raised from the dead (26:23–24). We should not think that ancient people were primitive and backward and that they easily believed whatever they were told. It doesn't matter who you are or where you were born or when you lived—most people have a hard time believing things they have never seen. And no one in first-century Palestine had ever seen a resurrection. Ancient people may have been superstitious (by our reckoning), but they did not easily believe in dead people coming back to life.

2. Paul insisted that his belief in the resurrection was true and rational (26:26). Miracles were not the product of wishful thinking; they were historical examples of God's direct involvement in the world. In defending the resurrection, Paul appealed to observable, verifiable evidence. The things Paul proclaimed had not been done in a corner. There were good reasons to believe in Paul's message.

3. Agrippa understood that accepting the miraculous was essential to being a Christian (26:28–29). The most important elements of our faith defy ordinary, natural explanations: the creation of the world, the inspiration of the Scriptures, the virginal conception, the incarnation, and the resurrection. Christianity is unembarrassed supernaturalism. Without the miraculous, there is no Christianity, and without belief in the miraculous events of redemptive history, we cannot be Christians.

DAY 70

Prayer

We don't always think of prayer as a doctrinal topic, but many of the best systematic theologies have a section on prayer, often as an aspect of God's providential care. This makes sense. In an ultimate sense, God doesn't need our prayers, but he has chosen to govern the world through secondary means, and one of those means is the prayer of his people. God has ordained prayer so that we may see our dependency upon him and so that he receives glory as the giver of all good gifts.

Calvin devotes seventy pages in his *Institutes* to prayer. As a part of this exploration, he gives four rules for right prayer:

- First rule: reverence.
- Second rule: sincerity and penitence.
- Third rule: we give up confidence in ourselves and humbly plead for pardon.
- Fourth rule: we "pray by a sure hope that our prayer will be answered."[1]

Drawing from texts like Mark 11:24 ("Therefore I tell you, whatever you ask . . . believe that you have received it, and it will be yours") and James 1:5–6 ("If any of you lacks wisdom, let him ask God. . . . But let him ask in faith, with no doubting") Calvin exhorts believers to be convinced that God is favorable and benevolent toward them. "It is amazing," Calvin writes, "how much our lack of trust provokes God if we request of him a boon that we do not expect."[2]

Of course, our prayers must be humble, and we should petition God according to his word (not according to all our whims and wants). But listen to godly Christians pray; they do not pray mealy-mouthed prayers. There are two great dangers in prayer: praying like we are God, and praying like there is no God. "Now what sort of prayer will this be?" Calvin asks in the same passage. " 'O Lord, I am in doubt whether thou willest to hear me, but because I am pressed by anxiety, I flee to thee, that, if I am worthy, thou mayest help me.' This is not the way of all the saints whose prayers we read in Scripture."

The most repeated command of Jesus, relative to prayer, is not how to pray or why to pray, but simply that we would pray. Ask, seek, and knock—that's what Jesus wants (Matt. 7:7). He wants us to trust that God cares and be confident that God can help. That's why prayerlessness is, at its core, unbelief. When Jesus comes again, will he find us praying and trusting (for the two are interconnected)? Or will he find us living and acting and planning and complaining and manipulating our own strategies as if there were no God at all?

Jesus knows that it is hard to keep praying and not give up (Luke 18:1). It is hard to pray for justice day after day and year after year with sometimes minuscule results. Prayer is first and foremost an act of faith—faith that there is a God, faith that he is a personal God, faith that we are able to come into his presence, faith that God moves the world through prayer, and faith that Christ intercedes for us at God's right hand. We believe, Lord. Help our unbelief.

---

1 Calvin, *Institutes*, 3.20.11.
2 Calvin, *Institutes*, 3.20.11.

ANTHROPOLOGY

Man as Created and Fallen

DAY 71

Created Being and Crowning Achievement

When we talk about man, we must keep two things in mind. First, we must never forget that man is *not* God. Second, we must remember that man is uniquely *like* God. As men and women, we are not only created beings; we are the crowning achievement of God's creation.

We see both of these truths in Psalm 8. On the one hand, David marvels that the God who made the moon and the stars should be mindful of man and care for him. We are not, after all, heavenly beings. On the other hand, David rejoices that we have been crowned with glory and honor. God has given man dominion over the works of his hands and has put all things under his feet.

We see the same two truths in Genesis 1. We are in a class of created beings along with the animals (with whom we were made on the sixth day), not in the "class" of uncreated beings we call God. And yet we are undeniably distinct from the animals, for unlike all the birds of the sky, fish of the sea, and beasts of the earth, man was made in God's image, after his likeness. (Gen. 1:26).

The biblical story is first of all about God, but it is everywhere about man in relation to God. The story of Scripture is not biocentric or geocentric but plainly anthropocentric. That is to say, the story is not about life in general or about the earth for its own sake. The story is about human beings. We matter to God not simply because God cares for all living things and we are one of those living things. God cares for us because we are the most important of his creative works and the pinnacle of his work in the creation week.

If there is one biblical insight missing from the modern environmental movement, it is this: human beings are not alien to the story of the created world, but the most important part of it. Too often a model is assumed where the earth is a healthy organism and humans are cancerous cells. If all we do is pillage, pollute, consume, and destroy, then the world would be better off without us, and the goal should be to minimize our "footprint" at all costs.

It is true: human beings can pollute and destroy, but we can also produce and develop. We are subcreators made in the image of the Creator, meant to tend to the garden in paradise and meant to work in the world still today. We can create beauty, build culture, and make a harsh planet more conducive for human flourishing. By God's grace, humans have learned to feed more people and help those people live longer, healthier, easier lives.

We must resist the temptation to think of humans as intruders from another world wreaking carnage in a pristine environment. Instead, we must see ourselves as stewards, called to subdue, protect, enjoy, and make more humane God's fallen creation. Christians should not seek a supposedly romantic ideal where the earth is untouched by human hands. Rather, we want to think carefully about how we can use our hands to make the earth more hospitable for more people, so that we might enjoy the beauty, grandeur, creativity, and productivity of our Father's world.

DAY 72

Man as Body and Soul

In Genesis 2:7, the Lord God forms the man from the dust of the ground. God breathes into his nostrils the breath of life, and the man becomes a living creature. The phrase "living creature" in the ESV is the Hebrew word *nephesh*, translated "living soul" in the KJV. Both translations can be justified—*nephesh* is the usual word for "soul" or the inner being of a person in the Old Testament, but it also can refer more broadly to a living, breathing person. The Greek word *psyche* can be similarly broad, often best translated simply as "life" (Matt. 6:25). We should not read technical, philosophical concepts back into every use of everyday words like *nephesh* and *psyche*.

At the same time, those who wish to deny any kind of body-soul dualism do not do justice to many verses elsewhere in the Bible. Although it is hard for us to conceptualize (since we have only experienced embodied existence), the apostle Paul clearly taught that upon death he would depart the body in order to be with Christ (Phil. 1:23–24). The body is an earthly tent that is destroyed at death, even as the believer inherits a new home with God in the heavens (2 Cor. 5:1–10). This is why Revelation 6:9, prior to our bodily resurrection, speaks of the "souls of those who had been slain for the word of God."

The position that affirms that man consists of body and soul is called *dichotomy* (i.e., two parts). There is an alternate position, however, called *tri-*

chotomy, which affirms that man is comprised of three things: body, soul, and spirit. Two texts, in particular, seem to support trichotomy: 1 Thessalonians 5:23, which says, "May your whole spirit and soul and body be kept blameless," and Hebrews 4:12, which says that the word of God pierces to the division of soul and spirit.

While trichotomy is not an unorthodox view, dichotomy has been the majority view throughout church history, and there are good reasons for accepting it. For starters, Paul often uses spirit and soul interchangeably (Rom. 8:10; 1 Cor. 5:5; 7:34; 2 Cor. 7:1; Eph. 2:3; Col. 2:5). Concerning 1 Thessalonians 5:23, Paul is heaping up synonyms much like Jesus does when he tells us to love God with all our heart, soul, mind, and (in Mark's Gospel) strength. Soul and spirit are used in parallelism in Luke 1:46–47 ("My soul magnifies the Lord, and my spirit rejoices in God my Savior"). Jesus also uses the two words as synonyms, saying that his soul is troubled in John 12:27 and then saying he is troubled in spirit in John 13:21. As for Hebrews 4:12, the text does not say "division of soul *from* spirit" but "division of soul and of spirit." The author is not making an intricate metaphysical point. Rather, he is saying that the word of God can penetrate to the deepest, most inward aspects of who we are.

The body-soul distinction can seem unimportant or even like an imposition of Greek philosophy. But Scripture often emphasizes that we would be foolish to live for the body (only) to the neglect of our souls or spirits (Matt. 10:28; 1 Cor. 5:5). Surely the danger in our day is not that we are too beholden to ancient ideas, but that too many of God's image bearers have forgotten that they even have a soul and that there is something more important and more eternal than satisfying the desires of the body.

DAY 73

Where Do Our Souls Come From?

We can understand easily enough that the human body is propagated through the organic process of sexual reproduction. A sperm unites with an egg, and a new biological life is conceived. But what about the soul? Where does that come from? Historically, there have been three different explanations for the origin of the soul.

The first explanation maintains that the soul transmigrates to the body from a *preexistent* state. On this view, each of us has an earlier immaterial existence. The church father Origen went so far as to argue that our current embodied life reflects the good or bad of our previous immaterial life. But besides Origen, few Christian theologians have taught that our souls come from a previous state. Such a view renders the body accidental to human existence, eliminates the distinction between men and angels, and is devoid of any scriptural support.

A second explanation teaches that the souls of men are propagated in the same way that bodies are propagated. That is, we receive both body and soul from our parents. This view is called *traducianism* (*tradux* being the Latin word for a shoot or a sprout from a vine). Several arguments can be put forward in support of traducianism. (1) God is depicted as breathing life into Adam, but the same process is not indicated for Eve. Might this suggest that God created a soul for the first man, but after that each soul would be formed by natural processes? (2) God ceased from his work after the sixth day. (3) If future descendants are said to be still in the "loins" of their ancestors (Heb. 7:9–10), then our whole person must be derived from our parents. (4) Traducianism best accounts for universal sin and depravity. God did not create for us a corrupt soul; we inherited depraved souls from our parents. Church fathers like Tertullian and Gregory of Nyssa held to traducianism. More recently, the Reformed theologian W. G. T. Shedd argued vigorously for the position.

The third explanation is called *creationism* because it teaches that each individual soul is owing to the immediate creation of God. This has been the most common view in church history, being the dominant view in the Eastern church, the prevailing view in the Roman Catholic Church, and at least the majority conviction among Protestants. Key arguments in favor of creationism include: (1) God is credited with being the Father of spirits (Heb. 12:9) and is said to have formed the spirit of man within him (Zech. 12:1). (2) The creation of Adam demonstrates that body and soul are two substances, one formed from created things and the other created directly from God. (3) Creationism best explains how Christ can possess a true human nature without inheriting the guilt and pollution from Adam's sin. (4) We do not inherit our depraved nature from the physical union of bodies, but because God has imputed to us Adam's original disobedience. God does not make for us polluted souls with evil tendencies, but God does withhold from us the gift of original righteousness, such that sin naturally follows.

With good theological and historical support for both traducianism and creationism, we should not be dogmatic about either view. But given the preponderance of support for creationism, and that it better accounts for Christ's sinlessness, I am inclined to favor the creationist view. On either account, we should recognize that both body and soul are good gifts from God, in need of redemption in our fallen state, but always meant to be used for his glory.

DAY 74

Faculty Psychology

The history of Western philosophy and theology has spent considerable time and energy trying to understand how the soul works. Just as the material part of us has different elements (eyes to see, ears to hear, mouths to speak), so the immaterial part of us has different elements. These elements (to use a nontechnical term) are referred to as faculties. Thus, faculty psychology has to do with the inner working of our immaterial selves.

A faculty can be defined as a power to exercise a specific operation in the soul. Throughout history, these faculties have been variously conceived. Plato believed in three faculties: intellect, affections (related to nobler inclinations), and appetites (related to sensual desires). Aristotle taught five faculties: a vegetative faculty (for the maintenance of organic life), and faculties of appetite, sense perception, locomotion (or movement), and reason. These five Aristotelian faculties were taken as a general starting place by Augustine, Aquinas, and Reformed scholasticism.

Although he often borrowed from Aristotle, Aquinas had his own way of understanding faculty psychology. First, there are intellective faculties (those that deal with the mind or understanding). Then there are appetitive faculties (those that deal with appetites). Here Aquinas distinguishes between two types: intellectual appetency (the will) and sensitive appetency (desires). Third, there is reason, which functions as the combination of intellect and will. Importantly, in Aquinas's scheme, reason can control the lower faculties.

Reformed theology follows the broader Western tradition in affirming that the faculty of intellect (sometimes called "understanding" or "reason") has primacy over other faculties. But, according to Reformed theology, reason cannot always be trusted. The Westminster Confession states that through original sin we "became dead in sin, and wholly defiled in all the parts and faculties of soul and body" (WCF 6:2). In other words, no part of us has been untouched and left untainted by the fall.

Reformed theologians have tended to be more modest and less exhaustive in exploring these issues. Consequently, they often reduce the faculties to two: intellect and will. Others include the mind, or memory, or conscience as distinct faculties. Crucially, when talking about our inner life, Reformed theologians have been careful to distinguish between affections and passions. While we tend to use *emotions* as a catchall term for the inner life, Christian theologians and philosophers have typically employed a more robust and nuanced vocabulary. In fact, the word *emotion* didn't become common until the nineteenth century.

Before that, thinkers spoke of sentiments, sympathy, and (especially) of affections and passions. Affections are motions of the will, while passions are motions of the sensual appetites. Passions render us passive. They come upon us and sweep over us, which is why the Westminster Confession says God is "without body, parts, or passions" (WCF 2:1).

Faculty psychology may seem like esoteric wrangling, but the concepts can be helpful for thinking about the operation of our inner world. In particular, the language of passions and affections can help reinforce that the Christian life must never be inert and that true faith is more than mere intellectual assent. At the same time, we are safeguarded against thinking that salvation depends upon a certain emotional feeling sweeping over us.

DAY 75

Male and Female

Man has both singularity and plurality. Humanity can be named singularly as "man" (*adam*), but humanity can also be named in the plural, as male and female. "Let *us* make man in *our* image" (Gen. 1:26). Just as God is a plurality, so in an analogous way is man. Of all the things that God could have mentioned about man in the garden of Eden, he wanted us to know that man is characterized by sexual differentiation.

Let me suggest five ways the Bible distinguishes between male and female. We can remember these differences using the letters ABCDE.

Appearance. The exegesis and application of 1 Corinthians 11:1–16 can be tricky. When Paul says that nature itself teaches that long hair is a disgrace to men (11:14), he's not making a universal statement about follicles. But he is making a universal statement about gender. There is a crucial principle in chapter 11 and one our world and our churches need to hear: men are not women, and when men look like women (or women look like men), it is off-putting and unnatural. God made us male and female on purpose, and he doesn't want the two sexes to be confused.

Body. Where the world wants us to believe that our bodies tell us nothing permanent or obligatory about our selves, the Bible says just the opposite. There is a fittedness to our bodily design. Part of being a man is that your body was designed for a woman; part of being a woman is that your body was designed for a man (Lev. 18:22; Rom. 1:26–27). The body must not be altered to fit our own sense of identity. Our bodies are given, not identified or chosen by us, and they are given to us to be used for God's glory (1 Cor. 6:19).

Crowning characteristic. The Bible often associates the pursuit of beauty with womanhood (1 Tim. 2; 1 Pet. 3) and the pursuit of strength with manhood (1 Kings 2:2; 1 Cor. 16:13–14). To be sure, beauty and strength are not uniquely feminine or masculine characteristics, but each is uniquely linked to one sex. God directs women to embrace the true beauty of godly character, and he directs men to embrace the true strength of noble courage and self-sacrifice.

Demeanor. Within the span of a few verses in 1 Thessalonians 2, Paul likens his pastoral approach to both mothering (vv. 7–8) and fathering (vv. 11–12). For the apostle Paul, mothering implies gentleness, affection, and sacrifice. Fathering implies exhortation, encouragement, and a spiritual charge. Men can be tender, and women can exhort. But still, there is a method behind the Pauline metaphors. There is a distinction in demeanor. For Paul, the picture of divinely aided gentleness is a mother, and the picture of divinely guided exhortation is a father.

Eager posture. According to God's design in the garden, the woman's posture is to help (Gen. 2:18), while the man's posture is to lead. Adam was created first, he named the animals, and he was held responsible for the couple's sin. The word *posture* is deliberate. We are not talking about an inflexible office, but about what men and women are intentional to find and happy to accept. These roles will be most clearly seen in marriage, but the attitudes should be present outside of marriage as well. Sexual differentiation is not a mistake or an afterthought, but God's good design from the very beginning.

<hr>

WEEK 16

DAY 76

Marriage

There has probably never been more confusion about the nature of marriage in the (once) Christian West than exists today. Thankfully, we can sketch out a basic understanding of marriage from three biblical themes: complementarity, covenant and kids, and Christ and the church. These themes arise, in turn, from three biblical texts: Genesis 2:18–25, Malachi 2:13–16, and Ephesians 5:22–33.

1. *Complementarity (Gen. 2:18–25).* By complementarity I don't mean everything about the roles of men and women that go under the heading "complementarianism," though I believe in that -ism. By complementarity I mean that in the Genesis account the man and the woman are uniquely fit for each other (2:18, 20). The woman is a suitable helper for the man because only with a woman can the man fulfill the creation mandate to be fruitful and multiply (1:28). The woman is taken from man (2:21–22) and named in relationship to man (2:23). Since the woman was created from the side of the man, the one-flesh union in marriage is really a kind of re-union. Only on this understanding of marriage do monogamy and exclusivity have any coherent moral logic.

2. *Covenant and kids (Mal. 2:13–16).* Marriage is a covenant bond (2:14). As a covenant, marriage was constituted in the ancient world (and still is today) by two things: a verbal oath and a ratification sign (i.e., sexual intercourse). One of the God-given purposes in marriage is godly offspring (2:15). While it would be wrong to say procreation is the sole purpose in marriage or that sexual intimacy is given only as a means to some reproductive end, it would also be wrong to think marriage can be properly defined without any reference to the offspring that should (and normally does) result from the one-flesh union of a husband and wife. This is why the Westminster Confession (Reformed) says marriage was given, in part, for the "increase" of "holy seed"; and the Book of Common Prayer (Anglican) says holy matrimony was "ordained for the procreation of children"; and *Humanae Vitae* (Roman Catholic) says "the unitive significance and the procreative significance" are "both inherent to the marriage act." Marriage is, by definition, that sort of union from which, if all the plumbing is working correctly, children can be conceived. This does not mean procreation is required for a marriage to be valid. What it does mean is that marriage—by nature, by design, and by aim—is a covenant between two persons whose one-flesh commitment is the sort of union that produces offspring.

3. *Christ and the church (Eph. 5:22–33).* The mysterious union of Christ and the church finds expression in a man and a woman becoming one flesh in Christian marriage. Notice that Paul's reference only works if there is differentiation in the marital union. It makes perfect sense that the coming together of heaven and earth in Revelation 21–22 is preceded by the marriage supper of the Lamb in Revelation 19. Marriage was created as a picture of the fittedness of heaven and earth or, as Paul puts, of Christ and the church. The meaning of marriage is more than mutual sacrifice and covenantal commitment. The mystical union of Christ and the church—each "part" belonging to the other but neither interchangeable—cannot be pictured in marital union without the differentiation of male and female. We cannot insert two men (or two women) into the logic of Ephesians 5 and get the same mystery, let alone a full-orbed picture of the gospel.

DAY 77

Transgenderism

The Bible teaches that God made us male or female, and that no matter our own feelings or desires, we should act in accordance with the biological reality of God's good design. Transgenderism falls short of the glory of God and is not the way to walk in obedience to Christ.

When God created the first human pair in his image, he created them male and female (Gen. 1:27). He made the woman to be a complement and help to the man (Gen. 2:18–22). Far from being a mere cultural construct, God depicts the existence of a man and a woman as essential to his creational plan. The two sexes are neither identical nor interchangeable. They do, however, belong together. When the woman, who was taken out of man, joins again with the man in sexual union, the two become one flesh (Gen. 1:23–24). The rare anomaly of intersex individuals does not undermine the creational design, but as an objective medical condition (as opposed to a subjective mental state) rather gives another example of creational "groaning" in a fallen world.

Where transgender inclinations are sincerely and deeply felt (as opposed to those who are merely trying on a new identity), Christians should respond with patience, kindness, and truth. The question is not whether transgender persons and feelings exist. The question is whether the *is* of our emotional or mental state equals the *ought* of God's design. Most Christians reject this thinking in other areas, from eating disorders to unbiblical divorces. We understand that following Christ means dying to ourselves (Matt. 16:24), being renewed in our minds (Rom. 12:2), and no longer walking as we once did (Eph. 4:17–18). Being "true to ourselves" is the wrong choice when it means going against God's word.

The Bible teaches the organic unity of biological sex and gender identity. This is why male and female are (uniquely) the type of pair that can reproduce (Gen. 1:28; 2:20). It's why homosexuality—a man lying with a man as with a woman (Lev. 18:22)—is wrong. It's why the apostle Paul can speak of homosexual partnerships as deviating from the natural relations or natural function of male-female sexual intercourse (Rom. 1:26–27). In each instance, the argument only works if there is an assumed equivalence between the biology of sexual difference and the corresponding identities of male and female.

If the binary of male and female is God's idea, and if we are meant to embrace, by divine design, our biological and creational difference as men and women, then it stands to reason that the confusion of these realities would be displeasing to God. So we see clearly in the Bible that men should not act sexually as women (Lev. 18:22; Rom. 1:18–32; 1 Cor. 6:9–10), that men should not dress like women (Deut. 22:5), and that when men and women embrace obviously other-gendered expressions of identity it is a disgrace (1 Cor. 11:14–15). We do not have an inalienable right to do whatever we want with our physical selves. We belong to God and should glorify him with our bodies (1 Cor. 6:19–20).

Image of God

Every human being is made in the image of God (*imago dei*), and as such each of us was made to represent God and be like God.

References to the image of God appear at three turning points in the opening chapters of Genesis. At creation, God decrees, "Let us make man in our image, after our likeness," and in the next verse we read that "God created man in his own image, in the image of God he created him; male and female he created them" (Gen. 1:26–27). After Adam and Eve are kicked out of the garden and the curse takes root on the earth, we are told again that "when God created man, he made him in the likeness of God" (5:1). And finally, after the flood the presence of the *imago dei* in man is reiterated a third time: "Whoever sheds the blood of man, by man shall his blood be shed, for God made man in his own image" (9:6). By these three references we are meant to see that man was created in the image of God, that the fall did not mean the end of the *imago dei*, and that the punishment of the flood did not wipe it out.

Although the concept is of paramount importance in Christian theology, the explicit language of the image of God does not occur again until the New Testament. In 1 Corinthians 11:7 man is called "the image and glory of God," and in James 3:9 we are warned against cursing "people who are made in the likeness of God." The latter passage reinforces the idea that the *imago dei* is not something that belongs only to God's people. We must be mindful that the person we are tempted to curse—whoever that person might be and whatever he has done to us—is someone made in God's image and likeness.

There are two important (and related) shifts in the way in which the image of God is talked about in the New Testament.

First, in the New Testament the focus is upon Christ as the man who perfectly displays the image of God. The gospel is the message about the glory of Christ, who is the image of God (2 Cor. 4:4–6). By this gospel we can be saved (5:17–21), and by it we can be transformed into the same image from one degree of glory to another (3:17–18). Likewise, in Colossians we are told that Christ, in his divine nature, is the unique image of the invisible God (Col. 1:15–20). Later, believers are told to put to death what is earthly and so be renewed in knowledge after the image of their Creator (3:5–10).

Second, in the New Testament the focus is less upon the image of God as our creational possession and more upon the image of God as our eschatological goal. As Paul says in Romans 8:29, "For those whom he foreknew he also predestined to be conformed to the image of his Son." Or, again, in 1 Corinthians 15:49, "Just as we have borne the image of the man of dust, we shall also bear the image of the man of heaven." The image of God is not only what we have and what we were given; it is what we are growing into and what will one day be realized in all those (and in only those) who belong to Christ. For Christians, the image of God is both our dignity and our destiny.[1]

1 See Kilner, *Dignity and Destiny.*

What Does It Mean to Be Made in the Image of God?

Considering its significance in Chrisitan thought and in Western civilization, the image of God has not always been easy to define.

Older theologians tended to emphasize the *structural aspects* of the image of God. They viewed man's capacity for intelligence, rationality, morality, beauty, and worship as that which distinguishes us from the animals. Even in unborn babies and persons with severe impairments, there is still a unique human capacity for these qualities, however limited by physical or psychological constraints.

More recent theologians have focused on the *functional aspects* of the image of God. That is, they identify God's image less with our essence than with our ethics. According to passages like Romans 8:29 ("predestined to be conformed to the image of his Son") and 1 Corinthians 15:49 ("as we have borne the image of the man of dust, we shall also bear the image of the man of heaven"), the image of God is not just what we have; it is what we are called to do and to be (1 John 3:2–3).

Both aspects teach us something important about the image of God, but the Bible allows us to say more about the functional (what we do) than the structural (what we have). Note, then, three further dimensions of how we live out the image of God.

First, human beings are *representatives* of God. Just as an ancient king would place a statue of himself throughout his realm, marking his ownership and rule, so our presence as image bearers in the world marks out the earth as belonging to God. Further, as representatives, we are called to be rulers and stewards. We are set apart from the animals in that we are given "dominion over the works of [his] hands" (Ps. 8:6; cf. Gen. 1:28).

Second, human beings are made to be in *relationship* with God. Unique among his creatures, Adam was created for covenant (Hos. 6:7). The image of God is not only something *in* us or something true *about* us; it is something that exists *between* us and God. Unique among all his creatures, God can see something of himself in us. To be an image bearer is to be the sort of creature who can know, serve, and self-consciously worship the Creator.

Third, human beings are made to reflect the *righteousness* of God. The New Testament defines the image of God as true knowledge, righteousness, and holiness (Eph. 4:24; WCF 4.2). Although sin has marred the divine image in man, we can still be renewed by God in Christlikeness so as to increasingly reflect his image (Col. 3:9–10).

This last point needs to be underscored. While we can understand something about human nature ontologically apart from Christ, only by virtue of the incarnation can we know what obedient human life looks like. The gospel is the message about the "glory of Christ, who is the image of God" (2 Cor. 4:4). By his Spirit we can be transformed into the same image from one degree of glory to another (3:17–18). To be made in the image of God means we ought to be—and can be—remade in the likeness of Christ.

DAY 80

What Are the Implications of Being Made in the Image of God?

The importance of the *imago dei* cannot be overstated. Its significance ought to touch every area of life. Let me mention six implications of being made in the image of God.

1. Being made in the image of God, human beings are unique among all God's creatures. We are qualitatively and constitutionally different from plants and

animals. We have been made a little lower than the heavenly beings and crowned with glory and honor (Ps. 8:5). The highpoint of all creation was not a mountain, a river, a badger, a beetle, a volcano, a fish, or a star. We were the climax, because we alone bear the image of God.

2. The image of God means that all human beings have inherent worth and dignity. This is one reason abortion is wrong. A person is a person no matter how small, no matter her development, no matter his environment, and no matter her degree of dependence on another human being. Innocent human life must be protected, even when that life is old or sick, even when the person wants to end his own life. Because every human being is made in God's image, descended from the same human pair, there is no place for racism, partiality, or feelings of ethnic superiority.

3. With a proper understanding of the image of God, we can see what it means to be fully human. We live out our deepest identity not in self-expression or sexual fulfillment, but in obedience to and love for the one who made us. When the serpent told Adam and Eve they would be like God on the day that they ate of the forbidden tree, he lied: they were already like God, made in his image.

4. The doctrine of the image of God reminds us that the world belongs to God. In the ancient world, a conquering king might put his statue in different locations throughout his realm to make clear that this was his dominion. In the same way, pagan temples in the ancient world always included images of the god who was said to dwell there. Our presence in the world as God's image bearers testifies that this is God's world. The God who made everything does not live in temples made by man (Acts 17:24). We are God's "idols," spread across the face of the earth (17:26), because the earth is the Lord's and the fulness thereof (Ps. 24:1 KJV).

5. The image of God in us means that we belong to God. When Jesus asked the Pharisees whose likeness was on the denarius, they said Caesar's (Matt. 22:20–21). They should have also stopped to consider whose likeness was on them. "Therefore render to Caesar the things that are Caesar's, and to God the things that are God's" (22:21). Caesar can have his taxes. Human beings belong to God, not to Caesar.

6. The image of God teaches us how to truly worship. All throughout the Old Testament, God's people were warned not to worship graven images (Ex. 20:4–6, 23). The God of Israel could not be seen. Until one day, he was. Worship now must be focused on Jesus Christ, a man like us (except for sin), the Son of God the Father, and the image of the invisible God (Col. 1:15).

DAY 81

The Essence of Sin

Sin is another name for that hideous rebellion, that God-defiance, that wretched opposition to the Creator that crouches at the door of every fallen human heart. Sin is both a condition, inherited from Adam (Rom. 5:12–21), and an action, manifesting itself in thought, word, and deed, which, when full-grown, gives birth to death (James 1:15).

In simplest terms, sin is lawlessness (1 John 3:4). It means we have broken God's commands and have fallen short of his glory (Rom. 3:23). But sin goes deeper than merely missing the mark. Sin is idolatry (Col. 3:5; 1 John 5:21). It is worshiping false gods, whether these deities are overt and physical, or more subtle and internal. Sin can also be considered adultery, a spiritual whoring after other lovers and other sources of satisfaction and meaning (Ezek. 16:15–42). Sin is pollution (James 1:27). Sin is pervasive (Rom. 3:9–20). And sin is the problem in the universe.[1]

We know very little about the first sin, except that it manifested itself in an angelic rebellion. Jude 6 explains that some angels "did not stay within their own position of authority, but left their proper dwelling" and these "he has kept in eternal chains under gloomy darkness until the judgment of the great day." First Timothy 3:6 suggests that the fall of the devil was the result of pride (see also Ezek. 28:11–19 for another possible allusion). However, Satan (the "adversary") fell. It's important to note that sin originated in the world of spirits, not in the world of human beings. Moreover, it is critical to see that these spirits did not sin by some external power or temptation, but in and by themselves. The devil's sin came out of the devil's own self-twisted arrogance and deception (John 8:44).

We know much more about the first sin in the human realm. We can't say just one thing about the first sin, but we can say that the first sin was prototypical of every other sin. Adam's sin in Eden involved disbelieving the word of God and pride in thinking he knew better than God. Adam sinned by pursuing illicit pleasure and by disregarding the consequences of sin.

The Old Testament uses several Hebrew words to speak of sin. The basic word is *chatta'ath*, meaning "to miss the mark." Other terms include: *hawon* (iniquity), *pesha* (rebellion), *habhar* (transgression), *resha* (wickedness), *ra* (evil), *ma'al* (trespass), and *awen* (idolatry). Likewise, the New Testament uses a variety of Greek words in relationship to sin. Sin is *hamartia* (falling short), *anomia* (lawlessness), *paraptoma* (trespass), *parabasis* (stepping over a boundary), *asebeia* (godlessness), *parakoe* (failing to listen to God), and *adikia* (unrighteousness).

Although the English words themselves are not inspired, it is worth noting the angularity and directness of the Bible. If we reduce sin to brokenness or struggle or mere weakness, we will miss the uncomfortable moral dimension and spiritual urgency of sin. The human problem is not simply that we make mistakes, or that we don't operate as we should, or that we are generically imperfect. No, our problem is that we are full of inquity, transgression, wickedness, lawlessness, and rebellion.

1 Some of this section comes from DeYoung, "Sin." Used by permission.

DAY 82

The Origin of Sin

The tree of the knowledge of good and evil was a probationary tree. It was there to test Adam. "Do this and live," God said. "Disobey and die." Adam disobeyed, so he died, and so we die. As a result of the fall, shame entered the world—Adam and Eve realized they were naked (Gen. 3:7). Fear entered the world—Adam and Eve hid from God (3:10). Blame entered the world—the man blamed God for giving him the woman, and the woman blamed the serpent for deceiving her (3:11–13). Pain entered the world too (3:16). Relationships turned sour (3:16). Work became a chore (3:17).

Because of Adam's sin, God cursed the serpent and cursed the ground. Although the man and the woman were not directly cursed, they were made to experience the curse in their particular spheres of responsibility. So serpents slither, women have pain in childbirth, men are frustrated by work, and the earth produces thorns and thistles. All of creation, in other words, was subjected to futility, such that creation itself now eagerly awaits freedom from its bondage to decay (Rom. 8:20–25).

Original sin, as a technical theological term, does not refer to the first (or original) sin in the garden, though that's bound up in the definition of the term. More precisely, original sin refers to that hereditary depravity and corruption that makes us guilty before God and yields in us sinful thoughts, desires, and actions. *Original sin* is what clings to us as fallen creatures because the whole human race was bound up in Adam. *Actual sin* refers to the sin we now commit as an act of the soul. The term *actual* does not refer to real sin as opposed to supposed sin, nor does it refer to external sin as opposed to internal sin. Actual sin is the sin we commit by our volition (in thought, word, and deed) as opposed to the sin we inherited from Adam.

Our fundamental problem is not bad parents, bad schools, or bad circumstances. Our fundamental problem is a bad heart. And every single one of us is born into the world with it. The Heidelberg Catechism puts the matter rather bluntly: "I have a natural tendency to hate God and my neighbor." As Scripture puts it, just as plainly, no one is righteous (Rom. 3:10). All have sinned and fall short of the glory of God (Rom. 3:23). The human heart is deceitful above all things, and desperately sick (Jer. 17:9). The natural man is dead in trespasses and sins (Eph. 2:1). By nature, we pass our days in malice and envy, hated by others and hating one another (Titus 3:3). We were conceived in sin and brought forth in iniquity (Ps. 51:5) We are inclined toward evil (Gen. 6:5). All of us like sheep have gone astray (Isa. 53:6). There is no one who does not sin (1 Kings 8:46). No one born of woman can be righteous before God (Job 15:14). No one can say, "I have made my heart pure; I am clean from my sin" (Prov. 20:9). Scripture has imprisoned everyone under sin (Gal. 3:22).

There is virtually no doctrine in the Bible taught more forcefully and more frequently than the natural man's inherited, all-pervasive sinfulness. And there is no doctrine we see more clearly in the world around us. There is no hope for any of us except to cry out, "Woe is me! For I am lost; for I am a man of unclean lips, and I dwell in the midst of a people of unclean lips; for my eyes have seen the King, the LORD of hosts!" (Isa. 6:5).

DAY 83

The Transmission of Sin

We've looked at the essence of sin (what is the nature of sin?), the origin of sin (where does our sin come from?), and now we come to the transmission of sin (how does sin spread?).

In some people's minds, there are only sinful acts, not sinful dispositions. That is, we don't inherit Adam's sinful nature; we only copy his sinful behavior. Against this view, the Bible teaches that we sin not only by imitation; we sin by imputation. In other words, we sin because we are sinners, and we are sinners because (to quote the old adage), "in Adam's fall, we sinned all."

Romans 5 is the classic text in dealing with the transmission of sin. Romans 5:12 says, "Therefore, just as sin came into the world through one man, and death through sin, . . . so death spread to all men because all sinned." When Paul says, "all sinned," he doesn't mean "all have sinned in our lifetimes." He means, "all sinned in Adam in the garden of Eden." Sin came into the world through Adam. Death came as a result of that sin. And death spread to everyone else in the human race because everyone else in the human race sinned in Adam at that moment in Eden in Genesis 3.

We know this is what Paul means because in verse 18 he compares the one trespass (Adam eating the fruit) with the one act of righteousness (Christ's death on the cross). Just as the one act of disobedience brought condemnation and death through our union with Adam (and not just as a result of our subsequent sin), so also the one act of obedience brings justification and life though our union with Christ (and not as a result of subsequent good works).

To use a homely analogy, it's like playing fantasy football. In fantasy football you pick your players, and when they get yards or receptions or score a touchdown, your fantasy team gets points. You're not physically doing anything. You didn't break a tackle. You didn't run into the end zone. Yet you talk about *your* team, *your* points, *your* wins and losses. The players are your representatives. That's Paul's argument in Romans. Every human being—past, present, and future—had Adam on his fantasy team, which means we all lost. When Adam sinned, we sinned. So Adam's punishment of death is our punishment too.

Theologians sometimes speak of the gospel as the story of three imputations. (1) Adam's sin and guilt were imputed to us. (2) Our sin and guilt were imputed to Christ. (3) Christ's obedience and perfect righteousness were imputed to believers. In each transaction, the guilt or obedience of another was reckoned or credited to us. That's what imputation means. In the first man, we became sinners. In the second Man, we become righteous. In the first man, we participated in sin and were reckoned as condemned. In the second Man, we participate in death for sin and resurrection unto life and are reckoned as holy.

All of human history is a tale of two Adams. The question is whether by faith we will be transferred from the dark kingdom of the first Adam to the eternal kingdom of the second Adam. "The wages of sin is death, but the free gift of God is eternal life in Christ Jesus our Lord" (Rom. 6:23).[1]

---

1 Portions of this section are reworked from DeYoung, *The Good News We Almost Forgot*, 33–35. Used by permission.

DAY 84

Total Inability

Pelagius (360–418) was a British monk famous in his day for his piety and austerity. For most Christians ever since, however, Pelagius has been infamous for his theology. Pelagius taught that humans must have the ability to overcome their sin. "How can we be blamed for sins we are powerless to resist?" Pelagius thought. He did not believe in inherited guilt and depravity. In particular, Pelagius opposed this phrase from Augustine's *Confessions*: "Grant what you command, and command what you will." He thought Augustine's view of human inability made man too passive and undermined human responsibility.

Throughout the controversy with Pelagius, Augustine proved himself to be the church's champion of sovereign grace. The fallen human will, Augustine taught, is in bondage to sin, utterly incapable of choosing the good. We can only be saved by grace. More than that, we can only accept God's grace by the regenerating power of grace itself.

The familiar phrase many Christians use to describe the fallenness of man is "total depravity." This is a fine phrase so long as we realize the "total" refers to the extent of our depravity (e.g., our will, our desires, our reason, all our faculties) and not the depth of our depravity (i.e., we are all as bad as we possibly can be). A better phrase might be "total inability" because it captures the helplessness (and hopelessness) of the human will apart from Christ.

Some Reformed theologians have made the distinction between natural inability and moral inability. Francis Turretin was not fond of the distinction, but his nephew and successor, Benedict Pictet, used the terms, as did John Witherspoon. The disciples of Jonathan Edwards took the distinction in a more liberalizing direction, sowing the seeds for a rosier view of the human will. But Pictet and Witherspoon used the distinction to underscore that the impotence of the sinner did not arise from a physical or natural defect, but from a depraved nature. They wanted to make clear that man had no excuse for his sin, since his sin was voluntary and moral.

The Canons of Dort provide the best succinct definition of total inability when it affirms that "all people are conceived in sin and are born children of wrath, unfit for any saving good, inclined to evil, dead in their sins, and slaves to sin; without the grace of the regenerating Holy Spirit they are neither willing nor able to return to God, to reform their distorted nature, or even to dispose themselves to such reform" (3/4.3). Such a low view of man does not sit well with many people in our age, but Dort's teaching is abundantly biblical. We are dead in trespasses and sin (Eph. 2:1). The natural person does not accept the things of the Spirit (1 Cor. 2:14). The mind of the flesh cannot submit to God's law (Rom. 7:18, 24; 8:7). No one can come to Jesus unless the Father draws him (John 6:44; cf. 8:34; 15:4–5).

There is no escaping the conclusion that we are utterly powerless to save ourselves. Not only that, but we are powerless to truly reform ourselves. We must be born from above. We must be born of the Spirit (John 3:5). Left to ourselves we would reject Christ, just as his fellow Jews did (1:12). But we are not without hope, for we who were born in sin can be born again, "not of blood nor of the will of the flesh nor of the will of man, but of God" (1:13).

DAY 85

Human Nature in Its Fourfold State

In 1720, Thomas Boston, a Scottish pastor and theologian, published what would become his best-known work, *Human Nature in Its Fourfold State*. The book proved immensely popular in Scotland, going through sixty editions by 1800, and served as one of the chief exports from the eighteenth century of Scottish and Reformed piety.

Boston's work was rooted in Augustine's famous fourfold description of man in relationship to sin:

- In the garden of Eden, man was able to sin and able not to sin (*posse peccare, posse non peccare*).
- After the fall, man was not able not to sin (*non posse, non peccare*).
- Once born again by the Spirit, man is able not to sin (*posse non peccare*).
- In heaven, the redeemed will be unable to sin (*non posse peccare*).

Boston described this taxonomy of Augustinian anthropology as: primitive integrity, entire depravity, begun recovery, and consummate happiness. More simply and more memorably, Boston speaks of human nature in four different states.

First, Adam was created in a *state of innocence*. Adam had the ability to obey God's command in the garden. There was nothing deficient in Adam's constitution that prevented him from keeping the probationary command and living a life pleasing to God. Adam was innocent of transgression—both original and actual.

Second, having disobeyed God, Adam plunged himself and the whole human race in a *state of nature*. According to Boston, this state is marked by sinfulness, misery, and inability. This is the inherited disposition of every human being born of natural descent. We are slaves to wickedness, unable to do what is truly good, unable to please God, and unable to save ourselves.

Third, for those who are saved by the sovereign work of the Spirit, by faith alone in Christ alone, we enter into a *state of grace*. Boston explains that two new realities mark this new state. (1) We are regenerated, and (2) we are joined in mystical union to Christ. True, we must still fight against indwelling sin. The state of grace is not free from temptation and the need for repentance. But we are not in the position we once were. We have a new principle at work within us. We are now slaves to righteousness instead of slaves to sin.

Fourth, upon death we enter into the *eternal state*. While Boston distinguishes between the righteous and the wicked in their deaths (and talks about both heaven and hell), this final state is usually remembered with respect to the believer. It is in this glorified state that we are fully restored, no longer sinning *and* no longer able to sin. This final state will be even better than man's first state, for whereas Adam had the ability to sin, in the eternal state the redeemed will be so unalterably consecrated and made new that no possibility of further transgression will exist. As the glory of God gives us light and the Lamb shines like a lamp, so we will walk in the brightness of the sun, never to return to the darkness again.

WEEK 18

DAY 86

Is Every Sin the Same in God's Eyes?

Many Christians hold to the mistaken notion that every sin is the same in God's eyes. Some Christians embrace this conviction by way of a misguided theological calculation: "If every sin deserves eternal judgment, then every sin must be equally heinous." Others promote the idea for apologetic reasons: "Don't worry, friend, your sins are no worse than anyone else's sins." Still others believe in the equality of every sin out of a genuine sense of humility: "Who am I to think that my sins are less vile than anyone else's sins?"

While these reasons are understandable, and in some sense commendable, the witness of Scripture tells a different story. Consider several examples:

- The Mosaic law prescribed different penalties for different infractions and required different sacrifices and payments to make restitution.
- The Mosaic law also distinguished between unintentional sins and high-handed sins (Num. 15:29–30).
- Sins of rank idolatry and willful rebellion were more serious indictments on the kings of Israel and Judah than was the sin of failing to remove the easy-to-overlook "high places" in the land.
- God's anger was often specifically directed against the leaders of the people. The sins of the king or the priests or the elders meant greater judgment than the sins of the laity.
- Jesus warned that cities in which he performed his miracles would be more severely judged than Sodom and Gomorrah (Matt. 10:15).
- Jesus considered Judas's betrayal to be a sin worse than others (Matt. 26:24).
- God's anger is especially roused by sins against children, the weak, or the helpless (Jer. 32:35; Matt. 18:6; Luke 20:47).
- Excommunication seems to have been reserved for only the most flagrant sins (1 Cor. 5:1–13).
- Cornelius, though not yet saved, was considered a devout man who feared God (Acts 10:2). Even among non-Christians there is a difference between being a decent person and being a dirty, rotten scoundrel.
- There is a sin that leads to death, but not all sins are unto death (1 John 5:16).

The Bible simply doesn't make sense—not the Mosaic law, not the exile, not church discipline, not the frequent warnings of judgment for specific transgressions—if all sins are equally vile in God's eyes.

In fact, life doesn't make sense if every sin is the same. Parents do not discipline their children the same for every act of disobedience. Employers do not inflict the same punitive measures for every violation of company policy. Law enforcement officers do not treat every offense the same. Our judicial system does not hand down the same punishments for every infraction. What we know to be true in ordinary life we must not forget in our spiritual lives. As much as it shows admirable humility or apologetic concern, we must not act or teach as if every sin is the same in God's eyes.

Sins Made More Heinous

The Westminster Larger Catechism teaches, "All transgressions of the law of God are not equally heinous; but some sins in themselves, and by reason of several aggravations, are more heinous in the sight of God than others" (WLC 150). The Larger Catechism goes on to provide a helpful analysis of what makes "some sins more heinous than others" (WLC 151). According to the Westminster divines, sins receive their aggravations from four different categories.

1. "From the persons offending." Sins are worse when they come from pastors or parents or public figures, when they come from those who teach and write books, and when they come from Christians who should (and do) know better.

2. "From the parties offended." Sins are worse when they expressly blaspheme God or demean Christ and the gospel, when they reject the work of the Spirit, when they show disrespect to parents and persons in authority, when they ignore our weaker brothers and sisters, and when they lead many astray.

3. "From the nature and quality of the offense." Sins are worse when they deal with matters that are black or white instead of gray; when they break forth externally, not just internally; when they are frequent; when they are celebrated; when they cannot be undone; when they are against nature, against conscience, and against the warnings of others.

4. "From circumstances of time and place." Sins are worse when they take place in connection with the gathering of God's people for worship, when they could have been avoided, and when they are committed in public so as to be well known to others.

Why does any of this matter? There are at least three benefits: public, pastoral, and personal.

When it comes to our *public* witness, we must have the courage to say that some sins are worse than others. Sins by pastors are worse than sins by parishioners. Sins by public figures with many followers are worse than sins by private individuals. And although all sexual sins are serious, we should not shrink back from teaching that sins against the light of nature are especially heinous, particularly when these sins are committed with delight and to the detriment of the common good.

Pastorally, distinguishing among various degrees of sin can help us apply the comfort and the warnings of Scripture more judiciously. Some preachers are quick to pull the punch when the Bible would have us issue a stern warning, while others are ready to thunder judgment against our people for every offense.

Likewise, when we learn to discern how "sins receive their aggravations," we will have the proper categories to hold people responsible for their lesser sins even as we may sympathize with them for having been more grievously sinned against.

And finally, there are *personal* benefits. Too many Christians have flattened the moral contours of the Bible such that we no longer distinguish between falling into sin and running headlong into sin. This means that some of us are too hard on ourselves (seeing no moral space between fallen temptations and flagrant disobedience), some of us are too easy on ourselves (believing our heinous sins to be little more than "struggles" or "mistakes"), and many of us give up striving after holiness because we know we will always be sinners. Let us keep fighting the good fight of faith, knowing that by God's grace in Christ, sanctified sinners can put to death the deeds of the flesh, grow in godliness, and do what is pleasing in God's sight.

Concupiscence

According to the Reformed tradition, we are held accountable not only for the sins we commit by an act of the will, but also for the original sin we inherited from Adam. "This corruption of nature, during this life," the Westminster Confession states, "doth remain in those that are regenerated; and although it be, through Christ, pardoned, and mortified, yet both itself, and all the motions thereof, are truly and properly called sin" (WCF 6.5). Later the confession declares that "every sin, both original and actual," is a "transgression of the righteous law of God," and does, "in its own nature, bring guilt upon the sinner" (WCF 6.6). The fall does not simply make us broken and disordered; it condemns us before God.

To be sure, many of us have desires that do not feel freely chosen. People may not wake up one day and make a conscious decision to be same-sex attracted, or to be lustfully distracted by scantily clad persons at the beach, or to be addicted to gambling, or to be angry all the time. While the reality of these not-asked-for desires should move us to compassion and understanding, it does not change the moral calculus of those desires. It is one of the hallmarks of Reformed anthropology that sin can be both unchosen bondage and willful rebellion at the same time. We all have disordered desires that arise in us unbidden.

How we describe our involuntary, disordered desires is a major difference between a Roman Catholic and a Reformed understanding of sin. According to the Catholic Catechism, the "inclination to sin that Tradition calls concupiscence" is "left for us to wrestle with," but "it cannot harm those who do not consent."[1] Elsewhere, the Catholic Catechism explains that "concupiscence stems from the disobedience of the first sin. It unsettles man's moral faculties and, without being in itself an offense, inclines man to commit sins."[2] In other words, disordered desire, though a result of the fall, does not become sin apart from a consenting act of the will.

The Reformed tradition has uniformly disagreed with this understanding of concupiscence. "The Reformation," writes Bavinck, "spoke out against that position, asserting that also the impure thoughts and desires that arose in us prior to and apart from our will are sin."[3] Calvin argues that these "inordinate desires" (*concupiscentiis*) should be called not merely "weakness" but "sin." "We label 'sin,'" he writes, "that very depravity which begets in us desires of this sort. We accordingly teach that in the saints, until they are divested of mortal bodies, there is always sin; for in their flesh there resides the depravity of inordinate desiring which contends against righteousness."[4] We repent of these sins, therefore, insofar as we grieve for our sin, hate our sin, and "turn from them all unto God" (WCF 15.2). Every desire for an illicit end is itself an illicit desire, whether we have are aware of choosing the desire or not. Concupiscence is not just disordered, but sinful. The good news is that as such it can be healed and forgiven.

1 Catechism of the Catholic Church, 1264.
2 Catechism of the Catholic Church, 2515.
3 Bavinck, *Reformed Dogmatics*, 3:143.
4 Calvin, *Institutes*, 3.3.10.

DAY 89

Temptation

James 1:14–15 is a key text when it comes to understanding the nature of sin and temptation: "Each person is tempted when he is lured and enticed by his own desire. Then desire when it has conceived gives birth to sin, and sin when it is fully grown brings forth death." It is important to understand what James is *not* saying. When James speaks of desire giving birth to sin, he is talking about observable outward sin. He is not declaring that every temptation is free from sin.

To understand what James is saying we need to look carefully at the word *temptation*. The word James uses for "tempts" (*peirazei*) and "tempted" (*peiraze-*

tai) in verses 13 and 14 is the same word (in noun form) translated as "trials" (*peirasmois*) in James 1:2 ("Count it all joy, my brothers, when you meet trials of various kinds"). Clearly, there are some "temptations" God gives us in the form of morally neutral trials, and some "temptations" God never gives us because they arise from within as morally illicit desires. The one who is experiencing temptation caused by his own desire (*epithumias*) is already experiencing the reality of indwelling sin, though that indwelling sin (in the Christian) can be resisted so as not to give birth to observable sin.

John Owen explains that temptations can be taken two ways: passively (as in James 1:2) and actively (as in James 1:13–14). Roughly speaking, passive temptation is that which entreats us from without, while active temptation is that which arises from within. Commenting on James 1:14–15, Owen argues: "Now, when such a temptation comes from without, it is unto the soul an indifferent thing, neither good nor evil, unless it be consented unto; but the very proposal from within, it being the soul's own act, is its sin."[1] Later in the same passage, Owen describes the tempting proposal from within as "this power of sin to beget figments and ideas of actual evil in the heart." In other words, when there is this kind of "temptation"—the kind that arises from within—it is no different from the lusts of the heart and indwelling sin itself.

This distinction—between passive and active temptation, or between temptation from without or within—helps make sense of Christ's temptations. Christ suffered real temptation (Heb. 2:18; 4:15), but it was a temptation that befell him in the form of trials and the devil's entreaties, not a temptation that was stirred up due to disordered desire. "Christ had only the *suffering* part of temptation, when he entered into it," Owen observes; "we have also the *sinning* part."[2]

For Owen, James 1:14–15 describes the process of (1) the mind being drawn away, (2) the affections being entangled, (3) the will consenting to actual sin, (4) the conversation wherein sin is brought forth into view, and (5) the stubborn course that finishes sin and ends in death.[3] Each step of the process is worse than the next. We should not think that the entanglement of the affections is equivalent to obstinately pursuing a life of sin. There *is* moral space to be found between each step. And yet this process is not one that moves from innocence to sin, but rather one that sees indwelling sin move from the mind to the affections to the will and finally to the outward working of sin in the life (and death) of a person.

1   Owen, *Overcoming Sin and Temptation*, 276.
2   Owen, *Overcoming Sin and Temptation*, 183.
3   Owen, "*Overcoming Sin and Temptation*, 297–98.

What Difference Does the Doctrine of Sin Make?

Reformed theology is (in)famous for having a robust doctrine of sin. We often emphasize—correctly and biblically—the depravity, lostness, and utter inability of man apart from God's grace. We also talk about the need to fight temptation and the power of indwelling sin in our lives as Christians. I imagine some people get tired of all the sin talk. But rightly understood and wisely communicated, a proper doctrine of sin is indispensable to mature Christian discipleship.

Let me mention four ways that the doctrine of sin should make a difference in our lives and in our thinking.

First, *the doctrine of sin should make us realistic about the world.* By God's saving grace for sinners and by his common grace for all of us, there is much to enjoy and celebrate in the world. And yet we should not be surprised when people sin. That's why we need mediating institutions, why we need an economic system that expects people to act according to self-interest, and why we need safeguards against concentrated power. The best government is the one designed to check its own inherent tendencies to tyranny, just as a prudent political philosophy embraces the realities of our fallen condition and plans accordingly. Throughout human history, many of the worst dictators and most murderous regimes were those that thought they could create heaven on earth.

Second, *the doctrine of sin should make us recognize our own fallen tendencies.* Most people believe in human sinfulness; they just believe that it's *other people* who are sinful. If Reformed theology reminds us that the powerful often oppress the weak, it also reminds us that all of us "have a natural tendency to hate God and [our] neighbor[s]" (Heidelberg Catechism Q/A 5). What many modern ideologies locate in certain races, sexes, classes, and sexual orientations, the Reformed tradition locates in every human heart. As Aleksandr Solzhenitsyn famously observed in his account of the Soviet prison system, "the line separating good and evil passes . . . right through every human heart."

Third, *the doctrine of sin should make us resolute in our mission.* We will not be Bible people—or Jesus people, or gospel people—if we are not salvation-for-sinners people. Though some may derisively call it a fire insurance gospel or an individualistic gospel, the unavoidable reality of Scripture is that at the heart of the message of the cross is the simple, wonderful, glorious good news that

Christ saves sinners like you and me. And if this message, and all that took place to accomplish what it announces, represents the climax of redemptive history—indeed, if all of history is about redemption—then we are right to conclude that this soteriological emphasis must shape the sound of our preaching, the priority of our ministry, and the mission of the church.

Fourth, *the doctrine of sin should make us rejoice in our salvation.* It is nothing less than a miracle that any of us believe in the Lord Jesus Christ and are saved from the wrath to come. Wherever we see genuine faith and repentance, we ought to give thanks for all that the Father appointed, all that Christ accomplished, and all that the Spirit is applying to God's elect. As John Stoker, the eighteenth-century hymn writer, put it, "Thy mercy of God is the theme of our song, the joy of my heart, and the boast of my tongue. Thy free grace alone, from the first to the last, hath won my affections and bound my soul fast."

COVENANT THEOLOGY

How God Relates to His Creatures

DAY 91

Centrality of Covenant

"As they were eating, he took bread, and after blessing it broke it and gave it to them and said, 'Take; this is my body.' And he took a cup, and when he had given thanks he gave it to them, and they all drank of it. And he said to them, 'This is my blood of the covenant, which is poured out for many'" (Mark 14:22–24).

Most Christians have heard these words hundreds of times—retold every time we come to the story of the Last Supper and repeated every time we partake of the Lord's Supper. And yet, for as important as these words are in redemptive history and in the church, we often pay little attention to them. Or more specifically, we often pay little attention to *one* of these words. As Jonty Rhodes has pointed out, many of us could put our thumb over the word "covenant" in Jesus's declaration and the verse wouldn't mean anything different.[1] We miss the fact that when Jesus explained the meaning of his saving death, he chose to do so explicitly in terms of covenant theology.

Covenant should be a central theme in any systematic theology. The word *covenant* is mentioned more than three hundred times in the Bible. It's there in the Christmas story (Luke 1:73) and the passion of Christ (Luke 22:20). It's there in the opening chapters of the Bible (Gen. 6:18; 9:17; cf. Hos. 6:7), and it's there near the end of the Bible where we learn of Christ's high priestly work (Heb. 8:6). It's no wonder the Jews were called "sons . . . of the covenant" (Acts 3:25). We would do well to imitate Spurgeon who waxed nostalgic when thinking about "our venerable grandsires [who] were at home conversing upon 'the covenants.'"[2]

In his introduction to *Economy of the Covenants*, the classic work by the Dutch theologian Hermann Witsius (1636–1708), J. I. Packer argues that covenant theology is a hermeneutic, a way of reading the whole Bible.[3] Biblical redemption starts with the covenantal relations among the persons of the Trinity. Biblical doctrine has to do with the covenantal relationship between God and man. And biblical ethics has to do with our covenantal relationships with others. We can't make sense of the gospel of God, the word of God, or the reality of God unless we view these through a covenantal frame.[4]

According to Packer, the Bible underlines the significance of covenant theology in four ways.[5] (1) By the story it tells—a unified story of grace unfolding in successive covenants. (2) By the place it gives to Jesus Christ as the one the covenants foretold and as the covenant-keeping Messiah for our sins. (3) By the specific parallels between the two covenant heads, Adam and Christ. (4) By the eternal covenant of redemption taught most clearly from Jesus himself in John's Gospel. Covenant theology is not an alien system that Reformed theologians have forced upon the Bible. Rather, covenant theology forces itself upon all who read the Bible thoughtfully and humbly from cover to cover.

1   Jonty Rhodes, *Raiding the Lost Ark: Recovering the Gospel of the Covenant King* (Nottingham, UK: Inter-Varsity Press, 2013), 17–18.
2   Quoted in Golding, *Covenant Theology*, 9.
3   Packer, "Introduction," 27.
4   Packer, "Introduction," 31–34.
5   These four ways are given in my words, but the four concepts come from Packer, "Introduction," 39–42.

DAY 92

Definition of Covenant

What exactly is a covenant? Turretin defines *covenant* in Scripture as "a pact and agreement entered into between God and man, consisting partly in stipulation of duty (or of the thing to be done) and partly in the promise of reward."[1] More verbose, Witsius states that a covenant "is an agreement between God and man about the way of obtaining consummate happiness; including a commination of eternal destructions, with which the contemner of the happiness, offered in that way, is to be punished."[2] The *c*-words there are confusing. *Consummate* means perfect; *commination* means threatening, and *contemner* refers to someone who holds something in contempt. In other words, God's covenant with man is about the promise of eternal happiness, a warning of eternal judgment, and how the person who rejects the former will get the latter.

There are more contemporary definitions as well. Richard Belcher argues that covenant refers to a legal agreement between two parties that is ratified by certain rituals that emphasize the binding nature of the agreement.[3] J. I. Packer defines covenant as "a voluntary mutual commitment that binds each party to each other."[4] Most well known, perhaps, is O. Palmer Robertson's definition of covenant as "a bond in blood sovereignly administered."[5]

My definition differs slightly from Robertson's memorable dictum. Roberton's definition is succinctly put and generally useful, insofar as his definition reminds us that covenants have to do with relationships bound by verbal oaths and symbolic actions. His definition also rightly stresses that God dictates the terms of all biblical covenants. But one can questions whether every biblical covenant is a bond in blood. To be sure, without the shedding of blood there is no remission of sins (Heb. 9:22), but it is hard to see how the Noahic and Davidic covenants involve the shedding of blood, or how the covenant of redemption is administered in blood (even if it commits the Surety to a bloody death). With all this in mind, I think we ought to define *covenant* more simply as "a promissory agreement between two or more parties."

Biblical covenants come out of an ancient world where political treaties and formal relational agreements were well known. The various covenants in Scripture, like many of the covenants of the same era, are composed of identifiable elements. In general, we see seven elements associated with biblical covenants. There are three *p*-words: promises, prescriptions, and penalties. And four *s*-words: swearing (of an oath), seeing, statements, and signs. These seven elements aren't present in every covenant, and they aren't the only way to categorize things, but taken together these elements represent a common template. In biblical covenants, God makes promises, lays out commands, and threatens punishment. And in establishing the covenant relationship, there is often an oath, eyewitnesses, written documents, and symbols of ratification. Everywhere throughout the Bible, God relates to his creatures by way of these promissory agreements.

1   Turretin, *Elenctic Theology*, 2:172.
2   Witsius, *Economy of the Covenants*, 1:45.
3   Belcher, *Fulfillment of the Promises of God*, 18.
4   Packer, "Introduction," 29.
5   Robertson, *Christ of the Covenants*, 4.

DAY 93

Berith and *Diatheke*

The Hebrew word for covenant is *berith*, and the Greek word is *diatheke*. Both are normally translated as "covenant" in modern English versions of the Bible, though they haven't always been understood as meaning the same thing. (The Latin word for covenant is *foedus*, which is why covenant theology is sometimes called federal theology.)

Everyone agrees that *berith* should be translated as "covenant," but scholars have not always agreed on whether the Greek idea of *diatheke* refers to a covenant, a testament (like a last will and testament that disposes of someone's possessions upon death), or something in between. Many older theologians assumed that the use of *diatheke* in the New Testament could refer (at least some of the time) to a last will and testament. Indeed, while the King James Version often translates *diatheke* as "covenant," it uses the word "testament" fourteen times. The RSV translates all of the uses of *diatheke* as "covenant," except for Hebrews 9:16. The ESV uses "will" for *diatheke* in verses 16 and 17. Given the statement that "a *diatheke* takes effect only at death" (9:17), it's possible that a will or testament is in view.

There are other reasons, however, to think that even in Hebrews 9, the author is thinking of a covenant rather than a last will and testament. (1) The use of *diatheke* in verse 15 and in verses 18–21 clearly refers to a covenant. The burden of proof rests with those who want to make the same word mean something different in verses 16 and 17. (2) The word "death" (*nekroi*) in the first half of verse 17 could be translated "dead bodies," referring to the slain animals often present in ancient covenant ceremonies. (3) The second half of verse 17 could refer to a symbolic death; namely, the one who makes a covenant must die because he swears a self-maledictory oath should he break the covenant. (4) Crucially, more recent New Testament scholars argue that Greek testaments did not work like our "last will and testament." They did not require death for the inheritance to be distributed (think, for example, of the parable of the prodigal son). In other words, we should see *diatheke* throughout the New Testament as largely synonymous with *berith* from the Old Testament.

Even if we see the testamentary idea, instead of covenant, in a few places in the New Testament—and many of the best theologians (e.g., Calvin, Turretin, Witsius) have—we should not confuse the two ideas. Both relate to death, but in a covenant, death stands at the beginning of the agreement (symbolized as potential cursing), whereas in a testament, death stands at the end of the relationship. Death activates a testament, while death vindicates a covenant. In a testament, death is presumed. In a covenant, there is the option of life or death. Most importantly, remember that Christ understood his death in covenantal terms. Our salvation is nothing less than the fulfillment of covenant theology: the death of our covenant-keeping Christ, through the shed blood of the covenant of grace, is as a substitutionary sacrifice for God's covenant-breaking people.

DAY 94

Worship as Covenant Renewal

Exodus 24 is a picture of covenant confirmation. After initiating the covenant (Ex. 19), establishing the constitutional obligations of the covenant (Ex. 20), and applying the constitution as case law (Ex. 21–23), God confirms the covenant with Moses. In addition to being a picture of covenant confirmation for Moses and the people of Israel, Exodus 24 provides a striking picture of worship as covenant renewal.

Exodus 24 begins with a call to worship as the Lord summons Moses and Aaron, Nadab and Abihu, and the seventy elders of Israel to draw near. Moses then includes the people in what can be described as a service of worship, a ceremony of covenant confirmation (and later renewal) focusing on three elements.

1. The service on Sinai centered on the *Book of the Covenant*. Moses told the people all the words of the Lord (the Ten Commandments) and all the rules applying those words (24:3). Then later Moses repeated the essence of these instructions, reading to the people from the Book of the Covenant (24:7). Importantly, we see that Moses was not just passing on oral tradition. Already at this early stage in redemptive history, Moses had written revelation to share (24:4). Twice in this passage, the people respond to the word of God with a commitment of obedience. This is the heart of worship as covenant renewal. God's word is read and taught—the stipulations, the promises, the blessings and curses. God's people hear it, receive it, understand it, and respond.

2. The service also involved the *blood of the covenant*. With an altar (24:4), sacrifices (24:5), and sprinkling (24:6), blood not only accompanies the administration of the covenant; it makes the provisions of the covenant possible. The shedding of blood represents substitution (there are twelve pillars for the twelve tribes of Israel) and propitiation (hence the mention of burnt offerings and peace offerings). The blood of the covenant also pointed to consecration as the people were set apart by the word and set apart for obedience to the word (24:8).

3. Finally, the service included the *bread of the covenant*. As Moses and Aaron, Nadab, and Abihu, and the seventy elders beheld God in his glory, they ate and drank (24:11). Covenant ceremonies often concluded with a meal (Gen. 26:30; 31:44, 46). Eating and drinking were an expression of fellowship, a sign and seal of the closeness the people had with each other and with their God.

Exodus 24 is a worship service, the first gathering of corporate worship depicted in the Bible. It contains the basic elements of a public service and sets the pattern for biblical worship. There is a call to worship, an approach to worship made possible by a bloody sacrifice, the reading of God's word, a response to God's word, a fellowship meal, and the promise of God's presence as he draws near in worship. As we gather Sunday by Sunday to rehearse the Lord's covenant promises and provisions (1 Cor. 11:23–26), the same elements should be regularly found in our services today.

DAY 95

Covenant of Redemption

The covenant of redemption—or in Latin, the *pactum salutis*—refers to the eternal agreement between the Father and the Son to save a people chosen in Christ before the ages began. In traditional Reformed theology, the *pactum* has been a critically important doctrine, helping to make sense of (and hold together) election in Christ, God's activity in history, and the intra-Trinitarian love of God. It has also been a pastoral doctrine meant to give the believer confidence that because our covenant relationship with God has its origin in the Father's pretemporal covenant relationship with the Son, we have every reason to rest secure in Christ our surety.

Despite its central place in the history of Reformed dogmatics, the *pactum* has often been criticized—both from without and from within the Reformed tradition. Three criticisms are most common.

First, it is argued that the *pactum* is sub-Trinitarian in that no role is given for the Holy Spirit. While it's true that the *pactum* has normally been construed as an agreement between the Father and the Son, this need not undermine the Trinity any more than Jesus's emphasis on the Father-Son relationship in the high priestly prayer undermines the Trinity. Many newer theologies make the Spirit an equal partner in the eternal *pactum*, defending the doctrine in explicitly Trinitarian terms. But even among older theologians the Spirit was not absent. Wilhelmus à Brakel, for example, taught that "the manifestation of every grace and influence of the Holy Spirit proceeds from this covenant [of redemption]."[1]

Second, others object that the *pactum* entails heterodox theology in that it undermines the singularity of God's will. If the Father truly covenants with the Son, it is said, then the Father must have one will and the Son another. Reformed theologians, in anticipating this objection, have argued that the one divine will can be viewed from a twofold perspective. The Father and the Son have the same aim and objective, but whereas the Father wills to redeem by the agency of the Son as surety, the Son wills to redeem by his own agency as surety.[2]

Third, and most critically, the *pactum* has been derided as metaphysical speculation. Karl Barth famously dismissed the covenant of redemption as "mythology," while more recently, one evangelical theologian has argued that the *pactum* "lacks clear biblical support" and is little more than "scholastic tinkering."[3]

On closer inspection, however, there is good evidence in Scripture for a salvation pact between the Father and the Son. We know that promises were made to Christ that he would be given a people by the Father (John 6:38–40; cf. 5:30, 43; 17:4–12) and that Christ, as the second Adam, is the covenant head of his people (Rom. 5:12–21; 1 Cor. 15:22). We also know that there was a decree whereby the eternally begotten Son was given the nations as his heritage and the ends of the earth as his possession (Ps. 2:7; cf. Ps. 110). This is why Zechariah 6:13 speaks of a covenant of peace between Yahweh and the Branch, and why Jesus in Luke 22:29 speaks of the kingdom the Father has assigned to him. Our salvation is sure: the covenant of grace in time was made possible by the covenant of redemption from all eternity.

1 À Brakel, *The Christian's Reasonable Service*, 1:262.
2 À Brakel, *The Christian's Reasonable Service*, 1:252.
3 Williamson, "The *Pactum Salutis*," 281.

WEEK 20

DAY 96

Covenant of Works

The covenant of works refers to the arrangement between God and Adam in the garden of Eden, whereby Adam, as federal head of the human race, was promised life upon obedience to the divine command and threatened with death upon disobedience.

This covenant with Adam has been called by various names: the covenant of nature (because it is founded on the *natura* of man as first created by God), the

Edenic covenant (because it was initiated in the garden of Eden), the covenant of creation (because it was established at the creation of man), and the covenant of life (because life was offered upon perfect and perpetual obedience). The covenant of works, however, is preferable because it underscores that the blessings and curses were to be meted out according to the principles of works instead of grace.

John Murray famously denied that God's arrangement with Adam in the garden was a covenant of works, calling it instead the "Adamic administration."[1] First, he argued that the word covenant is not used. Second, he did not believe there was a works principle in this arrangement. God would fulfill his promise to give life to Adam, but, Murray argued, this was not on the basis of works. It was according to God's faithfulness, not his justice.

Despite these and other objections, there are good reasons that Reformed theologians have typically defended and emphasized the covenant of works. For starters, most of the elements associated with biblical covenants are present in the garden. There is the prescription not to eat, the promise of eternal life, and the penalty of death. There is also the swearing of an oath ("You shall surely die"), the presence of witnesses ("Let *us* make man"), and the sign of the tree of life. Furthermore, the fact that Genesis 1–3 and Deuteronomy 28–34 act as bookends for the first five books of the Bible—with creational imagery repeated especially in chapters 33 and 34—suggests that the Pentateuch ends with the prospect of Israel breaking the Mosaic covenant just like the opening chapters of Genesis end with the reality that Adam broke the covenant of works.

The classic text used to defend the covenant of works is Hosea 6:7: "But like Adam they transgressed the covenant." Although some have understood *adam* in this passage as a place name or a reference to mankind generally, it is best to see the singular person of Adam in view. Apart from the possible parallel in Job 31:33 and the creational imagery elsewhere in Hosea, the immediate context is decisive. To compare Israel's sin to the sin of mankind would *minimize* their crime, when Hosea's point is to emphasize the magnitude of Israel's by pointing to Adam as the origin and example of their iniquity.

Finally, strong support for the covenant idea in Genesis 1–3 can be found in Romans 5 and 1 Corinthians 15. For Paul, Adam was a type of one to come (Rom. 5:14), meaning we have good reason to connect the nature of Jesus's accomplishment with the nature of Adam's failure. If Jesus's representative work is understood in covenantal terms (1 Cor. 11:25–26; 2 Cor. 3:4–11), and if Adam and Jesus stand in parallel as representative persons, we must see Adam's representative work also in covenantal terms.

1 Murray, *Collected Writings*, 4:217–22.

Covenant of Grace

Since the fall, man has been rendered incapable of living by the covenant of works. But God, being gracious, has established another covenant—a covenant of grace "wherein he freely offereth unto sinners life and salvation by Jesus Christ" (WCF 7.3). Louis Berkhof defines the covenant of grace as "that gracious agreement between the offended God and the offending but elect sinner, in which God promises salvation through faith in Christ, and the sinner accepts this believingly, promising a life of faith and obedience."[1]

Three further points.

1. The covenant of grace, depending on the meaning of our terms, can be considered conditional or unconditional. The covenant of grace is unconditional if you understand the condition to imply some sort of merit. There is nothing that we earn or come to deserve in the covenant of grace. It is, after all, not a covenant of works. On the other hand, many Reformed theologians have not shied away from calling the covenant of grace a conditional covenant. Entrance into this covenant is free. At the same time, faith is required of those who would enjoy all the benefits of the covenant (WCF 7.3). Importantly, this faith is itself a gift from the Holy Spirit.

2. There have always been two ways of existing within the covenant of grace. The covenant expressed in the Old Testament was always spiritual in nature. Circumcision of the flesh was supposed to have its counterpart in the circumcision of the heart (Lev. 26:40–42; Deut. 30:6; Jer. 9:25). Paul makes this point forcefully in Romans 4:11 where circumcision is called a sign and seal given to Abraham of the righteousness that comes by faith. It may seem strange that this sign was given to eight-day-old sons, until we realize that it was possible to be connected externally to the covenant without personally owning all the internal blessings (cf. Rom. 2:25–29; 9:6–8).

This same reality is possible in the new covenant. Those who are externally connected to the blood of Christ and set apart in a covenantal sense, can, in the end, "profane the blood of the covenant by which [they were] sanctified" (Heb. 10:29). Some theologians refer to this dynamic as the administration of the covenant and the essence of the covenant, or the conditional covenant and absolute covenant, or covenant as a legal relationship and covenant as a communion of life. Whatever language we use, the point is that in the Old Testament and the New Testament, the covenant of grace has both objective and subjective elements.

3. The covenant of grace, though differently administered throughout redemptive history, is "but one and the same, under various dispensations" (WCF 7.6). The new covenant is a fuller and clearer expression of the covenant of grace, but it is not different in substance from the various covenants in the Old Testament. The most fundamental and foundational covenant blessing—the promise of God's presence—is a scarlet thread woven through the Bible. From Genesis 17 and the covenant of circumcision, to the giving of the law in Exodus 20, to the renewal of the covenant in Deuteronomy 29, to the promise of a Davidic king in 2 Samuel 7, to the hope of the new covenant in Jeremiah and Ezekiel, to the consummation of the new heavens and the new earth in Revelation 21, we see God's gracious covenant promise: that he will be a God to us and we will be his people.

1   Berkhof, *Systematic Theology*, 277.

DAY 98

The Noahic Covenant

The Noahic covenant established in Genesis 9 is fundamentally a covenant of preservation. God promises a predictable regularity to days and seasons. He also promises that he will never again destroy the world with a flood. God will not "curse" the ground after the flood (8:21) as he did after the sin in the garden (3:17). The covenant arrangement in Genesis 9 indicated to all living things that the war of watery annihilation had ceased.

Famously, the sign of this promise is a rainbow, a natural sign (whether it had appeared in the sky before Genesis 9 we do not know) and a bloodless sign (unlike circumcision and Passover later to be revealed in the Pentateuch). Although the rainbow has been taken as a sign for the sexual revolution in our day, it was a Jewish-Christian symbol first, and we should not give it up. The rainbow is a sign to us, and even more explicitly a reminder to God himself (9:16), that God will never again destroy the world with a flood. God has hung his bow in the sky, and he will not send forth his cataclysmic arrows of judgment on the earth until the end of the age (8:22). A final judgment is coming, but it will be fire instead of water (2 Pet. 3:3–10).

Unique among the major covenants in the Bible, the Noahic covenant is not made with God's people alone. The covenant is made with Noah, his family, their descendants, and all living things (see the language of every/all in Genesis 9:10a, 10b, 11b, 12b, 15a, 15b, 17b). The Noahic covenant is a covenant of common grace, not special grace. It encompasses the godly and the ungodly. It even includes animals. To be sure, the Noahic covenant is an administration of the one covenant of grace, but it is not directly about redemption as much as it is about the cosmic preservation that makes God's later redemptive work possible. As Bavinck puts it, "This covenant with Noah (Gen. 8:21–22; 9:1–17), though it is rooted in God's grace and is intimately bound up with the actual covenant of grace because it sustains and prepares for it, is not identical with it. It is rather a 'covenant of long-suffering' made by God with all humans and even with all creatures."[1]

The Noahic covenant is both like and unlike God's covenant with Adam. There are undeniable similarities to the creation mandate of Genesis, but the covenant arrangement has been redrawn for a world of sin (8:21). In Genesis 9, there are no covenant conditions to be met, no curses invoked, no if-then formula. Instead, God unilaterally promises preservation for the world and reestablishes that man is made in the image of God (9:6), that he should be fruitful and multiply (9:1), and that he is God's vice-regent on the earth (9:2). The covenant of Genesis 9 reestablishes the blessings and dominion concerns of Genesis 1 but in a way that assumes a fallen world instead of a pristine garden paradise.

---

1 Bavinck, *Reformed Dogmatics*, 218.

DAY 99

Abrahamic Covenant

The Abrahamic covenant—God's promise to bless the world by grace through faith—unfolds over several chapters in Genesis.

First, we have *covenant introduction* in Genesis 12. Right away we notice the principle of election at work. Why was Abraham (technically Abram at this point) summoned? He and his household were not worshiping the true God; they were idol worshipers (Josh. 24:2). The mysterious Melchizedek seems a more worthy choice. Or maybe the righteous man Job (who might have been alive around this time). But the Lord chose Abraham because the Lord was up to something of his own planning and purpose. The Lord makes seven promises to Abraham encompassing three expanding circles of blessing: God will bless Abraham, God will bless the nation that comes from Abraham, and God will bless all the peoples on earth through Abraham. Galatians 3:8–9 calls this announcement nothing less than the preaching of the gospel. God had good news for Abraham and good news for all those who, like Abraham, trust in the promise.

Next, we have *covenant ratification* in Genesis 15. No sooner does Abraham receive the promise of blessing than that promise is immediately threatened. The promise is threatened by famine (Gen. 12), by Lot (Gen. 13), and by the eastern kings (Gen. 14). But after each ordeal Abraham comes out on top. Abraham is blessed in every way—except the one way that matters most. He does not yet have a child. So once again God promises to give Abraham a child and to make him into a mighty nation. Abraham believed the Lord, and Abraham was declared righteous through the instrumentality of his faith (Gen. 15:6). After this declaration of justification, the Lord cut a covenant with Abraham, ratifying the divine promise by passing through the strewn animals as an oath against himself that he should be torn limb from limb should he fail to keep his promises (Jer. 34:18–20).

Then we have *covenant signification* in Genesis 17. The word *berith* occurs thirteen times in nine different verses as the nature of the covenant is more explicitly detailed. We see again that the stipulation of the covenant calls upon Abraham to walk with God. We also see again that God promises land, offspring, and (above all) his presence. Importantly, we are introduced to the sign of the covenant. The covenant—made with Abraham and his children—is to be signed and sealed with circumcision, a symbol of the cutting away of sinful flesh for the blessed and a symbol of being cut off from God for the cursed.

Finally, we have *covenant confirmation* in Genesis 22. God tests Abraham's faith by ordering him to sacrifice his only son. When Abraham passes the test, God redoubles his commitment to the promise. More than a story about Abraham's faith, the (almost) sacrifice of Isaac is a story of God's provision. The God of Abraham can be counted on to keep his end of the bargain, which is why the Abrahamic covenant is so often an anchor point in the Old Testament (Ex. 2:24; 3:6; 6:8; 32:13) and so often used as a shorthand for the gospel in the New Testament (Rom. 4:13; Gal. 3:16, 26, 29). It's no coincidence that Matthew begins his Gospel as the story of the genesis of the son of Abraham (Matt. 1:1) and ends his Gospel with that Son announcing his mission to bless all the nations (28:19–20).

Mosaic Covenant

The Mosaic covenant was that arrangement established at Sinai whereby the nation of Israel was promised blessing upon the condition of obedience to the statutes of God and threatened with cursing should they prove to be persistently and resolutely disobedient. Although the Mosaic covenant became an instrument of death for God's sinful people, the covenant itself, with its numerous sacrifices and provisions for sin, was fundamentally an administration of the one covenant of grace (see WCF 7:4–6).

The Mosaic covenant was both more than what came before and less than what would come after. On the one hand, it was a step forward in God's plan of redemption insofar as the covenant was more comprehensive and more typologically rich than previous covenants. Moses introduced a totalizing and nationalizing covenant that showed forth God's holy character and was meant to humble God's people by showing them their sin. At the same time, the Mosaic covenant was much less glorious than the new covenant that would replace it (2 Cor. 3). One thinks of B. B. Warfield's famous statement that the Old Testament was like a room richly furnished but dimly lit. The presence of more light in the gospel did not add something new to the room of God's grace, but it did allow one to see God's grace more clearly and enjoy it more fully.

Though focused on laws, the Mosaic covenant was not legalistic. Law was significant in all the administrations up to Moses (there were commands to Noah and to Abraham) and in all the administrations after Moses. Even the new covenant came with commands to be obeyed (think of the Great Commission or Jesus saying that if you love me, you will keep my commands). To be sure, there were conditions present in the Mosaic covenant, but they functioned differently from the conditions in the covenant of works. One was a test of absolute obedience, the other a response of gratitude. One allowed for no failure, the other provided a rich remedy for transgression and impurity. One would yield entrance into eternal life, the other would yield the full blessedness of covenant life. In the garden, Adam and Eve were exiled for disobeying the one probationary command. Under Moses, there were remedies available for disobedience. Exile was not for a single sin, but for the failure to make use of the remedies for sin. Exile under the old covenant (like church discipline in the new covenant) was a punishment for the habitually impenitent.

The law is good if used lawfully (1 Tim. 1:8). The Mosaic covenant was meant to be a schoolmaster, but in the history of God's people it sometimes became a taskmaster. The law, insofar as it was tantamount to human effort and self-salvation, was not of faith (Gal. 3:12). But law as the moral code revealed in the Mosaic covenant was never meant to replace the good news preached to Abraham (WCF 9:6–7). The Mosaic covenant was not meant to render void the promise, but was meant as the gracious means for living in that promise.

WEEK 21

DAY 101

Republication

Republication refers to the notion that the Mosaic covenant in some sense republished the covenant of works given to Adam in the garden. Typologically, the argument goes, Israel was like another Adam, so that when Israel failed the covenantal test, he too was kicked out of the land. Leviticus 18:5 ("You shall therefore keep my statutes and my rules; if a person does them, he shall live by them") established the Mosaic covenant as an administration built on the works principle. So when Paul cites Leviticus 18:5 in Romans 10 and Galatians 3, he is not dealing with Israel's abuse of the law but with the law as it was given to Israel. Although the covenant at Sinai belongs to the covenant of grace, those in favor of the republication thesis insist that Paul makes a sharp antithesis between the covenant with Abraham and the covenant with Moses. The former is a covenant of promise, while the latter is a covenant characteristic of law and condemnation. In this way, the Mosaic covenant functions like a covenant of works.

How should we respond to the case for republication? Two points: the first exegetical, the second theological.

1. Exegetically, traditional Reformed exegesis has argued that Paul's claims in Romans 10 and Galatians 3 presume the faulty view of his opponents. Paul assesses the law negatively because he is making a kind of *reductio ad absurdum*

argument: "If you want to live by the law, how is that going to work? It's impossible to use the law as an instrument of self-justification before God." In commenting on Romans 10:5, Calvin distinguishes between "the whole of the doctrine taught by Moses" and that "part of it which belonged peculiarly to his ministry."[1] In his universal office, Moses taught nothing inconsistent with the gospel. But Moses also had a peculiar office to instruct people in their duties and obligations under the Sinai covenant. The law is contrasted with gospel, therefore, not in its entirety but specifically as a set of commandments that the Judaizers took to be the way to achieve a right standing before God.

2. Theologically, it is difficult to see how republication fits within bicovenantal understanding of covenant theology. In traditional bicovenantal structure, the covenant of grace is fundamentally, in its essence, not to be identified with the covenant of works. They operate on two entirely different principles. How can one type of covenant *in some sense* include the other? The Mosaic covenant may center on law, but the covenant must either function according to grace or according to works. Moreover, once you equate the moral law (i.e., the Ten Commandments given under Mosaic administration) with the covenant of works in any sense, how can one insist on the third use of the law (the law as the perfect rule of righteousness for a saved and grateful people)? Turretin's distinction between the covenant of works and the Mosaic covenant gets it right. Works were required in the covenant of works "as an antecedent condition by way of a cause for acquiring life." But in the Mosaic covenant, works were "only the subsequent condition as the fruit and effect of the life already acquired." In short, works "precede the act of justification" in the covenant of works, but in the Mosaic covenant, "they follow it."[2]

1 Calvin, *Commentaries*, 386.
2 Turretin, *Elenctic Theology*, 2:191.

DAY 102

Davidic Covenant

The Davidic covenant is a covenant of kingship. It marks out the arrival of the glorious kingdom in Israel, and it anticipates a glorious king to come. The Davidic covenant consolidates all the promises of the previous covenants and sets the stage for richer fulfillment in the years and centuries ahead.

The key text is 2 Samuel 7 and the parallel (but not identical) passage in
1 Chronicles 17. Neither passage uses *berith*, but the term is explicitly applied to
the arrangement with David in several other places (2 Sam. 23:5; Pss. 89:3, 28, 34;
132:11–12). The setting for 2 Samuel 7 is important. The permanent location for
the throne of God has been established (2 Sam. 5), the ark has been brought to
Jerusalem (2 Sam. 6), and God has given David rest from all his enemies (2 Sam.
7:1). The kingdom had arrived as never before. God was ready to reinforce his
old commitments and make new ones as well.

The Davidic covenant builds on previous covenant arrangements. The promises of many descendants and a great name are restated to David (2 Sam. 7:9–10)
and fulfilled in the early reign of Solomon (cf. 1 Kings 4:20, 24–25). The blessing
did not last because of his disobedience (11:1–8), but God did not take the whole
kingdom away (11:34–36). Several promises from the Mosaic covenant are also
fulfilled, including rest (Deut. 28:1–14; 1 Kings 4:25), the nations witnessing God's
blessing (Deut. 29:10; 1 Kings 4:30), and the promise of divine presence (Ex. 6:7;
2 Sam. 7:9; Ezek. 34:24).

Building on these earlier promises to Abraham and to Moses, God promises
that the kingdom would reach its zenith under David's son. Two themes are
especially crucial: sonship and kingship. God promises to establish his throne
in Jerusalem and to set on that throne a kingly son. Israel had been called God's
firstborn before (Ex. 4:23), but now the king of Israel will also be God's son. The
king will be accorded special status as a royal representative of God's people and
as a son of God.

Like much of the Old Testament, the promises of the Davidic covenant find
their fulfillment in type and antitype, in shadow and substance, in near fulfillment
and in ultimate fulfillment. The kingdom proves to be glorious and expansive
under Solomon, but ultimately the covenant finds its truest fulfillment in a greater
Son (Isa. 9:7; 11:1). About the only thing the Jews seemed to have reliably understood about the promised Messiah is that he would be a son of David. This is why
the crowds asked in amazement, "Can this be the Son of David?" (Matt. 12:23)
and why on Palm Sunday the pilgrims shouted, "Hosanna to the Son of David"
(Matt. 21:9). Matthew begins his Gospel by referring to "the genealogy of Jesus
Christ, the son of David" (Matt. 1:1). Mark 12:35 and John 7:42 explicitly reference
this same messianic expectation, as does the apostle Paul (Rom. 1:3; 2 Tim. 2:8).

Just as God lavished blessing on Abraham and revealed his commandments to
Moses, so God established through David that the plan of salvation would depend
upon a kingly and filial mediator to come. At its heart, the Davidic covenant was
about preparing God's people for Jesus the Christ.

New Covenant

The new covenant refers to a constellation of promises that find their "yes and amen" in Christ. These promises are rooted in all the covenants that came before but find their fulfillment in the work of Christ and in the age of the Spirit. Ultimately, the good news of the new covenant will be fully realized in the age to come.

The phrase *berith khadashah* (new covenant) occurs only once in the Old Testament, in Jeremiah 31:31. The larger section (Jer. 30–33) is sometimes called the Book of Consolation because it is a unique survey of good news in the midst of a book almost entirely comprised of bad news. These four chapters focus on "the days [that] are coming" (30:3; 33:14; 31:27, 31, 38), on the merciful restoration of Israel's fortunes (33:26), and most centrally on the promise of the new covenant (31:31–34).

In order to interpret Jeremiah 31:31–34 correctly—and thereby to properly understand the nature of the new covenant—we must keep in mind three realities.

First, the new covenant is new and, in another sense, not new. The new covenant is new with relation to the Mosaic covenant, but it does not erase everything that came before. As God explains the new covenant, he uses categories and symbols created by older covenants. We might say the covenant is refreshed more than it is made brand-new. "New" does mean "never happened before" or "never promised before." Rather, the new covenant intensifies and brings to completion elements already present within the covenant of grace, especially as seen in the Abrahamic covenant. The new covenant is immutable, like the Abrahamic covenant is immutable (Gal. 3:15–18). The new covenant promises a religion of the heart, like the Mosaic covenant did (Deut. 30:6) and the psalmists often did (Pss. 1; 19; 119). The new covenant promises the forgiveness of sins, like God offered throughout the Old Testament (Ps. 32). And the new covenant promises immediate knowledge of the Lord, not that such a faith did not exist already, but that in the days to come there would be direct access to God through a single mediator.[1]

Second, the new covenant is individual and corporate. To be sure, there is a personalized dimension to the covenant. The law will be written on our hearts, and each person will know the Lord. But the covenant was not made with individuals. It was made with a corporate body, with the house of Israel and the house of Judah (Jer. 31:31). In fact, Jeremiah 32:39 reinforces the familial principle, affirming that the good news highlighted by the new covenant will be "for their own good and the good of their children after them."

Third, the new covenant is already and not yet. Like the Abrahamic covenant had a near fulfillment (Isaac, prosperity, Canaan) and a far fulfillment (Christ, spiritual riches, heavenly inheritance), so the new covenant has elements that are inaugurated without being fully accomplished. Do we really want to suggest that in the new covenant there is no teaching and there are no teachers (Jer. 31:34), or might the literal fulfillment of that statement be in the future? We don't need teachers as mediators between God and man, but we have not reached the final consummation where our knowledge will be complete (1 Cor. 13:9–10). We enjoy the blessings of the new covenant now, but there is more yet to come.

1   See R. Scott Clark, "On the New Covenant," The Heidelblog, January 1, 2011, https://heidelblog.net.

DAY 104

The Fathers Have Eaten Sour Grapes

Jeremiah 31:29–30 is another key text for those who believe that the new covenant does not have the same corporate dimension as the old covenant. The text says, "In those days they shall no longer say: 'The fathers have eaten sour grapes, and the children's teeth are set on edge.' But everyone shall die for his own iniquity. Each man who eats sour grapes, his teeth shall be set on edge." Does this indicate that a new arrangement will be instituted in the new covenant whereby God deals with people only as individuals and no longer corporately?

We can note several things in response.

First, this proverb is also quoted in Ezekiel 18:2. It seems that the people of Judah believed God was being unjust in punishing them for the sins of past generations and not for their own sins (18:25). "Why should the children be punished for the sins of their fathers?" they asked. But Jeremiah and Ezekiel quote the proverb to reject it. They are not saying this is how God has dealt with his people.

Second, it is true that God had promised to visit "the iniquity of the fathers on the children to the third and the fourth generation of those who hate me" and to show "steadfast love to thousands of those who love me and keep my commandments" (Ex. 20:5–6). Do not miss the precise language of God's promise. God says he will visit the iniquity of *those who hate me* and will show steadfast love *to those who love me* and keep my commandments. God wasn't promising to curse or to bless the next generation regardless of how they lived. God was making a general statement about how God's blessing is more expansive than his cursing.

Third, it was already a principle in the Mosaic covenant that the corporate nature of the covenant did not consign children to the punishment of their fathers. "Fathers shall not be put to death because of their children, nor shall children be put to death because of their fathers. Each one shall be put to death for his own sin" (Deut. 24:16). It was never the case that children, irrespective of how they lived, were to be punished for their father's sins.

Fourth, throughout the Old Testament God often allowed a believing remnant to escape the destruction that the larger group deserved. God was willing to save Sodom for ten righteous persons, and he gave Lot's family a means of escape (Gen. 19). Elijah was shown favor as the last remaining faithful prophet (1 Kings 19:10). God spared the lives of the seven thousand who had not bowed the knee to Baal (1 Kings 19:18). God would often bless those who didn't deserve blessing, while providing a means of escape for those who did not personally deserve cursing.

In summary, Jeremiah and Ezekiel did not quote the proverb about sour grapes because the God of the Old Testament had a habit of punishing innocent children for the sins of their fathers. Rather, the prophets wanted Judah to see that God's people were guilty of sin, but the time would come when they would no longer complain of punishment because their sins would be forgiven and they would be given new hearts to follow God.

DAY 105

The Newness of the New Covenant

The new covenant is not dissimilar to every covenant that has come before. There are many elements of continuity between the new covenant and the old. For example, just as there were some of Israel who proved not to be true Israel (Rom. 2:28–29; 9:6–8), so it is possible to belong to the administration of the new covenant without participating in the essence of the new covenant. We can "profane the blood of the covenant" by which we were sanctified (Heb. 10:29).

This is not "losing your salvation." We cannot be un-regenerated or un-justified. But we can be set apart as members of the new covenant community and prove to false sons and false daughters who trample underfoot the Son of God, profane the blood of the covenant, and outrage the Spirit of grace.

There are also many elements of *discontinuity* between the new covenant and the old. Francis Turretin expounds eight differences between the Old and New Testaments.[1] The two differ:

1. As to time: the Old preceded Christ, the New follows him.
2. As to clarity: the New reveals what the Old had veiled.
3. As to easiness: the signs and service required were more burdensome under the Old.
4. As to sweetness: grace is greater and more extended under the New.
5. As to perfection: the shadows of the Old have given way to the substance of the New.
6. As to freedom: we know more fully the spirit of adoption as sons under the New.
7. As to amplitude: the Old was restricted largely to one nation while the New extends to every nation.
8. As to duration: the Old was temporary, where the New is without end.

The use of Jeremiah 31 in Hebrews 8 underscores that Christ is a better mediator, of a better covenant, enacted on better promises (8:6). This has rendered the first covenant obsolete (8:13). Likewise, the use of Jeremiah 31 in Hebrews 10 underscores that Christ's death was once for all. No other sacrifice for sin is necessary (10:14, 18).

Hebrews does not teach that every covenant arrangement has been annulled, only that the Mosaic covenant has been abrogated. This isn't because the law was a mistake. The two long comments about Moses in the book of Hebrews are both positive (3:1–6; 11:23–28). Moses isn't bad, but Jesus is better. That's what Hebrews wants us to see about the covenant Jesus executes. The covenant established in Christ is new (*kainos* in 8:8, 13; 9:15 and *neos* in 12:24); it is second (8:7; 10:9); it is better (7:22; 8:6); and it is eternal (13:20). What is said about the Spirit-regenerated Christian can be said about the age of the Spirit more broadly: the old has passed away; behold, the new has come (2 Cor. 5:17).

1 Turretin, *Elenctic Theology*, 2:237–40.

DAY 106

The Law and the Christian

How should we understand the Christian's relationship to the law? Clearly, even in the New Testament obeying God and his word remains of paramount importance (John 14:15, 21; 15:10–11). Law-keeping is not an optional extra for Christians, and an insistence on law-keeping is not antithetical to true, gospel Christianity (1 John 2:3; 3:24).

But what about the Old Testament law? What do we do with the commands of the Mosaic covenant? On the one hand, we are not under the curse of the law—Christ is the end of the law for righteousness to everyone who believes (Rom. 10:4)—nor is the law a nationalized covenant for us like it was for Israel. On the other hand, the commandments are holy and righteous and good (Rom. 7:12), and the law is good if one uses it lawfully (1 Tim. 1:8). As new covenant Christians do we have to obey the Old Testament law or not?

One answer to that question can be found by paying attention to what Jesus says in the Sermon on the Mount. There Jesus states plainly, "Do not think that I have come to abolish the Law or the Prophets" (Matt. 5:17a). Jesus is saying, "I have not come to thrown down or destroy the Scriptures of the Old Testament." To which we might reply, "Then what about all the commands in the Old Testament that we don't follow anymore?" After all, Jesus declared all foods clean (Mark 7:19), and food laws and holy days have been relativized (Rom. 14:14), and the whole temple system of priests and sacrifices has become obsolete (Heb. 7:1–9:10). It sure looks like parts of the law have been annulled.

The key to understanding what Jesus means by "Do not think that I have come to abolish the Law or the Prophets" is to appreciate what he says next: "I have not come to abolish them but to fulfill them" (Matt. 5:17b). "Fulfill" is the Greek word *plēroō*, and it is a very important word in Matthew, occurring fifteen times in the book (1:22; 2:15, 17, 23; 3:15; 4:14; 5:17; 8:17; 12:17; 13:35, 48; 21:4; 23:32; 26:54; 26:56). The word "fulfill" does not simply refer to accomplishing specific prophecies; *plēroō* means Jesus brings the Scripture to completion. Jesus brings the law to its climax and to its intended goal. So nothing of the law has passed away (Matt. 5:18), but all of the law must be now understood according to the person and work of Jesus Christ, the new Moses and messianic lawgiver.

The whole law still has to do with us, supremely so by pointing us to Christ, but also by transcendent moral principles and by the general equity of all that it commands. Thus Paul can cite Deuteronomy 25:4 ("You shall not muzzle an ox when it is treading out the grain") as a justification for paying gospel preachers (1 Cor. 9:8–10; 1 Tim. 5:17–18), and he can allude to Deuteronomy 19:15 in insisting that we should not admit a charge against an elder except on the evidence of two or three witnesses (1 Tim. 5:19). The law of Moses is not to be thrown out, but it has been transformed and repurposed by the coming of Christ.

Threefold Division of the Law

The Westminster Confession of Faith teaches that the law of Moses can be divided into three parts: the moral law given in the Ten Commandments, ceremonial laws abrogated with the coming of Christ, and judicial laws that expired with the nation of Israel (WCF 19:2–4). As common as this threefold division has become, especially in Reformed churches, many contemporary scholars argue that the New Testament never makes these distinctions and that no one living under the law of Moses would have thought in these terms. The threefold division, it is said, is too tidy, too arbitrary, too convenient. Are we right, then, to speak of the law as moral, ceremonial, and judicial?

In a word, yes.

The division is at least as old as Aquinas, who argued from the different terms used in Deuteronomy 4:13–14 and 6:1 that there were three kinds of laws under Moses. Centuries earlier, Clement of Alexandria divided the law into four parts: historic, legislative, sacrificial, and theological. Tertullian made a distinction between moral and ceremonial laws. Augustine distinguished between the moral precepts that are binding and the symbols that are not.[1]

Besides this historical precedent, there are good biblical reasons for accepting the threefold division of the law.

For starters, the Ten Commandments are unique. Unlike most of the other statutes, these commandments were already known in the world prior to Sinai (e.g., the people in Genesis and Exodus know that murder is wrong, that adultery is wrong, that lying is wrong). What's more, at Sinai, God spoke the words of the

Decalogue directly. The Ten Commandments were given in absolute form and addressed to the individual rather than to the nation. The words were written down by the finger of God and were preserved in stone as a constitution for God's people.

Second, the Ten Commandments are distinguished from other commands within the law of Moses itself. If the Decalogue was the constitution, the other commands functioned as case law (Ex. 21:1). Even under Moses, God's people did not take all 613 commandments as being essentially equal. There were lighter matters and weightier matters and different penalties for different infractions. The prophets often announced that the Lord desired mercy, not sacrifice, and that their sacrifices did not please him. God even "hates" their feasts and assemblies (Amos 5:21), but he is never said to hate obedience to the Ten Commandments.

Third, the language used by Moses suggests something like ceremonial and judicial laws. By using the word *pattern* so often in Exodus and Leviticus (and then in Hebrews), there is a built-in obsolescence to the commands associated with worship. The earthly form will eventually give way to heavenly reality. Likewise, the language of "in the land" (Deut. 4:5, 14) suggests that some commands were specific to the nation of Israel in Canaan. In short, the Mosaic law was never seen as an indivisible whole. Moses may not have explicitly taught the threefold division, but he would not be surprised by our insistence that the Ten Commandments are uniquely binding while the commandments related to worship and the regulation of life in Israel apply to God's people now in a different way.

1 See Philip S. Ross, *From the Finger of God: The Biblical and Theological Basis for the Threefold Division of the Law* (Ross-shire, UK: Mentor, 2010), 1–50.

DAY 108

Dispensationalism

Dispensationalism is a hermeneutical approach to the Bible that sees a clear distinction between Israel and the church and believes in the literal interpretation of Old Testament prophecies. Like covenant theology (which is, in many ways, its opposite), dispensationalism is not simply a matter of one or two specific doctrinal conclusions as much as it is a coherent, self-contained way of reading the whole Bible.

The history of dispensationalism starts with John Nelson Darby (1800–1882). Ordained in the Church of England, Darby later renounced his Anglican ordination when required to affirm allegiance to the crown and helped establish the Plymouth Brethren. Based on his study of Isaiah 32, Darby taught that Israel would experience future blessings different from those of the church. Darby also popularized the idea of a secret rapture before the seventieth week of Daniel 9. Following the rapture would come the seven-year great tribulation. At the end of those seven years, Darby taught, Jesus will return, the temple will be rebuilt, the Jewish people will turn to Christ, and the kingdom of Israel will be reestablished for a glorious thousand-year theocracy.

Undoubtedly the most important conduit for dispensationalism was the Scofield Reference Bible, first published in 1909. Named after Cyrus Ingerson Scofield (1843–1921), the Bible taught that seven dispensations can be found in the Bible: innocency (Gen. 1:28), conscience (Gen. 3:23), human government (Gen. 8:20), promise (Gen. 12:1), law (Ex. 19:8), grace (John 1:17), and kingdom (Eph. 1:10). Dispensation, in plain English, can mean either an exemption or a system of order existing at a certain time. The Westminster Confession of Faith speaks of the one covenant of grace existing under "various dispensations" (7:6). But Scofield meant something more specific. He used dispensation to mean a period of time during which man is tested in accordance with a specific revelation of God's will. Each dispensation has a specific revelation, a probationary testing, and then after failing that test, there is divine mercy and a new redemptive arrangement.

The history of dispensationalism is often described in three different stages. Following the classic dispensationalism of Darby and Scofield, the movement was revised in the second half of the twentieth century. "Essentialists" like Charles Ryrie spoke of the natural or plain meaning of Scripture, not just the literal meaning. In this period, many dispensationalists backed away from some of the more idiosyncratic doctrines, like that the Sermon on the Mount was only for the future millennial reign or that the kingdom of God and the kingdom of heaven were not the same thing.

More recently, scholars like Craig Blaising and Darrell Bock have issued further revisions, resulting in what has been called "progressive dispensationalism." This new form sees continuous development (i.e., progress) in redemptive history instead of distinct dispensations whereby God governs the affairs of men differently. Progressive dispensationalists also insist on one people of God and one plan of God. Even with this movement away from traditional Scofield-style dispensationalism, covenant theologians would still question whether dispensationalism applies its literal (or plain) hermeneutic consistently and would argue for more continuity between God's people in both Testaments. Surely it is good news worth celebrating that as the church, with divine blessings upon us, we have been constituted "the Israel of God" (Gal. 6:16).

DAY 109

Baptist Covenant Theology

Although covenant theology is usually associated with confessional Reformed churches and confessional Presbyterians, there is a long history of covenant theology in the Baptist tradition as well.

In October 1658 a group of Independents and Congregationalists met at the Savoy Hospital in London to draw up a revision of the Westminster Confession of Faith that reflected their commitment to congregational church government. The result was the (now little-known) Savoy Declaration. This document, in turn, would be revised two decades later and become the classic Baptist summary of faith known as the 1689 Baptist Confession of Faith (also called the London Baptist Confession or sometimes the Second London Baptist Confession to distinguish it from another Baptist confession written in 1644). Written in 1677 as a revision of a revision of the Westminster Confession, the London Baptist Confession is a Reformed document in many ways. It is Calvinist in soteriology and even includes some additions that Reformed Christians welcome (e.g., an augmented statement on the Trinity).

As one would expect, the most significant differences have to do with the doctrine of the church and the sacraments. These differences touch on covenant theology as well. To cite one crucial example, the London Baptist Confession says that the one covenant of grace is revealed—not administered, as the Westminster Confession puts it (WCF 7:5)—by various arrangements throughout redemptive history (LBC 7:3). In Baptist theology, the various covenants of the Old Testament bear witness to the covenant of grace, but the covenant of grace is only finally and truly administered in the new covenant. The various covenants of the Old Testament "communicate" the benefits of Christ not in terms of communion with Christ, but in that they impart information about Christ. In traditional Reformed covenant theology, by contrast, Christ is in, with, and under the types in the Old Testament.

More recently, some Baptists have sought to find a middle ground between dispensationalism and covenant theology. This middle ground has been called "new covenant theology" or, in a slightly different form, "progressive covenantalism." Unlike traditional dispensationalism, progressive covenantalism stresses that God has one unified plan in Scripture and that this plan is revealed through a serious of covenants that form the backbone of the Bible's redemptive storyline. And yet, unlike Westminster covenant theology, progressive covenantalism does not employ a bilateral covenant scheme (i.e., a covenant of works and a covenant of grace), it does not consider the Ten Commandments an expression of the binding moral law of God, and it does not consider earlier covenants to be an administration of God's redemptive plan like the new covenant is.

While Reformed Christians can appreciate some of the emphases in progressive covenantalism, they still disagree at the foundational level as to how new is the new covenant. To use an analogy, we might ask whether the establishment of the new covenant moves us, in God's redemptive economy, from a mouse to a cat or from a puppy to a dog. The nature of the covenant community, the recipients of baptism, and the way in which the church becomes visible (is it by God's promise or by our commitment?) are all related to the question of whether the new covenant is fundamentally something different or the same essential thing brought to fullness and completion. Covenant theology answers this question by seeing the new covenant as a grown-up dog, not a different animal entirely.

DAY 110

The Israel of God

God chose the people of Israel as his special treasure and agent of redemption (Deut. 7:6; cf. Gen. 12:3). In the Old Testament, to be a part of the Israel of God meant—mainly, but not entirely (Gen. 17:12)—that you were an ethnic Jew. The New Testament confirms that God's plan is still for Israel, but the definition of true Israel now centers on Jesus Christ. This does not mean God is done with ethnic Israel or that he may not have a plan to effect a widespread conversion of the Jewish people (depending on one's interpretation of Romans 11). Covenant theology is sometimes derided as "replacement theology" or as teaching "supercession." But that's not how Reformed theology describes itself. There is a faithful remnant of ethnic Jews, and the Gentiles have been grafted in. Israel has not been replaced but has been reconstituted around its Messiah, Jesus.

Jesus was one of a long line of prophets who rebuked Israel and pointed the way to their renewal and restoration. That basic message was familiar. What made Jesus unique is that he pointed to himself as the way to that renewal and restoration. He said, in effect, "You belong to Israel if you follow me." That's why he chose twelve apostles, to signal that he was drawing up a new Israel. That's what Jesus was communicating with his famous "I am" statements. Jesus was drawing attention to himself as the manna from heaven, the pillar of fire in the wilderness,

CHRISTOLOGY 1

The Person of Christ

DAY 111

Logos

John's Gospel begins with a deliberate echo of Genesis 1:1. Every Jew would have been familiar with the opening line of the Hebrew Scriptures: "In the beginning, God created the heavens and the earth." How striking, then, it must have been for John's audience to encounter his opening line: "In the beginning was the Word." Where the Septuagint has *en archē epoiesn ho theos* for Genesis 1:1, John 1:1 has *en archē ēn ho logos*. Instead of being introduced to *theos* (God) at the beginning, of the world, we are introduced to *logos* (the Word).

The Greek word *logos* can be translated "word," "talk," "speech," or "conversation." It was a common term in Greek philosophy. More importantly, it was a concept with clear Old Testament connections. In verse 3 John mentions creation, then life in verse 4, and light and darkness in verse 5. This is the mental terrain of Genesis. Just as God created by means of his word in Genesis 1, so the Word is heralded as the instrument of creation in John 1.

Crucially, John doesn't leave it to his readers to connect the dots between *theos* and *logos*. He states explicitly that "the Word was with God, and the Word was God" (1:1). The Word was not the first of God's created things; the Word was the means by which God created all things (1:3). There never was when the Word was not. Whatever we can say about the eternality of God in Genesis, you can say about the Word in John.

Some have argued that the Word in John 1 is not fully God because *theos* at the end of verse 1 does not have a definite article. Jehovah's Witnesses are particularly adamant on this point, translating John 1:1 in their New World Translation (NWT): "the Word was a god." This rendering, however, is hardly consistent through the NWT. There are 282 instances of the word *theos* without the definite article. In only sixteen places does the NWT say "a god" or "god" or "gods." In fact, *theos* occurs eight times in John's prologue (vv. 1 [2x], 2, 6, 12, 13, 18 [2x]) and only twice is the definite article used. And yet the NWT translates *theos* as God (instead of "a god" or "god") in six of those instances.

The grammatical construction at the end of John 1:1—an anarthrous preverbal predicate nominative, in technical language—is almost never indefinite.

This means that translating *theos* as "a god" is not warranted by the grammar. Rather, *theos* is best understood as a qualitative noun (i.e., *theos* describes the quality of the Word). This is how John can say that the Word was with *ho theos* (God, the Father), but also that the Word is *theos* (having the nature and essence of God).

John 1:1 could not have stated any more succinctly the wondrous theological truth that the Word who is not God the Father is, nevertheless, still God. As Luther put it, "the Word was God" is against Arius (who denied the full deity of Christ), while "the Word was with God" is against Sabellius (who believed the Father and the Son were only different modes of being). From the very beginning, John's Gospel is leading us inexorably to the same conclusion that Thomas reached when he said about the risen Christ, "My Lord and my God!" (20:28).

DAY 112

Virgin Birth

The accounts of Jesus's birth in Matthew (chapter 1) and Luke (chapters 1–2) are clear and unequivocal: Jesus's birth was not ordinary. He was not an ordinary child, and his conception did not come about in the ordinary way. His mother, Mary, was a virgin, having had no intercourse prior to conception and birth. By the Holy Spirit, Mary's womb became the cradle of the Son's incarnation (Matt. 1:20; Luke 1:35).

The doctrine of the virgin birth (or more precisely, the virginal conception) has been doubted by many outside the church and in modern times by not a few voices inside the church. Two arguments are usually mentioned.

First, *the prophecy about a virgin birth in Isaiah 7:14, it is argued, actually speaks of a young woman and not a virgin.* Many have pointed out that the Hebrew word in Isaiah is *almah* and not the technical term for virgin, *bethula*. It is true that *almah* has a wider semantic range than *bethula*, but there are no clear references in the Old Testament where *almah* does not mean virgin. The word *almah* occurs nine times in the Old Testament, and wherever the context makes its meaning clear, the word refers to a virgin. More importantly, the Septuagint translates *almah* with the Greek word *parthenos* (the same word used in Matthew 1:23 where Isaiah 7:14 is quoted), and everyone agrees that *parthenos* means "virgin."

Second, *many have objected to the virgin birth because they see it as a typical bit of pagan mythologizing.* This popular argument sounds plausible at first glance, but there are a number of problems with it. (1) The assumption that there was a prototypical God-man who had certain titles, did certain miracles, was born of a virgin, saved his people, and then got resurrected is not well-founded. In fact, no such prototypical "hero" existed before the rise of Christianity. (2) It would have been unthinkable for a Jewish sect (which is what Christianity was initially) to try to win new converts by adding pagan elements to their gospel story. (3) The other supposed virgin births are not convincing. From Alexander the Great to Dionysus to Mithra, the parallels either date after Christianity or only bear superficial resemblance to the supernatural birth of Christ (e.g., Mithra was born of a rock, not a virgin; Alexander's mother was not a virgin; Dionysus was the child of Zeus and a human princess).

The virgin birth has been an essential part of the Christian story since the earliest days of the church. And for good reason. The virgin birth demonstrates that Jesus is truly human and truly divine. The virgin birth also testifies that Jesus did not inherit the curse of depravity that clings to Adam's race. Jesus was made like us in every way except for sin (Heb. 4:15; 7:26–27). Sinners beget sinners (Ps. 51:5), which is why the Spirit's miraculous role in Jesus's birth is so important. The virgin birth is part of what Christians have believed in all times and in all places, and it is a key element in what it means for the incarnation to be "for us and for salvation."

DAY 113

Messianic Prophecies

When Jesus Christ came into the world, he did not come unannounced. For those who had ears to hear, God had long promised to send a deliverer: a seed of the woman to crush the head of the serpent (Gen. 3:15), a child of Abraham (12:3), a lion of the tribe of Judah (49:10), a star from Jacob and a scepter from Israel (Num. 24:17), a prophet like Moses (Deut. 18:15–19), a royal Son (Ps. 2:7), a son of David (132:11; 2 Sam. 7:12-13), a child born of a virgin (Isa. 7:14), a Prince of Peace (9:6), a shoot from the stump of Jesse (11:1), a revelation of the glory of the Lord (40:3–5), a light to the nations (49:6), an ancient one born in Bethlehem (Mic. 5:2), a speaker of peace whose rule shall extend from sea to sea (Zech. 9:10), and the God of justice and the Lord come to his temple (Mal. 3:1).

The Gospel of Matthew, in particular, depicts Jesus as the fulfillment of Old Testament prophecy, retelling Israel's story but casting Jesus as the main character. From the opening verse we see that Matthew understands Jesus to be a new generation, a new beginning for the nation of Israel (Matt. 1:1). Not only is Jesus the new genesis; his life embodies the new exodus. Shortly after Jesus's birth, he was rushed to safety to avoid the wrath of a jealous king who had ordered all the young boys to be killed. Like Moses, Jesus was spared the royal decree because his mother hid him in Egypt.

Following on the heels of Jesus's exodus out of Egypt, we come to his baptism in the Jordan (Matt. 3). Just as the Israelites left Egypt and then passed through the Red Sea (baptized into the sea according to 1 Cor. 10:2), Jesus too leaves Egypt and passes through the waters in his baptism. And after the Red Sea, the Israelites wind up in the desert where they wander for forty years. Where is Jesus in Matthew 4? He is in the desert about to be tempted after having fasted for forty days and forty nights.

Jesus is fulfilling Israel's history and bringing it to a climax. "When Israel was a child, I loved him, and out of Egypt I called my son" (Hos. 11:1). Matthew didn't think this was a direct prophecy about Jesus and his family going to Egypt, and Hosea certainly didn't mean it as such. The passage is about Israel's exodus out of Egypt and about her subsequent idolatries and adulteries. Matthew understood that. He wasn't trying to give Hosea 11 a new meaning, but he rightly saw something messianic in Hosea's words. Jesus would be the faithful Son called out of Egypt, filling up what was lacking in the first faithless son, Israel.

From his genesis, to his exodus, to his baptism in the Jordan, to his forty days in the wilderness, Jesus identified himself with God's covenant people. That's why Matthew can say, "This was to fulfill what was spoken by the prophet" (Matt. 8:17). But whereas the first Israel, God's son, broke the covenant and deserved God's wrath, when God beholds his only begotten Son Jesus Christ, he says in Matthew 3:17, "This is my beloved Son, with whom I am well pleased."

DAY 114

Names and Titles of Jesus

The English name "Jesus" comes from the Greek *Iesous*, which in turn comes from the Hebrew *Yehoshua* or *Jeshua* (think: *Joshua*). Jesus was a common name among first-century Jews. As Matthew 1:21 indicates, the name Jesus refers to the Lord (Yahweh) who saves.

The New Testament heaps up names and epithets for Jesus, too many to explore or even name in a short summary. Jesus is the Word made flesh (John 1:1–18), and Immanuel, God with us (Matt. 1:23). He is the Lamb of God (John 1:29), the bread of life (6:35), and the King of the Jews (19:21). He is a Helper (14:16) and the great I am (8:58). Jesus is the way, the truth, and the life (14:6). He is the image of the invisible God (Col. 1:15), the radiance of the glory of God, and the exact imprint of his nature (Heb. 1:3). He is our advocate (1 John 2:1), our great high priest (Heb. 4:14), and the founder and perfector of our faith (12:2). Jesus is the faithful witness, the firstborn of the dead, and the ruler of the kings of earth (Rev. 1:5). He is the Alpha and the Omega, the one who is and who was and who is to come, the Almighty (1:8). He is the first and the last, and the living one (1:17–18). Jesus is King of kings and Lord of lords (19:16).

Besides this glorious list of names and descriptions, there are many titles given to Jesus. We should mention five of the most important.

Jesus is the Christ. More than five hundred times in the New Testament Jesus is given this title. Christ means "anointed one" and is the Greek equivalent of Messiah. It is an official name more than a personal name, indicating that Jesus, like kings and priests in the Old Testament, is God's chosen one set apart to reign and to serve.

Jesus is the Son of God. Jesus's sonship is often given with reference to the Father. He is God's beloved Son (Matt. 3:17; 17:5), the only begotten Son (John 3:16), and the Son who is equal to the Father (5:19–29). Jesus is also called "Son" as the culmination of God's revelation (Heb. 1:1) and as the one who was raised from the dead in power (Rom. 1:4). In each of the four Gospels, the story climaxes with the recognition that Jesus is the Son of God (Matt. 16:16; 28:16–20; Mark 14:61; 15:39; Luke 22:70; John 20:31).

Jesus is the Son of Man. The title sounds like proof of Christ's humanity, but it is actually one of the best statements of his divinity. The imagery comes from Daniel 7:9–10 where the divine son of man approaches the divine Ancient of Days. Jesus often refers to himself as the Son of Man: in his ministry (Mark 2:10), in his suffering and resurrection (Mark 10:45), and in his coming again (Mark 8:38; 13:26; 14:62).

Jesus is Lord. Although *kyrios* can be used merely as respectful address (Matt. 8:2), the title normally speaks of Jesus's exalted divine status (Mark 12:36–37; Luke 2:11; 3:4). God has made Jesus both Lord and Christ (Acts 2:36). No one can say Jesus is Lord except by the Holy Spirit (1 Cor. 12:3). Every tongue will confess that Jesus Christ is Lord (Phil. 2:11).

Jesus is God. At least seven times, Jesus is explicitly called God. This is true in John (1:1, 18; 20:28), but in other books as well (Heb. 1:8). Christ is God over all (Rom. 9:5). He is our great God and Savior (Titus 2:13; 2 Pet. 1:1). The Son is God, and his throne is forever and ever (Heb. 1:8).

Jesus's Witness to Himself

Anyone wanting to understand Jesus should pay attention to Jesus's understanding of himself. In the Gospel of John in particular, we see that Jesus knew he was the fulfillment of Old Testament prophecy, the long-awaited Messiah, the only begotten Son of the Father, the divine Son of Man, and equal with God in power, rank, and glory.

Famously, he describes his identity and purpose with "I am" statements in John's Gospel.

Jesus is the bread of life (John 6:35, 41, 48). He is manna from heaven and food for the hungry. Unless we feast on him, we have no life in us.

Jesus is the light of the world (8:12). He is the pillar of fire in the wilderness and salvation in a dark world. Unless we believe in him, we will die in our sins.

Jesus is the gate for the sheep (10:7, 9). He is the Passover door and the entryway into the fold. Unless we come in by Jesus, we are thieves and robbers.

Jesus is the good shepherd (10:11, 14). He knows his flock, calls them by name, and lays down his life for the sheep. Unless he is our shepherd, we will not be safe from wolves and will not lie down in green pastures.

Jesus is the resurrection and the life (11:25). Whoever believes in him will never die. Unless we belong to him, we will not live forever in the age to come.

Jesus is the way, the truth, and the life (14:6). He is the Messiah, God in the flesh, and there is no other. Unless we know the Son and honor him, we neither know the Father nor him.

And Jesus is the true vine (15:1). He is the one in whom we must remain if we are to bear fruit. Unless we abide in him, we will be gathered up like dead branches, thrown into the fire, and burned.

Less well known, Jesus makes seven other "I am" statements throughout John's Gospel, but each of these is without a predicate. That is, instead of stating his identity by way of attributes and metaphors, Jesus simply and dramatically states that *he is*, a striking echo of the "I Am" declaration of Exodus 3:14.

- "I who speak to you am he" (4:26).
- "It is I; do not be afraid" (6:20).
- "Unless you believe that I am he you will die in your sins" (8:24).
- "When you have lifted up the Son of Man, then you will know that I am he" (8:28).

- "Before Abraham was, I am" (8:58).
- "I am telling you this now, before it takes place, that when it does take place you may believe that I am he" (13:19).
- "I told you that I am he" (18:8).

In all this, Jesus makes himself equal to God and the object of all saving faith. Indeed, Jesus does not hesitate to say, "Believe in God; believe also in me" (John 14:1). Jesus knew who he was. If we have ears to hear, we can know him too.

WEEK 24

DAY 116

Autotheos

John 5:19–26 is a crucial passage about the identity of Jesus Christ. At the heart of Jesus's teaching about himself is the statement he makes right in the middle of this section: "Whoever does not honor the Son does not honor the Father who sent him" (5:23b). The point is not simply that we should honor Christ because he is the Father's Son. Rather, we must honor the Son because he is equal with the Father.

It's hard to exaggerate how upsetting statements like this must have been to first-century Jews. They knew there was only one God, but now Jesus was calling God his own Father and making himself equal with God (5:18). No wonder they wanted to kill him. Everything about their religion as they understood it and their worship was being called into question.

So how can God be one and the Father and the Son be equal? How can Jesus say that whoever does not the honor the Son does not honor the Father? The answer is found in five "for" (*gar*) statements that follow (5:19b, 20a, 21, 22, 26).

- "For whatever the Father does, that the Son does likewise" (5:19b).
- "For the Father loves the Son and shows him all that he himself is doing" (5:20a).

- "For as the Father raises the dead and gives them life, so also the Son gives life to whom he will" (5:21).
- "For the Father judges no one, but has given all judgment to the Son" (5:22).
- "For as the Father has life in himself, so he has granted the Son also to have life in himself" (5:26).

This last statement from verse 26 is particularly important. The phrase "life in himself" refers to the life God has because he is God. It means God is dependent on no one and contingent on nothing for his existence. The Father has this life in himself *and* so does the Son. They are both marked by aseity.

Verse 26 supports Calvin's argument that the Son is *autotheos*; he is God in himself. Calvin insists that the Father was not the deifier of the Son. The Son is deity in himself. His divinity is in no way subordinate to the Father. To be sure, the Son's in-himself-life came from the Father in one sense, by an eternal grant (to use Augustine's language). But we must not take the language of "eternal grant" to support the contention (made by Arminius, among others) that only the Father was *autotheos*, and not the Son. As we might expect, Turretin's distinction is helpful: "So the Son is God from himself although not the Son from himself." That is to say, the Son is God-of-himself (*autotheos*) with respect to his essence, but not with respect to his person.

The phrase "life in himself" in verse 26 is a perfect, pregnant phrase. Jesus has both clarified the charge in verse 18 and reaffirmed it. He is not another God, an independent God, or a second God. He only does what the Father does. And consequently, he ought to receive what the Father receives; namely, glory and honor. The Son can exercise divine judgment and produce in us resurrection life because he is, himself, the self-existent one. We will not find the true God except in and through his Son, our Lord Jesus Christ.

DAY 117

Deity of Christ

The New Testament leaves no doubt that Jesus of Nazareth, Jesus the Christ, was and is fully God.

Many passages teach the preexistence of Christ. Melchizedek resembled the Son of God, suggesting that the Son of God predated the ancient king of Salem (Heb. 7:3). Christ was foreknown before the foundation of the world. Christ existed long before he took on human flesh and was born; he was manifested in the flesh (1 Tim. 3:16), in the last times for our sake (1 Pet. 1:20). Christ Jesus must be eternal since we were given grace in him before the ages began (2 Tim. 1:9).

Christ possesses the communicable attributes of God. He is filled with love (Eph. 3:17–19), and full of grace and truth (John 1:14). Christ is righteous and holy (Acts 3:14). He exercises the authority of God (Eph. 1:11) and is the eternal and perfect image of God (Col. 1:15).

Christ also possesses the incommunicable attributes of God. He is eternal (Mic. 5:2; John 17:5; Rev. 1:8; 22:13) and immutable (Heb. 1:11–12; 13:8). Christ exercises omnipresence—where two or three are gathered, there he is in the midst of them (Matt. 18:2). He exercises omnipotence—even the wind and waves obey him (Matt. 8:26–27). He upholds all things by the word of his power (Heb. 1:3), and all authority in heaven and on earth has been given to him (Matt. 28:18). He also exercises omniscience—perceiving the hearts of men (Mark 2:8), knowing what men are like (John 1:48–49) and what is in a man (2:25), knowing from the beginning who would not believe and who would betray him (6:64). In short, in Christ all the fullness of God dwells bodily (Col. 2:9).

Christ demonstrates divine rule and authority. He exercises dominion over all things (Rom. 14:9; Eph. 1:22; Rev. 1:5), including human and angelic authorities (Eph. 1:21; Phil. 2:10). He sits on God's throne (2 Cor. 5:10), at the right hand of the majesty on high (Heb. 1:3). He shares universal lordship with Yahweh over every rule, power, and dominion (Rom. 9:5).

Christ is also said to participate in the works of God. Creation: all things were made by him (John 1:3); by him all things were created visible and invisible (Col. 1:16–17); by him the worlds were made (Heb. 1:2). Providence: he upholds all things by the word of his power (Heb. 1:3); in him all things consist (Col. 1:17); his Father works and so does he (John 5:17). Judgment: the Son of Man will come with his angels to repay each person for what he has done (16:27); he will separate the sheep from the goats (25:31–33, 41, 46); the Father has given all judgment to the Son; whoever does not honor the Son does not honor the Father (John 5:22–23).

Finally, Christ often receives the worship of men. Elsewhere men reject being worshiped (Acts 14:14–15), or die from receiving worship (Acts 12:20–23), or it is considered the height of idolatry to worship created things (Rom. 1:18–23). Not so with Christ Jesus. After he calmed the storm, those in the boat worshiped him (Matt. 14:33). On Palm Sunday, the crowds cry Hosanna to the Son of David; "Out of the mouth of infants . . . you have prepared praise" (21:15–16). At his resurrection the women took hold of his feet and worshiped him (28:9). Later the disciples did as well (Matt. 28:17). Jesus Christ is not just another man. He is God in the flesh.

Humanity of Christ

The New Testament also leaves no doubt that Jesus of Nazareth, Jesus the Christ, was and is fully human. Christ possesses two natures, one divine and one human, so we are right to call him God and right to call him a man.

The humanity of Christ can be seen in his outer life. Jesus had a body, he grew and developed, and he looked like other members of his family (Luke 2:16, 40, 43–45). Like other children, he was subject to his parents, and as he grew he increased in wisdom and stature (2:51–52). He aged according to normal human years (3:23). He was born of woman (Gal. 4:4) and made like other human beings in every respect except for sin (Heb. 2:17). As the last Adam, Jesus Christ was as much man as the first Adam (Rom. 5:14–16; 1 Cor. 15:21).

The humanity of Christ can also be seen in his inner life. Jesus knew what it was to be genuinely distressed (Mark 14:33), angry (3:5), annoyed (10:14), surprised (6:6), and disappointed (8:17). He suffered hunger and thirst (Matt. 4:1–2) and experienced fatigue (8:23–24). Jesus was tempted (Luke 4:2). He cried (John 11:35), he bled, and he died (John 19:28–37).

In short, Jesus Christ was a real human being, with a real human mind, a real human body, and real human emotion. He is called the seed of the woman (Gen. 3:15), the son of Abraham (Acts 3:25), the son of David (Luke 1:32; Rom. 1:3), and the seed of the virgin and the fruit of her womb (Luke 1:31, 42).

Why did the divine Son of God become man? That's the question Anselm asked in his famous book *Cur Deus Homo?* (Why a God Man?). There are many right ways to answer that question, but perhaps the best and clearest explanation comes from Hebrews 2:5–18. Here we see three reasons that God became man. (1) Jesus was made for a little while lower than the angels so that by the grace of God he might taste death for everyone (2:9). (2) Christ was made to share in our flesh and blood so that through death he might destroy the one who has the power of death, that is, the devil (2:14). (3) Christ had to be made like his human brothers in every respect so that he might become a merciful and faithful high priest in the service of God to make propitiation for the sins of the people (2:17). In other words, God became man so that as the God-man he could conquer death, defeat the devil, and atone for our sins.

Centuries before Anselm, Athanasius answered the same question in his book *On the Incarnation.* The King, Athanasius argues, "has come into our country and dwelt in one body," with the result that "the designs of the enemy against mankind have been foiled, and the corruption of death, which formerly held them in its power, has simply ceased to be. For the human race would have perished utterly had not the Lord and Saviour of all, the Son of God, come among us to put an end to death."[1]

1 Athanasius, *On the Incarnation*, 35.

DAY 119

Eternal Sonship

There never was when he was not.

That was the bone of contention with Arianism, the fourth-century heresy that rejected the full deity of the Son of God. The issue was not whether the Son was divine in some sense, but whether he shared the same essence (*homoousios*) as the Father. In particular, Arius held that sonship necessarily implied having a beginning. While Arius affirmed that Christ was preexistent and that all things were created through him, he also believed that the Father created the Son. According to Arius, "If the Father begat the Son, he that was begotten has a beginning of existence; hence it is clear that there was when he was not."[1] Arius was careful not to use the word *time*, because he believed the Son existed before the ages began, but for Arius eternality and sonship could not go together. The Son was a divine being, but a created being with a derivative deity.

How should we respond to this claim? It's not enough to point to passages where Christ is worshiped or where the deity of the Son is broadly affirmed. Arius did not reject these conclusions, and neither do modern-day Arians. Where do we turn to defend the belief that there never was when the Son of God was not? Four passages are critical:

1. In John 8:58 Jesus says to his opponents, "Before Abraham was, I am." Not only does Jesus link himself to Yahweh's great "I Am" statement of Exodus 3:14; he also makes allusion to the "I am" declarations in Isaiah 40–55 (e.g., "I, the LORD, the first, and with the last; I am he" [41:4]). Jesus considered himself as eternal as the God of the Old Testament was eternal. Little wonder some unbelieving Jews thought him a blasphemer and tried to kill him (John 8:59).

2. Likewise, Philippians 2:5–11 places Christ Jesus right in the middle of the most exalted language of Isaiah 45–46. The prediction that every knee will bow

and every tongue confess that Jesus Christ is Lord (Phil. 2:10–11) comes from Isaiah 45:23. Jesus is identified with the God who says, "I am" and, "There is no other" (Isa. 45:22), with the God who declares the end from the beginning (Isa. 46:9–10).

3. Hebrews 7:3 describes Melchizedek, the mysterious king of Salem from Genesis 14, as "having neither beginning of days nor end of life." Whatever this means about Melchizedek himself (a preincarnate Christ or simply a type of Christ), for the analogy to hold ("resembling the Son of God"), Christ must also have neither beginning of days nor end of life.

4. Most convincingly, in Revelation 22:13 Jesus announces, "I am the Alpha and the Omega, the first and the last, the beginning and the end." Earlier in the book, God says the same thing, making specific reference to his eternality as the one who is and who was and who is to come (Rev. 1:8; 21:6). In whatever sense the Father is the beginning and the end, so is the Son. One cannot be more or less eternal than the other. Without eternal sonship, we cannot affirm that the Father has always been the Father. And without the eternality of the Son, we do not have a Christ who can fully save because we do not have a Christ who shares in all the attributes of deity.

1 Bettenson and Maunder, "The Arian Syllogism."

DAY 120

Incarnation

The incarnation refers to the embodiment of God in human form. More specifically, in Christian theology the doctrine of the incarnation affirms that the divine Son of God, the second person of the Trinity, assumed a human nature and came to earth as the God-man Jesus Christ. The Bible describes the incarnation in several different ways: as the appearing of our Savior Jesus Christ (2 Tim. 1:10), as Christ emptying himself and taking the form of a servant (Phil. 2:7), as Christ coming into the world with the body prepared for him (Heb. 10:5), and as manifestation of God in the flesh (1 Tim. 3:16).

It is important to underscore that only the Son of God could have become incarnate. The Father could not become incarnate, for he is first in order and cannot be sent by anyone or act as a mediator to the Son or the Spirit. The Father could not take on human flesh and be born of a virgin without becoming a son in an earthly sense, which would undermine his divine Fatherhood. Likewise, the Spirit could not be sent to be born as a man without becoming, as it were, a second Son. We should stress too that the Godhead—the divine essence in Father, Son, and Holy Spirit—did not become incarnate. As Aquinas writes, "It is more proper to say that a divine person assumed a human nature, than to say that the divine nature assumed a human nature."[1]

It is also critical that we understand what did and did not happen in the incarnation. The incarnation was not a transubstantiation, a transmutation, or a conversion. The incarnation was an assumption. Turretin explains that the communication of the hypostasis (the personal subsistence) of the Logos can be understood in three ways: effectively (the Logos was made in the flesh of another hypostasis), transitively (the Logos transferred his own hypostasis into the flesh), or assumptively (the Logos assumed flesh into the same hypostasis and united it to himself). The third sense, Turretin maintains, is true and orthodox.

In the incarnation, the divine nature did not undergo any essential change. The divine nature remained impassible, omniscient, and immutable. The incarnation was a personal act whereby the person of the Son became incarnate. This is better than saying that the divine nature assumed human flesh. In "becoming man" the second person of the Trinity did not cease to be God. He became what he was not without ceasing to be what he was. That's what is meant by assuming a human nature rather than being transformed into something new.

To put things somewhat inelegantly, we should think of the divine nature, not the human nature, as the "base" nature. That is to say, a human person did not become divine; a divine person assumed a human nature. Christ is humanized deity, not deified humanity. The divinity, not the humanity, is dominant in Christ's person.

All of this intricate theology is meant to explain and safeguard the astounding truth of John 1:14: "And the Word became flesh and dwelt among us." Shedd's summary is helpful: "The divine-human person, Jesus Christ, was produced by the union of the divine nature of the Logos with a human nature derived from a human mother."[2] The Son of God did not begin at the incarnation, but the incarnate personality of Jesus Christ did. There was no God-man until the moment of the incarnation. The second person of the Trinity descended as Logos and ascended as *theanthropos*.

1 Aquinas, *Summa Theologica*, 3.2.1–2.
2 Shedd, *Dogmatic Theology*, 617.

DAY 121

Hypostatic Union

The hypostatic union refers to the joining together of a human nature and a divine nature in the one person of Jesus Christ.

Let's define some terms. By nature, we mean the essential qualities of a thing. The "doggyness" of a dog is its nature. The nature of a thing refers to the substance possessed in common with others of the same nature. Consequently, the hypostatic union affirms that Christ possesses a real and full humanness in common with other human persons, and he possesses a real and full divinity in common with all other divine persons.

The word *person* is also important. We've already encountered the word *person* when talking about the Trinity. Here the stress is on the incarnate Son as *one* person. Christ has one "self," not two "selves." Christ is a unified person (*hypostasis*), belonging to which are two natures in perfect union such that there was a single agent in all that Christ did, said, suffered, and felt. While certain qualities can be predicated of either the human or divine nature, what Christ did he always did as one person.

The union of the divine and human natures in the incarnate Son is not like the oneness of the three persons of the Trinity. There is an I-thou relation to the latter that does not exist in the former. The divine and human natures do not talk to each other or act upon each other as the Father does with the Son. As Turretin puts it, "The union is personal, but not of persons, as the union of nature, not natural."[1]

To make matters more confusing, but also to steer clear of possible theological problems, we need to look at two other related terms. The first is *anhypostasia*. The *an-* (or *a-*) prefix in Greek often acts as a negation (like an a-theist doesn't believe in God). Here *an-hypostasia* means that the Logos was not united with a human person but with a human nature. Jesus Christ is the name of the incarnate Son of God. Jesus is not the name of a free-floating human person who was joined to deity. The human nature received from the Virgin Mary was personalized in its union with the Logos. The Son of God took upon himself a human nature, but not an individual *hypostasis*.

The second confusing but necessary term follows on the logic of the first. The term *enhypostasia* affirms that the human nature of Christ only ever subsisted in the single person of Christ. There was no independent existence of Christ's human nature (that would entail some form of adoptionism). The human nature was in-personal (*en-hypostasia*). While we must say that Christ's human nature was *anhypostasia*, we must also be clear that the human nature never existed as a generic nature. Christ's human nature was never impersonal. If *anhypostasia* safeguards that the Logos was not united to a human person, then *enhypostasia* safeguards that the Logos was not united to humanity in general. Put simply, the humanity of Christ exists only as the humanity of the Son in the incarnation.

1 Turretin, *Elenctic Theology*, 2:311.

DAY 122

Communicatio Idiomatum

The term *communicatio idiomatum* is Latin for the communication of idioms or the communication of properties. It's probably easiest to understand the term as referring to the sharing of attributes. The concept goes back to Cyril of Alexandria but has been used extensively by a number of theologians, including John Calvin.

The *communicatio idiomatum* provides a way of thinking about the two natures of Christ. According to the communication of properties, what can be said about either nature can be said about the person of Christ, but what can be said about the person of Christ cannot necessarily be said about either nature, and what can be said about one nature cannot necessarily be said about the other. Here's Calvin's helpful definition:

> Thus also the Scriptures speak of Christ, they sometimes attribute to him what must be solely referred to his humanity, sometimes what belongs uniquely to his divinity; and sometimes what embraces both natures but fits neither alone. And they so earnestly express this union of the two natures that is in Christ as sometimes to interchange them. This figure of speech is called by the ancient writers—the communicating of properties.[1]

The key distinction is between the way we attribute properties to the *person* of Christ and the *two natures* of Christ. For example, we can say Christ took a nap in the boat. But we should not say that the divine nature took a nap. We can say the world was created through Christ. But we should not say the world was created through the human nature. What Christ did, he did as a single person, the union of two natures. So what we can say about either nature, we can say about the person. But what we say about the person, we cannot automatically say about both natures.

To put it another way: Christological predication runs from the natures to the person but not automatically from the person to the natures. In Scripture, we sometimes see human attributes ascribed to Christ designated by a divine title. This is why Acts can speak of the blood of God (Acts 20:28). God as God doesn't have a body, and thus he doesn't have blood. But if we are referring to the incarnate Son of God, a divine being who can rightly be called by divine titles, then we can speak of the blood of God.

By the same reasoning, *theotokos* is a proper term for Mary if by "God-bearer" we mean the bearer of the God-man Jesus Christ, not the bearer of the triune God or the bearer of the divine nature. Likewise, we can say, "God died on the cross," if we are using that as a title for the God-man Jesus Christ. But we should not say, "God died on the cross," if we mean to communicate that the divine essence died, or that one-third of the triune Godhead perished. The temporal experiences of Jesus cannot automatically be assigned to one or the other nature. Rather the experiences of Jesus should be assigned to the divine Son in his human mode of existence. In all this we are trying to affirm the wonderful mystery that the person of the incarnate Son is visible and invisible, passible and impassible, mutable and immutable, temporal and eternal, mortal and immortal.

1   Calvin, *Institutes* 2.14.1.

How Do the Two Natures Relate to Each Other?

As we've already seen, the *communicatio idiomatum* allows that the properties of either nature can be predicated to the person of Christ. Attribution, we might say, flows from the natures to the person. But what about the relationship between the two natures? Do the human and divine natures of Christ affect each other in any way?

Reformed theologians have affirmed that the human nature of Christ receives a twofold grace (*communicatio gratiarum*) by virtue of union with the divine Logos. The human nature receives (1) the grace of union: a special dignity afforded to the human nature so that flesh becomes a property of the Son of God and therefore can be an object of worship. The human nature also receives (2) the grace of habit: those gifts of the Spirit (gifts of intellect, will, and power) whereby the human nature of Christ was exalted above that of other human beings. In these two ways, the divine nature of Christ radiates a special honor and glory to Christ's human nature.

At the same time, Reformed theology has insisted that this communication of grace in no way involves any change in the essential properties of either nature. Historically, this has been an area of sharp disagreement between the Reformed and Lutheran traditions. Lutheran theology teaches that Christ's human nature is so glorified by the divine nature that the human nature comes to possess certain divine properties like omnipresence. This, in turn, supports the Lutheran understanding of the ubiquity of Christ's resurrected body, which allows for the real physical presence of Christ's body and blood in the Eucharist. Reformed theology disagrees, arguing that there is no genuine sharing of attributes between the two natures. John Owen, for example, stresses that the graces (mentioned above) are communicated *by the Spirit* to Christ's human nature. The communication of grace involves the indwelling of the Spirit without measure, not the infusion of the human nature with divine properties.

Francis Turretin makes a compelling case against the communication of properties across Christ's two natures. The theology is complex but can be broken down into a series of interlocking arguments: (1) None of the essential properties of divinity can be communicated to the human nature. The same nature cannot be created and uncreated. (2) What can be made common to a nature is no longer a property. (3) The properties of the divine nature are inseparable and one. You cannot communicate some of the properties of the divine nature. (4) If it is a true communication of properties across natures, the communication must be reciprocal. The Logos should then now have the property of flesh. (5) If this were so, we would be guilty of Eutychianism where neither nature retains its whole and distinct properties of humanity and divinity. (6) And if the properties of each nature remain distinct, then there can be no real communication of properties. (7) As to omnipresence specifically, the body of Christ was not ubiquitous after Christ's resurrection (Matt. 28:5–6). (8) According to his human nature, Christ did not know everything, so his human nature must not have had the property of omniscience. (9) Likewise, Christ suffered, so his human nature did not have the property of omnipotence. (10) Finally, if Christ's human nature possessed the properties of the divine nature, it would not have been possible for him to die, for "the life of God cannot be extinguished, nor the personal union be dissolved."

In short, Christ's human nature was made uniquely eminent by his divine nature, but the human nature did not come to possess any attributes of deity.[1]

---

1   Turretin, 2.327.

DAY 124

The *Extra Calvinisticum*

The *extra Calvinisticum* teaches that in the Son's incarnation the divine Logos is fully united to, but never fully contained within, the human nature.

The term was originally a pejorative label given by Lutheran theologians in their debates with Reformed theologians over the real presence of Christ in the Lord's Supper. Whereas Lutherans affirmed the physical presence of Christ's body in, with, and under the elements, Reformed theologians spoke of a real spiritual presence. In order to maintain their position (later termed *consubstantiation*), Lutherans argued that the attribute of omnipresence should be predicated not just of Christ's divine nature, but also of his human nature.

Reformed theologians, by contrast, held to a different understanding of the *communicatio idiomatum* (communion of properties), insisting that the divine Logos is omnipresent, but Christ's human body is not. Importantly, they also affirmed that the Son, even in his incarnate state, is able to live a divine life beyond (*extra*) his human nature. Or as the Heidelberg Catechism puts it: "Since divinity is not limited and is present everywhere, it is evident that Christ's divinity is surely beyond the bounds of the humanity he has taken on, but at the same time his divinity is in and remains personally united to his humanity" (Q/A 48).

While the doctrine may seem like special pleading, the *extra Calvinisticum* is crucial for protecting a classic understanding of the incarnation. In fact, some have preferred the term *extra Catholicum* because even though the doctrine is attributed to John Calvin, it was the position of church fathers like Augustine, Cyril, and Athanasius, and was taught throughout the Middle Ages. The *extra* is an important doctrine in that it safeguards the transcendence of Christ's divine nature (i.e., it cannot be contained) and the genuineness of the human nature (i.e., it does not possess attributes reserved for divinity).

The *extra* also reminds us that in the incarnation "the Son did not cease to be what he had always been."[1] He continued to sustain the universe (Col. 1:15–17; Heb. 1:1–3) and to exercise his divine attributes together with the Father and the Spirit. When Mary conceived a child by the power of the Holy Spirit, the divine nature did not undergo any essential change. Better to say the person of the Son became incarnate than to say the divine nature took on human flesh (for the latter suggests the divine nature changed in its essential properties).

All this means, because the divine nature did not undergo essential change, that in coming to earth, the Son of God did not abdicate his rule but extended it. It also means, because the human nature was not swallowed up by the divine, that the Son's earthly obedience was free and voluntary. In short, the *extra* protects a Chalcedonian understanding of the incarnation that Christ's divine and human natures were indissolubly joined, yet "without confusion" and "without change."

1 Wellum, *God the Son Incarnate*, 332.

DAY 125

Christological Heresies

There are grave dangers if Christians stray from the faith that was once for all delivered to the saints (Jude 3). We must hold fast to the truth (1 Tim. 2:4; 3:15; 4:3), guard the good deposit (1 Tim. 6:20; 2 Tim. 1:14), and stick to the pattern of the sound words (2 Tim. 1:13). We must not deviate from the traditions (2 Thess. 2:15), from the apostles' teaching (Acts 2:42; 2 Tim. 2:2), or from what we have heard (Heb. 2:1; 1 John 2:24). We must beware the yeast of the Pharisees and of the Sadducees (Matt. 16:6); we must be on the lookout for "destructive heresies" (2 Pet. 2:1).

In the next several chapters, we will focus on four errors in particular (Arianism, Docetism, Nestorianism, and Eutychianism), but it might helpful here, if only as a reference point, to highlight the other main Christological errors that had to be sifted through in the early church.

Dynamic Monarchianism. There is only one ruler (or *archē*), God the Father. Jesus Christ was tested by the Father and then adopted as his Son. Consequently, Christ was filled with wisdom and power and worked miracles by the power (*dynamis*) given to him by the Father. This heresy is also called adoptionism.

Modalistic Monarchianism. There is one God who reveals himself in three modes (like the ill-advised water/ice/vapor analogy). Sometimes called Sabellianism in the West (after the theologian Sabellius) and patripassianism in the East (because the Father was said to suffer as the Son on the cross), modalism denies personal distinctions between Father, Son, and Holy Spirit.

Ebionism. This was a Jewish heresy that denied Christ's divine nature. The Ebionites believed Jesus was the natural son of Joseph and Mary and that he became the Messiah because he obeyed the law. "Christ" descended on Jesus at his baptism. We are meant to follow Jesus's example and, with the same supernatural assistance, keep the law for ourselves.

Monophysitism. This was the name given to a number of related heresies which asserted that Christ had only one (mono) nature (physis). Theopaschitism, for example, defended by Peter the Fuller of Antioch, was a monophysite heresy, insisting that Christ's deity and humanity were joined in one nature so that when Christ died the divine nature also suffered.

Monothelitism. According to this error, Christ had only one (*mono*) will (*thelema*). Usually this means that Christ had no human will, just one divine will. By contrast, the orthodox position believed that will was a property of nature, not of the person. This is why the triune God (three persons sharing one nature) has one will, while the incarnate Son of God (the union of two natures) has two wills. In John 6:38 Jesus says, "I have come down from heaven, not to do my will but the will of him who sent me." There is a metaphysical distinction between the human will and the divine will, and the possibility that the wishes of the human Christ may not always coincide initially with the Father's divine will.

As poisonous as heresies can be, God has often used them to refine the church and clarify the truth. As Paul reminded the Corinthians, sometimes there must be factions and divisions in the church "in order that those who are genuine among you may be recognized" (1 Cor. 11:18–19). This was certainly the case over the course of the second, third, and fourth centuries, as the Holy Spirit worked through the church to provide clarity on what sort of person Jesus Christ was and is.

WEEK 26

DAY 126

Arianism

Arianism is the heresy that denies the full deity of Jesus Christ. For two centuries the early church struggled with how exactly to speak about the person of Christ and how Father, Son, and Holy Spirit fit together. The simmering controversy erupted in 313 when Arius (256–336) was made a presbyter in Alexandria,

Egypt. He was well-educated, and displayed a strong ascetic discipline. He was confident and impressive in speech. As best as we can tell, he was sincere in his convictions and concerned that Christians follow the example of Christ in their daily lives.

But Arius did not believe Christ was fully God. His problem was not, "How could a man be God?" but, "How could God become a man?" He wanted to protect the majesty, the sovereignty, and the unity of God. So Arius reasoned that if the Son and the Father shared the same nature, then that must mean that God the Father could suffer, could change, and could die. Clearly, Arius thought, these things cannot be true of the divine nature.

Arius began airing his opinions in 318, teaching that although Christ was preexistent and all things were created through him, Christ was also a creature. Christ was a divine being, but with a derivative deity. The Son had an origin. This was Arius's most (in)famous contention, that there was when the Son was not. This led Arius to conclude, in his hymn-poem *Thalia*, that the members of the Trinity "share in unequal glories."

The whole Christian East was in turmoil over Arianism. Bishop arose against bishop, province against province, church against church. Constantine could not ignore the conflict raging in his Empire, so in 325 he called for a council to meet at Nicaea, a small town near his imperial capital of Constantinople. Of the 318 bishops present at the council, only seven were from the West (e.g., France, Spain, Carthage, Rome). The rest were from the East.

The bishops divided into three parties: a pro-Arius party, an orthodox party, and a middle party looking to find common ground everyone could agree on. The noted historian Eusebius of Caesarea proposed adopting an ancient formula called the Palestinian Confession, which acknowledged the divinity of Christ in the broadest terms. The orthodox party, however, wanted the creed to be more specific. They knew that the council would be a failure unless it *exposed* rather than covered up what the Arians believed. In particular, the orthodox party wanted the word *homoousios*—an affirmation that Christ was not just of a similar nature with the Father; he was of the same nature (consubstantial).

The most important point of debate at Nicaea was over a single word, but it was a mighty important word. In the end, the bishops affirmed that the Son was consubstantial with the Father. Consequently, Arianism was deemed heretical by the first ecumenical council at Nicaea. Although the debate was far from settled, Nicene orthodoxy, as we know it in the Nicene Creed, was established at the Second Ecumenical Council in Constantinople (381). Praise God for the "one Lord Jesus Christ, the only Son of God, begotten from the Father before all ages, God from God, Light from Light, true God from true God, begotten not made, of the same essence as the Father."

DAY 127

Docetism

Docetism does not refer to a specific teaching but to a group of theologies that deny the full humanity of Christ. The heresy is called Docetism because of the Greek word *dokein*, which means "to seem" or "to appear." Docetists were those who believed that Jesus only appeared to be human. If Arians had a hard time imagining that the man Jesus could have been fully God, the Greeks had difficulty imagining that the God they worshiped could have really been human.

One of the main variants of Docetism is called Apollinarianism after Apollinarius (d. 390), the bishop of Laodicea and friend of Athanasius. Apollinarius was a pious, devout, and intelligent man. He strongly opposed Arianism and defended Nicene orthodoxy and the full divinity of Christ. He spoke against the teachings of Paul of Samosata, who taught an early form of adoptionism. Apollinarius affirmed the full deity of Christ, rejecting any notion that Jesus was a mere man who became God or who was infused with the divine Logos at his birth.

But affirming the full humanity of Christ was unsettling to Apollinarius. How could God be joined with all the weaknesses and imperfections of a human nature? Apollinarius reasoned that the only way Christ could have a fully divine nature and fully human nature would be if the divine nature was the natural Son of God, while the human nature became, or was adopted as, the Son of God. But this would turn Christ into two Sons. Apollinarius knew this was the wrong answer.

His solution was to look at man as tripartite: body, soul, and spirit. The spirit, thought Apollinarius, was the seat of sin. By spirit, he was thinking of rationality and the higher faculties. If Christ had a completely human mind, then he couldn't be of one mind with the Father, and he would be able to sin. Consequently, reasoned Apollinarius, Christ must have had the divine Logos in place of a human mind. After all, the mind must be changeless, not "prey to filthy thoughts, but existing as a divine mind, immutable and heavenly."

In short, the Son of God took to himself an incomplete human nature. Apollinarius saw the incarnation as the Word becoming flesh rather than Word becoming man. Christ was the substantial union of one heavenly element (the Logos) and one earthly element (a human body). "He is not man," Apollinarius wrote, "though like man; for He is not consubstantial with man in the most important element."[1] Thanks in large part to Basil's objections, Pope Damascus excommunicated Apollinarius around 377. Apollinarianism was deemed heretical at the Council of Constantinople in 381.

Arianism and Docetism both started off with good intentions. Almost every heresy does. Arianism wanted to defend the majesty of God, so it argued that the human Christ could not be equally divine in the same way that the Father is divine. Docetism wanted to defend the perfection of God, so it argued that the divine Christ could not be fully human in the same way we are human. Both heresies were drawn to aspects of the truth, but their human logic and philosophical assumptions prevented them from seeing the whole truth. Too strenuously avoiding one heresy often leads you into another. We must pay careful attention to what the Bible says—in every direction, all at once.

1 Quoted in MacLeod, *The Person of Christ*, 159.

DAY 128

Nestorianism

The debate with Arianism clarified that the Son is fully God, sharing the same essence with the Father. The debate with Docetism (e.g., Apollinarianism) clarified that the Son is fully human, not just appearing to be a man, or like a man in most ways (e.g., no human mind), but human like us in every way except for sin. Following these two disputes came a second pair of heresies: Nestorianism (which held that the two natures were divided) and Eutychianism (which held that the two natures were mixed).

Nestorius was the patriarch of Constantinople. His teachings were condemned in 431 at the Council of Ephesus. Nestorius's error grew out of his concern that people were calling Mary *theotokos*, the God-bearer. It has happened since Nestorius and most likely was happening in his day too, that people took the step from "Mary the bearer of God" to "Mary the divine Mother of God." *Theotokos* is a proper term, but only with the proper qualifications. The emphasis must be on the Son, not on Mary.

In any event, Nestorius objected to the popular title. He could admit that Mary bore someone, and that the someone was Jesus of Nazareth. But he reckoned that she gave birth to only the human nature of Christ. After all, divinity is eternal, so how could the divine nature be born? Mary could be the mother of Jesus, but not the mother of God. If Mary was *theotokos*, Nestorius reasoned, then the Son of God had a beginning, which meant he was a creation, which meant we were right back at the Arian heresy.

Nestorius's solution was to argue for a dividing wall between the two natures. He knew the Son was God. He knew the Son was a man, and a whole man at that. Mary, therefore, must have been the mother of only Jesus. She brought forth a man who was accompanied by the Logos. The two natures of Christ existed more like a partnership than a union of being.

Nestorius was opposed by Cyril of Alexandria, who made two decisive arguments in favor of the title *theotokos*.

1. If Mary is not the God-bearer, then we must understand the incarnation as something other than God becoming man. Instead you have God coming alongside a man. Consequently, Jesus Christ would not be the God-man; he would be a man with God in him. And that would mean that in Nestorianism, God was in Christ in the same manner God is in us. The difference was only a matter of degree. Cyril showed how Nestorianism made too little of Jesus and made too much of us.

2. If Mary is not the God-bearer, then the relationship of Christ to humanity is changed. Nestorianism's problem was not with the two natures, but with the one person. Christ is fully God and fully man in Nestorianism, but he didn't really constitute a single person. Instead of two natures in a single self-conscious person, the two natures are next to each other with a moral and sympathetic union. And yet Romans 5 makes clear that our salvation is accomplished through "the one man's obedience" (5:19). It's only through the one man, Jesus Christ, the union of humanity and deity, that we are made righteous. If the two natures are divided, there is no way for the single person of the Son to "lay his hand on us both" (Job 9:33).

DAY 129

Eutychianism

Eutyches was an aged monk at a large monastery in Constantinople. He was born around 378 and died in 454. Like Nestorius, it's hard to determine what Eutyches actually taught and what ideas simply got attached to his name. Eutyches was older at the time of his controversy and a somewhat muddled thinker. So it's unclear how much of Eutychianism came from Eutyches.

What we do know is that Eutyches had a strong anti-Nestorian bias. He was loathe to fall into the error of dividing Christ's humanity from his divinity. So instead of division, Eutychianism came down on the side of mixture and confusion. Eutyches taught that there were two natures before the union, but only one nature (*physis*) in Christ after the union of his divinity and humanity. Eutychianism is a version of monophysitism, the belief that Christ had only one nature. Eutyches argued for the absorption of the human nature into the divine, the fusion of the two natures resulting in a *tertium quid* (a "third thing"), like mixing yellow and blue to get green. Eutyches believed that Christ's humanity was so united to his divinity that his humanity was not the same as ours (i.e., not consubstantial). Christ was "of one substance with the Father" but not "of one substance with us."

Eutyches was stubborn and not very careful. But he was also led astray by misunderstanding a particular phrase from Cyril of Alexandria. Cyril, who secured the condemnation of Nestorius at Ephesus in 431, was considered the standard bearer for orthodoxy. If you agreed with Cyril, you were orthodox. If you didn't, you probably were off track. Unfortunately, Cyril had grown fond of a particular phrase: "one incarnate nature of God the Word incarnate." He thought this phrase came from Athanasius, and who could possibly be more orthodox than Athanasius? But the phrase actually came from Apollinarius, whose ideas proved heretical. Cyril liked the phrase because he thought it safeguarded the unity of Christ against Nestorianism. In later years, Cyril was very clear that he still affirmed a full human nature and accepted the phrase "two natures" as long as it did not detract from the *union* of the two natures. Cyril meant something orthodox by the unfortunate phrase. Eutyches, however, had no room for subtlety. In his mind he concluded: "one nature" was good theology; "two natures" was bad theology.

Eutyches was deposed in 448 by a Synod that was led by Archbishop Flavian. Eutyches complained to Pope Leo that he was treated unfairly. Leo, after some back and forth, wrote a letter to Flavian where he brilliantly surveyed all the Christological heresies and concluded that Eutyches was wrong. "In Christ Jesus," he wrote, "neither Humanity without true Divinity, nor Divinity without true Humanity, may be believed to exist." For a short time, Eutychianism was vindicated—at the "Robbers' Synod" in Ephesus in 449. But two years later, in 451, the synod at Chalcedon clearly rejected Eutychianism and established orthodox Christology. The Son of God, the Lord Jesus Christ, ought to be recognized in two natures coming together to form one person (*prosopon*) and subsistence (*hypostasis*).

Chalcedonian Definition

For a concise and careful definition of the hypostatic union, the Chalcedonian Definition (451) is still unsurpassed. Take special note of the special terms we've looked at in previous chapters and at the four underlined phrases.

> Therefore, following the holy fathers, we all with one accord teach men to acknowledge one and the same Son, our Lord Jesus Christ, at once complete in Godhead and complete in manhood, truly God and truly man, consisting also of a reasonable soul and body; of one substance [*homoousion*] with the Father as regards his Godhead, and at the same time of one substance with us as regards his manhood; like us in all respects, apart from sin; as regards his Godhead, begotten of the Father before the ages, but yet as regards his manhood begotten, for us men and for our salvation, of Mary the Virgin, the God-bearer [*theotokos*]; one and the same Christ, Son, Lord, Only-begotten, recognized in two natures, <u>without confusion, without change, without division, without separation</u>; the distinction of natures being in no way annulled by the union, but rather the characteristics of each nature being preserved and coming together to form one person and subsistence [hypostasis], not as parted or separated into two persons, but one and the same Son and Only-begotten God the Word, Lord Jesus Christ; even as the prophets from earliest times spoke of him, and our Lord Jesus Christ himself taught us, and the creed of the fathers has handed down to us.

At the heart of this definition are the four negative statements (underlined above).

Without confusion. The Lord Jesus Christ is not what you get when you mix blue and yellow together and end up with green. He's not a *tertium quid* (a third thing), the result of mixing a divine nature and a human nature.

Without change. In assuming human flesh, the Logos did not cease to be what he had always been. The incarnation effected no substantial change in the divine Son.

Without division. The two natures of Christ do not represent a split in the divine person. Jesus Christ is not half God and half man.

Without separation. The union of the human and divine in the person of Jesus Christ is a real, organic union, not simply a moral sympathy or relational partnership.

This may seem like needless theological wrangling, but Chalcedon's careful definition is meant to preserve the biblical teaching that (1) the divine nature was united, in the person of the Son, with a human nature (John 1:14; Rom. 8:3; 1 Tim. 3:16; Heb. 2:11–14), and (2) the two natures are united in only one divine person (Rom. 1:3–4; Gal. 4:4–5; Phil. 2:6–11). As Chalcedon puts it, the characteristics of each nature are preserved—in no way annulled by the union—even as they come together in one person and one subsistence. We are not saved by two natures working together, but by one divine person consisting of a human nature and a divine nature.

WEEK 27

DAY 131

"Whatever Is Not Assumed Cannot Be Healed"

Chalcedon didn't settle everything. Some in the East still couldn't swallow the two natures doctrine. They wanted to honor the memory of Cyril and held on to one nature theology. This was the first significant split in the church. There are six churches known as the Old Oriental Orthodoxy (or Non-Chalcedonian churches): Syriac, Coptic, Ethiopian, Eritrea, Malankara (Indian), and Armenian. These six churches have a different hierarchy and are not in communion with the rest of Eastern Orthodoxy or with the Roman Catholic Church.

These churches have been called monophysite, but they reject the label, saying they too deny Eutychianism. They prefer to be called miaphysites (primarily one nature). Church leaders continue to debate whether the Oriental churches have different theology from the rest of the church or only a different way of saying things.

For the vast majority of the church, however, since the fifth century, the Chalcedonian Definition has served as the definitive statement of orthodox Christology because it so effectively and succinctly argued against a slew of heterodox beliefs:

- Against Docetism Chalcedon affirmed that the Lord Jesus was a true man, consubstantial with us in manhood, his manhood begotten from the Virgin Mary.
- Against adoptionism Chalcedon affirmed that Christ was begotten from the Father before ages began.
- Against modalism Chalcedon distinguished between the Father and the Son, with the former eternally begetting the latter.
- Against Arianism Chalcedon affirmed that Christ was perfect in Godhead, truly God, and the divine Word.
- Against Apollinarianism Chalcedon confessed that Christ was truly man, of a rational soul and body, in all things like unto us except for sin.
- Against Nestorianism Chalcedon called Mary *theotokos* and affirmed that there was one and the same Son, one person and one subsistence, the union of two natures without division and without separation.
- Against Eutychianism Chalcedon affirmed that the two natures were joined together without confusion or change, the difference of the natures not being removed in the union.
- Against monophysitism Chalcedon affirmed that two natures, with their properties, were preserved in the coming together in one *prosopon* and one *hypostasis.*

Why does all of this matter? It matters in order that we may truly know the true Christ, and it also matters for our salvation. Recall the famous words from Gregory of Nazianzus: "Whatever is not assumed cannot be healed."

Arianism cannot save us from God because its Christ is not God. Docetism cannot save us from our sin because its Christ is not fully human. Nestorianism removes the unity of God's work. The bridge doesn't meet in the middle. God can lay a hand on us both, but not at the same time. Eutychianism removes the human dimension of Christ's work. The bridge doesn't really touch either side. All of the theological wrangling and defining were meant to preserve the simple, eminently biblical truth that Jesus is God and man and as such is uniquely and solely capable of saving sinful human beings like us.

DAY 132

Christ's Divine Self-Consciousness

What did Christ know about himself? Did he know he was the Son of God, or did he have to learn this from someone or somewhere else? We aren't told what Jesus would have said about himself at five years old, but we see him as a twelve-year-old dazzling the teachers in the temple and telling his parents that he must be in his Father's house (Luke 2:49). Clearly, already as a boy, Jesus understood what his elders did not understand (Luke 2:50). We should not think, as some have argued, that someone (like his parents) sat down with him at some point and showed him who he was from the Scriptures. The clear picture in all the Gospels is that people were very fuzzy on his identity, including his parents.

Every picture we have of a communicating Christ in the Gospels is of a Christ who understands his divine and messianic identity. He frequently calls himself the Son of Man. He asks the disciples who he is and affirms their correct answer that he is the Christ, the Son of the living God. He goes up on the Mount of Transfiguration knowing who he is and what will be revealed.

He says, "Before Abraham was, I am" (John 8:58). He tells people that they must believe that "I am he" (John 8:24). He understands he is the Messiah, the Son of God, the Son of Man, the fulfillment of Old Testament prophecy, the one who will stand in judgment upon all people, the one who is deserving of worship, the one who must die and be raised to life on the third day, the one who will die for the sins of his people, the one apart from whom there is no eternal life, the one who has been with his Father from the beginning, the one who is one with the Father and shared in glory with the Father before time began. Jesus was not confused about who he was.

At the same time, Christ experienced a twofold consciousness (cf. John 5:16–30; Matt. 11:25–27). He could experience divine perception or human perception. He can say, "I and the Father are one" (divine consciousness; John 10:30), and he can say, "I thirst" (human consciousness; John 19:28). Shedd says that in the complex person of Christ there was a continual fluctuation of consciousness, according to divine or human nature. "At one moment, he felt and spoke as an almighty, self-existent, and infinite being. Finite and infinite, man and God, creature and Creator, time and eternity, met and mingled in that wonderful person who was not divine solely or human solely, but divine-human."[1]

This naturally leads to questions about whether Christ was omniscient: did Christ on earth know all things? Christ increased in wisdom and stature (Luke 2:52). The Son, as a man, did not know the day of the parousia (Mark 13:32). The human mind of Christ only knew what the divine Logos made known. Christ knew what was in a man. He knew the exact timing of Lazarus's death. He knew Nathanael under the fig tree. He knew who would betray him. As the divine Lord over all, he knew everything (John 21:17).

Christ never did not know what he should have known, but he had to fulfill his office with the limitations of a human body and the limitations of a human mind. The answer is once again to assert the mystery (which is different from the irrationality) of the two natures in one person. Turretin's summary is well put: "We acknowledge that Christ as God was indeed omniscient, but as man we hold that he was endowed with knowledge, great indeed beyond all other creatures, but yet finite and created, to which something could be added (and really was added)."[2]

1   Shedd, *Dogmatic Theology*, 652–53.
2   Turretin, *Elenctic Theology*, 2:349.

DAY 133

Kenosis

According to Philippians 2:6–7, though Christ "was in the form of God, he did not count equality with God a thing to be grasped, but emptied [*ekenosen*] himself, by taking the form of a servant, being born in the likeness of men." In the nineteenth century, the question of kenosis (Christ's self-emptying) became a topic of fierce debate. Motivated by a desire to explain how the results of higher criticism could square with the depiction of Christ in the New Testament, specifically his tacit assumptions about the Old Testament (e.g., that Moses wrote the Pentateuch, that there was only one Isaiah, that Jonah was true history, and that Old Testament chronology is straightforward), theologians in Britain and Germany put forward a Christ completely devoid of the attribute of divine omniscience.

The kenotic theories were not all of one kind. Some theologians argued that Christ abandoned the relative attributes of deity (omnipotence and omniscience), while retaining the essential attributes of holiness and love. Others argued the Christ divested himself of relative *and* essential attributes, to the point of disrupting the life of the Trinity and suspending the Son's cosmic functions. Still others tried to stay within the bounds of orthodoxy by arguing that Christ ceased to exercise divine functions, with the end result that Christ lived his earthly life entirely within the conditions of his humanity.

To be sure, there is a way to say that Christ is all-knowing and must learn, he is omnipresent and localized, and he is all powerful and has embraced finitude. Certain activities of the God-man Christ Jesus can be predicated of his human nature and some activities of his divine nature. Kenoticism goes further than this, however, and says that he truly emptied himself of these divine attributes, not merely that he sometimes did not exercise them or did not draw upon them.

So how should we understand Christ's self-emptying in Philippians 2? Kenosis, properly understood, means that though he was fully God, Christ did not cling to his Godhood as something to be used for his own selfish gain. Rather, he set aside his divine rights as God and came to earth as a servant. He came as a human being who willingly obeyed his Father in everything, even to the point of dying a shameful death on a cruel cross.

In short, Christ Jesus emptied himself not of the divine nature, nor of divine attributes, but of divine prerogatives. As God, Christ had certain rights or privileges exclusive to deity, but as God *in the flesh*, he often set aside those rights. We might best understand kenosis with another Greek word: *krypsis*, meaning "hidden." Christ emptied himself in that his divine glory was for a time veiled, obscured, hidden (John 17:5). In the incarnation, the Son of God became what he was not (a man) without ceasing to be what he was (fully God). It was temporary self-abasement by assumption (of a human nature), not by subtraction.

The cross is the turning point in human history because it was precisely in that moment of defeat and shame that God won the victory. At Calvary, humiliation paved the way for exaltation. It was the hour in human history when God's purposes and God's character were finally and fully revealed for all to see, even if few had eyes to see who he was on that day, and then only with an incomplete faith. Soon enough, however, the self-emptying one on earth would be exalted in heaven.

DAY 134

Spirit Christology

Spirit Christology is an umbrella term given to a number of theologies that put the Holy Spirit at the center of our understanding of the person and work of Christ. Some proposals are anti-Trinitarian, but others are quick to affirm traditional Trinitarian theology and the ontological deity of the Son.

It is easy to overlook how Jesus is presented in the Gospels as one supremely full of and empowered by the Holy Spirit. Jesus was conceived by the Holy Spirit

(Luke 1:35). At his baptism, the Holy Spirit descended on Jesus (3:22). Likewise, Luke records that Jesus was led by the Spirit into the wilderness to be tempted (4:1), and then returned in the power of the Spirit (4:14). In launching his public ministry at Nazareth, Jesus announced, in keeping with Isaiah's prophecy, that the Spirit of the Lord was upon him (4:18). Jesus is said to have rejoiced in the Holy Spirit (10:21), baptized with the Holy Spirit (3:16), and declared to be the Son of God in power according to the Spirit (Rom. 1:4).

Spirit Christology can be a positive insofar as it emphasizes the work of the Spirit in the life of Jesus. Spirit Christology also underscores the true humanity of Christ. Jesus was not a superhero who could simply switch on his divine nature whenever he was in a pinch. He had to overcome real human weakness. Finally, by highlighting the work of the Spirit in Christ's life, we are drawn to ask for the same Spirit to teach us, lead us, and empower us. We too must (and can!) live a life of faith in and dependence upon the Holy Spirit.

At the same time, there are a number of dangers we should be aware of under the broad teaching known as Spirit Christology. It's sometimes said that Christ's miracles cannot be used as proof of Christ's divinity. After all, Elijah and Elisha did great miracles. They multiplied food. They raised the dead. They were given supernatural insight into specific people and situations. That's true, of course, but we should not overcorrect our exegesis and act as if all of Christ's mighty works were done simply in reliance upon the power of the Spirit. The seven signs in John were explicit pointers to his messianic identity and divine power (see John 20:31). When Jesus feeds the five thousand, they say, "This is indeed the Prophet who is to come into the world" (John 6:14). When the disciples ask, "Who then is this, that even the wind and the sea obey him?" the expected response is not, "This is a man empowered by the same Spirit that we can have." The answer to the rhetorical question is, "This is the Lord God almighty" (Mark 4:41; cf. Ps. 89:8).

There are theological dangers too. We must not so emphasize the role of the Spirit in Christ's life that we end up with a functional kenoticism (if not hints of adoptionism), with a human Christ so dependent on the Spirit that there is no demonstrable evidence of divinity. Likewise, an overemphasis on the agency of the Spirit in the work of Christ can undermine the traditional notion of insepa-rable operations. It can also run counter to the priority given to Christ in the Trinitarian work of redemption. In short, while the Holy Spirit was integral in every part of Christ's work of salvation, it was still Christ who accomplished our redemption (not the Spirit), and the work he accomplished could not have been fulfilled had he not been fully God.

DAY 135

Impeccability

The doctrine of impeccability states that Christ was not only sinless; he was unable to sin (*non posse peccare*). As the incarnate Son of God, Christ faced real temptations, but these temptations did not arise in Christ due to sinful desires. Christ was not only able to overcome temptation; he was unable to be overcome by it.[1]

Christ's impeccability has been widely affirmed throughout the history of the church. In the last 150 years, however, many theologians have rejected the idea that Christ was unable to sin, arguing instead that peccability is necessary for Christ's temptations to be genuine and for Christ to sympathize with his people. Surprisingly, even the redoubtable Charles Hodge (1797–1878) went wobbly on impeccability, which may be one of the reasons his contemporary W. G. T. Shedd (1820–1894) offered an especially robust defense of the doctrine.[2]

In defense of Christ's impeccability, Shedd makes three broad points.

First, Christ's impeccability can be deduced from Scripture. If Jesus Christ is the same yesterday and today and forever (Heb. 13:8), he must be unchanging in his holiness. A mutable holiness would be inconsistent with the omnipotence of Christ and irreconcilable with the fact that Christ is the author and finisher of our faith (Heb. 12:2). If Christ were able to sin, his holiness would, by definition, be open to change—his obedience open to failure—even if Christ proved in the end to be faithful. A peccable Christ is a Savior who can be trusted only in hindsight.

Second, Christ's impeccability is tied to the constitution of his person. At the heart of this second point is the Chalcedonian conviction that whatever Christ did, he did as one undivided theanthropic person. Consequently, Shedd argues, Christ's ability to sin must be measured according to "his mightiest nature." Just as an iron wire by itself can be bent, but once welded to an iron bar is rendered immovable, so the God-man Jesus Christ is rendered impeccable by the union of the human and divine natures.

Third, impeccability is consistent with temptation. Some temptations arise from without as trials and sufferings—these Christ constantly endured. But also, temptations arise from within as sinful desires—these Christ never experienced. When Hebrews 4:15 says Christ was tempted in every respect as we are, yet without sin, we should understand the preposition "without" (*choris*) as extending both to the outcome of the temptations (unlike us, Christ did not sin) and to the nature of the temptations (unlike ours, Christ's temptations were not sinful). We are tempted by the world, the flesh, and the devil; Christ never faced temptation from the flesh.

Christ's inability to sin does not make his temptations less genuine. The army that cannot be conquered can still be attacked. If anything, Christ's temptations were more intense than ours because he never gave in to them. Our temptations wax and wane as we sometimes withstand them and sometimes succumb to them. But Christ never gave in, and as such the experience of temptation only mounted throughout his life. In all this, Christ is able to sympathize with us in our human experience of temptation, even though as the God-man, he was incapable of giving in to these temptations.

1   Shedd, *Dogmatic Theology*, 659.
2   See Hodge, *Systematic Theology*, 2:457. Shedd's points below come from *Dogmatic Theology*, 660–62.

CHRISTOLOGY 2

The Work of Christ

DAY 136

Two States

The work of Christ was carried out in two different states. Of course, we aren't thinking here of states like North Carolina and South Carolina. *State*, in the theological sense, refers to Christ's position as determined by his relationship to the law and then the condition that follows from this state. In one state, Christ lived under the law—facing all that it demands and dishes out. In the other state, Christ lived free from the law, having vanquished its curse. These two positions are called the state of humiliation and the state of exaltation.

The *state of humiliation* is the state wherein Christ laid aside his divine majesty (allowing it to be veiled and hidden), assumed human nature in the form of a servant, and became voluntarily subject to the demands and the curse of the law.

The *state of exaltation* is the state wherein Christ passed from under the penalty and the burden of the law (as a covenant of works), came to possess all the blessings of salvation, and was crowned with glory and honor.

Typically, there are said to be five stages in the state of humiliation: incarnation, suffering, death, burial, and descent into hell. We can hear each of these stages of Christ's humiliation in the Apostles' Creed: ". . . born of the Virgin Mary, suffered under Pontius Pilate, was crucified, died, and was buried; he descended into hell."

Similarly, there are said to be four stages in the state of exaltation: resurrection, ascension, session, and return. We can hear each of these stages in the next line of the Apostles' Creed: "On the third day he rose again from the dead; he ascended into heaven, where he sits at the right hand of God the Father Almighty from whence he shall come to judge the living and the dead."

The idea of two states—one in which Christ was brought low, and one in which Christ was lifted up—can be found in several biblical passages. Hebrews 2:7 tells us (applying the words of Psalm 8) that Jesus was made a little lower than the angels (humiliation) and was crowned with glory and honor (exaltation). Likewise, according to Psalm 118:22, the stone the builders rejected (humiliation) has become the cornerstone (exaltation). We read of the same dynamic—first the sufferings of Christ and then the subsequent glories—in Luke 24:26 and 1 Peter 1:10–11. The clearest example comes from Philippians 2 where we read that because Christ emptied himself, took the form of a servant, and became obedient unto death, God has highly exalted him and given him the name above every name (2:7–9).

No human existence has been marked by such undeserved and unrelenting humiliation as the life and death of the Lord Jesus. But humiliation is not the entire story. Christ suffered as one of us that he might suffer *for* us—the righteous for the unrighteous, the just for the unjust, the deserving for the undeserving. He was cast low so that we might be lifted up. He was humiliated so that in turn he might be exalted.

DAY 137

Incarnation and Suffering

There is disagreement among theologians about whether the incarnation should be considered an aspect of Christ's humiliation. On the one hand, there is nothing ignoble about possessing a human nature. If human nature itself were demeaning, Christ would be in a perpetual state of humiliation because the incarnation continues for all time.

And yet, for Christ, the incarnation was never simply the assumption of a human nature. To take on human flesh meant for the Son of God that he would be born into poverty and that his deity would be partially veiled. It also meant that Christ would be subjected to the weakness of fallen humanity, destined to live a life of privation, grief, and limitations (in knowledge and in power) according to his human nature. For Christ, the incarnation entailed being born in the likeness of sinful flesh (Rom. 8:3), being born under law (Gal. 4:4), and taking the form of a servant (Phil. 2:6–7). Since the incarnation—as it played out and was planned—cannot be separated from circumstances of abasement, we can label Christ's incarnation as an aspect of his humiliation.

The second aspect of Christ's humiliation is his suffering, about which we can note three things.

1. Christ's *whole* life was one of suffering. The heavenly Son of God occupied a position far beneath him and lived among sinful people in a depraved world. He faced hostility from enemies and misunderstandings from friends. He lived with an awareness that he would die as a young man and die in no ordinary way. He faced special temptations from the devil. He knew what it was to hunger, to thirst, to weep, and to mourn. Perhaps most heinously, the Word made flesh came to his own people, and his own did not receive him (John 1:11).

2. Christ suffered in body *and* in soul (not according to both natures, but according to his human nature). In body, Christ was flogged, beaten, spat upon, and crucified. In soul, he was, more than other men, deeply troubled (John 12:27) and exceedingly sorrowful, even unto death (Matt. 26:38).

3. Christ's suffering was *unique* in its intensity. No one felt the grief of moral evil like Christ. No one was as relentlessly and ruthlessly tempted. No one faced the wrath of God for the sins of the world as Christ did. No man ever suffered more fully and more excruciatingly than the Lord Jesus. *Man of sorrows—what a name for the Son of God, who came ruined sinners to reclaim: Hallelujah, what a Savior!*

DAY 138

Cry of Dereliction

In the last moments of his life, as he suffered the cruel torments of the cross, Jesus cried out with a loud voice, "'Eli, Eli, lema sabachthani?'" that is, 'My God, my God, why have you forsaken me?'" (Matt. 27:46). How are we to understand this cry of dereliction?

On the cross Christ experienced the absence of divine comfort and the weight of divine wrath. In his human consciousness, Christ experienced a true feeling of God-forsakenness. Death on the cross represented Christ becoming a curse for us (Deut. 21:23; Gal. 3:13). Yet even under the weight of this judicial sentence, Christ did not utterly despair, for he cried out to God in fulfillment of Scripture (Ps. 22:1).

While we never want to lessen the pain and passion of Christ's cry on the cross, we must be careful we do not read into it insuperable theological problems. According to à Brakel, Christ was not forsaken by the Father, whose union could not be severed. Neither was Christ forsaken by the Holy Spirit, with whom he had been anointed beyond measure. Instead, we ought to understand that Christ experienced the "withdrawal of all light, love, help, and comfort during the specific moment when his distress was at its highest and when he needed them to the utmost."[1] This may seem like a distinction without a difference, but à Brakel means to guard against any notion of intra-Trinitarian conflict. Later he says, "Christ was the Son of love, and as such God was not angry with Him. God was wrathful towards sin, however, and in righteously executing justice as Judge, caused Him who had taken sin upon Himself to feel this wrath."[2]

Francis Turretin is also helpful in parsing out what the cry of dereliction means (and does not mean). The desertion, insists Turretin, was not absolute as felt only by demons and by the reprobate. The desertion was temporal and relative, not in respect to the union of nature or the union of grace and holiness. God was always at Christ's right hand (Ps. 110:5), such that Christ was never truly alone (John 16:32). God did not leave his beloved Son (how could one subsistence of the divine essence forsake another subsistence of the same essence?). It was a "withdrawal of vision" not a "dissolution of union." Christ lacked the sense of divine love as he was overwhelmed by divine wrath and vengeance, but the Father's love was not truly extinguished. In scholastic terminology, Christ lost temporarily the "affection of advantage" but not the "affection of righteousness."[3]

As to the question of damnation, Turretin recognizes that many theologians have used condemnation and damnation somewhat interchangeably, but he argues that technically we should avoid the language of the latter—condemnation being a judicial sentence as opposed to the experience of damnation and despair in hell. "As he is properly said to be damned who in hell endures the punishment due to his own sins, this term cannot be applied to Christ, who never suffered for his own but for our sins; nor did he suffer in hell, but on earth."[4] Christ experienced pain that was hellish, and he bore the punishment of those deserving damnation. But he did not enter the place of the damned or suffer in hell as the damned do.

1 À Brakel, *The Christian's Reasonable Service*, 1.579.
2 À Brakel, *The Christian's Reasonable Service*, 1.580.
3 Turretin, *Elenctic Theology*, 2.354.
4 Turretin, *Elenctic Theology*, 2.364.

DAY 139

Death and Burial

Christianity is a religion irreducibly and uniquely fixated on the death of its Savior. Every Sunday, in every corner of the globe, Christians partake of the Lord's Supper and in so doing proclaim the Lord's death until he comes again (1 Cor. 11:26). We will have opportunity in the chapters ahead to think about Christ's death as an atonement for sin. It is worth reflecting here that Christ suffered on the cross not just for our sin but for our shame.

We tend to focus on the physical pain of crucifixion, and it was horrendous. It was an unbelievably cruel way to kill someone. You might hang on the cross for days before your heart finally gave out or until you couldn't get another breath and died of asphyxiation. It was a gruesome ordeal where naked criminals died in excruciating pain. Even many of the Romans spoke out against crucifixion as a hideous and barbaric instrument.

But the Gospels don't focus on any of that. Yes, Jesus suffered physical torment. But so did two other men on that hill, and so did hundreds of criminals who were crucified by Rome. In fact, what's physically remarkable about Jesus's death on the cross is that he died so quickly (Mark 15:44). The Gospels do not direct our gaze to the pain of the cross; they draw attention to the *shame* of the cross.

The abandonment of Jesus was comprehensive. Judas betrayed him. His three friends fell asleep in his hour of deepest need. A young man ran away naked into woods in the darkness of the night rather than have anything to do with Jesus. Peter denied him, the council schemed against him, and false witnesses spoke lies about him. The crowd cried out for Christ's death, and Pilate was too cowardly to stop them. He was laughed at by soldiers, mocked by the chief priests and scribes, derided by those passing by, and reviled by those who were crucified with him. Was there ever a man so utterly abandoned by friends, cheated by his enemies, and ridiculed by those who should have bowed to worship him? "He was despised and rejected by men, a man of sorrows and acquainted with grief; and as one from whom men hide their faces, he was despised, and we esteemed him not" (Isa. 53:3).

The creed tells us that Christ died *and* was buried. This may seem like an unnecessary tautology, but the burial should be seen as another aspect of his humiliation. The burial was not only a confirmation of Christ's death; it was an indication that Christ had received what men in their sins deserve. Like a man under the curse, he had returned to the dust (Gen. 3:19). The grave (*sheol* in the Old Testament) was the place of death, the place of corruption, the place where bodies go to decay (Ps. 16:10; cf. Acts 2:27, 31; 13:34–35). This was no resting place for the immortal King of glory.

Jesus's life was marked by suffering from start to finish. À Brakel says the first step in his suffering was prior to his baptism, the second step was from his baptism to Gethsemane, the third step was from Gethsemane to the cross, and the fourth step was his burial. "He, who prior to this had been mocked and despised of men, was now removed from their view as one unfit to be viewed by them."[1]

1 À Brakel, *The Christian's Reasonable Service*, 1.582–83.

⌂

DAY 140

Descent into Hell

No phrase in the Apostles' Creed has generated more controversy among evangelical Christians than the affirmation that Jesus "descended into hell." The phrase is not found in the earliest versions of the creed. It seems to have been first used around 390 and then not again until 650. Some early versions have "buried" but not "descended into hell." Others mention the descent but not the burial. The official Roman form of the creed has both, and Christians everywhere have been confessing the descent for almost all of church history. We should not dismiss the phrase lightly, even as we readily acknowledge that no human creed is infallible.

Three passages are often mentioned in connection with the phrase "descended into hell," but none of them should be used to defend a literal descent.

1. Ephesians 4:9 speaks of Christ descending into "the lower regions." The ESV translates the passage "the lower regions, the earth" instead of "the lower regions of the earth." The ESV rendering makes sense. The opposite of going up from earth into heaven is coming down from heaven to earth. The contrast is not with a descent into hell but with the incarnation.

2. According to 1 Peter 3:18–19, Christ preached to the spirits in prison. This is not a reference to the "harrowing of hell" (i.e., Christ freeing the souls in limbo in the underworld). Peter's argument is that Christ preached *through* Noah to the disobedient who lived in his day, that is, to those spirits who were alive then but are now in prison (3:20).

3. Likewise, 1 Peter 4:4–6 is not about Christ descending into Hades. The dead to whom Christ preached were not dead when Christ preached to them. The purpose in Christ's preaching is that the hearers would not be judged, and there is no evidence in Scripture to support postmortem repentance.

Jesus did not go to a literal underworld in the days between his death and resurrection. Jesus told the thief on the cross that they would be together that very day in paradise (Luke 23:46), a promise made difficult to deliver on if Jesus was on his way to hell. Plus it's hard to imagine Jesus crying out, "It is finished" (John 19:30), and, "Into your hands I commit my spirit" (Luke 23:46), if he had more suffering to endure in hell.

If Christ did not physically go into the underworld, how should we understand the language of the descent? Some believe "descended into hell" means nothing different than "he was buried." The different early versions of the creed might support this contention. Calvin argued, however, that "buried" and "descended" would not have both been accepted in the Roman form if they were redundant. The creed is such a compact statement; why waste a phrase saying the same thing again?

With good reason, many interpreters understand "descended into hell" to be a reference to the hellish torments Christ endured on the cross. This was the view of Calvin, Ursinus, and Turretin (among many others). "Surely no more terrible abyss can be conceived," writes Calvin, "than to feel yourself forsaken and estranged from God; and when you call upon him not to be heard."[1] As the Heidelberg Catechism explains, the phrase "descended into hell" is included "to assure me in times of personal crisis and temptation that Christ my Lord, by suffering unspeakable anguish, pain, and terror of soul, especially on the cross but also earlier, has delivered me from the anguish and torment of hell" (Q/A 44).

1 Calvin, *Institutes*, 2.16.11.

WEEK 29

DAY 141

Resurrection

Easter Sunday marks the movement from humiliation to exaltation in the work of Christ. During his earthly ministry, Jesus often predicted his resurrection, declaring himself to be the resurrection and the life (John 11:25) and announcing that he would lay his life down and take it up again (10:18; cf. 2:19–21). Jesus Christ rose from the dead by his own power.

But it was not by his power alone. The resurrection is frequently ascribed to the power of God (Acts 2:24, 32; 3:26; 5:30; 1 Cor. 6:14; Eph. 1:20) or more specifically to God the Father (Rom. 6:4; Gal. 1:1). Likewise, the work of the Spirit is implied in Romans 1:4 ("declared to be the Son of God in power according to the Spirit") and Romans 8:11 ("the Spirit of him who raised Jesus from the dead"). The resurrection took place according to the operation of each member of the Trinity.

Importantly, Christ's resurrection was more than a mere resuscitation of life. Jesus raised several persons from the dead (e.g., a young man; Jairus's daughter;

Lazarus). But none of these "resurrections" marked the turning point in history. We must ask the question: What makes Christ's resurrection different?

Six points.

1. Christ's body was raised incorruptible. Jesus will not die again. His body underwent a remarkable change (e.g., the disciples did not recognize him on the Emmaus Road). Christ's resurrected body could pass through walls and mysteriously appear or disappear. His body was not immaterial, but Christ's physicality had been adapted perfectly for spiritual use.

2. Through the resurrection, Christ became a life-giving Spirit (1 Cor. 15:45). Raised to life, he was now able to give the Holy Spirit to his disciples.

3. In fulfilling Israel's feasts by his death and resurrection (Lev. 25), Christ became the firstfruits of those who sleep (1 Cor. 15:20) and the firstborn from the dead (Col. 1:18; Rev. 1:5). Jesus's resurrection is often mentioned as an example of what awaits every member of Christ's body (Rom. 6:4–9; 8:11; 1 Cor. 6:14; 15:20–22; 2 Cor. 4:10–14; Col. 2:12; 1 Thess. 4:14).

4. The resurrection signified the accomplishment of Christ's mediatorial work on earth. Christ "was declared to be the Son of God in power according to the Spirit of holiness by his resurrection from the dead" (Rom. 1:4).

5. By his resurrection, Christ triumphed over death. Note carefully the wording in Acts 2:24: "God raised him up, loosing the pangs of death, because *it was not possible* for him to be held by it." The grave could not hold the Son of God because it had no claim on him. The wages of sin is death, but once sin is paid for, there is no obligation to pay the wages of sin. The resurrection announced that Christ's work on behalf of sinners was finished, and there was nothing left to pay.

6. Finally, the resurrection tells us that God's justice has been satisfied. Romans 4:25 says that Christ was raised for our justification. Like a convict being released from prison after his sentence has been fulfilled, the resurrection testifies that the penal and prescriptive requirements of the law have been paid for. Jesus lives, and so can we.

DAY 142

Ascension

Of all the aspects of Christ's work in his state of exaltation, the ascension is one of the most overlooked. And yet Christ's ascension is more prominent in Scripture than many realize. Luke describes the ascension in the most detail, first in his Gospel and then in Acts. Peter's Pentecost sermon is, in part, about the ascension and enthronement of Christ. Likewise, John's Gospel is full of references to the ascension of the Son of Man and the importance of Jesus returning to the Father.

The ascension is not simply about getting Jesus to heaven. It matters how Jesus ascended. He ascended locally (a real geographic place), visibly (in front of many witnesses), and bodily (not some ethereal disappearance). The manner in which Jesus ascended will be the manner in which he descends at the end of the age. The blessed appearing of our Lord and Savior will be an actual appearing—in the flesh, to the earth, witnessed by multitudes.

Just as important, the ascension is a further fulfillment and vindication of the triumph of the resurrection. It is no wonder that the ascension is highlighted throughout the New Testament as a necessary precursor to a number of blessings in this age of the Spirit. The ascension is linked to the giving of messianic gifts (Eph. 4:8–10), to the intercession of our high priest (Heb. 4:14–16), and to the subjection of all things under Christ's feet (1 Pet. 3:22). Because Jesus is our conquering King, he is positioned to gift us with the spoils of victory. Because Jesus is seated at the right hand of God the Father, he is able to plead his finished work on our behalf. And because Jesus is enthroned on high, he is able to rule over all things in heaven and on earth.

What, then, does the oft-overlooked ascension mean for us?

First, the ascension means that we have an advocate with the Father, Jesus Christ the righteous (1 John 2:1; cf. Rom. 8:34).

Second, the ascension means God's people are, in a manner of speaking, already in heaven. We set our minds on things that are above, because our lives are hidden with Christ who dwells above (Col. 3:2–3).

Third, the ascension means we can receive the gift of the Holy Spirit. Once ascended to heaven, Jesus sent another Helper (John 14:16; 16:7) to give us power from on high and to be with us forever.

Fourth, the ascension means human flesh sits enthroned in heaven. God has granted all power and authority to a man (Matt. 28:19; Eph. 1:21–22). Jesus Christ is exercising the dominion that human beings were made to have from the beginning (Gen. 1:28). The ruin of the first Adam is being undone by the reign of the second.

Because of Christ's ascension we know that the resurrection is real, the incarnation continues, Christ's humanity lives on in heaven, the Spirit of Jesus can live in our hearts, and a flesh-and-blood, divine human being rules the universe.

DAY 143

Session

Christ's session refers to his being seated in heaven at the Father's right hand. At his trial, Jesus predicted that he would sit at the right hand of power (Matt. 26:64). Peter made the session an important point in his sermons (Acts 2:33–36; 5:31; see also Eph. 1:20–22; Heb. 10:12; 1 Pet. 3:22; Rev. 3:21; 22:1). Psalm 110 is referenced more than any other Old Testament prophecy, and it makes Christ's session its central theme: "Sit at my right hand, until I make your enemies your footstool" (v. 1).

The session does not *make* Christ king. Rather, it represents the public inauguration of Christ in his kingly glory. Upon being seated in heaven, the administration of his reign and rule was formally committed to Christ. Considered as the divine Logos, Christ has always been at the right hand of God, working in accordance with the Father's omnipotent power. When considered as the incarnate mediator, however, Christ came at a moment in time to sit at the right hand of God. According to his divine nature, nothing new was bestowed upon Christ, but as the God-man, a new manifestation of power and a new installation of government was granted by virtue of his mediatorial work.

To be seated is not a literal statement, of course, because God has no right hand. We should not be concerned that Christ is sometimes said to be at the right hand (Rom. 8:34; 1 Pet. 3:22), is sometimes said to be standing (Acts 7:56), and is sometimes said to be walking (Rev. 2:1). Christ's session is a figure of speech, not an exact indication of personal geography.

But as a figure of speech, being seated signifies something important about the completion of Christ's atoning work. Jesus continues to exercise kingly rule, priestly intercession, and prophetical speech, but the work of satisfaction, upon which all the rest is based, has been accomplished. Hebrews 1 tells us that after making purification for sins, Jesus "sat down at the right hand of the Majesty on high, having become as much superior to angels as the name he has inherited is more excellent than theirs" (vv. 3–4). The imagery is striking. Picture an attorney making his closing arguments to the jury, and then after a crescendo of rhetoric he says, "I rest my case," and sits back down next to his notes. Or think of a mom who has had no time for herself all day. She's made meals, cleaned the house, changed diapers, folded clothes, helped with homework, played in the backyard, raced to the grocery store, and now finally has the kids snoozing in their beds. She walks wearily down the stairs, and for the first time since she woke up sixteen hours before, she sits down. Being seated, in both examples, is more than an act of rest. It represents completion. All that was needed has been accomplished.

That's why it's thrilling to think that Jesus is *seated* at the right hand of God. His saving work is finished. He accomplished all that was necessary for our salvation. And having proved himself to be the victor over sin, death, and the devil, it is granted to him to sit—not in any old place, but at the place of honor and exaltation at God's right hand. All things have been placed under his feet (Eph. 1:20–22). All authority in heaven and on earth has been given to him (Matt. 28:18). Therefore, Jesus can sit down.

Return

Christ's exaltation is to be located not only in all that he has accomplished in the past but also in the final act of judgment that is still to come. Jesus will return to earth in the same way he was taken up into heaven (Acts 1:11). His return will not be spiritual, or in secret. He will come visibly and bodily as King and Judge. The New Testament makes much of the fact that Christ has been appointed by God to judge the living and the dead (Acts 10:42). The Father has given all judgment to the Son (John 5:22; cf. 5:27).

Each stage in the state of exaltation is indispensable for the others. In Matthew 24, Jesus describes the Son of Man coming on the clouds of heaven with power and great glory (v. 30). In the next chapter he depicts the Son of Man sitting on his glorious throne, gathering all the nations, and separating people as a shepherd separates sheep from goats (25:31–32). Likewise, Acts 17:31 informs us that God has fixed a day in which he will judge the world in righteousness by a man whom he has appointed; and of this he has given assurance to all by raising him from the dead (Acts 17:31). The resurrection, ascension, session, and return are mutually reinforcing aspects of Christ's power and glory.

There are three main Greek words used to describe Christ's return.

- *Parousia* is the word for "coming." Jesus uses parousia to describe his return (Matt. 24:3, 27, 37, 39). Likewise, Paul refers to "his coming" (1 Cor. 15:23). This is the most common way the New Testament speaks of Christ's return (1 Thess. 2:19; 3:13; 4:15; 5:23; 2 Thess. 2:1; James 5:7, 8; 2 Pet. 3:4).

- *Apocalypsis* is the word for "revealing." At his return, the Lord Jesus will be revealed from heaven with his mighty angels (2 Thess. 1:7). The event itself can be described as the "revelation of Jesus Christ" (1 Pet. 1:7, 13). Importantly, it is the event where Christ's glory will be fully revealed (4:13).

- *Epiphaneia* is the word for "appearing." Jesus's return is described as "the appearance of his coming" (2 Thess. 2:8) and as "the appearing of our Lord Jesus Christ" (1 Tim. 6:14). God's people are those "who have loved his appearing" (2 Tim. 4:8) and those who are "waiting for our blessed hope, the appearing of the glory of our great God and Savior Jesus Christ" (Titus 2:13).

These three words remind us that we are waiting not merely for "God to show up" or for "the end of the world." We are waiting for the man Christ Jesus. He is, of course, no ordinary man. He is the God-man. But it is significant that judgment has been given to a man, for it means that the judge will be visible, and he will be one of us. That all judgment has been given to the Son also means that the mediator will be our judge, and the disbelieving will have to face the one they rejected.

The Lord Jesus is not to be trifled with. We must never skip his humiliation to get to his exaltation, but neither should we focus only on the state of humiliation as if this state were not meant to give way to the now-and-forever state of exaltation.

DAY 145

Prophet

Since at least the time of Calvin, theologians have spoken of Christ's work as fulfilling three offices. Christ simply means "anointed one," and in the Old Testament three types of office bearers were anointed with oil: prophets, priests, and kings.[1] For example, Elisha the prophet was anointed (1 Kings 19:16), as was Aaron the high priest (Ex. 29:7), and David the king (1 Sam. 16:13).

Jesus, for his part, was anointed not with oil but with the Holy Spirit beyond measure (John 3:34).

The three offices have other theological resonances as well. One can argue that man in his original state was a kind of prophet (endowed with knowledge and understanding), a kind of priest (set apart in righteousness and holiness), and a kind of king (meant to cultivate the garden and to exercise dominion on the earth). Likewise, Turretin argues that man in his fallen state has a threefold misery: ignorance (for which he needs a prophetic word from the Lord), guilt (for which he needs a priestly sacrifice), and tyranny (from which he needs a benevolent king to set him free).[2]

The prophetic office combined a passive and an active function. Passively, the prophet received divine revelation (in dreams, angelic visitation, and verbal communication). Actively, he revealed to others what God had given to him. The prophet's role was broad: he warned and admonished, he comforted and encouraged, he rebuked, he called for repentance, he gave assurance of grace, he made known God's will, he announced God's commands, he spoke of coming blessing and threatened coming judgment.

Although Christ is not wholly unlike the prophets of old, he exercises his office in three unique ways. (1) Christ exercises the prophetic office *infallibly* as one having total authority and unerring speech. (2) Christ exercises the prophetic office *immediately* with an authority that is direct and personal. (3) Christ exercises the prophetic office *unceasingly* by his Spirit through the teaching ministry of the church.

In fulfilling all these functions, Christ showed himself to be the prophet God's people had been waiting for (Deut. 18:18). During his earthly ministry Christ exercised a prophetic ministry by teaching the truth, preaching the gospel, and predicting the future. One of the marks of these last days is that God now speaks to us by his Son (Heb. 1:2). The fullness and finality of his redemption are connected to the fullness and finality of his revelation. We need no more prophets because Christ continues his work as the prophet par excellence. "Christ executes the office of a prophet in revealing to the church, in all ages, by his Spirit and word, the whole will of God in all things concerning edification and salvation" (WLC Q/A 43).

1 Calvin, *Institutes*, 2.15.2.
2 Turretin, *Elenctic Theology*, 2.393.

DAY 146

Priest

Priests in the Old Testament were mediators. If prophets represented God to the people, priests represented the people to God. The Levitical priests were taken from among men and appointed by God. They were given the task of acting on behalf of men. Their work was to offer gifts and sacrifices for sins (Heb. 5:1–9).

Although Christ fulfilled the work of the Levitical priesthood, the New Testament stresses that Christ was a priest after the order of Melchizedek (Ps. 110; Heb. 7). Turretin highlights several differences between the two priesthoods. One came from Aaron, the other from Melchizedek. One was associated with the Mosaic administration, the other with Abraham. One had a derivative power, the other had power in itself. One was temporal and of finite value, the other eternal and of infinite value. In short, the two differ in persons, in institution, in efficacy, in perfection, and in duration.[1]

Christ's work as priest chiefly consists of two things: atonement and intercession. "Christ executes the office of a priest, in his once offering himself as a sacrifice without spot to God, to be a reconciliation for the sins of his people; and in making continual intercession for them" (WLC Q/A 44). We will look at the atonement in more detail later, so we will focus here on the priestly work of intercession.

The nature of Christ's ongoing intercession is manifold. Christ not only prays for us; his perpetual presence in heaven is itself part of his mediatorial work (Heb. 7:25; 8:1–4; 9:24). Christ is also in heaven in a judicial capacity to be an advocate with the Father (1 John 2:1) and to turn away the accusations of the accuser (Zech. 3:1–2; Rom. 8:33–34). In all this, Christ's atonement and his intercession are inextricably linked. The suffering and death of Christ were "preparatory and antecedent to his intercession."[2] Suffering was the part of his priestly work done on earth; intercession is the part of his priesthood to be performed in heaven. Christ procured salvation by his suffering; he continues to apply it by his intercession.

Christ also ministers to us as a sympathetic high priest (Heb. 2:18; 4:15). We should not equate Christ's sympathy with the notion that the Son of God is weeping in heaven for our sakes. Any notion of Christ's continued suffering undermines the completed nature of his atoning work and confuses the state of exaltation with the state of humiliation. The sympathy of Christ is not the same as contemporary notions of sentimentality. Interestingly, Hebrews doesn't actually say Christ sympathizes with us, but with *our weaknesses*. The point is that because of the Son's identification with his brothers, he can help us. The emphasis is not on Jesus feeling the right thing in heaven. Rather, the good news is that because he has felt what we feel, he will surely come to our aid.

Our comfort is not that Christ is still bound up in our sorrow, but that because he suffered for our sake we can be caught up into his glory. Suffering itself is not sacred. Christ sanctified suffering because he suffered with a purpose. He suffered to save the lost. The aim of Christ's ongoing priestly intercession is not for Christ to continue to participate in the life of suffering on earth, but for believers to participate in the life of God in heaven.

1 Turretin, *Elenctic Theology*, 2.406–8.
2 Turretin, *Elenctic Theology*, 2.406.

King

Jesus Christ is the only king and head of the church. That is to say, there is no earthly magistrate and no supreme pontiff who rules over the church as sovereign, not even in a derivative sense. Christ is King, and there is no room on the throne for any other.

Christ exercises his kingly office in three ways: by establishing and governing the church, by saving and sustaining his elect people, and by taking vengeance upon those who do not know God and do not obey the gospel (WLC Q/A 45). Christ rules as a king of law, of love, and of lordly recompense. He calls the church out of the world, giving them officers, rules, and censures. He saves the elect, rewarding their obedience, correcting their faults, and restraining their enemies. And he judges the rebellious, executing his just wrath upon those who should have been his loyal subjects.

We should say something here about the relationship between the kingdom and the church. The two are not identical, but they cannot be separated.

We can think of the church as a kind of outpost or embassy of the kingdom. An embassy is a national outpost dwelling in a foreign land. The embassy, while it wants to dwell peacefully in the foreign land, exists to advance the interests of another country. So the church, dwelling on earth in various nations around the world, exists to advance the interest of another kingdom, a heavenly kingdom.

The church is the place where you expect to see the values and rules of the kingdom honored and upheld. The church is supposed to be the outpost of heaven on earth, which is why the poor should be provided for *in the church*, and why the wicked and unbelieving don't belong *in the church*. The reason the church is not mainly about societal transformation is the same reason the church does not throw sinners into the lake of fire. The heaven on earth we seek to create is the heavenly reality among God's people in the church.

Life in the church looks forward to the eternal life where God's redemptive presence will be enjoyed to the fullest. In the age to come, the kingdom will no longer be something that has broken in here or there; it will be all in. Think of the good news from Revelation 11:15: "The kingdom of the world has become the kingdom of our Lord and of his Christ, and he shall reign forever and ever." The kingdom of God is the heavenly world breaking into the our earthly existence. Do not think of the kingdom as a realm to which we are going as much as a reality that is coming to us. Both now and in the future, the kingdom comes when and where the King is known.[1]

---

1   These last few paragraphs are adapted from DeYoung, *The Lord's Prayer*, 40–41. Used by permission.

Christ's Kingdom

Christ's kingdom can be distinguished in three ways.

First, there is the *regnum potentiae*, the kingdom of power. This is the dominion of Jesus Christ over the universe, the providential and judicial administration of all things that Christ exercises by virtue of being the eternal Son of God.

Second, we can speak of the *regnum gratiae*, the kingdom of grace. This refers to Christ's reign over his saved people, the spiritual kingship that Christ exercises by virtue of being our mediator and the head of the church.

Finally, there is the *regnum gloriae*, the kingdom of glory. This is Christ's dominion in the age to come. The kingdom of glory is the kingdom of grace made perfect and complete.

In an absolute sense, the kingdom is one. We should not think of these distinctions crassly as three different nations. But the distinctions are important. As God, Christ rules over the kingdom of power, to which all creatures belong. As mediator, he rules over the kingdom of grace on earth, to which the elect belong. And as conqueror, he rules over the kingdom of glory in heaven, to which angels and the redeemed belong. To be sure, there is not one square inch in all the universe about which Christ does not cry out, "This is mine!" And yet, Christ does not reign over every square inch in the same way.

One reason for emphasizing these distinctions is to make sure that we are telling the right story when it comes to the kingdom. In explaining the petition "Your kingdom come" (Matt. 6:10), the Westminster Larger Catechism instructs us to "pray that the kingdom of sin and Satan may be destroyed, the gospel propagated throughout the world . . . the church furnished with all gospel officers and ordinances . . . that the ordinances of Christ may be purely dispensed, and made effectual to the converting of those that are yet in their sins, and the confirming, comforting, and building up those that are already converted: that Christ would rule in our hearts here, and hasten the time of his second coming, and our reigning with him forever" (Q/A 191). The catechism gives us a magnificent prayer for the growth, strength, and health of the church.

But that's not the end of the answer. Here's the last line of WLC 191: ". . . and that [Christ] would be pleased so to exercise the kingdom of his power in all the world, as may best conduce to these ends." Notice the ecclesial logic of the Larger Catechism. Christ rules over all things for the good of the church. The kingdom of power is subservient in purpose to the kingdom of grace (giving way to the kingdom of glory), *not* the other way around.[1]

This means the kingdom story we are telling is not the story of Christ saving his people so that they might change the world, transform the culture, or reclaim a nation. Instead, the story is of Christ so ruling over the nations of the world that the church might be built up. To be sure, we will be salt and light in a dark and decaying world, but the prayer the Westminster divines would have us pray is for God to so rule over the world *for the sake* of the church. We pray, then, for the success of the kingdom of power, but to the end that the kingdom of grace may flourish and the kingdom of glory may be brought near.

---

1 It is true that the catechism speaks of the church as "countenanced and maintained by the civil magistrate." Even if this implies a more expansive role for the state in the affairs of the church, the catechism still sees the kingdom of power as serving the purposes of the kingdom of grace.

Introducing the Atonement

We now turn to one of the great themes in all the Bible: Christ's atoning work for sinners. Here are five introductory comments.

1. *Christ's work of atonement is an aspect of his priestly work.* "For every high priest chosen from among men is appointed to act on behalf of men in relation to God, to offer gifts and sacrifices for sins" (Heb. 5:1). One could argue that of the three offices Christ fulfilled, the priestly office is the most essential—not more important, but more emphasized, and more central to the other two. His prophetic work was in large part announcing his priestly work, and the completion of his priestly work is the basis for his enthronement as King.

2. *Christ's work of atonement is primarily objective and only secondarily subjective.* That is to say, the purpose of Christ's death on the cross is not first of all to give us personal transformation. True, there is a wonderful subjective element that comes as a result of the cross, but the purpose of the atonement was to accomplish something objective. The priests did not offer sacrifices in order to effect something in the worshiper. They offered sacrifices to do something about sin. The work of the atonement is objective, to be subjectively appropriated by faith.

3. *The atonement is based on the active and passive obedience of Christ.* We are not talking about different temporal periods of Christ's work, but different aspects of his work. The distinction is between all that Christ did to observe the law (active obedience) and all that he did in discharging the debts that the law demanded (passive obedience). In his active obedience, Christ offered complete, intentional, heartfelt obedience to God's commands (Rom. 5:12–21; Heb. 4:14–16; 7:25–26; 10:1–5). In his passive obedience, Christ endured the suffering we deserve as sinners under the curse (Matt. 27:46; Luke 23:39–46; Phil. 2:7–8; Heb. 5:7–10). In short, Christ fulfilled all the prescriptive and penal aspects of the law.

4. *The motivation for the atonement is not one thing but many things.* Christ's sacrificial death on the cross was motivated by God's love (John 3:16; Rom. 5:8; 1 John 4:10), by God's justice (Isa. 53:10; Matt. 26:42; 2 Cor. 5:21), and by God's good pleasure (Gal. 1:4; Col. 1:19–20). We are right to emphasize any one of these motivations, so long as we do not elevate one at the expense of the others. When it comes to the atonement specifically or to the will of God more broadly, God's love, God's justice, and God's good pleasure are always complementary, and never competing, aspects of the divine character.

5. *Christ's work of atonement is at the heart of the gospel and the irreducible minimum of the apostolic message of salvation.* From the beginning of the Gospels, Jesus is announced as the one who will save his people from their sins (Matt. 1:21). Three times he will predict his death and resurrection. No other "biography" spends a third to half of its material on the subject's last week. Clearly we are meant to focus on the cross and the empty tomb as the climax of redemptive history. So important is the atonement that Paul's preaching can be summarized as "Christ crucified" (1 Cor. 1:23). There is more we can say about the good news besides the atonement, but we must never say less.

The Necessity of the Atonement

Louis Berkhof outlines three basic views on the necessity of the atonement.[1]

The first view holds that the atonement was *not necessary*. For Scotus, the atonement was unnecessary because it was arbitrarily chosen by God. For others, it was unnecessary because sin did not need to be punished (Socinus) and because God could have forgiven sins without judicial satisfaction (Grotius). The atonement may have been a moral necessity, but it was not a legal necessity (Schleiermacher).

The second view maintains that the atonement was *relatively necessary*. That is, the atonement was not inherently necessary, but it was necessary according to the divine decree. God determined that sin would be forgiven based on no condition other than a perfect atoning sacrifice. Many of the most important theologians (e.g., Athanasius, Augustine, Aquinas, Luther, Calvin, Bavinck) have favored this view, insisting that the atonement was only relatively or hypothetically necessary.

The third view argues for the *absolute necessity* of the atonement. According to this view, God's holiness and man's sinfulness demand that sin must be punished with an atoning sacrifice. Atonement is not just the way God has decreed to forgive sin; it is the *only* way sin can be forgiven. This view goes back to Irenaeus and (more prominently) to Anselm. Many Reformed theologians (e.g., Turretin, Owen, Voetius, Mastricht) have held to this view as well.

Berkhof highlights several reasons in support of the absolute necessity of the atonement. (1) God repeatedly says he will by no means clear the guilty. (2) The immutability of the moral law means punishment is necessary when the law's demands are not met. (3) God decreed death as the penalty of disobedience in the covenant of works, and God cannot be untrue to this statement of moral fact.

(4) Sin is lawlessness, making us debtors to the law and in need of a personal and vicarious atonement. (5) That God should send his beloved and only begotten Son suggests there was no other way for sin to be dealt with except by an atoning sacrifice.

There are two main objections to the idea that God demands satisfaction in order to forgive sin. First, it seems that the necessity of the atonement makes God less gracious than man. If it is a glory to overlook an offense (Prov. 19:11), shouldn't God simply determine to forgive and forget man's sin against him? The problem with this argument is that God is a judge, and in his official capacity he must follow the law. Moreover, our ability to overlook the faults of others depends upon God's eventual justice and the exercise of his wrath (Rom. 12:14–21). Finally, we should not pit God's justice against his love. It is because of the love of God that the atonement is even possible (John 3:16; Rom. 5:8; 1 John 4:10).

The second objection to the idea of divine satisfaction implies a schism in the Trinitarian life of God. This objection, however, ignores the intra-Trinitarian agreement expressed in the *pactum salutis*. The Father and the Son exhibit the most perfect harmony in the eternal planning and in the temporal carrying out of the atonement. The Son willingly gave up his life (John 10:18). The atonement was necessary because of the holiness of God and the gravity of sin, not because God the Father was implacably opposed to God the Son.

1 This section tracks with and summarizes Berkhof, *Systematic Theology*, 368–72.

WEEK 31

DAY 151

The Perfection of the Atonement

When we speak of the perfection of the atonement, we mean that nothing was lacking in Christ's sacrifice for sin and no one can contribute in any way to his work of satisfaction. The precious blood of Christ is without spot or blemish (1 Pet. 1:19). To think any angelic or human intermediary could contribute to the efficacy of the atonement is a perversion of the gospel. We cannot admit Mary to be a coredemptrix or comediatrix, even if her mediatorial role is said to be subordinate to Christ's. There is only one mediator between God and men, the man Christ Jesus (1 Tim. 2:5). Christ's atoning sacrifice was once for all, never to be repeated, as unique and perfect as the Son of God is unique and perfect (Heb. 9:25–26; 10:1–14).

The perfection of the atonement, however, seems to be at odds with Paul's contention that he was "filling up what is lacking in Christ's afflictions" (Col. 1:24). Surely Paul does not mean that the atonement was inadequate in some way, for the whole chapter is about the preeminence of Christ's person and work. When Christ said on the cross, "It is finished" (John 19:30), we can take him at his word. The "lacking" must be referring to something other than the work of atonement itself.

One option is to consider that the church has a definite measure of suffering to fill up, a kind of quota appointed by God that must be completed for Christ's suffering to be considered complete. After all, it seems that there is a fixed number of martyrs waiting to be filled up (Rev. 6:11). Moreover, we know that persecution against the church is also persecution against Christ (Acts 9:4). So Paul may be saying in Colossians 1:24 that his suffering is one part of contributing to the appointed whole.

And yet Paul doesn't say that the body of Christ fills up an appointed number of afflictions. Rather, Paul says he is filling up what is lacking in Christ's afflictions *for the sake* of Christ's body (i.e., the church). The option detailed in the last paragraph is not wrong, but it may be too broad if we take "affliction" to be a generic kind of suffering. The "filling up what is lacking" refers specifically to the personal presentation of the gospel in the midst of suffering *for* the gospel. Indeed, the rest of Colossians 1 puts verse 24 in a missions context. Paul has a stewardship from God to make the word of God fully known (1:25) and is struggling with all his energy as he powerfully proclaims the gospel (1:28–29). Just as Epaphroditus filled up by his personal presence what was lacking in the Macedonian gift, so Paul fills up the afflictions of Christ by suffering for the cause of the gospel among the Colossians.

In short, the work of Christ is not lacking in quality or quantity. Afflictions in Colossians 1:24 are not used of redemptive atonement, but of suffering more broadly, and of suffering as a messenger of the gospel more specifically. There is no imperfection in the atonement. What is lacking are people to present the afflictions of Christ to the world—no matter the cost.

DAY 152

Theories of the Atonement 1

Over the centuries, theologians have articulated several different theories or models of the atonement. Most of the models get something right, though some are much closer to the mark than others. We will look at ten models over two chapters, concluding with penal substitution, which is at the heart of the atonement and the "theory" that holds all the biblical insights of the other theories together.

Recapitulation theory (Irenaeus). According to this model, Christ lived out all the stages of human life in such a way that his life of obedience compensated for Adam's life of disobedience. Christ obeyed the Father, reversing the curse in Adam and setting us free from the tryanny of the devil. This understanding of the atonement is right in what it affirms, though there is nothing about the satisfaction of divine wrath and little about Christ bearing the penalty of sin.

Ransom to Satan (Origen). In this popular and well attested model, Christ's death is seen as a ransom to purchase man's freedom. The atonement is directed toward Satan, who was duped—like a fish is fooled by bait on a hook—into thinking the cross was his triumph when it was his defeat (think of the sacrifice of Aslan made to the White Witch in Narnia). The contemporary version is usually referred to as *Christus Victor*, meaning Christ is the one who vanquished the powers of hell. While this is certainly one important aspect of the atonement, the theory gives too much power to Satan in making him the object of the payment.

Commercial theory (Anselm). Anselm's theology of the atonement represented a major step forward in biblical reflection. In Anselm's thought, Christ's death brought infinite honor to God. In turn, God gave Christ a reward, which (needing no reward himself) he passed on to man in the form of forgiveness and eternal life. Importantly, Anselm understood that the atonement was directed toward God and that man's main problem was dishonoring God. And yet the nature of the transaction is somewhat vague. Christ's death is offered as a tribute—rooted in God's honor instead of God's justice—but it is not clearly a vicarious suffering for the penalty of sin.

Moral influence theory (Abelard). For the medieval theologian Peter Abelard, Christ's death showed God's great love, which in turn gave man the impetus to repent and believe. In Abelard's theory man's main problem is spiritual neediness, with the atonement directed toward man in order to convince him of God's love. This makes Christ's atoning work strictly voluntary rather than a necessity according to the logic of divine justice.

Example theory (Socinus). According to Faustus Socinus, the sixteenth-century anti-Trinitarian heretic opposed by every branch of the church, Christ's death was an example of obedience and piety that can inspire man to the same virtues. The Socinian view of the atonement is not only Pelagian in its conception; it devalues the deity of Christ and calls into question the necessity of the incarnation itself. If man only needs to be inspired, why did God have to become man, and why a violent death on the cross? Socinianism fails where all man-directed atonement theories fail: it underestimates the plight of sinners, overestimates the power of human ability, and does nothing to account for the holiness and justice of God.

DAY 153

Theories of the Atonement 2

We come to five other theories or models of the atonement, the last of which best articulates what the death of Christ accomplished.

Governmental theory (Grotius). In this understanding of the atonement, often associated with the seventeenth-century political theorist Hugo Grotius, the cross demonstrates that the law must be upheld and sin must be punished. Christ's death is not a vicarious sacrifice but a way for God to uphold his moral governance of the universe. Grotius so emphasized God's rectoral justice (maintaining moral rectitude) to the exclusion of God's retributive justice (inflicting penalties on those who fail to live by this moral rectitude) that it is hard to know upon what basis Christ specifically (as opposed to someone else) had to die.

Mystical theory (Schleiermacher). Like the moral influence theory, the atonement, in this model, is meant to effect a change in man. Unlike the moral theory, which is merely ethical in inspiration, the mystical theory argues that a change was wrought in man deep in his subconciousness. Like the liberal theology he inspired, Friedrich Schleiermacher's theory had no real place for man's inherent guilt and depravity.

Vicarious repentance (Campbell). According to the nineteenth-century Scottish theologian John McLeod Campbell, the atonement represented Christ's identification with us. Christ lived a life of self-sacrifice, identified with us by suffering on the cross, and repented on our behalf, thereby leading God to be merciful to sinners. The problem with Campbell's theology is that it makes mercy a necessary attribute of God and justice an arbitrary one. And yet justice that can be set aside (rather than satisfied) is not really justice, and mercy that must be administered is not really mercy.

Elect and effective (Barth). According to Karl Barth, since Christ assumed human nature, his death must have been intended for all those with that nature. Similarly, because God decreed to make himself known to the world in Christ, the atonement must be effective in all people. Barth and his followers are notoriously difficult to pin down when it comes to the universalist implications of their views, but it is hard to see how the incarnation and the atonement don't effectively save everyone upon a Barthian understanding.

Penal substitution (Protestant Reformers). This view was emphasized by Calvin and Luther, but traces can also be found in Justin Martyr and Tertullian. It continues to be the dominant understanding among confessional Reformed Christians and among other evangelicals. On this view, Christ's death was a substitutionary sacrifice meant to satisfy the demands of God's justice. Man's main problem is depravity, and thus the atonement is directed toward God as a payment for the law's prescriptive and penal demands. This understanding of the atonement does not eliminate every aspect of the other views, but it most fully explains the biblical data for the meaning of the cross. The atonement may be more than a substitutionary sacrifice, but it is not less. None of the other theories make sense if Christ did not die in our place to assuage the wrath of God. As John Stott puts it, "Substitution is not a 'theory of the atonement.' Nor is it even an additional image to take its place as an option alongside the others. It is rather the essence of each image and the heart of the atonement itself."[1] In penal substitutionary atonement we find hope for sinners, the heart of the gospel, and the good news without which all other news regarding the cross is null and void.

1   Stott, *The Cross of Christ*, 199.

DAY 154

Obedience and Conquest

Having outlined ten different theories or models of the atonement we now turn to examine in more detail the nature of the atonement. As we've already seen, the atonement is not one thing, but many things. What it accomplished was not singular, but manifold. In exploring the nature of the atonement we will see that many insights from the various models emphasize important aspects of Christ's work.

The atonement is an expression of Christ's *obedience*. Turretin puts it well:

> Some restrict [satisfaction] to the sufferings or punishments which Christ endured for us. . . . But the common opinion and the one received in our churches is that the satisfaction of Christ, which is imputed to us for righteousness before God, embraces not only the sufferings which he endured either in his life or at his death, but also the obedience of his whole life, or the just and holy actions by which he perfectly fulfilled the demands of the law in our place.[1]

We see the importance of Christ's work of obedience in many places in Scripture. We read of the obedience of the one man (Rom. 5:19), his fulfilling the righteous requirement in the law (8:3–4), and his obedience unto death (Phil. 2:8). There is satisfaction in Christ's righteousness (Rom. 1:17; 3:21; 5:8; Phil. 3:9). The reason Christ can be sin for us is that he knew no sin (2 Cor. 5:21). Jesus Christ is the Lord our righteousness (Jer. 23:6).

The obedience of the Son of God is a key element of Paul's second-Adam Christology (Rom. 5; 1 Cor. 15) and an important theme in the Gospels. Luke, for example, pays careful attention to the ways in which Jesus and his family strictly adhere to the law. Luke also presents Jesus as the son of Adam (Luke 3) who fulfilled the covenant of works by passing the test of temptation that Adam (and Israel) failed to keep (Luke 4).

The atonement can also be seen as the manifestation of Christ's *conquest* over the devil. This is sometimes called *Christus Victor* after Gustaf Aulen's book by that title published (in English) in 1931. Aulen reinterpreted the ransom theory as Christ's victory over all the powers of evil (i.e., sin, death, and the devil). The *Christus Victor* model can be problematic insofar as some advocates use the theory to supplant traditional models of substitution and propitiation, but Christ's conquest over the forces of evil is certainly one (often overlooked) aspect of his atoning work. The Old Testament makes much of Yahweh's conquest over the gods of Egypt (Ex. 12:12; 15:1–21). The Psalms often celebrate the trampling of God's enemies (Pss. 44:5; 47:3; 92:8–11). The Scriptures promise that the Messiah will crush the head of the serpent (Gen. 3:15) and receive the spoils of victory (Isa. 53:12). Likewise, the New Testament speaks of Christ's work as overpowering Beelzebul (Luke 18:15–20), destroying the works of the devil (1 John 3:8), disarming the rulers and authorities and putting them to open shame, by triumphing over them (Col. 2:15).

Though the final conquest remains, the great dragon has already been defeated and thrown down (Rev. 12:8–9). There is a great battle to be fought, but the final victory is secure. Christ has routed the devil and his army.

---

1 Turretin, *Elenctic Theology*, 2.445.

Reconciliation and Redemption

The English word *atonement* was coined by Tyndale to signify how estranged parties are brought together (at-one-ment). The nature of Christ's work is inescapably concerned with *reconciliation*. God is reconciling the world in Christ by not counting our sins against us (2 Cor. 5:18–21). This reconciliation is first of all personal and vertical (in relation to God), but also moves horizontally toward others (Eph. 2:11–22). God's work of reconciliation is ultimately cosmic in scope (Col. 1:19–20).

Importantly, the New Testament never speaks of God being reconciled. That is to say, the "barriers" are all on our side. Yes, God's justice is a "barrier" in a way, but it's not as if God and sinners must each give a little and learn to love each other. We are told to go and be reconciled to God (2 Cor. 5:20) in the same way Jesus tells the sinner to leave his gift at the altar and go be reconciled to his brother, meaning: "God has something legitimate against me. I must go and seek reconciliation." God is always the reconciler, not strictly speaking the reconciled.

We also need to be clear that the atonement did not make God love us (Rom. 5:8). The hostility is ours; the movement toward reconciliation was all from God. In one sense, our reconciliation was accomplished at the death of Christ (5:10), though we must personally receive it (5:11). Reconciliation is not an inward state but an objective change in our status before God.

The atonement is also a work of redemption. *Redemption* is an economic term, meaning to purchase, to buy back, or to set free. In the Old Testament, redemption is often used with reference to the exodus from Egypt (Ex. 6:6; Deut. 7:8), but the language is eventually used more broadly to refer to divine deliverance and salvation. "Fear not, for I have redeemed you; I have called you by name, you are mine" (Isa. 43:1). As Hosea bought back Gomer from the auction block after she had prostituted herself, so the Lord purchases his people from their bondage to sin and the devil.

The New Testament also underscores the importance of our redemption. Christ has freed us from our sins (Rev. 1:5–6) and redeemed us from the curse of the law (Gal. 3:13). We have been rescued from the domain of darkness (Col. 1:13) and redeemed from an empty way of life (1 Pet. 1:18).

Finally, we should note that the purchase of our freedom was not free. We were bought with a price (1 Cor. 6:20). And over and over we are told that the price was the blood of Christ. We have redemption through his blood (Eph. 1:7). God purchased the church with his blood (Acts 20:28). Considering the heinousness of our sin, the sufferings of Christ, and the promised blessings we enjoy now (and are yet to come), it is no wonder that the redeeming blood of Christ is lauded, above all, as "precious" (1 Pet. 1:18–19).

WEEK 32

DAY 156

Sacrifice and Satisfaction

We've already seen that penal substitution is at the heart of Christ's work on the cross, so it's no surprise that sacrifice and satisfaction are key concepts when considering the nature of the atonement. If reconciliation is a relational term, and redemption is an economic term, then sacrifice and satisfaction are cultic terms. Cultic here does not mean something evil or something heterodox. The word *cultus* has to do with religious ritual and liturgy. Sacrifice and satisfaction come from the world of Old Testament worship.

Jesus Christ is not just a *sacrifice*; he is a substitutionary sacrifice. In laying down his life for his friends (John 15:13), Jesus did more than give himself up, being willing to die so that others can live. Many heroes past and present have done the same. What made Jesus's sacrifice unique is that he became a curse for us (Gal. 3:13). The work of the high priest was to offer gifts and offer sacrifices for sin (Heb. 5:1; 8:3). But Christ is the best and true and final high priest because through the eternal Spirit he offered himself without blemish to God (9:14).

Time and again we are told that Christ died in the place of sinners. Christ died for our sins (1 Cor. 15:3), gave himself for our sins (Gal. 1:4), and bore our sins in his body on the tree (1 Pet. 2:24). Christ gave his life as a ransom for many (Mark 10:45; cf. 2 Tim. 2:6). Christ loved the church and gave himself up for her (Eph. 5:25). As the apostle Paul, the chief of sinners, puts it, "the Son of God . . . loved me and gave himself for me" (Gal. 2:20).

Christ's death was also a *satisfaction*. Think of the gratification of a well-made meal or a thirst-quenching drink. Better yet, think of a punishment incurred and a payment made. Satisfaction is God's delight in Christ's atoning death. Like the sacrifices of the Old Testament, Christ's death was a pleasing aroma to God (Lev. 1:9, 13, 17). God takes no pleasure in the blood of bulls and goats in and of themselves, but only in what they prefigured (Eph. 5:2). The death of Christ is enough to win for us appeasement and approval. Sin is lawlessness (1 John 3:4), but because of Christ's death, God is faithful and *just* to forgive us our sins and cleanse us from all unrighteousness (1:9). Forgiveness is what we *deserve* in Christ because Christ's death was a substitutionary sacrifice that satisfied all the Father's righteous demands. The atoning work of Christ is like the "very good" of Genesis 1:31—a "well done" in which God rejoices, and therefore so can we.

DAY 157

Expiation and Propitiation

The final two words to describe the nature of the atonement go together. Although some liberal theologians have privileged the notion of *expiation* above *propitiation*, both concepts are biblical, and neither should be used to cancel out the other.

Expiation is the work of Christ to cover our sins, to expunge our guilt, and to remove our transgressions from us. We can think of expiation as God's exit strategy for sin. It is a general term referring to the cleansing power of the atonement. Christ's sacrifice purged away sin (Heb. 1:3), did away with sin (9:26), and took away sin (10:4). Jesus is the Lamb of God who takes away the sins of the world (John 1:29).

If *expiation* is a general and moral term, *propitiation* is personal and relational. *Propitiation* is used in the New Testament to describe the pacifying, placating, or appeasing of God's wrath. An easy way to remember the term is that in propitiation God is made pro-us. Unlike expiation, propitiation has a relational component to it. Christ's death not only removed the moral stain of sin; it also removed the personal offense of sin.

The English word *propitiation* comes from the *hilasmos* word group in Greek and almost always refers in the ancient world (when applied to God) to appeasing or averting divine anger. The root word is used several times in the New Testament—as *hilasmos* (1 John 2:2; 4:10), as *hilaskomai* (Luke 18:13; Heb. 2:17), and as *hilasterion* (Rom. 3:25; Heb. 9:5). The term is undoubtedly a biblical word and a biblical concept.

Over the years, many have objected to propitiation, arguing that notions of God's anger are not befitting a God of love. Critics think propitiation makes God rather like some petty, blood-thirsty pagan deity who must be bought off with a bribe. But God's wrath is not arbitrary and capricious; it is part of his immutable justice and holiness. In the Old Testament there are more than twenty different words used to express Yahweh's wrath, totaling more than 580 occurrences. And with John the Baptist's warning about the wrath to come (Matt. 3:7), Jesus's declaration that wrath remains on the unbelieving sinner (John 3:36), and John's imagery of the wrath of the Lamb (Rev. 6:16), we cannot make the New Testament a "good cop" to the Old Testament's supposed "bad cop."

The wrath of the biblical God is distinct from the peeved god of the pagans in at least three ways.

1. The God of the Bible is eternal and immutable, never losing his temper, flying off the handle, or judging his creatures capriciously.

2. The God of the Bible is not appeased by a bribe but by his own blood (Acts 20:28).

3. The God of the Bible, though justly angry with sin and with sinners, nevertheless sent his Son to be our propitiatory sacrifice out of love. The death of Christ did not make God love us. The electing love of God planned for the once-for-all sacrifice of Jesus. "In this is love, not that we have loved God but that he loved us and sent his Son to be the propitiation for our sins" (1 John 4:10). The God who has always been for us in eternity sent his Son in time to be the wrath-absorbing sacrifice that we might enjoy peace with God for ages unending.

DAY 158

Limited Atonement

The doctrine of limited atonement teaches that Christ effectively redeems from every people "only those who were chosen from eternity to salvation" (Canons of Dort, 2.8). The death of Christ was sufficient to atone for the sins of the whole world, but God willed that it should effectively redeem those and only those who were chosen from eternity and given to Christ by the Father.

Particular redemption or *definitive atonement* are often considered more favorable terms because the point of the doctrine is not to limit the mercy of God but to make clear that Jesus did not die in the place of every sinner on the earth, but definitively for his particular people. This is why John 6 says Jesus came to save those the Father had given to him, and why Matthew 1:21 says he died for his people, and John 15:13 says for his friends, and Acts 20:28 says for the church, and Ephesians 5:25 says for his bride, and Ephesians 1:4 says for those chosen in Christ Jesus.

The most significant exegetical objection to limited atonement centers on the word *world* (*kosmos*). What should we do with the scriptural language of God loving the world (John 3:16) or Jesus being the propitiation for the sins of the whole world (1 John 2:2)? Most often, *world* refers to badness instead of bigness, and when it refers to bigness, *world* means everyone without distinction, not everyone without exception. So when 1 John 2:2 says Christ is the propitiation for the sins "of the whole world" (*holou tou kosmou*), it's a reference to all parts or all regions or all peoples of the world. The phrase is not used in Scripture to mean every person on the planet, which is why Paul can say to the Romans, "Your faith is proclaimed in all the world" (Rom. 1:8), when every individual on the planet did not know their faith; and Luke can tell us that "a decree went out from Caesar Augustus that all the world should be registered" (Luke 2:1), when the decree only covered the Roman Empire. *World* can mean people everywhere or all kinds of people, but it does not mean every person everywhere.

The doctrine of limited atonement is worth defining and defending because it gets to the heart of the gospel. If the atonement is not particularly and only for the sheep, then either we have universalism—Christ died in everyone's place and therefore everyone is saved—or we have something less than full substitution. Christ does not come to us merely saying, "I've done my part. I laid down my life for everyone because I have saving love for everyone in the whole world. Now, if you would only believe and come to me, I can save you." Instead he says to us, "I was pierced for your transgressions. I was crushed for your iniquities" (see Isa. 53:5). "I have purchased with my blood men for God from every tribe and language and people and nation" (see Rev. 5:9). "I myself bore your sins in my body on the tree so that you might infallibly die to sins and assuredly live for righteousness. For my wounds did not merely make healing available. They healed you" (see 1 Pet. 2:24). The good shepherd didn't die indiscriminately for the goats; he sustained the anger of God in body and soul, bore the curse, and laid down his life for the sheep (John 10:11).[1]

1 Parts of this section are adapted from DeYoung, *The Good News We Almost Forgot*, 82–84; and from DeYoung, *Grace Defined and Defended*, 59. Both volumes used by permission.

Dort and Definite Atonement

It is sometimes assumed that the doctrine of definite atonement originated during the Reformation era of the sixteenth and seventeenth centuries, but the idea can be traced through the patristic and medieval periods as well. Although the doctrine was not articulated as clearly as it would be in later centuries, we can find versions of definite atonement from Augustine (354–430) to a theologian named Gottschalk (808–878) to medieval schoolmen like Peter Lombard (1100–1160) and Thomas Aquinas (1225–1274).

Of particular importance is the classic distinction given by Lombard that Christ's death was sufficient for all, but efficient only for the elect. Even though Lombard's view, taken as a whole, was consistent with a Reformed view of the atonement, the sufficient/efficient distinction by itself was ambiguous enough to be affirmed by most parts of the church. The debate between the Arminians and the traditionally Reformed at the Synod of Dort (1618–1619) was about the relationship between the sufficiency of the price and the efficacy for the elect.

The two key words are *intention* and *effectively*. At issue were these two questions: What outcome did God purpose to achieve by the cross? and, What did the death of Christ actually accomplish on the cross?

To the first question Dort said, "It was the entirely free plan and very gracious will and intention of God the Father that the enlivening and saving effectiveness of his Son's costly death should work itself out in all the elect, in order that God might grant justifying faith to them only and thereby lead them without fail to salvation." The issue was not whether Christ's death was sufficiently capable of saving all men, but whether God's *intention* was to put forth Christ as an effectual atoning sacrifice for every person. Arminians acknowledged that the atonement was only efficient in the elect. Dort, however, maintained that the decisive factor in making the death of Christ efficacious for only some was not human will, but God's will. The Arminians may have agreed on the outcome—an atoning sacrifice for the elect—but they denied a particular and divinely ordained intention in Christ's death. The issue could not be clarified by sufficiency and efficiency, but by sufficiency and *intentionality*.

The second crucial question is about the death of Christ and what it actually accomplished. Here the key word is *effectively*. "It was God's will that Christ through the blood of the cross (by which he confirmed the new covenant) should effectively redeem from every people, tribe, nation, and language all those and only those who were chosen from eternity to salvation and given to him by the Father." Both sides at Dort actually taught a "limited" atonement. While the Reformed famously limited the extent of the atonement, the Arminians limited the nature of the atonement. Christ's death for the Arminians became the means of removing original sin and granting men the prevenient grace necessary to believe. And yet there was no guarantee—not by human experience, let alone by divine decree—that anyone would enjoy the redeeming power of the cross. In order to defend the notion that Christ died for "all men and for every man," the Arminians championed an atonement that allowed for the potential salvation of everyone but actually secured the salvation of none. Definite atonement is such good news because it doesn't just make sinners save-able; it makes them saved.[1]

1 Parts of this section are adapted from DeYoung, *Grace Defined and Defended*, 50, 56–57.

DAY 160

Crushed for Our Iniquities

Isaiah 53 begins with a question: "Who has believed what he has heard from us?" (v. 1). Considering all that happens to the suffering servant, it's a fair question. How can such violence, such tragedy, such injustice be tolerated? How can the righteous suffer and the guilty go free? Why was the promised deliverer crushed for our iniquities? Verse 10 gives the answer to these mounting questions: "It was the will of the LORD to crush him."

This may seem like an unsatisfying answer. "This only makes it worse," we may think. "I could scarcely accept such punishment befalling an innocent man. I could barely embrace the idea that the righteous would suffer in the place of the guilty. But this is altogether too much. How does it help to know that it was the *Lord's* will to crush him?"

But this *is* good news, and worth reflecting upon as a fitting summary to this entire section on the work of Christ.

Because it was the Lord's will to crush him, we can behold the glory of our triune God in planning and procuring our redemption. The Father did not punish the Son as a helpless victim of cosmic child abuse. The Son *went* to the cross freely and willingly. Likewise, the Son did not appease an angry God as some sort of divine good cop to the Father's divine bad cop. The Father *sent* his Son to the cross freely and willingly. The good news of Good Friday is that the Father did not spare his own Son but gave him up for us all (Rom. 8:32) and that the Son drank the bitter cup of God's wrath for our sakes (Mark 14:36).

Because it was the Lord's will to crush him, we can rest secure in the love of God. The cross did not change the mind of God. Good Friday did not happen so that God *could* love us, but because he *already* loved those whom he had chosen in Christ. For God so loved the world, that he gave his only Son, that whoever believes in him should not perish but have eternal life (John 3:16). God shows his love for us in that while we were still sinners, Christ died for us (Rom. 5:8). In this is love, not that we have loved God but that he loved us and sent his Son to be the propitiation for our sins (1 John 4:10).

And finally, because it was the Lord's will to crush him, we can be sure that full satisfaction has been made for our sins. If the cross is something other than divine judgment upon the divine Son of God, if Good Friday is not the eternal, redemptive plan of God executed fully and finally on a hill outside Jerusalem, then we cannot know if our sins have truly been forgiven. We cannot be sure that Christ's death was enough. We cannot be certain that it is finished.

But if Isaiah 53:10 is the answer to all the problems mounting in verses 1–9, then we can say with the psalmist the words that Jesus himself quoted: "The stone that the builders rejected has become the cornerstone. This is the LORD's doing; it is marvelous in our eyes" (Ps. 118:22–23; Mark 12:10–11). And then we can say with all our might and savor with all our hearts the very next verse in that psalm: "This is the day that the LORD has made; let us rejoice and be glad in it" (Ps. 118:24).

SOTERIOLOGY

Salvation in Christ

DAY 161

Ordo Salutis

Soteriology is the great theme of Scripture. If the storyline of the Bible is creation-fall-redemption-consummation, one could argue that we have two chapters of creation, one chapter of fall, two chapters at the end of the Bible on consummation, and in between we have 1,184 chapters about redemption. Simply put, the Bible is about salvation—how we get saved, how we live when we are saved, and how we stay saved.

One of the best ways to understand this great salvation is by studying the *ordo salutis*, a Latin phrase meaning "order of salvation." Although the phrase itself, as a deliberate theological term, may only be three hundred years old, the concept can be found throughout the history of the church. In fact, support for the *ordo salutis* can be found in the New Testament. Ephesians 1:3–14 talks about salvation in terms of predestination, adoption, faith, and perseverance. More precisely, Romans 8:29–30 summarizes the "steps" of salvation as predestination, calling, justification, and glorification. When we talk about the *ordo salutis*, we are talking about a more detailed version of this "golden chain" found in Romans 8.

Not everyone finds the *ordo salutis* helpful. Critics point out that Scripture does not spell out an elaborate *ordo* in detail and that by explaining salvation in "steps" we can give the wrong impression that there is a tidy, temporal sequence to every aspect of the Christian life. Moreover, critics worry that by focusing on a supposed *ordo salutis*, we are not paying sufficient attention to the redemptive-historical storyline of Scripture, that we aren't matching Paul's eschatological focus, and that we are not anchoring salvation in the death and resurrection of Christ. These are fair concerns, but they need not be decisive. Surely, there is room to talk about the story of salvation *and* the order of salvation, to explain the logical distinctions in salvation *without* understanding them to be strict temporal distinctions.

The *ordo salutis* helpfully reminds us that salvation is a unitary process with various aspects and movements (though we may not be conscious of each step). We can distinguish between what man does (faith and repentance) and what God alone does (regeneration and justification). We can distinguish between judicial acts (justification), filial acts (adoption), and acts of moral renewal (regeneration and sanctification). We can distinguish between elements of our salvation that are instantaneous (regeneration, definitive sanctification) and elements that are ongoing (progressive sanctification, perseverance). The Westminster Confession of Faith works through the various aspects of salvation in nine chapters: effectual calling, justification, adoption, sanctification, saving faith, repentance unto life, good works, perseverance of the saints, and assurance of grace and salvation. We are going to work through twelve categories (with several subpoints along the way): the work of the Holy Spirit, union with Christ, calling, regeneration, conversion, repentance, faith, justification, adoption, sanctification, preservation, and glorification.

The Bible is a big book, and it is about a lot of things. But there is a central plotline. The big idea in Scripture is not that the cosmos is going to be renewed (though it will) or that God must be obeyed (though he should). Even less is the Bible about a mystery to be explored or a journey to be experienced. The central plotline in Scripture is about sinners being saved. Salvation should be the theme of our preaching, the mission of the church, and the priority of our ministry.

DAY 162

The Work of the Holy Spirit 1

The work of the Holy Spirit is not so much a separate aspect of the *ordo salutis* as it is the means by which all that Christ accomplished comes to benefit the elect. The Holy Spirit does (at least) seven things in and for our salvation.

1. *The Holy Spirit convicts.* The word often translated "convict" (*elegcho*) is used in John 3:20 with the sense of bringing sins to light: "For everyone who does wicked things hates the light and does not come to the light, lest his works should be exposed [*elegchthe*]." The Holy Spirit acts like a giant searchlight, exposing the world's wickedness, calling people to repentance, and convicting the world of sin, righteousness, and judgment (John 16:8–11).

2. *The Holy Spirit converts.* As Jesus famously told Nicodemus, "unless one is born of water and the Spirit, he cannot enter the kingdom of God" (John 3:5). Titus 3:5 calls this work "the washing of regeneration and renewal of the Holy Spirit." There is no Christian life without the converting work of the Spirit. He enables us to understand and spiritually discern the things of God (1 Cor. 2:12–14). He grants us repentance that leads to life (Acts 11:18). He pours God's love into our hearts so we can be assured that in Christ God is for us and not against us

(Rom. 5:5). The Holy Spirit enables us to believe in the promises of God (John 1:12–13; 3:36; 6:63–65).

3. *The Holy Spirit applies.* Calvin begins book 3 of the *Institutes* with a question: "How do we receive those benefits which the Father bestowed on his only-begotten Son—not for Christ's own private use, but that he might enrich poor and needy men?" The answer: "The Holy Spirit is the bond by which Christ effectually unites us to himself."[1] This is the logic of Romans 8:9–11. When we have the Spirit, we have Christ. And when we have Christ, we have the Spirit. The Holy Spirit applies to the believer the benefits won by Christ, because the Holy Spirit is the Spirit of Christ.

4. *The Holy Spirit glorifies.* "He will glorify me," Jesus told the disciples, "he will take what is mine and declare it to you" (John 16:14). This truth can help us avoid the common mistake of pitting the Spirit against Christ, as if we dishonor the Spirit by putting a relentless focus upon Christ. The Holy Spirit is a serving Spirit. He speaks only what he hears (16:13). He declares what he is given (16:14b). His mission is to glorify another (16:14a). All three persons of the Trinity are fully God, yet in the divine economy the Son makes known the Father and the Spirit glorifies the Son. Yes, it is a mistake if we know nothing about the Spirit. But when we focus on Christ we give evidence of the Spirit's work. We cannot worship Christ without the work of the Spirit. And the Spirit does not want to be magnified except insofar as he points to Christ. This is why the notion of anonymous Christians is so mistaken. The work of the Holy Spirit is to bring glory to Christ by taking what is his—his teaching, the truth about his death and resurrection—and making it known. The Spirit does not work indiscriminately without the revelation of Christ in view.

1   Calvin, *Institutes*, 3.1.1.

DAY 163

The Work of the Holy Spirit 2

Having outlined the work of the Spirit to convict, convert, apply, and glorify, we now come to the work of the Spirit in three other aspects of salvation.

5. *The Holy Spirit sanctifies.* The Spirit gives the believer a new position in Christ—set apart in Christ and sprinkled with his blood—and a new power in Christ (Eph. 3:16). The Spirit works in us "for obedience to Jesus Christ"

(1 Pet. 1:2). Peter elsewhere says that through God's precious and very great promises we may "become partakers of the divine nature" (2 Pet. 1:4). This is the doctrine of *theosis*, or deification, often emphasized in the Eastern Orthodox Church. So long as we don't think of Christians as becoming gods or being swallowed up in God in an ontological sense, the doctrine should be affirmed as an important aspect of our salvation. Peter isn't thinking about "nature" as the divine essence so much as the nature of God's character. That's why the next phrase speaks of "having escaped the corruption that is in the world because of sinful desire." The point is that we can share in the qualities that are characteristic of God himself.

6. *The Holy Spirit equips.* By the work of the Spirit, believers are given gifts for ministry. Sometimes called "service" or "activities," the purpose of these gifts is to build up the church. The manifestation of the Spirit is for the common good (1 Cor. 12:7) and the edification of the church (14:12, 26).

7. *The Holy Spirit promises.* Ephesians 1:13–14 states that in Christ we "were sealed with the promised Holy Spirit, who is the guarantee of our inheritance until we acquire possession of it." A seal in the ancient world did three things: it authenticated, it secured, and it marked ownership. All three elements are probably in view here. The seal of the Spirit authenticates us as true believers, secures our eternal safety, and marks us out as belonging to God.

This sealing is not a second blessing subsequent to salvation; it happens the moment when we become a Christian. The sealing at the end of Ephesians 1:13 is connected to hearing the word of truth and believing the gospel earlier in the verse. That's when the sealing takes place. Being sealed with the Spirit means that God has clamped down his embosser on us and promises to protect us and preserve us as he would his most prized possession. The Spirit is our guarantee (2 Cor. 5:5), like an engagement ring prior to the wedding, or like a down payment on a house before the final move-in date (Eph. 4:30).

The sealing is, first of all, a declarative fact, true of every Christian. But this doesn't mean there cannot also be an experiential dimension. Subjectively, being sealed with the Spirit means we experience an inner authentication that we are indeed forgiven and loved by God. "The Spirit himself bears witness with our spirit that we are children of God" (Rom. 8:16). Or as Paul puts it earlier in Romans, "God's love has been poured into our hearts through the Holy Spirit" (5:5). The Spirit assures us that we belong to God. Ideally, this assurance will be believed *and* felt.

⧉

DAY 164

Union with Christ

There has been some controversy in recent years about where union with Christ fits into the *ordo salutis*, with some thinking that union with Christ ought to supplant the *ordo salutis* and others nervous that an overemphasis on union with Christ might undermine the central role that justification has held in the Reformation tradition. I don't think we have to choose between an appreciation for union with Christ and a profitable use of the *ordo salutis*.

We've seen how the Westminster Confession lays out the *ordo salutis*, but it doesn't mention union with Christ. And yet the same basic *ordo salutis* is explained in more detail in the Westminster Larger Catechism, except there it *starts* with union with Christ. John Murray places union with Christ after perseverance and before glorification. We could look at union with Christ last, but like the Larger Catechism we are going to look at it first, insisting that the other benefits of salvation are only ours *in* Christ.

Union with Christ is not a single specific blessing we receive in our salvation. Rather, it is a necessary phrase to describe *all* the blessings of salvation, whether in eternity (election), in history (redemption), in the present (effectual calling, justification, and sanctification), or in the future (glorification). To use biblical metaphors, union with Christ is like a marriage (where the church is the bride and Christ is the groom), like a body (where Christ is the head and we are members of that body), and like a plant (where we are grafted into Christ, receiving from him new vitality, new life, and new power). Every blessing in the order of salvation flows from our union with Christ. As John Murray said, "It is not simply a step in the application of redemption; when viewed, according to the teaching of Scripture, in its broader aspects it underlies every step of the application of redemption. Union with Christ is really *the central truth of the whole doctrine of salvation* not only in its application but also in its once-for-all accomplishment in the finished work of Christ."[1]

The doctrine of union with Christ is so common in the New Testament that we can easily miss it. Over two hundred times in Paul's letters and more than two dozen times in the writings of John we see expressions like "in Christ," "in the Lord," or "in him." We are found in Christ (Phil. 3:9), preserved in Christ (Rom. 8:39), saved and sanctified in Christ (1 Cor. 1:30; 2 Tim. 1:9). We walk in Christ (Col. 2:6), labor in Christ (1 Cor. 15:58), and obey in Christ (Eph. 6:1). We die in Christ (Rev. 14:13), live in Christ (Gal. 2:20), and conquer in Christ (Rom. 8:37)—just to name a few examples. Another thirty-two times Paul speaks of believers participating together with Christ in some aspect of redemption, whether it's being crucified with Christ, being buried with Christ, being raised with Christ, or being seated with Christ. The whole of the Christian life from election to justification to sanctification to final glorification is made possible by and is an expression of our union with Christ. That's why Jesus's final request in the high priestly prayer is that "I [may be] in them" (John 17:26) and why Paul says "Christ in you" is the hope of glory (Col. 1:27).

1   Murray, *Redemption*, 161. Parts of this section, including the Murray quotation, are also found in DeYoung, *The Hole in Our Holiness*, 94–96. Used by permission.

General Calling

General calling refers to the free offer of the gospel announced to all sinners, both elect and nonelect. This calling is general instead of effectual, external instead of internal, and visible (insofar as we "see" the word being proclaimed) instead of invisible. The church should go into all the world to make disciples (Matt. 28:19–20); and we should bear witness to the ends of the earth (Acts 1:8). God now commands people everywhere to repent (Acts 17:30). And yet not all will obey the Son (John 3:36). Almost everywhere Paul went, large crowds rejected him and rejected his message (Acts 13:46). The gospel will be an aroma of life to some and a fragrance of death to others (2 Cor. 2:15–16). Same gospel perfume, different noses.

Throughout the New Testament we see many references to the sin of unbelief (Matt 10:15; 11:21–24; John 5:40; 16:8–9; 1 John 5:10). In the parable of the marriage feast, many are called but few are chosen (Matt. 22:1–14). In the parable of the great banquet, none of those who were called ended up coming (Luke 14:16–24). In other words, Jesus taught that there would be a general, external call of the gospel that would often not correspond with a special, internal, effectual call.

Importantly, this general call is a bona fide gospel call. The promise of forgiveness and eternal life is equally true for the reprobate, even if God does not intend in his secret will to effectually give them the gift of faith. Some Calvinists (often called hyper-Calvinists) have denied that we ought to preach a universal call, arguing that the double decree of election and reprobation means God does not desire all to come to faith and repentance. God's desire is only to prepare the reprobate for damnation. Preaching therefore is a presentation of the facts of the gospel, a declaration of the way of salvation, but it is not a plea to repent and believe.

This logic does not fit the example of Scripture (as seen above), nor does it arise from the teaching of the Reformed confessions. For example, the Canons of Dort affirm that "this promise [of the gospel], together with the command to repent and believe, ought to be announced and declared without differentiation or discrimination to all nations and people, to whom God in his good pleasure sends the gospel" (2.5). The Arminians believed that God could not seriously call sinners to salvation if their reprobation was already unconditionally decreed. This is why Dort uses the language of a "serious" gospel call (3/4.8). The promise is still true. The invitation is still sincere. This is what Jesus teaches in John 6: "I am the bread of life; whoever comes to me shall not hunger, and whoever believes in me shall never thirst.... All that the Father gives me will come to me, and whoever comes to me I will never cast out" (vv. 35, 37). That is the general call. But an effectual call is also necessary. As Jesus says, "No one can come to me unless the Father who sent me draws him" (6:44).

WEEK 34

DAY 166

Effectual Calling

Effectual calling is the initial act of salvific application whereby we are joined to Christ and made sharers in all his benefits. In contrast to general calling, effectual calling doesn't just make our embrace of Christ possible; it makes it certain (WCF 10:1). All those God electingly knows he calls, and all those who are called will be justified and glorified (Rom. 8:29–30). Effectual calling is where the grace decreed in eternity begins to find expression in time.

The New Testament describes the effectual calling of the gospel in several ways. It is a holy calling (2 Tim. 1:9), a heavenly calling (Heb. 3:1), and a high calling (Phil. 3:14). It is a calling from darkness, from sin, from condemnation, and from the world. Conversely, it is a calling to light, to holiness, to eternal life, and to Christ. The Shorter Catechism describes effectual calling as "the work of God's

Spirit, whereby, convicting us of our sin and misery, enlightening our minds in the knowledge of Christ, and renewing our wills, he doth persuade and enable us to embrace Jesus Christ, freely offered to us in the gospel" (WSC 31).

One way to think of effectual calling is to consider how God works in and on all our faculties. The eyes of the heart are enlightened (Eph. 1:18). The stony heart is replaced with a heart of flesh (Ezek. 11:19; 36:26–27). The mind is given the Spirit that we might understand the things of the Spirit (1 Cor. 2:12–13). The will is moved and renewed by the God who shows mercy (Rom. 9:16).

The terms *effectual calling* and *regeneration* are almost interchangeable. For example, the Westminster Confession does not have a separate chapter for regeneration but describes the quickening and renewing work of the Holy Spirit under effectual calling (WCF 10.2). Later, under *sanctification* the Confession speaks of those "who are once effectually called, and regenerated, having a new heart, and a new spirit created in them" (13.1). At the very least, the two terms are inextricably linked.

Still, there may be some warrant for distinguishing between effectual calling and regeneration. We might think of effectual calling as God's known work upon the consciousness of man, while regeneration is God's secret work on the subconscious life of man. If the two terms are distinguished, effectual calling usually comes before regeneration in the *ordo salutis*. On the one hand, one could argue that regeneration comes first because the call cannot be effectual unless there is new life in the heart. On the other hand, it makes sense to think that effectual calling comes first, and regeneration is the result of that calling.

Both orders can be theologically true. We can say that God opens the heart so that sinners can respond to the gospel, and we can also say that God uses the preaching of the gospel to effectually give the sinner new life. We are born again through the living and abiding word of God (1 Pet. 1:23). At the same time, the Lord must open our hearts so we can pay attention to the preaching of the gospel (Acts 16:14).

DAY 167

Irresistible Grace

How do we account for the fact that only some respond to the gospel call? Like the Calvinists at the Synod of Dort, the Arminians taught that sinners need the Spirit's work in their lives in order to exercise faith and repentance. The difference lies in how both sides understood the Spirit's work in conversion. The Arminians maintained that all people have been given sufficient grace for conversion. Faith is a gift offered to all, but unilaterally infused in none.

By contrast, Dort concluded that sinners are in need of more than enlightening or enabling grace. God doesn't effect conversion by a "gentle persuasion" (3/4, Rejection of Errors, 7). Rather, God "penetrates into the inmost being, opens the closed heart, softens the hard heart, and circumcises the heart that is uncircumcised." God does more than provide the opportunity for conversion. He "infuses new qualities into the will, making the dead will alive, the evil one good, the unwilling one willing, and the stubborn one compliant" (3/4.11). God pours grace into the human heart so that we can *and will* believe.

Another way to approach the question is to ask whether efficacious grace works in man in such a way that he can either receive it or reject it. The question is not whether we can reject the gospel, or spurn the light of truth, or grieve the Holy Spirit, or disbelieve the promises of God. We know from the Bible and from experience that people can do all these things. The question is, as Turretin puts it, "whether all the operations of grace being supplied . . . still that conversion remains so in the power of man that he can close or not close the door (i.e., receive or reject it) and thus convert or not convert himself?"[1]

The answer is no, man can neither convert himself nor reject the converting grace of God. The Scriptures do not grant to man any power of cooperation in the grace that quickens, makes alive, and effectually calls. God makes us alive (Eph. 2:5). God grants us repentance (Acts 11:18). God works in us to will and to act (Phil. 2:13). Just as the uncreated cosmos could not resist the omnipotent power of God's command, so God has irresistibly shone in our hearts to give us the light of the knowledge of the glory of God in the face of Jesus Christ (2 Cor. 4:6).

This means that saving faith is worked in us by God's grace. While we must exercise faith as an act of the will, faith "is a gift of God, not in the sense that it is offered by God for people to choose, but that it is in actual fact bestowed on them, breathed and infused into them" (Canons of Dort 3/4.14). Faith is not the gift of a healing antidote we can take if we are smart enough to take it. Faith is like a blood transfusion poured into our veins when we were utterly helpless to help ourselves. In other words, faith is not something outside of us that we grab hold of. It is a work that God works in us, producing "both the will to believe and the belief itself" (3/4.14).[2]

---

1   Turretin, *Elenctic Theology*, 2.547–48.
2   Parts of this section are adapted from DeYoung, *Grace Defined and Defended*, 73–75. Used by permission.

⊞

Regeneration

In the past, *regeneration* sometimes referred to the moral renewal of the whole person throughout the Christian life. That's how John Calvin and early Protestants often used the term. Later, the term came to be used more narrowly to refer to the supernatural work of new birth at the beginning of the Christian life. That's how most systematicians use the term today, and how I am using it here.

Regeneration is often associated with the idea of newness. The word *palingenesia*, translated "regeneration" in Titus 3:5, is used in Matthew 19:28 to describe the new world ushered in by the Son of Man. The Christian is called a "new creation" (2 Cor. 5:17; Gal. 6:15) or a "new self" (Eph. 4:24).

The other key concept, closely related to newness, is life or birth. The New Testament often stresses the importance of being born again (John 1:13; 3:3–8; 1 Pet. 1:23; 1 John 2:29; 3:9; 4:7; 5:1, 4, 18). The Christian is someone who has been brought forth (James 1:18), created anew (Eph. 2:10), and made alive (Eph. 2:5; Col. 2:13).

We can distinguish between two elements in regeneration: the begetting of new life and the bringing forth of new life. The former is often called "the seed of regeneration." Just as desire when it has conceived gives birth to sin, and sin when it is fully grown brings forth death (James 1:15), so we can think of God as invisibly quickening new life in the heart *and* as bringing us forth by the word of truth (1:18). If it isn't pressing the biological analogy too far, we can say there is both divine conception and supernatural birth. In regeneration, the sinner is endowed with new spiritual life, and that life is first called into action.

This distinction plays a role in the debate over presumptive regeneration. The debate was particularly heated in the Netherlands at the end of the nineteenth century, with Abraham Kuyper arguing for presumptive regeneration and Herman Bavinck arguing against presumptive regeneration as a proper ground for baptism. Importantly, Bavinck did not reject the *possibility* of regeneration for infants, nor did he want the church to presuppose *nonregeneration*. He believed covenant children were not strangers and aliens to the promises of God, but he also worried about giving covenant families false assurance. The frequent warnings and pleadings in the Old Testament, the preaching of faith and repentance to the covenant community in the New Testament, and the way Jesus spoke to Nicodemus—all these mitigate against the notion that those who belong to the covenant externally should be presumed to be internally renewed. While the seed of regeneration may be present at a young age, we normally wait years to see the first signs of new birth.

This does not mean believers cannot have confidence when covenant children die at an early age. As Dort puts it, "godly parents ought not to doubt the election and salvation of their children whom God calls out of this life in infancy" (1.17). That David comforted his wife after the death of their child (2 Sam. 12:24) and expressed the hope "I shall go to him" (12:23) supports Dort's conclusion. Likewise, the examples of David, Jeremiah, and John the Baptist teach us that regeneration apart from the ordinary means of the preached word is possible, even if we should not presume it to always be the case.

DAY 169

Monergism

The work of God in regeneration is *monergistic* (by the one working) not *synergistic* (by a work of cooperation). That is to say, regeneration is God's work and his alone. Being dead in our sins and trespasses, we are passive, helpless, acted upon in the new birth, rather than working jointly with God. The Reformed confessions all reject the synergism of the Council of Trent whereby the will is said to be "excited and assisted" by divine grace. The Bible does not share the theology of Miracle Max from *The Princess Bride*. We are not *mostly dead*; we are all the way dead. If we contribute or cooperate in any way in our regeneration, then we can be proud of contributing some small part to our salvation, of which Paul says, "But far be it from me to boast except in the cross of our Lord Jesus Christ" (Gal. 6:14).

Given the monergistic nature of the new birth, we must also conclude that regeneration precedes faith. We don't believe unto new life; we are given new life that we may believe. If we are to put our faith in Christ, God must work in our hearts so that we are "certainly, unfailingly, and effectively reborn" (Canons of Dort 3/4.12). In the miracle of regeneration, we bring nothing and do nothing. That's why Paul likens regeneration to a new creation (2 Cor. 5:17) and to a resurrection (Col. 2:12). If we want to see a miracle, go to any true church on any Sunday. We will see men and women and children who were dead and are now alive. As Dort puts it, this "inexpressible work" is "not less than or inferior in power to that of creation or of raising the dead."

It is important to add that regeneration does not impart a new substance in man, but a new principle. We are given a new inclination, disposition, direction, and movement. In regeneration the human will is renewed, not removed. People often criticize Reformed theology for reducing men and women to robots or puppets on a string, but this is not accurate. Puppets have no will of their own. Their movements are manipulated by an outside force. This is not what Calvinists believe (or not what they should believe) about God's sovereignty. The "divine grace of regeneration does not act in people as if they were blocks and stones; nor does it abolish the will and its properties or coerce a reluctant will by force, but spiritually revives, heals, reforms, and—in a manner at once pleasing and powerful—bends it back" (Canons of Dort 3/4.16).

This is a key point. Calvinists believe in making choices. They should not hesitate to call people to repent and believe. We believe in human willing and doing. We *also* believe that God must infuse the will with new properties if we are to will or do anything pleasing to him. Regeneration is what God supernaturally accomplishes by the internal and effectual power of the Spirit, not what God forces upon us by external compulsion and coercion.[1]

1 These two paragraphs are adapted from DeYoung, *Grace Defined and Defended*, 78–79.

Conversion

Regeneration and conversion were often used by older theologians as synonyms. But now they are used more specifically to refer to God's activity in us and the action we take as a result. Regeneration is an act wrought unilaterally within is; while conversion is a process worked out cooperatively by us. Turretin distinguishes between two kinds of conversion.[1] The first kind is passive, the infusion of supernatural habits by the Holy Spirit. We now call this regeneration. The second kind is active and involves the exercise of these new habits. We now call this conversion.

We see at least three different types of conversion in the Bible. Most obviously, we see true individual conversions. That's what we mainly want to talk about.

But we also see national conversions where representative leaders or a large percentage of the population turn to God in such a way that the nation, people, or tribe can be said to have turned to God. These conversions—like the ones seen in the days of Moses, Joshua, Hezekiah, Josiah, and Jonah—tend to be short-lived, depending as they do upon the moral exertions and example of a key leader.

The Bible also understands there will be false conversions. The seed of God's word may flourish for a time, only to wither away on account of suffering and persecution or to get choked out by the cares of the world and deceitfulness of riches (Matt. 13:20–22). Hebrews tell us that those who have been enlightened, who have tasted the heavenly gift, have shared in the Holy Spirit, and have tasted the goodness of the word of God can fall away (Heb. 6:4–6). Likewise, John indicates that some who start out among the faithful do not stay among the faithful and so prove they never really were among those who had been truly converted (1 John 2:19). In 2 Timothy, Paul laments that Hymenaeus and Philetus have swerved from the truth (2:17–18) and that Demas fell in love with the world and deserted him (4:10). It is possible for people to turn to God temporarily only to turn away from him permanently (demonstrating that the initial turning was not genuine).

At the most basic level, conversion refers to turning. The Bible captures this idea with various terms. In the Old Testament, the most common word used to express this idea is *shub*, meaning turn, turn about, or return. The New Testament uses *epistrophe* (turn, return), *metameleia* (changing one's mind), and *metanoia* (repentance). Although *metanoia* is often explained as a change of mind, the word indicates a new outlook and disposition on life. It signifies a change in intellect, affections, and will. Conversion may not be remembered or experienced as a crisis or as accompanied by deep emotion. The evidence of conversion is not a feeling but a turning from sin and turning to God.

1 Turretin, *Elenctic Theology*, 2.522–23.

WEEK 35

DAY 171

Repentance

Conversion involves turning from sin and turning to God. This is another way of saying that conversion entails repentance and faith. We will deal with repentance first because faith leads naturally into the doctrine of justification. The danger in putting repentance first is that one might think we first have to feel sufficient sorrow for our sins before flying to Christ for salvation. The gospel calls for an evangelical repentance, not a legal repentance. Repentance entails sorrow for sin and the forsaking of sin (2 Cor. 7:10–11), but it is not groveling before a stingy God, or a meritorious work that convinces God to forgive us. Repentance unto life is a saving grace whereby a sinner not only has a sense of his sin, but he also has a sense of the mercy of God in Christ (WSC 87).

Repentance in the Christian life is twofold. We must distinguish between repentance as turning to Christ in an act of saving faith, and repentance in the ongoing life of Christian discipleship. Martin Luther famously began his Ninety-Five Theses by insisting that the entire life of believers is to be one of repentance. Repentance is necessary in becoming a Christian, and it is necessary in living as a Christian.

Even a cursory glance at the New Testament demonstrates that we have not understood the message of the gospel if we do not understand repentance. When John the Baptist prepared the way of the Lord, he preached repentance (Matt. 3:8, 11), just as Jesus launched his Galilean ministry by preaching, "Repent, for the kingdom of heaven is at hand" (Matt. 4:17). Jesus understood the purpose of his ministry to be calling sinners to repentance (Luke 5:32). Just before his ascension, the resurrected Christ implored the disciples to be his witnesses, that "repentance for the forgiveness of sins" would be preached in his name to all nations (Luke 24:47). In fact, if there is a one-sentence summary of Jesus's preaching, Mark gives it at the beginning of his Gospel: "Now after John was arrested, Jesus came into Galilee, proclaiming the gospel of God, and saying, 'The time is fulfilled, and the kingdom of God is at hand; repent and believe in the gospel'" (Mark 1:14–15).

Notice that pair: repent and believe. The two are virtually synonymous in the New Testament, not that the words mean the same thing, but that they are signs of the same Spirit-prompted work and lead to the same eschatological inheritance. Strictly speaking, the proper response to the gospel involves both faith and repentance (Matt. 21:32; Acts 20:21). If only one item in the pair is mentioned—which happens often in the New Testament—we should realize that the other half is assumed. You can't really believe without also repenting, and you haven't really repented if you don't also believe.

Any gospel that never speaks of repentance is not the authentic gospel. The gospel message is sometimes presented as a straightforward summons to repent. Other times forgiveness is linked to a singular act of repentance (Acts 5:31; Rom. 2:4; 2 Cor. 7:10). The message of the apostolic good news is that repentance leads to life (Acts 11:18). "Repent therefore, and turn back, that your sins may be blotted out" (Acts 3:19).

⁜

DAY 172

Faith

The Bible sometimes talks about faith as that which is believed (*fides quae creditur*). Think Jude's exhortation to contend for the faith (Jude 3; cf. Gal. 1:23; 1 Tim. 4:1). As an aspect of *ordo salutis*, however, we are thinking of the faith by which we believe (*fides qua creditur*). The New Testament is relentless in its emphasis on the need for faith. Without faith it is impossible to please God (Heb. 11:6). We are saved by believing (Rom. 10:9). God commands us to believe (1 John 3:23). The purpose of John's Gospel is that we may believe that Jesus is the Christ, the Son of God, and that by believing we may have life in his name (John 20:31).

It would be hard to exaggerate the importance of faith. The noun *pistis* (faith, faithful) and the verb *pistuein* (to believe) occur over 240 times. Christians are, by definition and designation, believers (Acts 2:44). Abraham believed God and it was credited to him as righteousness (Gen. 15:6). As the man of faith, Abraham is the father of all those who believe (Rom. 4; Gal. 3; Heb. 11; James 2). Indeed, the gospel age is called "the coming of faith" (see Gal. 3:23, 25).

Faith can be described in many ways. Most well-known is the definition in Hebrews: "Now faith is the assurance of things hoped for, the conviction of things not seen" (11:1). That's not all the New Testament tells us about faith. Faith is the fruit of election (Acts 13:48), the result of regeneration (1 John 5:1), the work of the Spirit (1 Cor. 12:3), enabled by the Father (John 6:65), and authored by Jesus (Heb. 12:2). Faith is a gift from God (Eph. 2:8; Phil. 1:29), and it is the responsibility of man (John 3:16; 1 John 3:23).

We can distinguish among four different types of faith in the Bible.

1. *Historical faith* involves mental assent to many of the facts about God. King Agrippa may not have been converted, but he believed the prophets (Acts 26:27–28). On the level of mental assent, even the demons believe—and shudder (James 2:19).

2. *Faith of miracles* can be taken in a passive sense ("I believe God will work a miracle for me") or in an active sense ("I believe that a miracle just happened"). This type of faith may or may not be accompanied by saving faith. The crowds often marveled at the signs and wonders performed by Jesus, but they did not follow him as disciples. It is possible to "believe" in Jesus only for the signs and not for Jesus himself (John 2:23–25).

3. *Temporary faith* is short-lived, springing up for a time before withering away or being choked out (Mark 4:16–19).

4. *Justifying faith* is a saving grace, wrought in our hearts by the Spirit and the word of God, whereby we are convinced of our sin and misery, assent to the truth of the gospel, and receive and rest upon Christ and his righteousness (WLC 72).

Finally, we should say something about the object of faith. General faith (*fides generalis*) means accepting God's word (John 2:22) and trusting in the Scriptures (John 5:45–47). Special faith (*fides specialis*) involves trusting in Christ and the promise of salvation (Gen. 15:6; Heb. 11:6). It means hungering and thirsting after Jesus (John 6:50–58). In the exercise of special faith, the sinner comes to Jesus and receives him and all his benefits (John 1:12; 5:40; 6:44, 65; 7:37).

DAY 173

Acts of Faith

Given the importance of faith as the instrumental cause in our justification, it is not surprising that Reformed theologians have been extremely careful in describing what exactly faith *does*. The "acts of faith" and the "experience of faith" are not the same. (1) An act of the soul is active, while an experience suggests something that passively is true of us. (2) An act of the soul originates in one of the faculties, either the intellect or the will (or both). An experience may involve the intellect and the will but is not necessarily an activity from them. (3) An act of the soul terminates on an object—what we know, what truth we assent to, what person we trust—while an experience suggests that we ourselves are the object.

This is not an esoteric point of theology. It's one thing to say, "Faith treasures Christ." That is the language of act. It is another thing to say, implicitly or explicitly, "Faith must be experienced as treasuring or it is not saving faith." In simple terms, faith consists of *notitia* (knowledge), *assensus* (assent), and *fiducia* (trust). This classic definition is one helpful way to describe what faith does: faith knows, faith assents, faith trusts. The last element is key. It's not enough to understand that the chair exists or believe that the chair can hold you; you actually have to sit down in the chair trusting that it will hold you.

Other theologians have explained these basic categories in different ways. Turretin lists six acts of justifying faith: knowledge, theoretical assent, practical assent and persuasion, refuge arising from persuasion (e.g., running to Christ), reception (e.g., embracing Christ), and a reflex act whereby we conclude that Christ certainly died for us. He also mentions an act of consolation and comfort that arises from possession of Christ, but this seventh act is not, strictly speaking, part of the essence of faith.[1] Similarly, Ursinus says, "the act which belongs to faith is to apprehend and apply to itself the righteousness of Christ; yea, faith is nothing else than the acceptance itself, or the apprehension of the merits of Christ."[2] Likewise, John Owen argues that there are two acts essential unto faith: assent of mind (which he says takes "precedency") and approbation (which entails renunciation, consent, acquiescency of heart, trust in God, and composure of soul).[3] Owen is perfectly happy to talk about the varied experiences of faith, but when it comes to detailing the formal *acts* of faith, his definition narrows. Wilhelmus à Brakel gives a wonderful eightfold description of saving faith, but he does not enfold this experience of saving faith into the act of faith, which he defines as "trust in Jesus, and in entrusting oneself to Him."[4]

In short, while the Reformed tradition sometimes describes the acts of faith with affectional language (to guard against bare cognition or heartless assent), the tradition does not include the experience of love or joy or treasuring as constitutive elements of justifying faith. The "principal acts of saving faith are accepting, receiving, and resting in Christ alone" (WCF 14:2). It is the nature of saving faith to look away from itself. Faith does not rest in what it does or what it experiences. Faith rests in Christ and receives blessing from all that he has accomplished for our sakes.

1   Turretin, *Elenctic Theology*, 2:560–64.
2   Ursinus, *Commentary*, 332.
3   Owen, *Doctrine of Justification by Faith*, 113–15.
4   À Brakel, *The Christian's Reasonable Service*, 2:282.

DAY 174

Faith and Assurance

Many Protestants think of the Reformation as being chiefly about justification, and there is truth in that common assumption. But one could also make the case that pastorally the Reformation was first about assurance. The Council of Trent declared, "No one can know with a certainty of faith, which can not be subject to error, that he has obtained the grace of God." Likewise, one modern, Catholic dictionary of theology defines "certainty of salvation" as "a concept of Protestant theology which signifies a belief in justification so firm that this belief is inconsistent with any doubt of man's ultimate salvation." The dictionary insists that while we should not doubt what God has done in Christ, we cannot have absolute certainty of one's own eternal salvation.[1]

The Reformers strenuously opposed this repudiation of assurance. Faith, for Calvin, is "a firm and certain knowledge of God's benevolence toward us."[2] Or as the Heidelberg Catechism puts it, "true faith is not only a knowledge and conviction" that God's word is true; it is also "a deep-rooted assurance" that "I too, have had my sins forgiven, have been made forever right with God, and have been granted salvation" (Q/A 21). The Bible teaches that we can know that we know Christ (1 John 2:3). We ought to be persuaded of God's favor toward us (2 Tim. 2:12). Faith results in confidence (Eph. 3:12), boldness (2 Cor. 3:12; Heb. 3:6; 4:16), and full assurance (1 Thess. 1:5; Heb. 6:11).

According to the Canons of Dort, assurance of salvation comes from three sources: (1) from faith in the promises of God, (2) from the testimony of the Holy Spirit testifying to our spirits that we are children of God, and (3) from a serious and holy pursuit of a clear conscience and of good works (5.10). These are not three ways to *get* saved; they are three ways to be confident that we *are* saved.

Assurance is a gift available to every true believer. Although it is possible for "hypocrites and other unregenerate men" to deceive themselves with false hope of eternal life, God wants his children to be "certainly assured that they are in the state of grace." This certainty is possible for those who truly believe in the Lord Jesus, love him in sincerity, and endeavor to walk in a good conscience before him (WCF 18.1). Assurance is both an exhortation and a comfort for the Christian. We ought to strive for good works and a good conscience, always remembering that even endeavoring and pursuing are signs of God's grace in us.

To be sure, believers may not always experience assurance in this life. Even the regenerate can be shaken and tempted to despair (WCF 18.4), for infallible assurance is not part of "the essence of faith" (WCF 18.3). We can wound the conscience and grieve the Spirit. God may, for a season, remove the light of his countenance from us. And yet it is the duty of everyone to pursue assurance. We do not need "extraordinary revelation," but only the "right use of ordinary means" (WCF 18.3) This means we should be diligent to make our calling and election sure that our hearts may be enlarged in peace and joy, in love and thankfulness, in strength and cheerfulness in obedience, which are the proper fruits of assurance.

---

1 Rahner and Vorgrimler, *Dictionary of Theology*, 63.

2 Calvin, *Institutes*, 3.2.7.

⊞

DAY 175

Justification

In 2 Corinthians 5:18–20, Paul explains that he has a ministry of reconciliation. This invites the question: How are we reconciled to God? That may seem like a silly question to us. "What do you mean, how are we reconciled? We say we're sorry for our sins. God says it's not a problem. And everything's all better." But God's forgiveness doesn't work like that. It would be a violation of his own nature. God is loving, but he is also just. God cannot simply pass over our sins because he feels like it.

Sin is a personal offense to God. If God were to simply look past our sin just because he really likes us, he would be treating his own name with contempt. There needs to be some kind of restitution for our wrongs, some kind of satisfaction of divine justice. Proverbs 17:15 says he who justifies the wicked is an abomination to the Lord. So how is God to justify us without committing an abomination? The answer lies in the great exchange (2 Cor. 5:21). For our sake, because he loved us, God sent his Son Jesus Christ, who never did anything wrong, never failed his heavenly Father in the slightest way, to be counted as sin, so that we who have nothing to offer God but our sin might be counted as righteous as Christ.

The gifts conveyed in justification are both negative and positive. Negatively, justification is the declaration that our sins have been forgiven and our guilt removed. This divine acquittal is not a process, but a once for all judicial verdict of innocence (Rom. 5:1; 8:30). The declaration is based on the substitutionary work of Christ (Gal. 3:13–14) and is grounded in an alien righteousness, that is, not in our righteousness but in Christ our righteousness (1 Cor. 1:30). Positively, justification entails our adoption as children of God (Eph. 1:5–6; 1 John 3:1) and our legal right to eternal life (Titus 3:7). We are no longer slaves but heirs (Gal. 4:7). Eternal life is now our present possession (John 3:36) and that for which we are kept (John 12:25).

As we can see, *justification* is a forensic term. That's why it is used in the context of judgment or used as the opposite of condemnation (Deut. 25:1; Rom. 4:5; 8:33). The Greek word for "to justify" (*dikaioo*) speaks of something declarative, not transformative. Justification refers to a judicial pronouncement that one is righteous or that one is in right standing with the requirements of God's law. We took the test of obedience and got an F. Christ took the test and got an A+. God is a fair teacher. He can't give us an A+ just because he likes our smile. We have to get what we deserve. And an F deserves his wrath.

But that's not the end of the story, because by faith we are joined to Christ. Consequently, instead of giving us the wrath we deserve for our F, God determined that Christ's A+ would be credited to us, and our F would be credited to Christ. He got what we deserved, so that we can get what he deserves. And in that way, God and sinners are reconciled. We are justified before God, and God's justice is satisfied.

WEEK 36

DAY 176

Imputation

"Justification is an act of God's free grace, wherein he pardons all our sins, and accepts us as righteous in his sight, only for the righteousness of Christ imputed to us, and received by faith alone" (WSC 33). That word *imputed* is essential to a biblical understanding of justification. The controversy between the Reformers and Rome was whether the righteousness whereby we are forgiven and made right with God is a righteousness working in us or a righteousness reckoned to our account. That's the difference between an infused (or inherent, or imparted) righteousness and an imputed righteousness.

The question is not whether an inherent righteousness from Christ is infused in us. The God who justifies always sanctifies. God is at work within us to make us holy in thought, word, and deed. The question is whether any part of that infused righteousness contributes to our justification or forms some part of the foundation of our forgiveness before God. According to the Catholic Catechism, "Justification is not only the remission of sins, but also the sanctification and renewal of the interior man." Also, "Justification detaches man from sin which contradicts the love of God, and purifies his heart of sin." And justification "makes us inwardly just by the power of [God's] mercy."[1] It is no wonder, then, that the Council of Trent anathematized anyone who says "that men are justified, either by the sole imputation of the justice of Christ, or by the sole remission of sins, to the exclusion of the grace and the charity that is poured forth in their hearts by the Holy Ghost" (Art. 11).

By contrast, the Reformers insisted that the formal cause of our justification is the righteousness and obedience of Christ imputed to believers by faith alone. An inherent righteousness cannot be the cause of our justification because our best deeds are always imperfect. The Pharisee confessed that he had done his good works by God's grace, but still he could not be justified by them (Luke 18:9–14). Moreover, if our works contributed (even in some small way) to the basis of our justification we would have reason to boast. Anything other than justification by imputation denigrates the work and merit of Christ, implying that it is somehow insufficient or incomplete.

Imputation is essential to the storyline of Scripture. Adam's disobedience was imputed, our sin was imputed to Christ, and Christ's obedience is imputed to the elect. Abraham believed and it was *credited* to him as righteousness (Gen. 15:6; Rom. 4:23–25; Gal. 3:6). The logic of 2 Corinthians 5:21 teaches that we must become righteous in the same way that Christ became sin. Righteousness is not the moral quality of the justified soul, just like sin was not the moral quality of Christ's soul. Though without sin, Christ was reckoned to be a sinner. In the same way, though still sinners, we are reckoned to be righteous.

Our justification is not an act of legal fiction. God does not turn a blind eye toward our sin and declare us to be what we are not. Rightly understood, we can say that justification is a declarative and a constitutive act. Righteousness is constituted of us—by imputation—in order for "righteous" to be justly declared of us. God did not set aside the law in judging us. He fulfilled it. Christ bore the curse of the law so that in him we might become the righteousness of God—sinners, but at the same time justified (*simul iustus et peccator*).

1 Catechism of the Catholic Church, 1989, 1990, 1992.

DAY 177

Sola Fide

No Christian denies that justification is by faith. That is an obvious biblical teaching. The controversy is about whether justification is by faith alone (*sola fide*).

In Roman Catholic theology, justification is a process begun at baptism, after which we are obliged to cooperate with grace in hopes of receiving a favorable verdict from God at the end of our lives. "The Protestant doctrine of justification by faith alone contradicts Scripture," writes Peter Kreeft, a winsome and articulate spokesman for Catholic theology. Nevertheless, argues Kreeft, Protestant theology reminds us "that none of us can deserve heaven" and that if God were to ask us why he should let us into heaven, "our answer should not begin with the word 'I' but with the word 'Christ.'"[1] Don't overlook the word *begin* in that sentence, because works do eventually enter into the equation. Later Kreeft writes, "To the world's most practical question, 'What must I do to be saved?', God has given us clear answer: Repent, believe, and live in charity."[2] That's what Kreeft means when he says that justification is not by faith alone.

By contrast, the Bible stresses that we are justified by faith apart from works of the law (Rom. 3:28). "For by works of the law no human being will be justified in his sight" (Rom. 3:20). "We know that a person is not justified by works of the law but through faith in Jesus Christ" (Gal. 2:16). "It is evident that no one is justified before God by the law, for 'The righteous shall live by faith'" (Gal. 3:11). In short, the righteousness by which we are acquitted comes through faith in Christ, not through the law on account of our own righteousness (Phil. 3:9).

It is important to note that faith is not itself virtuous. Faith is not the basis or the ground by which we are justified, as if the righteous act of believing outweighs all our unrighteous deeds. Faith has value because of the object to which it connects us. Think of skating on a frozen pond. Faith is the means by which we get out on the ice, but it is not the reason we do not sink. We are kept out of the dangerous water below by the *object* of our faith. It is the thickness of the ice that saves us.

To put it in Aristotelian terms, faith is the *instrumental cause* of our justification. "We compare faith to a kind of vessel," Calvin writes, "for unless we come empty and with the mouth of our souls open to seek Christ's grace, we are not capable of receiving Christ."[3] Faith is the outstretched empty hand ready to receive Christ and all his benefits. The act of believing, in itself, does not save. Faith "is only the instrument by which we embrace Christ our righteousness" (BC Art. 22).

Finally, we should be clear that although we are justified by faith alone, the faith that justifies is never alone. Good works do not contribute to the root of our justification, but they must be found as fruit of our justification. As Turretin observes, "it is one thing for works to be connected with faith in the person of the justified; another, however, in the matter of justification."[4] In other words, sinners are not justified by works, but works will always be evident in the lives of justified sinners.

1   Kreeft, *Catholic Christianity*, 26.
2   Kreeft, *Catholic Christianity*, 130.
3   Calvin, *Institutes*, 3.11.7.
4   Turretin, *Elenctic Theology*, 2.682.

⊹

DAY 178

Does James Contradict Paul?

The book of James seems to repudiate the Protestant doctrine of *sola fide*. How does Romans 3:28 ("For we hold that one is justified by faith apart from works of the law") square with James 2:24 ("You see that a person is justified by works and not by faith alone")? This seems like a plain contradiction. Paul thinks we are justified by faith alone; James thinks we are justified by faith and works. No wonder Luther once called James a "right strawy epistle."

Rightly understood, however, there is no contradiction between Paul and James. Here are five reasons why.

1. James and Paul are addressing different concerns. The foolish person in James 2:20 is not the apostle Paul. James was likely written before Paul's letters to the Romans or Galatians. They are dealing with different issues. Paul is asking the question, "How are we right with God?" James is asking, "What does genuine faith look like?" For Paul the issue is: "How do Gentiles get into the church?" For James the issue is: "Why are people not caring for their brothers and sisters in the church?"

2. James's argument presupposes the importance of faith. The necessity of faith is presumed in verse 17 and in verse 20, and again in the example of Abraham in verses 22 and 24. James does not want faith to be *supplanted* by works or even *supplemented* by works. He wants faith to be *demonstrated* by works. The equation in James is not "faith plus works equals justification." The equation is "faith minus works does *not* equal justification." Think of salvation as F(aith)=J(ustification)+W(orks). Paul says, "Don't you dare put 'W' on the left side of the equation." James says, "Don't you dare leave out 'W' on the right side of the equation."

3. Paul and James use "works" in two different ways. Paul is talking about works of the law, especially Jewish rites like circumcision, holy days, and food observance. Those were the typical ways, for a Jewish audience, that one would be tempted to place their confidence in something other than Christ. James is talking about the works of faith, acts of charity operative in the body of Christ without preferential treatment.

4. Paul and James use the word *justify* in two different ways. Paul is dealing with people who trust in the works of the law for their standing with God. James is dealing with people who think that mere intellectual assent is real Christianity (James 2:19). Paul is talking about a forensic declaration of righteousness. James is talking about practical evidence that faith is real (2:16, 18).

5. Paul teaches the same point James teaches. Paul speaks of the obedience of faith (Rom. 1:5) and of faith working through love (Gal. 5:6). Paul understands that dead faith is no faith at all (1 Cor. 6:9–11; Gal. 5:16–26). James is talking about the kind of "belief" that even demons have (James 2:19). Neither Paul nor James believes that such empty, untrusting belief constitutes justifying faith.

In the end, there is no conflict between Paul and James. It is right to say we are justified by faith alone apart from works of the law, provided we understand, as James reminds us, that the faith that justifies will always work itself out in love.

DAY 179

Should We Take a "New Perspective" on Paul?

The term "New Perspective on Paul" refers to a constellation of ideas that critique the traditional Protestant understanding of the apostle Paul and his theology of salvation as too beholden to Luther's personal conversion story and his understanding of justification.

The New Perspective on Paul was, first, a new perspective on Judaism. This new view was pioneered by E. P. Sanders, who began arguing in the 1970s that the justification debates in the New Testament were not about getting into the covenant, but about staying in the covenant. The Jews had a view of the law Sanders called "covenantal nomism" (i.e., law-keeping as covenant faithfulness). The Jews, therefore, were not proto-Pelagians trying to earn their way into heaven. They were God's covenant people arguing about what it meant to keep the covenant.

Building on Sanders's new appraisal of Second Temple Judaism, New Testament scholars James Dunn and N. T. Wright popularized a reinterpretation of Paul's theology. They pointed out that Paul's teaching on justification came in the context of his Gentile mission. The issue, they argued, was about the practical realities of table fellowship, not some abstract theorizing about how to get right with God. Likewise, the controversy surrounding the "works of the law" was not about meriting eternal life. The debate was about distinctly Jewish rites and ceremonies and what duties were required (or not) as God's covenant people. In simplest form, the "new perspective" is that we've read Paul too much like a Lutheran when we should read him as a first-century Jew.

While the New Perspective on Paul is helpful at points to remind us of the Jewishness of the New Testament, there are several problems with its overall ideas and aims.

For starters, Second Temple Judaism was not one thing, but many things. Even if some extant sources sound a gracious note, this does mean most Jews thought that salvation was all of grace. It's true that the law was never supposed to be a means for earning favor with God. But many Jews—like human beings tend to do—had turned law-keeping in a legalistic direction. Likewise, works of the law may refer most immediately to Jewish boundary markers, but the underlying heart issue was boasting in those boundary markers and finding confidence in doing those works of the law.

Crucially, the New Perspective has often been marked with studied ambiguity and imprecision when it comes to key theological issues. For example, Wright argues that the Messiah bore the covenantal curse in himself so that the blessings of the covenant might flow out to the world. At the same time, Wright does not want to say that Jesus fulfilled the law in a way that can be "reckoned" to us.[1] Similarly, Wright insists that the future verdict of justification will surely match the present verdict of justification.[2] But Wright does not make clear on what basis this future declaration of innocence will be made. He simply does not think debating the word *basis* is helpful.[3] Traditional Reformed theology teaches one justification with a final judgment in which our works will serve as corroborating evidence. It is hard to know if the New Perspective affirms this, or, as it seems, if they posit an initial justification by faith alone *and* a subsequent justification on the basis of our obedience. These differences are not mere quibbles but get at the heart of the gospel and assurance before God.

1 Wright, *Justification*, 135–36.
2 Wright, *Justification*, 251, 260n11.
3 Wright, *Justification*, 258n7.

DAY 180

Time and Adjuncts

Two final items merit discussion before turning our attention in the *ordo salutis* from justification to adoption.

The first issue concerns the *time* of our justification. Some theologians have argued that justification takes place in eternity. If God's mercy is from everlasting, our justification must also be from eternity. After all, the *pactum salutis* puts the plan of redemption in eternity, so wouldn't justification take place there as well? On this understanding, the grace of regeneration is given as a consequence of the sinner being declared righteous and "deserving" (in a positional sense) of God's favor.

Most theologians, however, maintain that justification takes place when the sinner actually believes. This is the much better position. True, the decree is from eternity, but that should not be confused with the execution of that decree in time. Justification is one of the benefits of Christ applied to the believer by the Holy Spirit's joining us to Christ. This takes place in our personal history, not in "eternity past." Moreover, justification takes place by faith, which requires human activity. And finally, we should note the logical and temporal sequence in Romans 8:30. Justification stands before two acts that happen in time: calling and glorification. It would not make sense for the salvific element in the middle (justification) to have been carried out in eternity.

The second issue involves the *adjuncts* or qualities that accompany justification. We can mention three.

1. *Unity.* The unity of justification is twofold. First, there is unity relative to believers among themselves. No genuine Christian is more or less justified than another Christian. There is only one species of justification, and it is equal in all believers, in all times, and in all places. Second, there is unity with respect to the individual who is justified. The judgment to come will not render a new justification, but a final corroboration of the justification that has already taken place. Our good works will be brought forth not as the basis for a second justification but as signs, marks, and effects of the first (and only) justification.

2. *Perfection.* Justification cannot be added to or subtracted from. Even if our apprehension of justification may wax and wane, there can be no progression in the actual possession of justification or the nature of it. The negative removal of the curse and the positive attribution of righteousness cannot be augmented or diminished.

3. *Certainty.* The believer need not fear that Christ is coming again to judge the living and the dead. Once justified, always justified. While we must demonstrate that our profession was genuine, this is not the same as suggesting there is a final judgment based on "the whole life lived." There can be no judicial sentence other than righteous for those who have already been declared righteous in Christ. The gifts and calling of God are irrevocable (Rom. 11:29).

DAY 181

Adoption

We've already seen that justification gives us two positive rights: the right to adoption as sons and the right to eternal life. Now we want to look briefly at adoption itself. The Westminster Confession has only one paragraph in the *ordo salutis* on adoption, but the article is especially rich.

> All those that are justified, God vouchsafeth, in and for his only Son Jesus Christ, to make partakers of the grace of adoption, by which they are taken into the number, and enjoy the liberties and privileges of the children of God, have his name put upon them, receive the Spirit of adoption, have access to the throne of grace with boldness, are enabled to cry, Abba, Father, are pitied, protected, provided for, and chastened by him, as by a father: yet never cast off, but sealed to the day of redemption; and inherit the promises, as heirs of eternal salvation. (WCF 12.1)

Notice the who, the why, and the what.

The who: all those who are justified. This is not a blessing for the special few, but for all those who are truly justified. Adoption is distinct from justification, but never separate from it. If justification is the change in a legal verdict, adoption is the change in our legal status. Adoption is the familial change of status that is conjoined to our judicial change of status. Adoption reminds us that we do not relate to God only as Judge, but also as Father.

The why: our adoption is *in* Christ and *for the sake* of Christ. He is the older brother, a Son by natural right, who makes the way for us to be sons by grace. "But to all who did receive him, who believed in his name, he gave the right to become children of God, who were born, not of blood, nor of the will of the flesh, nor of the will of man, but of God" (John 1:12–13).

The what: the Confession lists thirteen blessings we enjoy as God's adopted children.

1. We are counted in the number of God's children.
2. We are no longer slaves, but free people.
3. We have the privilege of being at home.

4. We have God's name upon us as members of his family.
5. We have access to the throne of grace.
6. We can speak intimately to God, crying out, "Abba, Father."
7. We are pitied by our heavenly Father.
8. We are protected by our heavenly Father.
9. We are chastened by our heavenly Father.
10. We will never be cast off or disowned.
11. We are sealed and secure for all time.
12. We have an inheritance coming full of unspeakable blessings.
13. We are heirs of eternal life.

And so we exclaim: "See what kind of love the Father has given to us, that we should be called children of God" (1 John 3:1).

DAY 182

How Does Sanctification Differ from Justification?

The Bible typically uses the language of "sanctified" or "sanctify" to refer to the believer's positional holiness as one set apart unto God. In systematic theology, however, sanctification usually means the renovation of men and women by which God takes the joined-to-Christ, justified believer and transforms him more and more into the divine image. That is the sense we are talking about in this chapter and in the next several chapters—progressive sanctification rather than definitive sanctification.

Sanctification can be understood passively and actively—passively, inasmuch as the transforming work "is wrought by God in us," and also actively, inasmuch as sanctification "ought to be done by us, God performing this work in us and by us."[1] This is a crucial point. In sanctification, God is doing the work in us, but at the same time we are also working. Any theology that ignores either the passive or the active dimension of sanctification is going to be lopsided and unbiblical.

From this definition, we can already see that justification and sanctification, though related, are different gifts. The most serious, and potentially damning, errors surface when the two are not carefully distinguished. According to Turretin, justification and sanctification differ in at least five ways.[2]

1. They differ with regard to their *object.* Justification is concerned with guilt; sanctification with pollution.

2. They differ as to their *form.* Justification is a judicial and forensic act whereby our sins are forgiven and the righteousness of Christ is imputed to us. Sanctification is a moral act whereby righteousness is infused in the believer and personal renewal is begun and over a long process carried to completion.

3. They differ as to the *recipient subject.* In justification, man is given a new objective status based on God's acquittal. In sanctification, we are subjectively renewed by God.

4. They differ as to *degrees.* Justification is given in this life fully, without any possible increase. Sanctification is begun in this life but only made perfect in the next. The declaration of justification is once for all. The inward work of sanctification takes place by degrees.

5. They differ as to the *order.* God only sanctifies those who are already reconciled and justified by faith.

Some Christians have argued that sanctification is also "by faith alone." While we are right to stress that sanctification is a gift that comes only to those who put their faith in Christ, and that we grow in godliness by believing in the promises of God, the phrase "by faith alone" is not helpful. Both justification and sanctification are by faith, but whereas faith is the *instrument* through which we receive the righteousness of Christ, faith is the *root* and *principle* out of which sanctification grows.[3] We say that justification is by faith alone, because we want to safeguard justification from any notion of striving or working. But sanctification explicitly includes these co-operations, making the description of "alone" misleading at best and inaccurate at worst. We are apt to misunderstand both justification and sanctification if we describe them in ways that are too similar.

1 Turretin, *Elenctic Theology,* 2:689.
2 Turretin, *Elenctic Theology,* 2:690–91.
3 Turretin, *Elenctic Theology,* 2:692–93.

DAY 183

Three Uses of the Law

The Heidelberg Catechism is largely composed of three elements: the Apostles' Creed (Lord's Day 7–22), the Ten Commandments (Lord's Day 34–44), and the Lord's Prayer (Lord's Day 45–52). In covering these traditional elements, Heidelberg famously uses three section headings: guilt, grace, and gratitude (or less alliteratively: misery, deliverance, and thankfulness). It's worth noting, as many have, that the catechism includes its exposition of the law in the section on gratitude, not in the section on guilt. This choice reflects the widespread Reformed belief in what has come to be known as the third use of the law.

- The first use of the law is to show us our guilt, convict us of sin, and lead us to Christ.
- The second use of the law is given to restrain wickedness through fear of punishment for disobedience.
- The "third and principal use" of the law (as Calvin put it) is as an instrument to learn God's will.[1] The law doesn't just show us our sin so we might be drawn to Christ; it shows us how to live as those who belong to Christ.

In one sense Christians are no longer under the law. We are under grace (Rom. 6:14). We have been released from the law (Rom. 7:6) and its tutelage (Gal. 3). On the other hand, having been justified by faith, we uphold the law (Rom. 3:31). Even Christ recoiled at the idea of coming to abolish the Law and the Prophets (Matt. 5:17). Christians are free from the law in the sense that we are not under the curse of the law—Christ is the end of the law for righteousness to everyone who believes (Rom. 10:4)—nor is the law a nationalized covenant for us like it was for Israel.

But the law in general, and the Ten Commandments in particular, still give us a blueprint for how we ought to live. The Ten Commandments were central to the ethics of the New Testament. Jesus repeated most of the second table of the law to the rich young man (Mark 10:17–22). The apostle Paul repeated them too (Rom. 13:8–10) and used them as the basis for his moral instruction to Timothy (1 Tim. 1:8–11). There can be no doubt that the commandments, even under the new covenant, are holy and righteous and good (Rom. 7:12).

We obey the commandments, therefore, not in order to merit God's favor, but out of gratitude for his favor.

Don't forget that the Ten Commandments were given to Israel after God delivered them from Egypt. The law was a response to redemption, not a cause of it. We must never separate law from gospel. In one sense, the law shows us our sin and leads us to the gospel, but in another sense, the law ought to follow the gospel just as the giving of the Decalogue followed salvation from Egypt. Likewise, Ephesians 2 first explains salvation by grace and then instructs us to walk in the good deeds prepared for us (v. 10). Romans first explains justification and election, and then tells us how to live in response to these mercies (Rom. 12:1).

In short, we obey the law in gratitude for the gospel. As Louis Berkhof observed, we distinguish between the law and the gospel, but always as "the two parts of the Word of God as a means of grace."[2]

1   Calvin, *Institutes*, 2.7.12.
2   Berkhof, *Systematic Theology*, 612.

DAY 184

Trusting and Trying

J. C. Ryle's classic book *Holiness* was written in response to the Higher Life theology that was popular in England at the end of the nineteenth century. Sometimes called Keswick theology because the movement used to be associated with the Keswick Conventions, the Higher Life movement taught that the cure for sin was found in moving from one class of Christians to another. In a moment of crisis—a second conversion of sorts—the believer was supposed to move from being a carnal Christian to a spiritual Christian, from not abiding in Christ to abiding in Christ, from a believer to a disciple, from having Jesus as Savior to having Jesus as Lord, from a defeated Christian to a victorious Christian, in short, from a lower life to a higher life.

Crucially, in the original Keswick theology there were only two conditions for the victorious life: surrender and faith. Sanctification took place through consecration; that is, by surrendering unconditionally to the mastery of Jesus. Victory did not come through effort but through confirming over and over one's consecration and surrender. Sanctification meant trusting, *not* trying.

By contrast, it is the consistent witness of the New Testament that growth in godliness requires exertion on the part of the Christian. Romans 8:13 says by the Spirit we must put to death the deeds of the flesh. Ephesians 4:22–24 instructs us to put off the old self and put on the new. Ephesians 6 tells us to put on the full armor of God and stand fast against the devil. Colossians 3:5 commands us to put to death what is earthly in us. First Timothy 6:12 urges us to fight the good fight. Luke 13:24 exhorts us to strive to enter the narrow gate. Second Peter 1:5 puts it plainly: "Make every effort."

Christians work—they work to kill sin, and they work to live in the Spirit. They have rest in the gospel, but never rest in their battle against the flesh and the devil. As J. C. Ryle put it, the child of God has two great marks about him: he is known for his inner warfare and his inner peace.[1]

Of course, our effort can never win God's justifying favor. Whatever we manage to work out is really what God purposed to work in us (Phil. 2:12–13; cf. 1 Cor. 15:10; Heb. 2:11). The gospel is truly the A to Z of the Christian life. But let us not misunderstand what it means to be gospel-centered. As gospel Christians, we are not afraid of striving, fighting, and working. These are good Bible words. The gospel that frees us *from* self-justification also frees us *for* obedience. God did not tell the Israelites, "Work hard and I'll set you free from Egypt." That's law without a gospel. But neither did God tell them, "I love you. I set you free by my grace. I ask nothing more except that you believe in this good gift." That's gospel with no law. Instead, God redeemed the people by his mercy, and that mercy made a way for obedience.

Let us not make the mistake of the old Keswick theology with its mantra of "Let go and let God." Justification is wholly dependent on faith apart from works of the law. But sanctification—born of faith, dependent on faith, powered by faith—requires moral exertion. Mortify and vivify (put to death and make alive) is how older theologians used to put it. When it comes to growth in godliness, trusting does not put an end to trying.[2]

---

1 Ryle, *Holiness*, 69.
2 Parts of this section were adapted from DeYoung, *Hole in Our Holiness*, 88–91. Used by permission.

DAY 185

Good Works and Salvation

Are good works necessary to salvation? The question is not a simple one.

In addressing this issue, Turretin argues that there are three main views when it comes to the necessity of good works. Some are like modern Libertines, who make good works arbitrary and indifferent. Others are like ancient Pharisees, who contend that works are necessary to justification. In trying to hold the orthodox middle ground between these two extremes, Turretin maintains that good works are necessary but not according to the necessity of merit. The question is not "whether good works are necessary to effect salvation or to acquire it of right" but whether good works are "required as the means and way for possessing salvation." It is in this last sense that Turretin affirms the necessity of good works.[1]

According to Turretin, the necessity of good works can be proved from several factors. (1) God commands good works. (2) The covenant of grace requires good works. (3) The gospel is a rule of faith and of life. (4) The state of grace sets us free to do good works. (5) The blessing of God includes sanctification unto good works.

In the covenant of grace there are still stipulations and obligations (some call them conditions). There are duties man owes to God and blessings that are connected to the exercise of these duties, even if—and this is important—God is the one who sees to it that these duties are carried out. Heaven cannot be reached without good works (Heb. 12:14; Rev. 21:27), which is why it is such good news that he who began a good work in us will be faithful to complete it (Phil. 1:6).

To insist on the necessity of good works is not to become a legalist or a neonomian. This question about the necessity of good works has often perplexed Christians. If, on the one hand, we say that, no, good works are not necessary, we can hardly make sense of the warnings and moral imperatives of the New Testament. But if we say good works are necessary to salvation, it strikes many Christians as though heaven is what we earn by our effort and obedience. But that's not what Hebrews 12:14 ("Strive for . . . the holiness without which no one will see the Lord") means, nor what Turretin means.

> Works can be considered in three ways: either with reference to justification or sanctification or glorification. They are related to justification not antecedently, efficiently and meritoriously, but consequently and declaratively. They are related to sanctification constitutively because they constitute and promote it. They are related to glorification antecedently and ordinatively because they are related to it as the means to the end.[2]

That's a dense paragraph, but wonderfully concise and crucially important. Good works are inextricably linked to justification, sanctification, and glorification, but they are related in different ways. Good works come after justification as a result and a declaration. Good works are identified with sanctification as its definition and cheerleader. And good works come before glorification as God's appointed means to a divinely secured end. As Turretin puts it, "grace is glory begun, as glory is grace consummated."

1 Turretin, *Elenctic Theology*, 2:702.
2 Turretin, *Elenctic Theology*, 2:705.

DAY 186

Good Works and the Believer

The good works of the believer are never perfect in this life, but they can still be truly good.

Let's deal first with the question of perfection. Interestingly, when it comes to obeying the law, Turretin thinks certain kinds of perfection *are* possible. The question about fulfilling the law absolutely is not about the *perfection of sincerity* (serving God with a whole heart), nor the *perfection of parts* (being sanctified in body and soul); neither is it about *comparative perfection* (that some believers would be more advanced than others), nor *evangelical perfection* (whereby God in paternal forbearance perfects our works with his grace). Turretin affirms "all these species of perfections," noting that the Bible often speaks of believers being "perfect" and "upright." The question for Turretin is not about these things, but about *legal perfection*, and in this matter the answer is clearly no. The renewed believer can never so scrupulously obey the divine law such that God would have nothing to accuse and condemn in him.[1]

That we are unable to fulfill the law absolutely can be seen from several realities taught clearly in Scripture: the remains of sin in the believer in 1 John 1, the struggle between flesh and the Spirit in Romans 7, the unbearable yoke of the law in Acts 15, the command to pray daily for the remission of sins in the Lord's Prayer, and the example of the saints throughout the Bible. There are many ways in which the Bible *does* talk about the believer being obedient, righteous, and holy, but we must not understand any of these to imply that we can so fulfill the law that God has nothing proper against us were he to judge strictly and legally.

Let's turn, then, from the perfection of good works (which, in a legal sense, is an impossibility for the believer) to the possibility of good works. When believers do what God commands, from a heart of faith, for the glory of God, God is pleased with us (Rom. 12:1; Col. 1:10; 1 John 3:22). Reformed Christians sometimes make the mistake of thinking that if they are to be *really* Reformed they must utterly denigrate everything they do as Christians. To be sure, as we have seen, we cannot fulfill the law absolutely. But here's where careful distinctions are helpful: good works can be *truly* good without being *perfectly* good.

Acting like holiness is out of reach for the ordinary Christian doesn't do justice to the way the Bible speaks about people like Zechariah and Elizabeth, who "were both righteous before God, walking blamelessly in all the commandments and statutes of the Lord" (Luke 1:6). It doesn't take seriously the Lord's commendation of Job as "a blameless and upright man, who fears God and turns away from evil" (Job 1:8), or of Paul, who frequently commends his churches for their obedience and godly example. Likewise, Jesus teaches that the wise person hears his words and does them (Matt. 7:24). James says the same thing (James 2:22–25). There's no hint that doing God's word was only a hypothetical category. Quite the contrary, we are told to disciple the nations that they might *obey* everything Jesus commanded (Matt 28:19–20).[2]

Christians *can* be rich in good works (Acts 9:36; 1 Tim. 6:18). We *can* walk in a way worthy of our calling (Eph. 4:1). Looking upon our good works in his Son, God "is pleased to accept and reward that which is sincere, although accompanied with many weaknesses and imperfections" (WCF 16.6).

1 Turretin, *Elenctic Theology*, 2:694–95.
2 This paragraph is adapted from DeYoung, *Hole in Our Holiness*, 65–66.

DAY 187

Good Works and Merit

We've already seen that good works are necessary (as the consequence of, not the grounding for, justification) and that good works can be truly (though not perfectly) good. Now we turn to the question of merit.

Roman Catholic theology distinguishes among three kinds of merit. *Strict merit* is when the reward given is equal to the action performed. This kind of merit is like a paycheck for services rendered; it refers to what is owed and earned. *Condign merit* is when the reward given is according to the promise made, not the intrinsic value of the act. Believers are said to perform good deeds with condign merit; that is, performed with the dignity of Christ and in the state of grace. This merit is owed but not strictly earned. *Congruent merit* is similar to condign merit, but not performed in a state of grace. This is the category of merit for the unregenerate person. When someone does something of value, but not something that God has promised to reward, the merit is neither owed nor earned.

The problem with this system is not that the distinctions themselves are illogical or completely unhelpful but that the word *merit* is not the right category to describe more decent behavior or Christian good works. As Turretin explains, *merit* can be used in two ways.[1] Broadly we might use *merit* simply to refer to a sequence of events. In this sense, the verb "to merit" was used by the church fathers for "to gain," or "to obtain," or "to attain." This broad use is understandable but misleading. Strictly and properly, *merit* denotes a work to which a reward is due on account of that work's intrinsic value. When most people speak of merit, they are thinking of something earned or owed.

In this sense, good works, even of the justified believer, do not possess any merit. For a good work to be meritorious in the strict and proper sense, at least five characteristics must be present:

1. The work must be "undue." That is, we are not merely doing what we owe.
2. The work must be ours and not owing to the work of another.
3. The work must be absolutely perfect.
4. The work is equal to the payment made.
5. The payment or reward is owed because of the intrinsic worth of the work.[2]

Our good works do not meet any of these requirements. For even our best works are (1) merely what we owe, (2) from God's grace in us, (3) imperfect, (4) much less than the reward of eternal life, and (5) not worthy in and of themselves. Good works are necessary to salvation, but not in order to effect salvation or acquire it by right. The necessity is one of connection and sequence, not of causality and efficacy.

In short, while our good works are often praiseworthy in Scripture—pleasing to God and truly good—they do not win for us our heavenly reward. God is always true to his promises, but he never "owes" us anything. There is a true and necessary connection between good works and final glorification, but the connection is not one of merit.

1 Turretin, *Elenctic Theology*, 2:710–11.
2 Turretin, *Elenctic Theology*, 2:712.

DAY 188

Perseverance

Of the so-called five points of Calvinism—total depravity, unconditional election, limited atonement, irresistible grace, perseverance of the saints—the *P* is the one most people want to affirm. It's also the one many people misunderstand. A lot of Christians will gladly hold to the doctrine of "eternal security" or "once saved, always saved." But those slogans can be misleading and are easily misapplied. We need a more careful understanding of perseverance. Too often Christians have a mechanical view of salvation and, therefore, an unbiblical view of eternal security. They see "getting saved" as something that infallibly took place when they walked the aisle, raised their hand, and prayed the sinner's prayer. As long as you took that magical step of salvation, you have your "get out of jail free" card forever, and God is obliged to redeem you on the last day.

That's not exactly what the Bible teaches. Those who "believe in the name of the Son of God" already "have eternal life" (1 John 5:13). So, yes, we absolutely cannot become unregenerate once born again, or unjustified once justified. At the same time, those who do not "continue with us" demonstrate that "they were not of us" (see 1 John 2:19). We cannot lose our salvation, but we can be deceived about having it in the first place. The perseverance of the saints is not a doctrine to encourage spiritual lethargy and moral laxity. It is a doctrine that encourages the Christian to actively *persevere* in faith, in repentance, and in godliness because we have confidence that God will unfailingly *preserve* the elect.

The hymn writer was right: "Prone to wander, Lord I feel it; prone to leave the God I love." Left to ourselves, we would not remain in God's grace. Apart from God's intervention, it would not only be possible for men and women to forfeit saving faith, argues the Canons of Dort; it "undoubtedly would happen" (5.8). But praise God, we are not left to ourselves. Although we sin and struggle and may even stray from the path, God's purpose in election will stand (Rom. 9:11). In the end, it is not possible to destroy and deceive the elect (Matt. 24:24; 1 Pet. 1:5). "The power of God strengthening and preserving true believers in grace is more than a match for the flesh" (Canons of Dort 5.4). Or as John puts it, "He who is in you is greater than he who is in the world" (1 John 4:4).

This preserving grace is more than a passive protection. God *causes us* to persevere by actively working in what we need to keep walking with Christ. The seed of the word cannot finally be removed in the elect. God does not let the seed of the word die in us. God keeps those sermons and those Bible studies and those memory verses doing their good work in our hearts. God also renews our hearts unto repentance. True believers will always come back to a "heartfelt and godly sorrow for their sins." We will, then, "through faith and with a contrite heart" seek and obtain forgiveness in the blood of the mediator. And finally, we will "experience again the grace of a reconciled God" (Canons of Dort 5.7). As "Amazing Grace" reminds us, the grace that saves a wretch like me is also the grace that will lead us home.[1]

---

1 Parts of this section were adapted from DeYoung, *Grace Defined and Defended*, 81–82, 86–87. Used by permission.

⌇

DAY 189

Warning Passages

The New Testament contains many threats and warnings for God's people. Jesus told the disciples not to build their house on the sands and so be washed when the rains come (Matt. 7:26–27). Paul told the Corinthians that the unrighteous will not inherit the kingdom of God (1 Cor. 6:9) and that anyone who thinks that he stands should take heed lest he fall (1 Cor. 10:12). Hebrews, in particular, is full of warning passages. God's people are told not to neglect so great a salvation (2:1–4), not to harden their hearts like Israel did in the rebellion (3:7–4:13), not to be like those who have tasted the heavenly gift and have fallen away (5:11–6:12), not to profane the blood of the covenant (10:19–39), and not to be those who squander their birthright like Esau (12:14–29).

How do we make sense of these warning passages? Surely, part of the answer is to recognize that while it is possible to make shipwreck of the faith (1 Tim. 1:19), those who do so were never really of the faith (1 John 2:19). But that still doesn't tell us how genuine believers should appropriate (or not) the Bible's threats and exhortations. If the elect will infallibly persevere to the end, should they simply ignore the dire warnings about those who fall away? What role (if any) do those five passages in Hebrews, and others like them, play in the life of God's regenerate, justified people?

The Canons of Dort provides the best succinct answer to that question.

And, just as it has pleased God to begin this work of grace in us by the proclamation of the gospel, so he preserves, continues, and completes his work by the hearing and reading of the gospel, by meditation on it, by its exhortations, threats, and promises, and also by the use of the sacraments. (5.14)

Notice two things. First, God causes us to persevere by several means. He makes promises to us, but he also threatens. He works by the hearing of the gospel and by the use of the sacraments. He has not bound himself to one method. Surely this helps us make sense of the warnings in Hebrews and elsewhere in the New Testament. Threats and exhortations do not undermine perseverance; they help to complete it. God keeps us from stumbling (Jude 24), and he does so in part by telling us to keep ourselves in the love of God (Jude 21).

Second, notice the broad way in which Dort understands the gospel. In a strict sense we can say that the gospel is the good news of how to be saved. But in a wider sense, the gospel encompasses the whole story of salvation, which includes not only gospel promises but also the threats and exhortations inherent in the message of the cross. The God who keeps us means to keep us by means, and this includes not only the sacraments and discipline but also the "holy admonitions of the gospel" (3/4.17).

Glorification

Those whom God foreknew he also predestined, those he predestined he also called, those whom he called he also justified, and those whom he justified he also glorified (Rom. 8:29–30). Glorification is the completion of sanctification, the fruit of justification, and the enjoyment of adoption.

Like the rest of the *ordo salutis*, glorification is in and with Christ (Rom. 8:17). Glorification does not mean absorption into the divine, but it does mean a perfection in heaven we have not yet enjoyed here on earth (Heb. 12:23). We are not going back to the beginning of things, nor continuing in a cycle of reincarnation. There is a telos to human existence, and it ends, for the Christian, with a fuller humanity than we've had before, as we are renewed in the image of the God-man, Jesus Christ.

Biblically, we can think of glorification in several different and complementary ways. Romans 8 refers to our final glorification as "the revealing of the sons of God" (v. 19). Creation waits for this revelation with eager longing, knowing that only then will it be set free from bondage to corruption and obtain the glory of the children of God (8:21). Notice that creation is said to be caught up in *our* glory, not the other way around. We are the headline; the restoration of the cosmos is below the fold.

Revelation 21:1–8 provides another glimpse of glorification. When all things are made new, our lives will finally be free from three realities. We will be without suffering (no more tears, no more death, no more pain), we will be without sin (all will be holy in the heavenly city), and we will be without separation (God will dwell with us, and we will be his people).

Theologically, we can say that glorification makes us physically, morally, and conceptually perfect. Physically, we will experience the redemption of our bodies (Rom. 8:23) as we are raised in glory and in power (1 Cor. 15:43–44). Morally, we will be unalterably fixed in a state of holiness so that we might properly inhabit a new heavens and a new earth in which righteousness dwells (2 Pet. 3:13). Conceptually, we will be given a perfect and clear knowledge of God and of divine things, so that the one we now see dimly, we will then see face-to-face (1 Cor. 13:12).

This final perfection is sometimes called the beatific vision, the ability to see God in all his blessedness. Of course, God will still be God, and we will still be his creatures. That ontological gap will not be erased. We will not penetrate into the essence of God. But we will be given a supernatural vision—by perfection of intellect and consummation of will—so that we might see what no eye has seen (1 Cor. 2:9). This vision will beget love because we are beholding what is most lovely. The vision will also lead to joy, because joy answers to hope, and once glorified we will then have the thing hoped for. Our joy "will arise from the possession of God himself, which, as he is the supreme good, embraces all the universality and perpetuity of blessing."[1] Or as the Belgic Confession says about the reward for the elect, "the Lord will make them possess a glory such as the heart of man could never imagine" (BC Art. 37).

1 Turretin, *Elenctic Theology*, 3:612.

ECCLESIOLOGY

The Nature, Mission, and
Ordering of the Church

DAY 191

Church

For the Christian, there are few words more common than *church*. As a pastor, I'm sure I say the word hundreds of times each week. My kids learned to say "church" as one of their first words. Every week we talk about going to church, being part of a church, or what we learned at church.

But what does the word mean?

Before we get to our English word *church*, let's start with some Hebrew and Greek. There are two Hebrew words used in the Old Testament that mean assembly or gathering—*qahal* from the root meaning "to call" and *edhah* from a root meant "to appoint" or "to meet together." These two words are often translated when appearing side by side as "assembly of the congregation" (Ex. 12:6; Num. 14:5; Jer. 26:16). Sometimes the two words signify a meeting of the people's representatives (1 Kings 8:1–5).

The two Hebrew words are usually rendered in the Septuagint (the Greek translation of the Old Testament) as *synagoge* or *ekklesia*. The word *synagoge* means "to meet together" and can be used for the place of meeting (Matt. 4:23) or for the gathering itself (Acts 13:43). The word *ekklesia* could be translated woodenly as "called out ones" but by the time of the first century the word simply referred to a public assembly (Acts 19:32, 39, 41). Jesus was the first to use the word in an explicitly Christian sense when he promised, "I will build my church" (Matt. 16:18).

Our word *church*, like the words *kirk* (Scotland) or *kirche* (Germany), is not related etymologically to *ekklesia* but to *kuriake*, a Greek word meaning "belonging to the Lord." Although people sometimes get bent out of shape if you call your building a "church," there is good reason for doing so. The church is an *ekklesia* (an assembly), but it is also a *kuriakon* (a place that belongs to the Lord).

The New Testament employs a number of images for the church. Most prominently, the church is likened to three B's. The church is like a *building*, with Christ as the cornerstone, the apostles and prophets as the foundation, and each of us built together into a dwelling place for God (Eph. 2:19–22;

cf. 1 Cor. 3:16–17). The church is like a *body*, with Christ as the head and each of us connected to one another and members of that body (Rom. 12:4–5; 1 Cor. 12:12; Eph. 5:23). The church can also be compared to a *bride*, with Christ as the groom and God's people collectively as the wife of the Lamb (Eph. 5:31–32; Rev. 19:7–8; 21:9). While we should not press any of the images too far, we can see how a building emphasizes the church's solidity in Christ, a body emphasizes our connection to Christ, and a bride emphasizes our relationship to Christ.

The church is not an optional extra but an essential element of what it means to be a Christian and to grow in Christ. When we confess, in the Apostles' Creed, our belief "in the holy catholic church" we do so as a part of our belief in the Holy Spirit, right before stating our belief in the forgiveness of sins, the resurrection of the body, and the life everlasting. Believing in the church is no small matter; such faith cannot be separated from salvation itself and from trust in our triune God.

DAY 192

Nature of the Church

Believe it or not, many of the most heated debates among Christians today come back to ecclesiology. We are often arguing about the mission of the church or the witness of the church or the posture of the church because we haven't gotten squared away on the nature of the church. At the heart of a healthy ecclesiology is a series of both/and distinctions about the church.

The church is militant and triumphant. God's people must fight and travail here on earth. At the same time, there is a church in heaven gathered in glorified repose. The church must be at war—against sin, the flesh, and the devil—while also enjoying the Sabbath rest won for us in Christ.

The church is visible and invisible. This important distinction does not refer to two churches, as if we could choose to be a part of the invisible church but not the visible church. Instead, the distinction draws our attention to the church as she is (visible) and the church as she is called to be (invisible). The distinction can also contrast the church in an outward and external relationship to Christ and the church in an internal and spiritual relationship to Christ. Finally, the distinction is sometimes used to describe the professing church we can see on earth compared to the church of all the elect—in heaven and on earth—that we cannot see.

The church is catholic and local. On the one hand, the church cannot be confined to any one place or people. It is universal (which is what "catholic" means). On the other hand, the church finds tangible expression among an identifiable group of people. God does not give us the option to belong to the church universal without also belonging to a local church.

The church is organism and organization. Some Christians hear "church" and think of nothing but buildings and budgets. They need to be reminded that the church is a living, breathing, growing organism. At the same time, the church is also an institution, with officers, doctrines, rites, and orders.

The church is gathered and scattered. What the church looks like on Sunday in a specific time and place—that is the church gathered. But the church doesn't disappear after the last service on Sunday only to reappear in another week. The church also exists as believers spread abroad in their homes, in their workplaces, and in their communities.

Many mistakes in the church are the result of celebrating one half of each pair at the expense of the other side. We need both sides of the *and* lest we become unrealistic about what the church will be or skeptical about what Christ says she is. The church is bigger than the physical location where we are, but we need to belong to the church wherever we are. The church is more than an institution, but it cannot be less. The church needs trellis and vine. We should not expect every meaningful thing in the Christian life to happen on Sunday or in the walls of the church building. And yet the corporate gathering is a unique time for edification, covenant renewal, and reflecting the glories of heaven.

For realism without cynicism, for structure without lifelessness, for rejoicing in the big picture and in small places, we need the church with all of its both/and splendor.

DAY 193

Unity

Most of us have thought about the attributes of God, those qualities and characteristics that describe the Godness of God. But fewer Christians have considered the attributes of the church. Fortunately, many of us have learned these attributes without realizing it. The Nicene Creed confesses: "We believe in one holy, catholic and apostolic Church." The four attributes of the church are found in that one sentence: unity, holiness, catholicity, and apostolicity.

Because God is one, the church is one (John 17:11). Though diverse in many ways (1 Cor. 12:4–31), the church is bound together as one body. The dividing wall of hostility between Jews and Gentiles has been torn down (Eph. 2:14–18), and by that same unifying blood of Christ other estranged peoples can be reconciled in Christ. So important is the unity of the church that Jesus made it a central theme in his high priestly prayer (John 17:21).

The unity of the church is not primarily external, but internal and spiritual in character. That is to say, the presence of many congregations, or even many denominations, may not necessarily be a violation of "one" church. Not all divisions are schismatic. Many are caused by unavoidable differences in language, culture, and location. Berkhof puts it well: "It is quite possible that the inherent riches of the organism of the Church find better and fuller expression in the present variety of Churches than they would in a single, external organization."[1] Moreover, according to the apostle Paul, some factions—when the result of moral laxity or theological heterodoxy—can be an occasion for true Christians and true churches to stand apart from counterfeits (1 Cor. 11:19). The oneness of the church depends upon the church also being holy, catholic, and apostolic.

The logic of Ephesians 4:1–16 is crucial. Unity is a relational good we are called to maintain where true spiritual unity is already present. Having just finished explaining how the mystery of the gospel brings together Jews and Gentiles, Paul exhorts the Ephesians to "maintain the unity of the Spirit in the bond of peace" (4:3). All true Christians, at all times and in all places, share in one body, one Spirit, one hope, one Lord, one faith, one baptism, one God and Father of all (4:4–6). This is what theologians call the essential unity of the church. Paul wants the Jewish and Gentile Christians in Ephesus to get along because, despite their historic, ethnic, and cultural differences, they have these deep, essential, spiritual realities in common. The goal, then, is to be patient with each other and bear with one another in love (4:2).

There is no unity of the Spirit without a shared allegiance to our one Lord Jesus Christ and a shared commitment to our one faith (4:13). If we do not share "one faith" with Mormons or liberals or Unitarians (and we do not), then we have no unity to maintain. Paul celebrates unity in the midst of diversity, but the diversity is not theological. Unity is something true, orthodox Christians have in Christ; something we strive to maintain in the church; and something we grow into now and in the future (4:13).

1 Berkhof, *Systematic Theology*, 574.

Holiness

The holiness of the church is both a present positional reality—ours through union with Christ—and an ideal for which we must labor and toil. Holiness, for the Christian as well as for the church, is both gift and calling. We who are perfected in Christ are also being sanctified in Christ (Heb. 10:14). Holiness is what the church already has (Heb. 10:10), what the church will one day become (12:10), and what the church must presently strive after (12:14).

It's important that we keep in mind the positional and progressive aspects of the church's holiness. The church already *is* holy. The church is Christ's body and Christ's bride. We are a chosen race, a royal priesthood, and God's own treasured possession. Once we were not a people, but now we are God's people (1 Pet. 2:9–10). Despite the church's many failings and sins, she is still a holy temple in the Lord, being built together into a dwelling place for God by the Spirit (Eph. 2:21–22).

At the same time, the church that is holy is called to *be* holy (1 Pet. 1:16). We must abstain from the passions of the flesh, keep our conduct honorable, and live such good lives that the critics of the church will be proven wrong when Christ returns (2:11–12). In an age that prizes "authenticity" more than authority, and "messiness" more than godliness, we must never forget that Christ gave himself up for the church—to save us from sin's penalty *and* from sin's power. Christ did not die so that we can revel in our brokenness and be vulnerable regarding our rebellion. The Lord Jesus died to sanctify us, to cleanse us, and to wash us with the word (Eph. 5:25–26). The church that God called into existence and the church that God blesses is the church that reflects God's character.

In a similar vein, we can also affirm that the true church is *indefectible*: God's holy church will not ultimately fail. This does not mean that the church cannot act in ways repugnant to its own nature or that the visible church cannot be snuffed out (by persecution or by perfidy) at various times and in various places. But the church scattered across the globe cannot fail altogether. The promises of God, the preservation by the Spirit, and the power of Christ all ensure that there will never cease to be a true church on the earth (Matt. 16:18; 28:19–20). Nations will come and go. Great men and women will rise and fall. Powerful institutions will wax and wane. There is no institution save the church that Jesus promises to build, and no other organization whose ultimate mission is so indissolubly assured of success. The church will press on. Her perpetuity—like her present and future holiness—is guaranteed by Christ himself.

DAY 195

Catholicity

As a Protestant pastor I've lost track of how many times a congregant has asked me after we've recited the Apostles' Creed in worship, "Why do we profess to believe in the holy *catholic* church?" The answer is simple. The Greek word *katholikos* means "general," "universal," or "pertaining to the whole." While we do not confess our faith in the *Roman* Catholic Church, we do confess to believing in the catholic, or universal, church.

We can think of the church's catholicity in four different ways.

1. *With respect to places.* The church is not limited to one specific location. Believers everywhere can worship God in Spirit and in truth (John 4:21). God's people are scattered around the globe, yet truly one in Christ. What's more, the church to which we belong on earth is a part of the same universal church reigning in heaven.

2. *With respect to persons.* The church is, and was always meant to be, a global body. Even now, worshipers from various tribes, languages, peoples, and nations are gathered around the throne (Rev. 5:9). Membership in the true church is not restricted by race or ethnicity, by sex, or by social standing (Gal. 3:28; Col. 3:11).

3. *With respect to times.* The church is diffused across geographic, political, and cultural boundaries. It is also diffused across the centuries. We are a part of the church that has existed since the beginning of the world and will exist unto the consummation of all things. No matter his personal age or the age of his church or denomination, the Christian belongs to the oldest, most diverse, most global institution on the planet.

4. *With respect to truth.* The word *catholic* is not found in the New Testament but was used often by the church fathers to distinguish the church that was bound by the apostles' teaching from various sects and heretical groups. To be "catholic" does not mean we are in allegiance to an ecclesiastical hierarchy and an earthly pope. It means we are in allegiance to the faith that was once for all delivered to the saints (Jude 3).

A proper understanding of catholicity can help the church avoid a number of sins and errors. Racism, for example, is a fundamental rejection of the church's catholicity, as are our church-growth strategies that try to build a church with only certain kinds of people. Catholicity can also be threatened when national concerns become confused as necessarily Christian concerns.

In its proper place, patriotism can be a Christian expression of loving our neighbor, celebrating self-sacrifice, and giving honor to whom honor is due. But as a pastor I should not lead my people on Sunday morning in saying, praying, or singing things that they would only believe as Americans and not in common with Christians from Poland, Japan, or Mexico.

Perhaps the greatest threat to the church's catholicity is the defense and promotion of grave theological error. To be sure, the church has made plenty of doctrinal and ethical mistakes in its history. And yet our default should be to trust the work of the Spirit teaching the church over the centuries. When, for example, churches move to bless same-sex unions or sanction abortion on demand, they not only presume to know more than any Christian communion prior to the second half of the twentieth century; they also do great harm to the catholicity of the church. If the church in the West really believes in one holy, catholic church, it will cease to undermine doctrinal commitments that have been held, until a few decades ago, by Christians at all times and in all places.

WEEK 40

DAY 196

Apostolicity

The attribute of apostolicity does not refer to an apostolic succession of bishops but to an apostolic succession of truth. The New Testament is infinitely more concerned that the church remain fixed to the gospel handed down by the apostles than it is concerned with a supposed hierarchy of ecclesiastical primates descended from Peter. From the very beginning, the church devoted itself to the apostles' teaching (Acts 2:42). The church that is truly one, holy, and catholic is the church built upon the foundation of the apostles and prophets (Eph. 2:20).

The Pastoral Epistles in particular show the importance of the church anchoring itself in the apostolic deposit of truth. Paul tells Timothy to "charge certain persons not to teach any different doctrine" (1 Tim. 1:3). He warns against false teachers who have swerved from the truth and don't really understand what they are so confidently asserting (1 Tim. 1:6–7; 2 Tim. 3:7; Titus 1:16). According to Paul, these false teachers have made shipwreck of the faith (1 Tim. 1:19–20) and departed from the faith by devoting themselves to deceitful spirits and the teachings of demons (1 Tim. 4:1). They are opposed to the truth, corrupt in mind, and disqualified regarding the faith (2 Tim. 3:8). Their teaching "will lead people into more and more ungodliness, and their talk will spread like gangrene" (2 Tim. 2:16–17).

The importance of apostolic doctrine cannot be overstated. Anyone who thinks doctrine doesn't matter is not paying attention to the Bible. Timothy is enjoined repeatedly to guard the deposit of apostolic truth entrusted to him (1 Tim. 6:20; 2 Tim. 1:13, 14) and to pass it on to others (2 Tim. 2:1–2). He must keep a close watch on his life and his teaching so that he and his hearers may be saved (1 Tim. 4:16). As the Lord's servant, Timothy must be able to teach (1 Tim. 3:2), correct his opponents with gentleness (2 Tim. 2:25), and reprove, rebuke, and exhort from the Scriptures (2 Tim. 4:2; 3:16). In short, he must be "able to give instruction in sound doctrine and also to rebuke those who contradict it" (Titus 1:9, 13). Church people may not always endure sound teaching, but that's what they desperately need (2 Tim. 4:1–5).

Clearly, then, for the apostle Paul, there is a core of apostolic teaching that must be embraced by the Christian, a deposit of truth without which our gospel message is no longer the gospel. The early church believed orthodoxy was crucially important, and it was more than just living the right way; it involved holding certain truths about God, Christ, and salvation: God is glorious, we are sinners, and Jesus Christ is our Savior and God. Jesus Christ is the son of David and God in the flesh; he died and rose again; he ascended into heaven; he is coming again. Salvation is by sovereign grace, according to the converting power of the Holy Spirit, through faith, not according to works. Jesus Christ saves us from sin, saves us for eternal life, and saves us unto holiness. This is the gospel of the early church. It is rooted in Scripture, and it is not to be deviated from. This unchanging message must be proclaimed confidently by any church that would lay claim to apostolic authority.

DAY 197

Marks of the Church

It was Cyprian, the third-century bishop of Carthage, who famously said, "No one can have God for his Father who has not the Church for his mother."[1] He was right. The church is not incidental to God's plan of salvation, nor can it be incidental in our lives as Christians.

But Cyprian's famous dictum leads to an important follow-up question: Which church? From the earliest days of the church, Christianity has been beset by heresies, schisms, and sects. Therefore, distinguishing the true church from the false church has always been critical. This was especially the case during the Reformation as Protestant theologians, wary of Rome, tried to determine—from Scripture and from the logic of the gospel—what was absolutely necessary for a church to be a church. How many marks of the church are essential, and what are they?

The debate about the marks of the church is not about the well-being (*bene esse*) of the church but about the essence (*esse*) of the church. If we were to consider what constitutes a healthy church, we would want to mention dozens of things, from prayer to missions to expository preaching. The Reformers were interested in reforming every aspect of the church's work and worship.

But the question about the marks is more narrowly focused on what constitutes a church (in name) as a church (in reality). Some Roman Catholic theologians taught only one mark (being in submission to and in communion with the Roman pontiff), while others like Cardinal Bellarmine increased the number of marks to fifteen. Not surprisingly, Reformed theologians insisted on a different set of marks.

While Reformed theologians agree that right doctrine is the fundamental mark of the church, they have not always agreed on the exact number of marks. Some have enumerated three marks: right preaching of the word, right administration of the sacraments, and right exercise of discipline (Ursinus, De Bres). Others have preferred only two marks: preaching and sacraments (Calvin, Bullinger, Turretin, Mastricht, à Marck). And some have argued for only one mark: pure preaching of the word of God (Beza, Bannerman).

In the end, Turretin is right to see more harmony than discord in these different schemes so long as each scheme, no matter the number, is centered on right doctrine:

> In the first degree of necessity is the pure preaching and profession of the word, since without it the church cannot exist. But the administration of the sacraments does not have an equal degree of necessity which so depends upon the former that I may nevertheless be wanting for a time. . . . The same is the case with discipline, which pertains to the defense of the church, but which, being removed or corrupted, the church is not immediately taken away.[2]

In other words, the sacraments and discipline are also essential, but they are dependent upon the word in a way that the word is not dependent upon the sacraments and discipline. The essence of the true church is its proclamation and profession of the whole council of God.

1 Cyprian, *Unity of the Catholic Church*, chap. 6.
2 Turretin, *Elenctic Theology*, 3.87–88.

DAY 198

Preaching

Given its importance as one of the marks—if not *the* mark—of the true church, it is worth reflecting some more on the centrality of preaching.

The sermon was not stolen from the pagans or inherited from the Enlightenment. The sermon came from Judaism, which developed and refined the practice of exegesis and expositional preaching in the centuries leading up to Christ. The cardinal characteristic of Jewish worship was the reading and preaching of the inspired Scriptures.

We can see this in nascent form throughout the Old Testament. The Levites were to teach Israel the law (Deut. 33:10). The true priest did not just offer sacrifices; he was a teaching priest (2 Chron. 15:3). Ezra read the law to the returning exiles, giving them the sense of it (Neh. 8:6–8).

We see the same development in the New Testament. We know John the Baptist preached and Jesus preached. We know Paul preached and instructed his apprentice Timothy, with the most solemn warning, to also preach (2 Tim. 4:1–2). Even Jesus himself, we should remember, was a trainer of preachers, sending his disciples out not just to facilitate group discussions or inductive Bible studies, but to preach (Mark 3:14). The apostles considered the ministry of the word such a full-time job that they appointed other men to care for the physical needs of the church (Acts 6:1–7).

We can trace the same priorities in the early church. The Didache—one of the earliest noncanonical writings—speaks of daily services of the word and a large body of prophets, teachers, bishops, and deacons who devoted themselves full-time to preaching and teaching. Likewise, Justin Martyr recalled, "And on the day called Sunday, all who live in cities or in the country gather together to one place, and the memoirs of the apostles or the writings of the prophets are read, as long as time permits; then, when the reader has ceased, the president verbally instructs, and exhorts to the imitation of these good things." From the very beginning, preaching has been central to the worship of God's gathered people.

God has always been a revealing God, a God who speaks to his people. By the word he created the heavens and the earth. By the word he formed the nation of Israel at Sinai. By the word he instructed his people through the prophets. By the word he gathers and instructs the church. Christ, the Word made flesh, is present in God's speech to his people. That is why the Thessalonians were right to receive Paul's preaching "not as the word of men but as what it really is, the word of God" (1 Thess. 2:13).

God meets with and rules over his people through the authoritative preaching of the word of God. The Greek word for preacher is *kerux*. It is different from the word for teacher or apostle (2 Tim. 1:11). A *kerux* is a herald, the king's messenger. When Amos predicted a "famine" of "hearing the words of the LORD" (Amos 8:11), he wasn't thinking of the lack of personal impressions or a still, small voice inside of us. He was thinking about the absence of God's appointed mouthpieces to declare his word. Faithful gospel preaching is not an optional extra in God's plan for the church. Indeed, there is no true church without it.

DAY 199

Members of the Church

The question at hand is not, Who are the members of the invisible church? The invisible church consists of the whole number of the elect. That is not the issue before us. We want to consider who are the members of the visible church.

The Westminster Confession of Faith puts the matter succinctly: "The visible church . . . consists of all those throughout the world that profess the true religion; and of their children" (25.2). Let's take each of these two statements in turn.

First, the confession says that the visible church is made up of those who profess the true religion. This means that mere outward conformity to church authority and the sacramental system is not enough to be counted a member of the visible church (at least, that is the case for adults; more on children in a moment). If the essence of a true church is the right preaching of the gospel, then it stands to reason that the one thing required for entry into the visible church is a profession of faith in this true gospel. Sitting in church services, partaking of Christian rituals, even giving money to the church—these things by themselves do not constitute membership in the visible church.

Notice, however, that the confession makes the line of membership a right profession rather than regeneration per se. Of course, we don't want hypocrites and nominal Christians to feel falsely self-assured by membership in the church. And yet the confession recognizes that determining inner conviction and experience is extremely difficult. We are more competent to judge what can be seen and heard instead of the invisible realities of the heart. Adult church members must make a credible profession of faith that can be seen in their character and patterns of life.

But what about children? While I respect my Baptist friends who argue that the new covenant differs from the old covenant in that the new (unlike the old) includes only those who truly know the Lord (citing Jer. 31:34), we should remember that the new covenant replaced the Mosaic covenant, not the Abrahamic covenant (31:32; cf. Gal. 3:17). What Jeremiah promises is the fulfillment of the promises to Abraham that "I will be their God, and they shall be my people" (Jer. 31:33; cf. Gen. 17:7–8).

As we move from the old covenant to the new covenant, no new principle regarding children is introduced. The covenant promises still include children (Acts 2:39), children of believers are still considered holy to the Lord (1 Cor. 7:14), and God still deals with whole households (Acts 16:13–15). For two millennia—from Abraham to Christ—the visible church included believers and their children. If children were suddenly excluded from membership in the family of God, surely there would have been howls of protest from confused parents in the early church. We see great controversy over the expanding nature of the visible church, now bringing in the Gentiles, but we do not see a contraction that would cut children out. In fact, virtually every congregation and every Christian family treats their children as inside the church, even if their theology might suggest they are outsiders. While we undoubtedly ought to insist on children making their own profession of faith when they are of the age to do so, there is no good reason to think that covenant children do not belong to the visible church today, as the children of the covenant did before Christ.

DAY 200

Church and State

In his 1802 letter, Thomas Jefferson wrote to the Danbury Baptist Association in Connecticut offering his interpretation that the Constitution erected a "wall of separation between Church & State." Although Jefferson's phrase has been often misapplied, and his gloss on the First Amendment can be criticized, Jefferson was right to recognize that church and state are different institutions whose aim and approaches must not be confused or conflated.

The church is the visible society of professing Christians (and their children) on earth. This society has an order and government designed primarily for the spiritual well-being of its members, though not without all reference to the temporal interests of the community.

By contrast, the state is the visible society of all the members of that body (e.g., a country). This society has an order and government designed primarily for the temporal well-being of its members, though not without reference to the spiritual well-being of its members.[1]

While the church and the state will overlap in aims and functions at times, and both societies are ultimately accountable to God and will be judged according to the divine law, the two institutions are fundamentally different and independent.

The two societies differ in their origin. The church owes its origin to Christ as mediator. The state is founded in nature, not in grace. That is, the state is common to all people, whereas the church is a part of God's redemptive plan.

The two societies differ in the primary objects for which they were instituted. The church was ordained by God for the salvation of souls and for the spiritual good of its heavenly citizens. The state was ordained by God for the outward order and good of human society.

The two societies differ in the power committed to them. The church's power does not involve the exercise of physical force. The church exercises its power by the force of truth upon the convictions and consciences of men. To the magistrates of the state belongs the power of the sword.

The two societies differ in the administration of their respective authorities. The church has its own office bearers to exercise authority over its own affairs. The state, while not being prescribed a specific form of government in Scripture, has its own office bearers appointed by God to exercise authority as a government over the governed.

If these four points are true, then we must reject any Erastian system (based on the Swiss physician Thomas Erastus, 1524–1583) whereby the state exercises supreme authority over the church, and any medieval system whereby the church attempts to exercise supreme authority over the state. In the best of circumstances, the church and the state will pursue their unique aims in ways that are mutually reinforcing of the other, but the two societies must not be confused as being the same.

---

1 These definitions, as well as the points that follow, summarize Bannerman, *The Church of Christ,* 101–13, though it should be noted that Bannerman, who defended the establishment principle, argues for a more pronounced role for the state in establishing, supporting, and promoting true religion.

DAY 201

Nature and Extent of Church Power

God has ordained two great agencies of divine authority on the earth: the state and the church. They are both governed by God and accountable to God, but the way in which God exercises his power through the state and the church differs significantly. In keeping with the distinction laid out in Matthew 22:16–21 ("Render to Caesar the things that are Caesar's"), the state has been given authority to exercise power relative to the outward and temporal rights and privileges of men. The church, by contrast, has been given authority to exercise power relative to the inward and spiritual state and consciences of men.

The nature of church power is *ministerial* and *declarative*. This means all church power—whether exercised by the whole body, pronounced from the pulpit, or bound up in representative officers—must be in service to Christ (ministerial) and involves stating and enforcing the word of God (declarative). In Presbyterian polity, a group of elders exercising church power (in a session, a presbytery, or a general assembly), is called a "court" of the church, because the power vested in church officers is never legislative. The elders are only called to declare the mind of Christ, not to speak their own mind on whatever they deem important. Church power is a spiritual power, pertaining to believers, exercised in a moral and spiritual way, and never resorting to force.[1]

Reformed theologians have typically described church power using three categories.

1. *Potestas dogmatike* (power of dogma) is the authority the church possesses in regard to doctrine and faith. The power is not absolute but consists in the church's calling to interpret the Scriptures, draw up subordinate standards (i.e., confessions), and press the claims of Christ upon the consciences of men. The church has been given power to bear witness to the truth of God to those inside and outside the church.

2. *Potestas diataktike* (power of ordaining) is the authority the church possesses in regard to its own ordinances and government. While the church cannot bind the conscience to any man-made law, it does have power to adopt rules for effective operation that are in accord with the teaching of Scripture. Like every

society, the church is well served by doing things "decently and in order" (1 Cor. 14:40; cf. 14:26).

3. *Potestas diakritike* (power of distinguishing) is the authority the church possesses in regard to the discipline of its members. The church is not given a sword (as the state is), but rather keys that it might open and close membership in the church (as an expression of entrance into or expulsion from Christ's heavenly kingdom).

The function of the church, as distinct from the state, is "to proclaim, to administer, and to enforce the law of Christ revealed in the Scriptures."[2] The church *qua* church (i.e., the church in its capacity as the church) has not been granted authority to address every topic, settle every controversy, or right every wrong. The nature of church power extends to all those under its care but is limited to doctrine, order, and discipline.

1 Berkhof, *Systematic Theology*, 594.
2 PCA *Book of Church Order*, 3–3.

DAY 202

Establishment Principle and Voluntary Principle

As Reformed ecclesiology developed in the modern world, few theologians advocated final state authority over the church or final church authority over the state. Anything too close to the former was dismissed as Erastian, who argued for state supremacy in ecclesiastical affairs, and anything too close to the latter was considered dangerously Catholic.

But this doesn't mean the relationship between church and state was easy to figure out. Far from it. Even in countries with deep Protestant roots, church leaders and theologians often disagreed on whether the church should be organized according to the establishment principle or the voluntary principle.

According to the establishment principle, the church should be supported, defended, and promoted by the state. Even in a country like Scotland, which had long emphasized the distinction between church and state as two kings and two kingdoms, the assumption was that Scotland was a Christian nation and ought to be governed as a godly commonwealth. The church alone had authority to determine its worship, doctrine, and discipline, but the state was obligated to recognize and support the church by means of tax revenue and by upholding certain fundamental principles of true piety (e.g., Sabbath observance). The magistrate was afforded a power about religion (*circa sacra*) but not a power in religion (*in sacris*).

By contrast, those holding to the voluntary principle insisted upon a sharper separation of church and state. Most practically, this meant that the church was to be supported by the voluntary contributions of church members rather than out of the state coffers. Likewise, no one would be considered a member of the church simply by virtue of being a citizen of that country. Churches would be formed by the voluntary association of those wanting to belong to a given congregation. Among paedobaptists, "those" included parents and their children.

Given the fact that many of the greatest Protestant theologians in history have belonged to and believed in an establishment church, I'm hesitant to insist that the idea cannot mesh with biblical principles. And yet (as a Presbyterian), I'm glad that American Presbyterians, in forming a national denomination in 1788, altered the Westminster Standards in several places so as to give the civil magistrate much less of a role in the affairs of the church (WCF 20.4, 23.3, 31.1; WLC 109), sowing the seeds of disestablishment (which took almost fifty more years to play out in the individual states). This formal change cemented what had already taken place informally when chapters 20 and 23 of the confession were curtailed with the Adopting Act of 1729.

While the separation of church and state has often been misconstrued as the separation of the church *from* the state (or, in more recent years, the hostility of the state toward the church), I nevertheless see good reasons for the voluntary principle. (1) In an establishment, the church normally depends, to some degree, upon state revenue. This makes true ecclesiastical independence impossible. What the state giveth, the state can also taketh away. (2) The state that can establish my religion can later change its mind and establish someone else's religion. Given our belief in human depravity and corruptibility, I'd prefer not to give the state authority concerning religious matters. (3) The early church was clearly not an establishment church. The voluntary nature of gathering, belonging, and financially giving to the church—without which the church cannot flourish—seems more the spirit of the New Testament and should be considered a vital part of Christian discipleship.

Liberty of Conscience

When Martin Luther was summoned before the Diet of Worms and told to repudiate his views on theology and the church, he famously refused to recant, claiming that it was "neither right nor safe" to go against his conscience. More than a century later, the Westminster Confession of Faith stated just as emphatically, "God alone is Lord of the conscience" (WCF 20.2). Liberty of conscience has been ever since not just a hallmark of Protestant Christianity but one of the defining marks of the Western world.

But what did Luther and the Westminster divines mean by liberty of conscience? For starters, Luther declared that his conscience was "captive to the *Word of God*." Luther did not use "conscience" as shorthand for "doing whatever I want to do." His statement was about fidelity to the Bible, no matter the cost, not about cruising through life with "conscience" as a "get out of jail free" card.

Further, the Westminster Confession makes clear that "conscience" is not an excuse for sin and lawlessness. When, "upon the pretense of Christian liberty," we "practice any sin, or cherish any lust," we dishonor God and destroy the purpose of Christian liberty (WCF 20.3). Likewise, Christian liberty is not meant to overthrow the lawful power of civil and ecclesiastical authorities (WCF 20.4). The God-given authority of the civil magistrate and of the church is designed to work in concert with the God-given authority of the individual's conscience—each supporting, and at times limiting, the others.

How this all works out in practice is often complicated, but the principle that "God alone is Lord of the conscience" is worth preserving. It means that we should not press others (nor capitulate to pressure) to do what their conscience (or ours) has concluded from the Bible is wrong. It means that the church should not require of its members (in worship or elsewhere) what the Bible does not require. And it means that wherever possible the government should look to accommodate the sincerely held beliefs of its citizens.

The Reformation view of the conscience means that religious freedom is not just an Enlightenment value or a pragmatic consideration. John Locke's famous *Letter Concerning Toleration* (1689) argued chiefly on *Christian* grounds that the Protestant nations of Europe should show love, forbearance, and goodwill to all people.[1] Locke said that there is "but one truth, one way to heaven," but we cannot lead people there by coercion and by making them violate their consciences.[2] The care of souls does not belong to the civil magistrate. The magistrate is to secure men's possessions; the church is to secure men's salvation. They have distinct roles and operate in distinct spheres. To be sure, this may mean that the state has to tolerate false religion, but Locke feared that any power "given to the magistrate for the suppression of an idolatrous Church" could in time be used for "the ruin of an orthodox one."[3]

The revolutionary notion that the individual conscience should be respected and that there should be freedom of religious belief and practice is one of the great legacies of Reformation principles. May God be gracious to preserve these freedoms in our day and for generations to come.

1 Though, admittedly, Locke was thinking mainly about all *Protestant* people. Locke was actually more in favor of toleration for Jews and Muslims than for Catholics, because, like almost all Protestants at that time, he viewed Catholicism as a dangerous geopolitical power hostile to the interests of Protestant Europe.

2 Locke, *Two Treatises of Government*, 153.

3 Locke, *Letter Concerning Toleration*, 175.

DAY 204

Regulative Principle

The regulative principle states that "the acceptable way of worshiping the true God is instituted by himself and so limited by his own revealed will" (WCF 21.1). In other words, corporate worship should be comprised of those elements, and only those elements, we can show to be appropriate from the Bible. The regulative principle says, "Let's worship God as he wants to be worshiped" (see, for example, HC Q/A 96).

At its worst, this principle can lead to constant friction between believers as they try to parse out every jot and tittle of a Sunday service. When we expect the New Testament to give an exact layout of the *one* liturgy that pleases God, we are asking the Bible a question it doesn't mean to answer. It is possible for the regulative principle to be applied poorly.

But the heart of the regulative principle is not about restriction. It is about freedom.

Freedom from cultural captivity. When corporate worship is largely left to our own designs, we quickly find ourselves scrambling to keep up with the latest trends. The most important qualities become creativity, relevance, and newness.

But the freshness never lasts. What starts out as cutting edge ends up in the same generational or cultural captivity we were trying to avoid.

Freedom from constant battles over preferences. I once worked at a church whose worship committee loved to dream up new ideas. The problem was their personal dreams were not tethered to any objective standard. So the committee decided to open one service with the theme song from *Cheers.* Another service on Labor Day had people come up in their work outfits and talk about their jobs. If an idea seemed meaningful to someone on the committee, they gave it a try. But acceptable worship must be measured by more than sincerity and good intentions.

Freedom of conscience. Coming out of the Roman Catholic Church with its host of extrabiblical rituals, churches in the Reformation had to figure out how to worship in their own way. Some were comfortable keeping many of the elements of the Mass. Others associated those elements with a false religious system. This was the dynamic that made the regulative principle so important. Reformed Christians said in effect, "We don't want to ask our church members to do anything that would violate their consciences." This doesn't mean that Christians will *like* every song or every sermon, but at least with the regulative principle no one will be given words to say or actions to perform that God hasn't revealed to us in his word.

Freedom to be cross-cultural. Many people think of worship according to the regulative principle as culturally limited. But at its best, the regulative principle means we have simple services with singing, praying, reading, preaching, and sacraments—the kinds of services whose basic outline can "work" anywhere in the world.

Freedom to focus on the center. What do we know about early Christian worship services? We don't see dramas or pet blessings or liturgical dance numbers. We see mainly singing and sacraments, preaching and praying. Why try to improve on the elements we know were pleasing to God and practiced in the early church? The regulative principle gives us the freedom to unapologetically go back to basics. And stay there.

DAY 205

Mission of the Church

The mission of the church is the task given by God for the people of God to accomplish in the world. In simplest terms, the mission of the church is the Great Commission (Matt. 28:19–20). Our task as the gathered body of Christ is to make disciples, by bearing witness to Jesus Christ the Son in the power of the Holy Spirit to the glory of God the Father.[1]

In talking about the mission of the church, we are not trying to enumerate all the good things Christians can or should do to love their neighbors and to be salt and light in the world. The issue at hand relates to the church as church. What collectively as an organized institution must we be about as God's people if we are to faithfully accomplish his purposes for us in the world?

If the word *church* is important, so is the word *mission*. While *mission* does not appear in most English Bibles, it is still a biblical word. The Latin verb *mittere* corresponds to the Greek verb *apostellein*. The apostles, in the broadest sense of the term, were those who had been sent out. Likewise, the first thing Jesus notes about his mission is that he was *sent* to proclaim a message of good news to the poor (Luke 4:18). While it is certainly true that we should all be ready to give an answer for the hope we have (1 Pet. 3:15), and we should all adorn the gospel with our good works (Titus 2:10), and we should all do our part to make Christ known (1 Thess. 1:8; 2 Thess. 3:1), words like *mission* and *missionary* ought to imply intentional movement from one place to another.

There are ditches on either side of the road when trying to define the mission of the church. On the one hand, we want to avoid the danger of making our mission too small. Some well-meaning Christians act like conversion is the only thing that counts. They put all their efforts into getting to the field as quickly as possible, speaking to as many people as possible, and then leaving as soon as possible. And yet Paul did not practice blitzkrieg evangelism, nor was he motivated by an impatient hankering for numbers to report back home.

On the other hand, we want to avoid the danger of making our mission too broad. Some well-meaning Christians act like *everything* counts as mission. They put all their efforts into improving job skills, digging wells, setting up medical centers, establishing great schools, and working for political victories—all of which can be wonderful expressions of Christian love but bear little resemblance to what we see Paul and Barnabas sent out to do on their mission in Acts.

We see over and over in Paul's missionary journeys, and again in his letters, that the central work to which he was called was the verbal proclamation of Jesus Christ as Savior and Lord (Rom. 10:14–17; 15:18; 1 Cor. 15:1–2, 11; Col. 1:28). That's why in Acts 14:27 the singular summary of his just-completed mission work is that God had opened a door of faith to the Gentiles. His goal as a missionary was the conversion of Jews and pagans, the transformation of their hearts and minds, and the incorporation of these new believers into a mature, duly constituted church (14:21–23). What Paul aimed to accomplish as a missionary in the first century is an apt description of the mission of the church for every century.

1   This section is a condensed version of DeYoung, "The Mission of the Church."

DAY 206

Essential Reign and Mediatorial Reign

It's become one of the favorite lines of Christians everywhere: "There's not a square inch in the whole domain of human existence over which Christ, who is Lord over *all*, does not exclaim, 'Mine'!" These words from Abraham Kuyper's 1880 speech opening the Free University in Amsterdam—though perhaps overused and often misquoted—wonderfully announce that all things were created by Christ, through Christ, and for Christ (Col. 1:16). Christ does indeed reign over every square inch.

But he does not reign over all those square inches in exactly the same way. Christ is head of all things in his capacity as universal sovereign, but he reigns uniquely over the church as redemptive Savior. The first half of the previous sentence refers to Christ's natural or essential reign, while the second half of the sentence is often called Christ's economical or mediatorial reign. These two aspects of Christ's reign are similar to the three-part distinction we saw earlier with Christ's kingdom (kingdom of power, kingdom of grace, kingdom of glory).

Christ's twofold reign—essential and mediatorial—cannot ultimately be separated, but neither should these two senses of Christ's reign be confused. According to his essential reign, Christ rules over all creatures with glory and majesty. As the divine Logos, Christ reigns equally over all things by the decree of providence. No creature is more or less subject to the essential reign of Christ because this reign is tied to Christ's divine being. According to his mediatorial reign, Christ rules over the church, not only as eternal God but as the incarnate God-man who died for the sins of his people. Christ's reign over the church, though always guided by providence, is founded more specifically upon the decree of election. This reign is called "mediatorial" or "economical" because "it is a dominion peculiar to the Mediator" and is his according to the economy of grace.[1]

This distinction between Christ's essential reign and mediatorial reign reinforces two important truths. First, it reminds us that Christ's reign over the church is not a mere subset of being sovereign over all things, as if Christ is King over the church because he is King over everything. If anything, Christ's essential reign exists for the advancement of his mediatorial reign, not the other way around (see WLC 191). Christ has been made head over all things *to the church* (Eph. 1:22). That is, all things have been placed under his feet for the welfare and triumph of the church, which is his body.

Second, the distinction can help us avoid the mistaken assumption that because Christ is Lord over all, the exercise of that lordship will look the same everywhere. Earthly kingdoms are subject to Christ, but Christ's kingdom is not an earthly kingdom (John 18:36). We should not expect that because every square inch belongs to Christ that the kingdom of this world has already become the kingdom of our Lord and of his Christ (Rev. 11:15). Christ reigns "differently in the pious and in the wicked," and in both it is by "a spiritual, not an earthly sway."[2] As the risen Son who conquered sin and death, all authority in heaven and on earth has been given to Christ (Matt. 28:18). Christ's mediatorial reign, therefore, is also universal, but unlike the essential reign, Christ's mediatorial reign must be extended by proclamation and discipleship (28:19–20).

1 Turretin, *Elenctic Theology*, 2:486.
2 Turretin, *Elenctic Theology*, 2:489–90.

DAY 207

Spirituality of the Church

The spirituality of the church teaches that given the nature of the church under the mediatorial reign of Christ, there are limits to church power and that this power must not be confused with the power of the state. The aims of the church are first and foremost spiritual and eternal. Through most of Reformed history, the spirituality of the church has not entailed a silence on all political matters but rather a commitment to the uniqueness of the church's mission and a principled conviction that the eternal concerns of the church should not be swallowed up by the temporal concerns of the state.

The theology behind the spirituality of the church was present in Geneva with Calvin and Beza, but the doctrine took definitive shape in Scotland. Unlike its neighbor to the south, Scottish Presbyterianism—finding early expression in the Second Book of Discipline (1578)— insisted that the jurisdictions of church and state should not be confounded and that the head of the church and the head of the state were not the same. When a pastor makes a declaration "in the name of Jesus Christ, the only King and Head of his Church," he is not only denying the authority of the pope; he is repudiating the authority of every earthly monarch over the church.

One of the classic statements (if not in name, then in essence) on the spirituality of the church comes from the Westminster Confession of Faith.

> Synods and councils are to handle, or conclude nothing, but that which is ecclesiastical: and are not to intermeddle with civil affairs which concern the commonwealth, unless by way of humble petition in cases extraordinary; or, by way of advice, for satisfaction of conscience, if they by thereunto required by the civil magistrate. (WCF 31.4)

Notice the principle: the church should not meddle in civil affairs, and except in extreme situations should limit itself to ecclesiastical matters.

It must be admitted that in the American South the spirituality of the church was used to justify silence and inaction on the issue of slavery. This unfortunate application has given the doctrine a bad name. But not all Presbyterian theologians of the nineteenth century used the spirituality of the church to the same effect. Charles Hodge, for example, argued that while the Bible did not give the church the right to make pronouncements about tariffs, a national bank, and states' rights, the Bible did give principles by which the church could speak about the slave trade and slave laws. The spirituality of the church was not an injunction to stay silent on political matters when the Bible clearly had something to say.

Rightly applied, the spirituality of the church is an important part of biblical and Reformed ecclesiology. The doctrine (1) warns ministers against forgetting their gospel charge in a flurry of civil concerns, (2) calls churches not to transgress their God-given powers (and step outside their area of expertise), and (3) reminds denominations and ecclesiastical institutions not to pronounce too exactly and too confidently upon matters that demand extrabiblical knowledge and prudential judgment. The doctrine of the spirituality of the church is not a cure-all for politicization and polarization in the church, but wisely administered, it is a helpful antidote to many of the controversies that plague the church today.

Creeds and Confessions

Throughout the course of this book, I've cited many times the different creeds, confessions, and catechisms of the church. In particular, I've referenced different Reformed confessions like the Westminster Confession of Faith or the Heidelberg Catechism. For the first thirteen years of pastoral ministry, I made vows subscribing to the Heidelberg Catechism, the Belgic Confession, and the Canons of Dort (the Three Forms of Unity). Since 2015, my ordination vows have required me to affirm the system of doctrine taught in the Westminster Confession of Faith and the Westminster Larger and Shorter Catechisms (the Westminster Standards). That makes me a confessional Presbyterian minister serving in a confessional church.

And yet many Christians and many Christian traditions don't make use of creeds, confessions, and catechisms. In fact, some Christian traditions are positively opposed to these subordinate standards. Their motto is: "No creed but the Bible!" (which, as is often pointed out, is a creed in itself). While one can appreciate the desire to be thoroughly biblical, there are good reasons to use creeds and confessions as subordinate standards under the Bible.

For starters, we see already in the New Testament the development of early creedal and confessional formulas. Think of the "trustworthy sayings" in the Pastoral Epistles (1 Tim. 1:15; 3:1; 4:7–9; 2 Tim. 2:11–13; Titus 3:7–9) or John's tests of confessional faithfulness (1 John 4:2–3; 2 John 7). And this is to say nothing of the Jerusalem Council in Acts 15, which met to decide a matter of theological controversy and then offered an authoritative pronouncement on that matter.

Second, many of the most important doctrinal advances in the church would not have been possible (and subsequently would have been lost) were it not for creeds and confessions. Athanasius originally wanted the Nicene statement to use only scriptural language, but he realized this approach would allow people to give dishonest affirmations of the creed. They needed extrabiblical words like *homoousios* if they were to protect biblical teaching about the full and equal deity of the Son.

Third, the use of subordinate standards, insofar as they are drawn from Scripture, does not undermine liberty of conscience. The same Luther who appealed to his conscience at Worms went on to draw up confessions and catechisms. Even the simplest statement of faith on a church website will have to use "nonbiblical" language.

Fourth, the proper use of creeds, confessions, and catechisms reinforces important virtues in the church. Humility, because in submitting ourselves to older, often ancient, statements of faith, we acknowledge that we are part of a Spirit-led tradition bigger than ourselves. Clarity, because in subscribing to doctrinal statements, we make our theological commitments obvious instead of obscure. And unity, because in affirming the same confessions as others, we not only express our oneness with other orthodox Christians (and with those of our denominational tradition) across the centuries; we also communicate to our local church, "This is what you can expect to be taught from this pulpit; this is what your leaders believe and will defend."

We must be Bible people first and last. But in between, we would do well—for the propagation and the defense of the faith—to learn from the past and make good use of creeds, confessions, and catechisms.

DAY 209

Gifts of the Spirit

The key text when it comes to understanding spiritual gifts is 1 Corinthians 12:4–11. Let me make five comments about spiritual gifts from this passage.

1. Spiritual gifts can be controversial. Most of our information about spiritual gifts comes from 1 Corinthians 12 and 14, and the reason Paul writes so much about spiritual gifts in these chapters is that the Christians at Corinth were fighting over them. It should be a warning to us: if we find ourselves interested in who has more gifts or who has the more noticeable gifts, we've fallen into the Corinthian error and have completely missed the purpose of the Spirit's gifts.

2. The word *gift* (*charisma* in Greek) is a flexible term. We see this throughout the New Testament (Rom. 1:11; 5:15–16; 6:23; 11:29; 2 Cor. 1:11; Heb. 2:4), and we see it most obviously in 1 Corinthians 12. Notice the Trinitarian structure. Paul says there are varieties of gifts from the same Spirit, varieties of service from the same Lord, and varieties of activities from the same God. A gift is virtually synonymous with service and activity. *Charisma* is no more and no less than what the triune God does in the church.

3. Paul's lists of gifts are not exhaustive. Here in 1 Corinthians 12:8–10, he mentions nine gifts (though only healing is technically labeled a gift): the utterance of wisdom, the utterance of knowledge, faith, healing, the working of miracles, prophecy, distinguishing between spirits, various kinds of tongues, and

the interpretation of tongues. The other three major lists of gifts (Rom. 12:6–8; 1 Cor. 12:28; Eph. 4:11) repeat some of these gifts and add others to the list. First Corinthians 7:7 and 1 Peter 4:11 mention other gifts as well. These lists are not precise, and they are not meant to be complete. Paul is simply saying, "The church is made up of all sorts of people doing all kinds of things by the grace of God, and here are some examples." In short, wherever God's grace is evident, there we see spiritual gifts at work.

4. The purpose of the gifts is to build up the church. The manifestation of the Spirit is for the common good (1 Cor. 12:7). God's gifts in the church are not for the exaltation of the one exercising those gifts. God does not distribute gifts so the individual Christian can feel fulfilled in ministry or experience a sense of closeness to God. While those may be side-effects of spiritual gifting, we must always keep in mind that gifts are for building up the church (1 Cor. 14:12, 26).

5. Every Christian has gifts from the Spirit (1 Cor. 12:7). This is both a challenge and an encouragement. The challenge is that we *should* serve. The church is not a place to be entertained or to only receive from others. The encouragement is that we *can* serve. If we hang our heads and protest that we can't do anything for others or anything useful for God, we aren't being humble. We are calling into question the reality of the Holy Spirit and his empowerment for ministry. We are all members of the body of Christ, and each member has a part to play in helping the body function properly (1 Cor. 12:12–27).

DAY 210

Miraculous Gifts

What are we to make of the so-called miraculous gifts? Does God still empower Christians with the ability to heal diseases? Or the ability to speak in other languages? Or in an ecstatic prayer language? Does God still speak words of revelation through living prophets? Does he still guide us by dreams, impressions, and Spirit-led nudges? Christians are not of one mind when it comes to assessing these gifts.

On the one side are continuationists, who claim that all of the New Testament gifts are available today. They argue: (1) Without a clear word to the contrary, we should assume all the gifts are still in effect and earnestly desire them (1 Cor. 14:1). (2) The "perfect" in 1 Corinthians 13 refers to the return of Christ, so until that time the gifts will not pass away. (3) Revelatory gifts, though still present, do not have the same authority as Scripture. They must always be tested. (4) Whether the gifts are identical with the first century or not, we should welcome the Spirit's work in our midst.

On the other side are cessationists, who claim that some of the gifts, like tongues and prophecy, ceased after the apostolic age. They contend: (1) The miraculous gifts were only needed as authenticating signs for the initial establishing of the gospel and the church (Heb. 2:2–4). (2) First Corinthians 13:8–10 says that prophecy, tongues, and knowledge will cease "when the perfect comes," but this leaves open whether they might cease before that time. (3) Revelatory gifts like tongues and prophecy undermine the sufficiency of Scripture and the unique way in which God speaks to us in these last days (Heb. 1:1–2). (4) The miraculous gifts we see today are not the same as the gifts exercised in the New Testament.

Though the differences between these two positions are important, we should not overlook what the best representatives of both sides can agree on: (1) Every proclamation must be tested against Scripture. (2) Nothing can be added to Scripture. (3) We should be open to the Spirit working in nondiscursive ways, whether that's called prophecy, a word of knowledge, or a Spirit-prompted illumination and application of the Scriptures.

For my part, several additional considerations lead me to embrace the cessationist position. For starters, in Acts 19:6 tongues and prophecy are linked, just as they are throughout 1 Corinthians 12–14. We should not think that Corinthian tongues were different from Acts tongues, which were known foreign languages. And yet almost all the tongue-speaking today is in the form of ecstatic utterances without any fixed interpretative content (i.e., does anyone think that two interpretations of the same tongues message would be the same?). In fact, Gordon Fee, an excellent scholar on the continuationist side, has acknowledged that contemporary tongue speaking is only analogous to the kind in the Pauline churches.[1]

Most importantly, Ephesians 2:20 includes prophecy as part of the once for all nonrepeatable foundation of the church. Just as there are no more capital-A apostles, so there are no new revelatory utterances and no more prophets, and if no more prophecy, then no more tongues. The Spirit of God speaking through the word of God is more than enough to supply all we need for life and godliness.

---

1 Fee, *Empowering Presence*, 890.

DAY 211

Baptism in the Spirit

"For in one Spirit we were all baptized into one body—Jews or Greeks, slaves or free—and all were made to drink of one Spirit" (1 Cor. 12:13). Christians continue to debate the meaning of this verse. Is this baptism something all Christians experience or a special blessing that only some Christians receive? The answer is fairly straightforward.[1]

The phrase "baptism in [with/by] the Spirit" (*en pneumati*) occurs seven times in the New Testament. Four instances are in the Gospels where John the Baptist prophesies that the Lord Jesus will baptize with the Holy Spirit (Matt. 3:11; Mark 1:8; Luke 3:16; John 1:33). The fifth occurrence is in Acts 1:5, where Jesus alludes to John's prediction. The sixth instance is in Acts 11:16, when Peter recalls Jesus's words from before his ascension in Acts 1:5. So all six of these references to baptism in/with/by the Spirit look forward or back to the same thing, the outpouring of the Spirit at Pentecost. The seventh passage, 1 Corinthians 12:13, is unique because it does not refer directly to Pentecost (the Corinthians and Paul weren't there to be baptized with the Spirit in Jerusalem). Some Christians, therefore, have taught that 1 Corinthians 12:13 speaks of a "second blessing" experience, one that comes subsequent to conversion and only some Christians enjoy.

But the "second blessing" explanation will not work. For starters, the verse emphasizes that *all* were baptized in the Spirit, and *all* were made to drink of the Spirit. Whatever Paul is talking about, it's clear that he assumes everyone at Corinth has experienced it. Furthermore, given the larger context, Paul could not possibly be talking about a unique second blessing only experienced by some Christians. After emphasizing the diversity of gifts in the body, Paul now turns his focus on the unity the Corinthians share. They may all have different gifts, but they have all been baptized in one Spirit.

Baptism in the Spirit is something every Christian has experienced because every Christian has been born again and joined to Christ through the indwelling of the Holy Spirit. Baptism with the Spirit is nothing less than our union with Christ. The same Spirit first poured out at Pentecost now dwells in every believer, joining us to Christ and immersing us in all his benefits. If you'll permit a homely illustration, baptism in the Spirit is like that wonderful waterfall of glaze that pours over a Krispy Kreme doughnut moving down the conveyor belt. Every doughnut gets it, and every doughnut is much better for it. In a similar way, Jesus baptizes us in the Spirit that we might know his power and be awash in his blessings. Or as John Stott summarizes it: Spirit baptism is a distinctive blessing (only realized in the new covenant), an initial blessing (given at conversion), and a universal blessing (poured out on every genuine believer).[2] Spirit baptism is not something that should divide Christians; it is a blessing true of every Christian and a blessing that should unite us in thanksgiving to God for the powerful outpouring at Pentecost.

1   This section is adapted from DeYoung, *The Holy Spirit*. Used by permission.
2   Stott, *Baptism and Fullness*.

DAY 212

Filled with the Spirit

Being filled with the Spirit means being under the influence or sway of the Spirit. Sometimes the filling is more general, and other times it is more specific (e.g., in Acts 4 where the disciples are filled with the Spirit and spoke the word boldly) but in each case "filling" refers to the Spirit's work in empowering someone for godliness. Being filled with the Spirit not only equips you for boldness and courage; it also empowers you with wisdom (Acts 6:3), faith (11:24), and joy (13:52).

The Bible's most direct teaching on being filled with the Spirit comes in Ephesians 5. In verses 15–18, Paul highlights three contrasting behavioral pairs. The believer should walk not as unwise but as wise (5:15), he should not be foolish but understand the will of the Lord (5:17), and he should not get drunk on wine but be filled with the Spirit (5:18). Just like the other two pairs, this last one sets two opposite behaviors side by side. Being drunk with wine and being filled with the Spirit both exert influence on our whole person. But whereas drunkenness makes us out of control, the Spirit's influence gives us self-control. Wine in excess is a depressant; the Spirit is a stimulant to love and good deeds. Drunkenness leads to debauchery; the Spirit's work leads to devotion.

Verse 18 is really the heart of this paragraph and in some ways the main command in chapters 4–6. These chapters are all about godliness, about being marked by maturity, purity, and Christian character. Being filled with the Spirit is not about being an emotional person, a spontaneous person, or a demonstrably enthusiastic worshiper (though a Christian may be all three things). Being filled with the Spirit means we are imitators of God and we look like Jesus. It is worth noting the Trinitarian structure to "filling" in the book of Ephesians: first there is mention of being filled with Christ (1:23), then we hear of being filled with God (3:19), and finally we are told to be filled with the Spirit (5:18).

Spirit-filled worship is worship where Christ is made much of and Christians are built up in devotion to God and obedience to his commands. Again, we see nothing in Ephesians 5 about "Spirit-filled" implying a certain personality or experience or emotional register. We see instead in verses 19–22 four results (in the form of four participles) of the Spirit's filling. When we are filled with the Spirit, (1) we address one another in psalms, hymns, and spiritual songs, (2) we sing and make melody to the Lord with our hearts, (3) we give thanks to God the Father in the name of our Lord Jesus Christ, and (4) we submit to one another out of reverence for Christ. In other words: external speaking, internal singing, upward praising, and a proper respect for those in authority over us (as articulated in the rest of chapter 5 and chapter 6).

Let's keep in step with the Spirit. And let's ask for the Spirit's fullness in our lives. "If you then, who are evil, know how to give good gifts to your children, how much more will the heavenly Father give the Holy Spirit to those who ask him!" (Luke 11:13).

DAY 213

Calling

There is a long tradition in the church of speaking about a call to ministry. After all, Paul often talks of being called as an apostle or called to preach the gospel (Rom. 1:1; 1 Cor. 1:1). And yet we must be careful lest we expect an unmistakable divine impression before one can truly be "called" as a pastor (or missionary?). Conversely, we must not think that because an individual has had a powerful experience in the soul that he is necessarily called to vocational ministry.

The language of calling in the New Testament is almost always applied to all Christians. We have an upward call in Christ to be with Jesus and to be like Jesus (Phil. 3:14). We have been called to freedom, not bondage (Gal. 5:13). God has saved us and called us to a holy calling (2 Tim. 1:9). He has called us to his own glory and excellence (2 Pet. 1:3). Not many of us were called to noble things (in the world's eyes), but, amazingly, we have been called to Christ (1 Cor. 1:26). And if called, then justified, and if justified, then glorified (Rom. 8:30).

Does this mean we should abandon the language of a "call to ministry"? I don't think so, provided we understand *calling* to mean something like, "How do I know this is a wise, appropriate step for me to take?" as opposed to, "How do I know that I've received a special word from God that I must be a pastor?" Paul was "called" to be an apostle, and on one occasion he received a special call to go to Macedonia (Acts 19), so there is biblical warrant for *calling* as something more than just salvation, even if Paul's apostolic call is not necessarily normative.

Most theologians and ministry leaders talk about three aspects of a call: an internal call ("I desire to do this"), an external call ("I have recognized gifts for ministry and discernible fruit of maturity"), and a formal call ("I have been offered a position by a particular church or ministry"). Similarly, James Bannerman describes the call to ministry as an agreement of three wills: God's will (as a safeguard against presumption), the will of the office bearers (as a safeguard against fanaticism), and the will of the church (as a safeguard against encroachment).

If *calling* involves waiting for promptings, listening for still, small voices, and attaching divine authority to our vocational decisions, then we'd be better off dropping the language altogether. But if *calling* means knowing yourself, listening to godly men, and listening to the church, then we are wise to discern a call to ministry. Bannerman's summary is well put: "There is needed no supernatural call personally addressed to a man to assure him of his warrant to serve the Church of Christ in its ministry. There is no miraculous light thrown across the path, no voice from on high, like that which met Paul on the road to Damascus, sent to meet a man now, and summon him to the public service of Christ. But the gifts and graces for the office, when conferred, are God's commission and call to the office."[1]

How does a man know if he is called to ministry? By looking for gifts and graces to do the job and by listening for God's commission communicated through the church.

1 Bannerman, *Church of Christ*, 452.

DAY 214

Means of Grace

God can be gracious to us in a thousand different ways, and he can use a hundred different things for the gracious good of his people. But that's not what we mean by "means of grace." God has seen fit to use certain regular, reliable means of communicating his grace. These objective means of grace have been instituted by Christ to be dispensed through the ministry of the church for the saving and sanctifying of his people.

The outward and ordinary means of grace are those ordinances by which Christ communicates to us the benefits of redemption. The Westminster Shorter Catechism lists these ordinances as "especially the Word, sacraments, and prayer" (WSC 88). The Heidelberg Catechism, by contrast, places prayer in the section on gratitude rather than grace (HC 116) and mentions only two ordinances in connection with the communication of saving faith: "the preaching of the holy gospel" and "the holy sacraments" (HC 65). Without wanting to denigrate the central importance of prayer (Acts 6:4), one can make a more obvious case from the Great Commission for the word and sacraments as means of grace (Matt. 28:19–20). Several other passages directly link the preaching of the word and the administration of the sacraments with the communication of saving and sanctifying grace (Rom. 10:17; 1 Cor. 10:16; Titus 3:5; 1 Pet. 1:23–25).

Four other observations are in order.[1]

1. *These are means of special grace, not common grace.* We are not talking about seeing the good, the true, and the beautiful while hiking a national park or walking through an art museum. We are talking about the grace that brings about redemption.

2. *These are means of grace in themselves.* Many believers will testify to God's grace in holding a newborn infant, in laughing with friends, or in watching a sunset. But these experiences—no matter how enjoyable or beneficial—are not means of grace in themselves (and may not be channels of grace at all). Certain experiences may be used by God, but they only communicate grace insofar as they are interpreted in light of God's word or bring to mind God's word. In every instance, the word is the channel of special grace, not the babbling brook or snow-capped peak.

3. *The means of grace do not confer grace by mere external application.* The word of God never returns void, but it may not always confer saving grace. The same sun that melts the butter also hardens the clay. Likewise, the sacraments must be joined with faith if they are to be channels of divine grace. All this is to say, the means of grace do not work *ex opere operato* (by the working of the work), as if the mere preaching of a sermon or the mere administration of the sacraments automatically save and sanctify. God alone is the efficient cause of salvation.

4. *These are continuous instruments of God's grace.* Word and sacraments (and, if you like, prayer) are not occasional and accidental, but regular and perpetual channels of divine grace. We call the means of grace "ordinary" because we believe God has instituted them as the usual and perpetual means whereby he intends to administer his saving grace. Our churches would do well to major on these ordinary means and make minor everything else.

---

1 See Berkhof, *Systematic Theology*, 605–8.

Semper Reformanda

Whenever there is a push to alter the church's historic understanding of the faith (regarding sexuality or biblical authority or the historicity of Adam and Eve or whatever), you are bound to hear someone appeal to the Reformation slogan *semper reformanda*. We are told that the Spirit reveals new truths for a new day, that Jesus is pouring old wine into new wineskins, that the church must be "always reforming."

While it's true that we all see through a glass dimly and must be open to changing our minds, the Latin phrase *semper reformanda* was not about reforming the church's confessions to keep up with the times. The saying first appeared in 1674 in a devotional book by Jodocus van Lodenstein. As a key figure in the Dutch Second Reformation, van Lodenstein wanted to see the members of the Dutch church, which had seen its doctrine become Reformed during the Reformation, continue to pursue reformation in their lives and practices. His concern was personal piety, not doctrinal progressivism.

It is important to see the entirety of van Lodenstein's phrase: *ecclesia reformata, semper reformanda secundum verbi Dei.* In English: "the church is Reformed and always [in need of] being reformed according to the Word of God." Notice three things about this dictum.

First, it begins by addressing the church that is Reformed. Van Lodenstein was addressing the Dutch church that had identified as confessionally Reformed, specifically in subscription to the Three Forms of Unity (i.e., the Belgic Confession, Heidelberg Catechism, and Canons of Dort). Far from encouraging doctrinal innovation, the original phrase presumes doctrinal stability. It is not an encouragement to figure out your theological standards on the fly.

Second, the Latin verb *reformanda* is passive, which means the church is not "always reforming" but is "always being reformed." The difference is consequential. The former sounds like the pursuit of new enlightenment, while the latter suggests adhering to the proper standard. The passive construction also implies that there is an external agent operating upon the church to bring about the necessary reform.

This leads to the third and most important point: the church is always being reformed *according to the word of God.* There is nothing Reformed about changing the church's theology and ethics to get on "the right side of history," or to stay current with the insights of the social sciences. The point of van Lodenstein's phrase was that the church must constantly resubmit to the lordship of Christ exercised in his word.

Semper reformanda is not about constant fluctuations, but about firm founda-tions. It is about a personal devotion to match our doctrinal precision. It is about radical adherence to the Holy Scriptures, no matter the cost to ourselves, our traditions, or our own fallible sense of cultural relevance.

If people think the Bible is wrong, they should say so. But they must not claim the mantle of the Reformers in so doing. The only Reformation worth promoting and praying for is the one that gets us deeper into our Bibles, not farther away.

WEEK 44

DAY 216

Sacraments

"A sacrament is a holy ordinance instituted by Christ; wherein, by sensible signs, Christ, and the benefits of the new covenant, are represented, sealed, and applied to believers" (WSC 92). If you want a simpler version, we could say that a sacra-ment is a sign and seal of the covenant blessings we receive by faith. Or if you want something shorter still, we can go with Augustine's oft-cited definition: a sacrament is a visible sign of invisible grace.

Let's work with the middle definition and focus on the words *sign* and *seal*.

A sacrament is a sign. God gave us pictures for our benefit, not in replacement of the word, but as a complement to the spoken gospel. The word is adapted to the ear, and the sacraments are adapted to the eye.

Sometimes critics knock Protestant worship, especially Reformed worship, by saying, "God gave us all these senses, and the only one we use in worship is hearing. We listen to prayers and listen to music and listen to sermons and listen to Scripture. What about the other senses God gave us? We need multimedia. We need art. We need video. We need drama." My response is, "Sure, let's have visuals in worship. Let's have more drama. But let's stick to the visuals and the drama that the Lord instituted." God gave us the sacraments as spiritual signs so that we can see, smell, taste, and touch the promises of the gospel.

A sacrament is also a seal. Think about the purpose of an official seal—like a stamp from a notary public or the raised insignia on a legal document. A seal constitutes a formal engagement by two parties—an engagement where actions, instead of words, confirm the compact or covenant. When Jesus said, "This cup that is poured out for you is the new covenant in my blood" (Luke 22:20), he didn't mean that the cup itself was the covenant. He meant that by drinking the cup, the disciples participating in the new covenant would be authenticated.

The language of signs and seals comes from Romans 4:11, where Paul describes circumcision as a sign of the covenant and a seal of the righteousness that Abraham had by faith. As signs, the sacraments point to spiritual realities and divine promises. As seals, the sacraments presuppose a covenant transaction between God and the one who participates in the sacrament. In other words, sacraments are attestations and confirmations of God's grace, which, like the example of Abraham, are received by faith (whether faith must be operative *at the time of the sacrament's administration* is a matter we will consider when we come to the chapter on infant baptism).

The sacraments are overlooked and underappreciated in too many churches. Granted, we can ascribe too much significance to the sacraments, making them necessary for salvation or assuming they work like magical rites through the mere administration of the sign. And yet many of us are probably in danger of ascribing *too little* to baptism and the Lord's Supper. We do not expect much from the sacraments. We do not look for assurance, comfort, and strength. The God of all grace means to help us with these signs and seals, if only we would have the eyes of faith to see and believe.

How Many Sacraments?

Sacraments are not just pictures of spiritual realities (like marriage is a picture of the gospel) or powerful symbols of Christian virtues (like foot washing is a powerful picture of humble service). Sacraments are those ordinances (1) instituted explicitly and directly by Christ, which (2) act as signs and seals of special grace. In other words, they are not just pictorial representations of grace, but actual *means* of grace.

Given these definitional parameters, there are only two sacraments given by Christ to the church: baptism (Matt. 28) and the Lord's Supper (1 Cor. 11).

To these two sacraments the Catholic Church adds five more.

In Roman Catholic practice, *confirmation* is a sacrament of strengthening grace administered by the bishop when he lays hands on a baptized person who is at least seven years old. While it is important to make a public profession of faith (Rom. 10:9–10), there is no indication in the New Testament that Christ has instituted this practice as a means of grace. It is better to understand a child's profession of faith as the means by which the promises of baptism are ratified rather than as a means of grace in its own right.

The Catholic practice of *penance* offers forgiveness upon confession of sin and the satisfaction of certain compensatory works assigned by the priest. In many churches, Sunday worship includes the confession of sin and assurance of pardon. But these should be seen as applications of the word, not as a separate sacrament, and certainly not tied to indulgences or any form of works righteousness.

The Roman Church practices an elaborate system of *ordination* with three degrees of holy orders: the Diaconate, the Presbyterate, and (as the fullest expression of the sacrament) the Episcopate. Ordination is clearly a New Testament practice (Acts 6:6; 1 Tim. 4:14; 5:22; Titus 1:5) and can be tied to the conferring of spiritual gifts (1 Tim. 4:14). But ordination does not operate as a means of special grace available to all. Indeed, according to Catholic teaching, the sacrament infuses a special character to the ordinand, making him qualitatively different from the rest of the baptized. This is at odds with the priesthood of all believers and with the nature of the sacraments as ordinary means of grace.

The sacrament of *extreme unction* (or last rites) is derived from James 5:14, where the elders of the church are called to pray over the sick and anoint them with oil. As important as the symbolism of oil may be (likely depicting the power of the Holy Spirit at work), it would be strange for one verse from one apostle to introduce a new sacrament, especially when we don't find evidence of extreme unction as a sacrament in the early church, and we don't find it practiced in Christ's earthly ministry.

The Catholic Church also considers *marriage* a sacrament. This is, in part, based on a mistranslation of the Greek word *mysterion* with the Latin word *sacramentum* (Eph. 5:32). Marriage may be used in our sanctification, but it is never put forward in the Bible as an ordinary means of grace. In fact, marriage is a creation ordinance (Gen. 2) shared in common with non-Christians.

While the rites above contain elements of biblical truth and practice, baptism and the Lord's Supper are unique in that they are so obviously and directly instituted by Christ. To add to them in number, or subtract from them in importance, is to dishonor Christ and miss the grace he means to give us in the two sacraments of the church.

DAY 218

Baptism

When Christ commanded the eleven disciples to baptize in the name of the Father and of the Son and of the Holy Spirit (Matt. 28:19), he was not only instructing them in the Great Commission; he was instructing them in the nature of baptism. Baptism is a sign of initiation, part of what it means to be a disciple of Christ. That baptism is administered in the triune name signifies identity and inclusion. Baptism names us as belonging to God, as having a relation to him and being in relationship with him.

If union with God is key to a proper understanding of baptism, then the other foundational element is the washing of sin. This makes sense given the role water plays in the rite. Baptism symbolizes spiritual cleansing and purification. Baptism is tied to the forgiveness of sins (Acts 2:38) and the washing away of sins (Acts 22:16). Whether a reference to baptism or not, the Christian's life is often described as having been washed (1 Cor. 6:11; Heb. 10:22). Elsewhere baptism is explicitly called the washing of regeneration and renewal (Titus 3:5). Baptism saves us, not by removing physical dirt, but as an appeal to God for a good conscience through the resurrection of Jesus Christ (1 Pet. 3:21). Baptism is a sign and seal of the forgiveness of sins.

While the meaning of baptism is mainly positive, there is also an element of warning in the symbolism of water. The water that saves the righteous is also the water that overwhelms the wicked. Noah and his family were brought safely through water, while the rest of the world perished in the flood (1 Pet. 3:20; 2 Pet. 3:5–6). When the spiritual import of baptism is ignored, rejected, or despised, the blessing can turn to cursing, just as things will turn out worse for those who profane the blood of the covenant (Heb. 10:29).

The Old Testament practice of circumcision helps illumine the meaning of the New Testament practice of baptism. Although there is certainly discontinuity as we move from the shadows of the Old Testament to the substance of the New, the sacramental symbolism in both Testaments is largely the same. This is why circumcision and Passover can be ascribed to the New Testament church (1 Cor. 5:7; Col. 2:11), and baptism and the Lord's Supper can be ascribed to the Old Testament church (1 Cor. 10:1–4). Just as circumcision pointed positively to forgiveness and renewal (in the cutting away of the flesh) and negatively to the punishment of being cut off, so baptism signifies the same two realities. In the minor key, there is the threat of judgment. In the major key, baptism, like circumcision, is a sign and seal of the righteousness that comes by faith (Rom. 4:11).

Recipients of Baptism

There is no debate that believers should be baptized. As the gospel spreads in the book of Acts, we often see baptism linked to faith in Christ (Acts 2:41; 16:31–33). All those unbaptized persons who come to saving faith in Christ ought to be baptized. Baptism is for believers.

And their children.

That's the controversial part. That's what distinguishes credobaptists (*credo* referring to faith or belief) from paedobaptists (*paedo* referring to children). In the Old Testament, God marked his covenant people with the sign of circumcision. The cutting away of physical flesh was a symbol of the cutting away of fleshliness from the heart. This sign was administered to adult followers of the Lord and their children, even though some of the children never came to know the reality to which the sign pointed. In the same way, baptism—the washing away of sinful flesh—is administered to adult followers of Jesus and their children, even though some of the children never come to know the reality to which the sign pointed.

Consider several key passages.

Mark 10:14. If Christ lays hands on the children and blesses them as partakers of the covenant and welcomes them as citizens in the kingdom—if in word and deed he demonstrates that the children belong to him and are sanctified by him—why would we not apply the sign that signifies all this?

Acts 2:39. Peter uses obvious covenant language from the Old Testament ("for you and for your children"). The Abrahamic covenant had not been annulled (Gal. 3:15–18). Rather, the covenant community had expanded to include the Gentiles ("and for all who are far off").

Romans 4:9–12. Circumcision was always a sign of spiritual realities (Lev. 26:40–42; Deut. 10:16; 30:6; Jer. 4:4; 6:10; 9:25; Rom. 2:25–29). Here Paul links it explicitly with justification by faith. Abraham received the sign after he had faith, *and* he was instructed to administer the same sign to his sons before they had faith. Circumcision, like baptism, pointed to belonging, discipleship, and covenant obligations, and it allowed for future faith that would take hold of the realities symbolized.

Ephesians 6:1–3. Children were assumed to be members of the church who could rightly receive a commandment "in the Lord." God still deals with us as families, which is why we see household baptisms in the New Testament (Acts 16:13–15, 32–34; 18:8; 1 Cor. 1:16).

Colossians 2:11–12. In one sentence, Paul move seamlessly from circumcision to baptism, writing from the assumption that the two signs have the same spiritual import.

Hebrews 10:16, 26–31. It is still possible to belong externally to the covenant and prove to be a covenant breaker. Not all who start out with the church really belong to the church (1 John 2:19).

To be sure, there is no explicit mention of infant baptism in the New Testament (no infant dedication either!). But that is to be expected in a first-generation missionary context. What's more striking by its absence is any record of Jewish parents being shocked to see their children now excluded from the covenant. Surely, in an era where God's promises are more expansive and more inclusive, it would be surprising to discover that children were now on the outside looking in. This would be like a new, fabulous medical insurance plan that no longer covered children as a part of the policy. That would hardly seem like a better plan. It makes more sense to think that the sign of forgiveness and belonging, for centuries applied to eight-day-old males, has now been graciously applied to believers and their sons and daughters.

DAY 220

Mode of Baptism

The Bible speaks of several different actions whereby God's people are ritually cleansed by water. One can make the case that sprinkling was the most common purification rite in the Old Testament (Ex. 24:6–8; Lev. 14:7; Num. 8:7; 19:18–19; Isa. 52:15; Ezek. 36:25) and that this would have naturally carried over to the New Testament (Heb. 12:24). Indeed, Hebrews 9:10, in referencing various ceremonial washings (*diaphorois baptismois*), mentions the sprinkled blood of bulls and goats as one of these "washings" or "baptisms" (v. 13). Most Reformed churches practice baptism by sprinkling, though other paedobaptist traditions insist on pouring or immersion.

Most Baptists believe immersion is central to the act of baptism and inherent in the meaning of the word itself. A closer look at the pertinent texts, however, suggests that the word *baptism* need not imply the physical act of immersion. In fact, there is not a single example of baptism in the New Testament that demands immersion, and several examples that positively do not allow for it.

We read of three thousand believers being baptized in Jerusalem on Pentecost (Acts 2:41). And yet there is no large body of water near the old city. Baptism here was almost certainly by some means besides immersion.

In Acts 9:18, Ananias baptizes Paul, seemingly on the spot, after which Paul took food and was strengthened. There is no indication that they went looking for a body of water to be immersed in and then returned later for food (see also the baptism of the Philippian jailer and his family [Acts 16:32–33]). Likewise, the question in Acts 10:47, "Can anyone withhold water for baptizing these people?" suggests that water was being brought *to* the Gentiles, not Gentiles being brought to a large body of water.

The best case for baptism by immersion can be found in Acts 8 where Philip and the Ethiopian eunuch "both went down into the water" (v. 38). But even here the case for immersion is not strong, for both men go down into the water (8:38) and both come up out of the water (8:39). Surely Philip did not immerse himself along with the Ethiopian eunuch. It is better to think they both walked down into water, then Philip baptized by sprinkling or pouring, and then both men walked up out of the water.

"But," someone might ask, "doesn't the down and up of immersion best capture the symbolism of death and resurrection?" Not necessarily. The imagery of Romans 6 is about union with Christ more than it is about literally going up and down. After all, Jesus was not buried underground, but (sideways!) in a cave.

Baptism is about identification. Were the Israelites literally immersed (*baptizō*) into Moses (1 Cor. 10:2), or does the word connote a spiritual reality more than a specific physical rite? We see from the related word *bapto* that "baptism" can refer to nonimmersive acts. In Leviticus 14:6, a live bird is to be dipped (LXX: *baptō eis*) into the blood of a dead bird. In Luke 11:38, we read that Jesus had not first washed himself (*ebaptisthe*) before dinner. This was likely a washing of the hands, certainly not a full-body immersion.

Baptism does not have to be by immersion. Washing with water is the important part. "For if the blood of goats and bulls, and the sprinkling of defiled persons with the ashes of a heifer, sanctify for the purification of the flesh, how much more will the blood of Christ" (Heb. 9:13–14).

DAY 221

What Does Baptism Seal?

Baptism does not by itself confer grace. The sacramental signs do not communicate divine blessing. Rather, they are signs and seals of the grace that comes to the believer by faith.

This raises the question, however, of what the sign of baptism seals for the infant. For the Baptist, the issue is straightforward: baptism authenticates the believer's forgiveness and new life in Christ. But what does baptism seal according to the paedobaptist understanding of the sacrament?

For starters, we reject any notion of baptismal regeneration. (1) Should we think that Paul had not truly been born again on the road to Damascus because he had not yet been baptized? Or that the thief on the cross—though about to be admitted into paradise—needed baptism in order to be born again and saved? (2) Titus 3:5 does not mean that regeneration is inseparably tied to baptism. If the "washing" refers to baptism, it likely means that baptism is a sign of regeneration. But the verse may not be a reference to baptism at all, in which case it would mean "we are saved by that spiritual washing *that is regeneration*, namely, by the renewing work of the Holy Spirit." (3) The Bible everywhere teaches that the one indispensable condition of salvation is faith in Christ. Moreover, in the case of adults, faith is a prior requirement for baptism. (4) Experience contradicts the doctrine of baptismal regeneration. Were most people in the West, for the better part of fifteen hundred years, truly born again by virtue of their baptism? The evidence suggests otherwise. Sadly, many who have been baptized, at whatever age, do not persevere in spiritual vitality.

So what does baptism seal in the infant if not the assured regenerating work of the Spirit?

One option is to think that the sacrament is a seal of the parents' faith. This is not the best explanation. While the administration of baptism should be an encouragement to the parents as they "improve" upon their own baptism, it would be strange for the sacrament to seal something for someone who is not presently receiving the sign.

Some theologians have argued for presumptive regeneration. This view does not teach that baptism is the means of regeneration (as in baptismal regeneration), but that the sign is administered *presuming* that the child has already been born again. The examples of David (Ps. 22:9–10), Jeremiah (Jer. 1:5), and John the Baptist (Luke 1:15, 41–44) show that children can be born again in the womb, but there is no suggestion in Scripture that we should assume these cases are the norm.

Many Reformed Christians would describe baptism as a seal of the covenant. Surely this is part of the equation. There are objective and subjective realities to the covenant. Baptism, like circumcision, marks out the child as belonging to God's covenantal family in an outward and external sense.

Most crucially, baptism is a seal of the remission of sins, regeneration by the Spirit, and resurrection unto everlasting life (WLC 165). On this, the credobaptist and paedobaptist agree. We differ on whether this seal can be applied in *anticipation* of the child making these realities his own by faith. Baptism is a seal of the righteousness that comes by faith, but that faith may not be present at the exact moment the initiatory sign is applied. Membership in the covenant community comes with privileges, promises, and obligations.

DAY 222

Who Can Baptize?

We are used to discussing the question, "Who can be baptized?" But fewer Christians have thought through the question, "Who can *administer* baptism?" Some theologians argue that "there seems to be no need in principle to restrict the right to perform baptism only to ordained clergy" and that it is appropriate for "mature believers to baptize new converts."[1] Since Scripture does not make explicit any restrictions and since we believe in the priesthood of all believers (1 Pet. 2:4–10), the argument goes, why should we limit the administration of baptism to the ordained pastors (and possibly elders) of the church?

Let me see if I can make a persuasive case for restricting the administration of baptism to the ordained shepherds of the congregation.

Biblically, we see that those who perform Christian baptism in the New Testament have been set apart by Christ for an office in the church (e.g., Peter, Paul, Philip). There is no evidence to show that private members baptized. Yes, the

Great Commission mentions baptism, but we must remember that the Great Commission was given to a specific group of men—to those who would wait in Jerusalem for power from on high, to those who would give eyewitness testimony to the resurrection. The Great Commission is ours by implication, not by immediate application. If every aspect of the Great Commission is directly for every individual believer (rather than for the church corporately), then most of us are disobeying the Great Commission by not going to the nations of the world.

Theologically, we must take into account how Christ rules his church. In the truest sense, the one who administers baptism is Christ. And yet, as the only King and head of his church, Christ has instituted the office of presbyter (elder) by which he governs the church (Acts 20:28; 1 Pet. 5:1–4). Moreover, since the sacraments are inextricably linked to the task of preaching, we should expect that the one who gives the congregation the spoken word would also give the congregation the visible word. The sacraments involve the administration of grace and exercise of church power which belong to the office bearers of the church.

Exegetically, an appeal to the priesthood of all believers does not support the administration of baptism by every church member. The reference to the church as "a royal priesthood" affirms the holy nature of God's people (1 Pet. 2:9). It does not suggest that now in the New Testament there are no rites reserved for ordained officers. God's people in the Old Testament were also called a kingdom of priests (Ex. 19:6), and they had a whole tribe of priests set aside for functions that only the priests could perform.

Practically, for baptism to be responsibly administered, there must be some church oversight. There must be a process of accountability and evaluation, lest the sacrament becomes little more than a freely chosen, oft-repeated expression of personal commitment instead of a churchly means of worship and initiation. If presbyters superintend the process whereby someone is deemed fit for baptism (as they do in almost all churches), then it stands to reason that these same presbyters should exercise their Christ-given authority in administering the baptism.

In short, baptism by ordained pastors (and possibly elders, depending on one's understanding of the office) makes best sense of the nature of the church authority, the centrality of the preaching of the word, and the means by which God reigns and rules in his body.

1 Grudem, *Systematic Theology*, 983–84.

How Many Times Should I Be Baptized?

As the sacrament of naming, belonging, and inclusion (as opposed to the sacrament of covenant renewal), baptism is to be administered only once. We who were baptized into the death of Christ cannot be put to death again (Rom. 6:3–11). We cannot be born twice. We cannot be justified twice. We cannot be joined to Christ twice. We should not be baptized twice.

Of course, Baptists would argue that infant baptism is not a valid baptism, so to apply the sign again (from a Reformed perspective) to a believing adult who was baptized as a baby is really administering baptism for the first time (from a Baptist perspective). Baptism must take place upon a credible profession of faith. If you weren't a true believer when you were baptized, then you weren't really baptized. Thus, credobaptists will likely agree with paedobaptists that baptism should only be administered once. The two sides disagree as to what constitutes a valid baptism in the first place.

This raises a perennially difficult question for the paedobaptist: are Roman Catholic baptisms valid? Or to put it another way, "Do those who were baptized in the Catholic Church need to be baptized again?" During the middle decades of the nineteenth century, the southern Presbyterian theologian James Henley Thornwell, among others, made a strong case against the validity of Catholic baptism. They argued that Catholic priests were not duly ordained ministers of the gospel and that the Catholic Church was not a true church; consequently, baptisms from this "church" and by these priests should not be considered valid.

Against these arguments Charles Hodge made several points that I find persuasive.[1]

1. The nature of baptism is not defined by the character of those administering the baptism. Baptism by a Catholic priest is irregular (i.e., not according to Christ's design), but not invalid (i.e., not inauthentic).

2. Whether Rome be a true church or not, Hodge insisted that there was enough truth in the Catholic Church for a person to be saved. Rome is certainly not a pure church, but it does not follow that it is in no way a church. Just as Paul could deal with the Galatians and Corinthians as "saints," we can approach the Catholic Church from a judgment of charity.

3. Most importantly, Hodge appealed to the threefold definition of baptism from Westminster Shorter Catechism Q&A 94: baptism must be with water, it must be in the name of the Trinity, and it must be administered as a sign and seal

of our ingrafting into Christ (i.e., baptism is spiritual in intent and not applied in jest). Baptism in the Catholic Church meets all three criteria.

4. Finally, Hodge pointed to the history of the church. Calvin and Luther did not consider their baptisms in the Catholic Church invalid. The French, Genevan, and Dutch churches agreed with them, as did the Church of England. Shall we say that most Protestants have been wrong on this question? Shall we conclude that millions of persons converted from Catholicism to Protestantism since the Reformation have lived and died unbaptized? Or might the sign of baptism be more durable than that? To insist on the validity of irregular baptisms, even from impure churches, does not undermine the nature of baptism but, in the end, upholds it.

1 Hodge, "The Validity of Romish Baptism," 191–215.

DAY 224

The Lord's Supper

With the possible exception of justification, no point of theology during the Reformation was more debated, prompted more writing, and led to more vehement controversy than the Lord's Supper. Whether between Protestants and Roman Catholics, or Protestants and other Protestants, the debate over the Lord's Supper was at least as intense and acrimonious as debates over gender and sexuality are in our day. Calvin devoted one hundred pages of his fifteen-hundred-page *Institutes* to the Lord's Supper. By contrast, Louis Berkhof spent fifteen pages out of eight hundred in his *Systematic Theology*, and Wayne Grudem set aside about the same number of pages out of his twelve-hundred-page volume, to discuss the Lord's Supper.

The importance of the Lord's Supper is so obvious in Scripture and in church history that it's amazing the sacrament has become so unimportant in so many churches today. The celebration of the Last Supper and the corresponding institution of the Lord's Supper ("Do this in remembrance of me") occur in detail in all four Gospels. The breaking of bread (likely a reference to Communion) played a central role in the worship of the early church (Acts 2:42; 20:7). So important was the Lord's Supper that some died by partaking of it in an unworthy manner (1 Cor. 11:17–34). The liturgies of the early church, the Middle Ages, the Lutherans, the Anglicans, and the Reformed all made the Lord's Supper a central feature of corporate worship.

The names given for the sacrament tell us something about its meaning. It is the "Lord's Supper" (1 Cor. 11:20–21) because Christ meets us at his table as both meal and host. We call it the "breaking of bread" (Acts 2:42) because in the sacrament we have fellowship with one another. The meal is a thanksgiving (1 Cor. 11:24), a *eucharistesas* in which we gratefully receive grace from the Lord. We also call the sacrament "Communion" because in it we participate in the body and blood of Christ and have *koinonia* with him (1 Cor. 10:16).

Let me briefly highlight four characteristics of the Lord's Supper.

1. Like baptism, the Lord's Supper is a sign and seal—a sign of Christ's death on the cross and a seal of the remission of sins we have by faith through Christ's atoning sacrifice.

2. The Lord's Supper is a family meal and a covenantal meal. God not only gathers into his family those who were once strangers and aliens; he also feeds us as his children. Just as the leaders of Israel ate and drank on Mount Sinai as a sign of the Mosaic covenant (Ex. 24:1–11), so we eat and drink in renewal of the new covenant.

3. The Lord's Supper is for our help. It is a cup of blessing (1 Cor. 10:16). God supports our earthly life with physical bread and physical drink; he nourishes and strengthens our spiritual life with living bread and the cup of life. John 6:47–58 may not be about the Lord's Supper, but it is what the Lord's Supper is about. "This banquet is a spiritual table at which Christ communicates himself to us with all his benefits" (Belgic Confession 35.4).

4. The Lord's Supper orients us in two directions. It orients us vertically as we remember the body and blood, give thanks for his sacrifice, commune with him by faith, and proclaim the Lord's death until he comes again. It also orients us horizontally as we are moved in grace toward our fellow believers. We discern the body of Christ upward in glory and outward in love.

DAY 225

Real Presence

There are four major views concerning Christ's presence in the Lord's Supper.

Roman Catholics believe in *transubstantiation*. Relying on Aristotelian categories, Catholic theology teaches that the substance of the elements is transformed into the physical body and blood of Christ, while the accidents (i.e., the external qualities) retain the characteristics of bread and wine. Catholics take

Christ's words "this is my body" (*hoc est corpus meum* in Latin) with extreme literalness. But it's hard to imagine, with Jesus right in front of them, that he would have expected the disciples to think the bread was also his body. If you hold up a picture of yourself and say, "This is me," no one thinks the picture has been transformed. Everyone understands that you mean, "This picture is a representation of me." Moreover, in the normal Passover liturgy the Jews recalled, "This is the bread of affliction which our ancestors ate when they came from the land of Egypt." Did anyone really think the Passover bread was literally the same bread their ancestors ate fifteen hundred years earlier? When 1 Corinthians 10:4 says, "The Rock was Christ," no one thinks the rock literally became the body of Christ. Some mysteries are above comprehension, but the doctrine of transubstantiation is less a mystery than it is a violation of the laws of reason.

The Lutheran position is usually referred to as *consubstantiation* (though not all Lutherans like this term). In Lutheran theology, the bread is real bread and the wine is real wine, but the physical presence of Christ is also there, "in, with, and under" the elements. This position requires the ubiquity of Christ's glorified human body, which throws into question whether Christ's divine and human natures were indissolubly joined, yet "without confusion" and "without change."

The *memorial view* is often attributed to Ulrich Zwingli, though some scholars insist that his beliefs were not all that different from Calvin. Zwingli wanted to rid the Lord's Supper of unintelligible mysticism. He strongly denied the bodily presence of Christ in the Supper and emphasized that the sacrament is commemoration of the Lord's death.

The Reformed view argues that Christ is *spiritually present* in the Supper. The Catholic, Lutheran, and Reformed views do not dispute the real presence of Christ. They disagree as to whether that presence is corporal, local, or spiritual. Clearly, the Lord's Supper is a memorial. We remember Christ's Last Supper (1 Cor. 11:23). We remember his sacrifice and proclaim his death (1 Cor. 11:26). But the Lord's Supper is not just a commemoration; it is also a communion. First Corinthians 10:16 says, "The cup of blessing that we bless, is it not a participation [*koinonia*] in the blood of Christ? The bread that we break, is it not a participation [*koinonia*] in the body of Christ?" When we drink the cup and eat the bread, we participate in, and have fellowship with, the body and blood of Christ. We are joined to him and experience a deep, spiritual *koinonia* with him. When we feast in faith, Christ is our nourishment and strength. In celebrating the Lord's Supper, we do not simply remember the work of Christ in his death; we are also lifted up into heaven by the Spirit to enjoy fellowship with the living Christ in glory.

DAY 226

A Table or an Altar?

On July 25, 1593 Henry of Navarre, in order to secure his place as King Henry IV of France, renounced the Protestant faith in which he was raised and became a Catholic. As justification for his religious conversion, it is said that Henry declared, "Paris is well worth a Mass."

Henry's political calculation aside, how should Protestants assess the Catholic Mass, in particular the notion that at the heart of the service is a re-presentation of Christ's atoning death? Technically, Catholic theology does not consider the Eucharist a resacrifice of Christ. Instead, according to Catholic doctrine, "The sacrifice of Christ and the sacrifice of the Eucharist are *one single sacrifice*."[1] The Mass does not repeat the atoning sacrifice of Christ, because the sacrifice is "ever present."[2]

This understanding of the sacrament goes hand in hand with the doctrine of transubstantiation. If the bread and the wine are literally the body and blood of Christ, then Christ can be offered again as a sacrifice for sins, only this time in an unbloodied manner. If transubstantiation is true, then Catholics are right to kneel before the eucharistic procession and worship the monstrance (the receptacle in which the consecrated Host is displayed) as it passes by.

In their book *Rome Sweet Home*, popular apologist Scott Hahn and his wife, Kimberly, tell their story of converting from conservative Presbyterianism to Roman Catholicism. At one point in the book, Kimberly tells how she started looking at the Eucharist differently. She realized that if transubstantiation were true, the only response would be to kneel before the consecrated elements, but, she recalled thinking, "if that is not Jesus in the monstrance, then what they are doing is gross idolatry."[3] Likewise, Peter Kreeft, a well-regarded Catholic writer, argues that "if the doctrine of the Real Presence of Christ in the Eucharist were not true, this adoration would be the most momentous idolatry: bowing to bread and worshipping wine! And if it *is* true, then to refuse to adore is equally monstrous."[4]

But what if "This is my body" should not be taken any more physically than "I am the door" (John 10:9)? What if the once for all nature of Christ's propitiatory sacrifice is undermined—if not technically, then practically—when Christ's death on the cross is said to take place during every Mass (Heb. 10:1–18)?

However much orthodox Protestants and orthodox Catholics may agree on crucial articles of the faith and may be cobelligerents on certain cultural issues, there remains a mutually exclusive understanding of what takes place in Communion. The propitiatory work of Christ is finished, complete, in the past, never to be repeated or re-presented. The state of humiliation has given way to the state of exaltation (Phil. 2:5–11). The same person who died on Calvary two thousand years ago is not sacrificed for our sins during the eucharistic celebration. The Lord's Supper is a meal, not a sacrifice. And so we gather around a table, not an altar.

1   Catechism of the Catholic Church, 1367.
2   Catechism of the Catholic Church, 1364.
3   Hahn and Hahn, *Rome Sweet Home: Our Journey to Catholicism*, 142.
4   Kreeft, *Catholic Christianity*, 329.

DAY 227

Who Should Receive the Lord's Supper?

Those who come to the Lord's Supper must be sincere, instructed, and accountable believers. Note several points from Paul's instructions in 1 Corinthians 11:17–34:

1. Partaking in Communion requires an act of remembrance on the part of the recipient (11:24–25).
2. In eating the bread and drinking the cup, we proclaim the Lord's death until he comes (11:26). This implies a personal and self-conscious intention.
3. The elements can be consumed in an unworthy manner (11:27). This suggests an active participation in the Supper, not a merely passive reception.
4. The person who eats and drinks must examine himself (11:28). This is why most older liturgies call for a due season of self-reflection in advance of the sacrament.
5. Anyone who eats and drinks without discerning the body brings judgment upon himself (11:29).

In other words, 1 Corinthians 11 presumes a certain level of maturity for those who come to the table. We must not partake of the Supper lightly. Death and judgment are at stake. Berkhof says three kinds of people are excluded from the Lord's Supper: the sacrament is not for children, not for unbelievers, and not for hypocrites.[1]

Some Reformed Christians argue that the requirements in 1 Corinthians 11 are for adults only and were not meant to keep children away from the table. They insist that if children partook of the Passover under the Mosaic covenant, they should not be excluded from the Lord's Supper under the new covenant. As attractive as this reasoning may sound, there are several problems with this argument.

For starters, it is not clear at what age children partook of the Passover. Certainly, nursing infants were not participating in a meal that included roast meat, unleavened bread, and bitter herbs. Eight-day-old circumcised sons were not full participants during the Passover. Moreover, those who believe in a fundamental continuity between the Old and New Testaments must still allow for areas of discontinuity. Surely it is significant that Jesus instituted the Lord's Supper not as part of a family meal in Bethany but in the upper room with his disciples.

Most importantly, arguments for paedocommunion misunderstand the nature of the covenant and the nature of the two sacraments. To be sure, children are included in the covenant in both Testaments. But there is a distinction between the covenant as a legal relationship and the covenant as a communion of life. Children are heirs to the promises of God (and so they receive the initiatory sign of baptism), but apart from faith they are not heirs of salvation (of which the Lord's Supper is the sign and seal). The two sacraments are not identical. As the sacrament of naming and inclusion, baptism allows for passive recipients. As the sacrament of remembering and renewal, the Lord's Supper requires active participants. We recognize and honor the nature of baptism when we administer the sign to believers and their children. We recognize and honor the nature of the Lord's Supper when we welcome to the table only those who feast on Christ in repentance and faith.

1 Berkhof, *Systematic Theology*, 656–57.

DAY 228

Church Membership

For some Christians, membership sounds stiff and unnecessary, something you have at your bank or the country club, but too formal for the church. Why bother joining a local church when I'm already a member of the universal church? Why all the hoops? Why is local church membership such a big deal? Here are several reasons.

1. *Our God is a keeper of lists and names.* The Bible is full of membership rolls with names of covenant families and covenant heads. There is even a book called Numbers that contains an authorized census of God's people.

2. *Membership is a biblical category.* The church did not steal the idea of membership from the guild or the country club. "For just as the body is one and has many members, and all the members of the body, though many, are one body, so it is with Christ" (1 Cor. 12:12). Christians are members of the body of Christ. Unpopular as it may sound, you can belong or not belong to the family of God (Matt. 18; 1 Cor. 5). As Cyprian famously said, "Outside of the church, there is no salvation" (*extra ecclesiam nulla salus*).

3. *In joining a church you make visible your commitment to Christ and his people.* Membership is one way to raise the flag of faith. You state before God and others that you are part of *this* local body of believers. It's easy to talk in glowing terms about the invisible church—the body of all believers near and far, living and dead—but it's in the visible church that God expects you to live out your faith. Real fellowship is hard work, because most people are a lot like us—selfish, petty, and proud. But that's the body God calls us to.

4. *Church membership keeps us accountable.* When we join a church, we are offering ourselves to one another to be encouraged, rebuked, corrected, and served. We are placing ourselves under leaders and submitting to their authority. We are saying, "I am here to stay. I want to help you grow in godliness. Will you help me to do the same?"

5. *Joining the church will help your pastor and elders be more faithful shepherds.* Hebrews 13:17a says, "Obey your leaders and submit to them." That's the part for the congregation. Here's the part of the leaders: "for they are keeping watch over your souls, as those will have to give an account" (13:17b). The pastors and elders should take seriously their responsibility before God to care for the souls of their people. They must be diligent in getting to know their members, in following up with them, in praying for them, and in being available in times of distress. If the elders are to "shepherd the flock of God" that is among them (1 Pet. 5:2), they must know who belongs to that flock.

6. *Joining the church gives you an opportunity to make promises.* When people become members at your local church, they make promises to pray, give, serve, attend worship, accept the spiritual guidance of the church, obey its teachings, and seek the things that make for unity, purity, and peace. These are solemn vows. And we must hold each other to them. When Christians don't join a local church, they miss an opportunity to publicly make these promises and commit before God to be a blessing to the church and to each other.

Church Discipline

We have already seen that the church possesses *potestas diakritike*, power with respect to discipline. This power involves the inclusion and exclusion of persons in the fellowship of the church. It is a power only over those who have submitted themselves to the communion of the body of Christ, and the penalties are only those connected to membership in this communion. This power does not belong to the church by itself but is Christ's power exercised through the church.

The word *discipline* sounds negative to most of us. And yet discipline in the Bible is usually positive. It is the way the Lord (and those in authority under him) lovingly corrects us (Job 5:17; Prov. 12:1: Eph. 6:4; Heb. 12:11). We need to make the connection between discipline and discipleship. Discipline is a necessary element of discipleship, and discipleship is the motivation behind discipline.

The key text for understanding formal church discipline comes from Jesus's instructions in Matthew 18:15–20. We see in these verses four basic steps in the disciplinary process, three promises, two big ideas, and one overarching goal.

Four basic steps. (1) Go to the person alone. (2) Take one or two others with you. (3) Tell it to the church. (4) Treat the person as an outsider. These steps should not be understood or undertaken woodenly. They deal with personal (as opposed to public) offenses, and do not envision situations where someone's safety may be in jeopardy. The general rule of thumb is to keep the circle as small as possible and give the guilty party every opportunity to repent and change. As a last resort, the unrepentant sinner is excommunicated. The New Testament language of treating as a pagan (Matt. 18:17) or removing from your midst (1 Cor. 5:2, 13), or handing over to Satan (1 Cor. 5:5; 1 Tim. 1:20) is the spiritual and ecclesiastical appropriation of the Old Testament's civil penalty of putting someone "outside the camp" (Deut. 17:7; 19:19; 21:21; 22:24; 24:7).

Three promises. God promises to those who properly exercise church discipline: (1) Heaven will stand by you (Matt. 18:18). (2) God will act for you (18:19). (3) Jesus will be in the midst of you (18:20). God gives to the church the keys of the kingdom so that the heavenly membership of God's kingdom above might be reflected in the earthly membership of his church below.

Two big ideas. (1) Discipline is what we do as followers of Christ. Mutually correct, rebuke, repent, discipline, bind, and loose are not optional for the church (Gal. 6:1). (2) Discipline is what we do as the family of God. Notice the deliberate familial language in Matthew 18. We are dealing with siblings (18:15), and the discipline ultimately comes from our Father (18:19). Discipline is the merciful act of a Father who loves his children too much to let us go our own way.

One overarching goal. Discipline is for the purity of the church and for the honor of the Lord Jesus. We must never overlook these ends. And yet the New Testament emphasizes a complementary goal: the restoration of the sinner. We do not want to punish our brother; we want to win him back. We want to see our friends return to the right path (James 5:19–20). Anytime the church delivers someone "to Satan," it is in hope and in prayer that his spirit may be saved on the day of the Lord (1 Cor. 5:5).

Church Officers in the New Testament Church

When Christ ascended into heaven, he gave gifts to men, and chief among these gifts was the officers he commissioned for the edification of the church. "And he gave the apostles, the prophets, the evangelists, the shepherds and teachers, to equip the saints for the work of ministry, for building up the body of Christ" (Eph. 4:11–12).

The *apostles* were to be eyewitnesses to the Lord Jesus and his work. When it came time to replace Judas, the church looked for men who had been with them during Christ's ministry and could bear witness to his resurrection (Acts 1:21–22; cf. Luke 24:46–48; 2 Pet. 1:16). Importantly, the church drew lots for this vacancy because the commission was to come directly from Jesus himself. Although Paul saw the resurrected Christ by a different route, he still qualified to be an apostle because Christ appeared to him on the road to Damascus (1 Cor. 15:8; cf. Acts 22:14; 26:16). The apostles were granted supernatural power to perform miracles and signs that would authenticate the gospel message (2 Cor. 12:12; Heb. 2:3–4). The apostles also wielded a unique and unrivaled authority in the church (Acts 15:28; 1 Cor. 15:3; 1 Thess. 4:8). Given their special calling, qualifications, power, and authority, apostles are no longer operative in the church in an official sense, though by way of analogy the church still has "sent out" ones who engage in pioneering gospel work (Acts 13:3–4).

The New Testament often speaks of active *prophets* in the midst of the church (Acts 11:28; 13:1–2; 15:32; 1 Cor. 12:10; 13:2; 14:3; Eph. 2:20; 3:5; 4:11; 1 Tim. 1:18; 4:14; Rev. 11:6). Like their Old Testament counterparts, New Testament prophecy needed to be weighed and could be proven true or false (1 Cor. 14:26–40; 1 Thess. 5:20–21). The one congregational prophet we hear from directly—Agabus in the book of Acts—sounds like an Old Testament prophet when he declares, "Thus says the Holy Spirit" (Acts 21:11). This suggests that while God may still give supernatural insight to believers, and preachers may still speak with prophetic power, it is best to think of prophets as having ceased along with the apostles. Indeed, New Testament apostles and prophets are part of the once for all, nonrepeatable foundation of the church (Eph. 2:20).

The New Testament says less about *evangelists*, but we know that Philip was an evangelist (Acts 21:8). Likely, Timothy was too (2 Tim. 4:5). Given his authority to appoint elders, Titus was probably an evangelist as well (Titus 1:5). We don't know for certain what being an evangelist entailed, but Berkhof's supposition makes sense: "Their authority seems to have been more general and somewhat superior to that of the regular ministers."[1] Since we hear nothing else about the office of evangelist in the New Testament, it was probably not meant to be a perpetual office but was unique to the initial establishment of the church.

Of the four offices listed, the office of *pastor-teacher* is the only one that continues today. Some exegetes have argued that these two words should be understood as two offices, but the absence of the definite article before "teachers" suggests that Paul is thinking about one who is both a shepherd (pastor) and a teacher. Surely, we ought to highly esteem the faithful pastor-teacher, considering that the Lord Jesus himself has given him to us as a generous gift.

1 Berkhof, *Systematic Theology*, 585.

WEEK 47

DAY 231

The Work of Ministry

Most Christians understand Ephesians 4:12 to be a wonderful statement about every-member ministry in the church. Paul asserts that Christ gave pastor-teachers to the church so that they might equip the saints, who then do the work of ministry, all for the edification of the body of Christ.

This sense of verse 12 is conveyed by the way the ESV (along with most modern translations) punctuates the passage. With a comma after "ministry" but not after "saints," the ESV has decided that the three clauses are subordinate. That is, "for building up" and "for the work of ministry" line up under "to equip the saints." The last two clauses are subordinate to the first (or possibly each new clause is subordinate to the last). The best argument in support of this interpretation is that the Greek prepositions are not identical in the three clauses: to (*pros*) equip . . . for (*eis*) the work . . . for (*eis*) building up.

There is, however, another way of understanding verse 12. The King James Version inserts another comma (remember, there are no commas in the original Greek): "for the perfecting of the saints, for the work of ministry, for the edifying of the body of Christ." With this translation, the three clauses are coordinate. That is, each clause stands next to the others as a description of why God gave pastor-teachers to the church. On this reading, the pastors do not equip the saints who then do the work of ministry; pastors equip the saints *and* do the work of ministry *and* build up the church.

Both readings can be justified from the Greek. One could argue that the change in prepositions is significant, or that the change (as often happens in the New Testament) is merely stylistic. Although I grew up hearing many lessons about ordinary church members doing the real work of ministry, I now lean toward the second (older) interpretation.

For starters, the previous verses are all about God giving gifts to men by giving them the officers in the church (4:8–10). It would seem strange to shift so dramatically from all that the officers do in the church to then maintain that the saints do the real work of ministry. If the clauses in verse 12 are subordinate, the pastor-teachers are not actually doing the work of ministry. They are only equippers. Such an emphasis feels out of place, given the larger context. Moreover, to make the change in prepositions carry all that theological freight is more than the grammar alone can bear.

Surely it is significant that most Reformed theologians have assumed a coordinate understanding of the clauses. Calvin, for example, insists that the preaching office "is the chief sinew by which believers are held together in one body." It is through the ministers that the saints are renewed, the body is built up, and we are brought into the unity of Christ.[1] This is a word both pastors and congregants need to hear today. "There is nothing more notable or glorious in the church than the ministry of the gospel."[2]

1 Calvin, *Institutes*, 4.3.2.
2 Calvin, *Institutes*, 4.3.3.

How Many Offices in the Church?

Among Reformed theologians there is a longstanding debate as to the number of continuing offices in the church. Calvin listed four: elders, deacons, pastors, and teachers (sometimes called "doctors" of the church, what we would probably call "seminary professors"). Most theologians have not followed Calvin in this regard, arguing instead that there is no developed office of teacher in the New Testament and that "the shepherds and teachers" in Ephesians 4:11 refer to one office, the pastor-teacher.

More commonly, many Reformed thinkers have insisted on three offices: elders, deacons, and pastors. The key contention here is that the pastor is not simply a certain kind of elder (i.e., a teaching elder) but a different office altogether. There are good reasons for this view. (1) Ephesians 4:11 refers to pastors but not to elders. (2) Paul's letters to Timothy and Titus suggest that these men held an office distinct from the office of elder. Indeed, would Titus be called upon to appoint elders if he was also an elder? (3) The Old Testament had elders to rule over the people and the priests to teach and administer the sacraments. These two functions were carried out by two different offices. (4) Even in churches that have teaching elders and ruling elders, the teaching elder (i.e., the pastor) functions more like he holds a separate office.

There are also good reasons for the two-office view that sees pastors as teaching elders rather than a distinct office. (1) Grammatically, Ephesians 4:11 is better understood as one class of officer with two different orders. (2) First Timothy 5:17 envisions a certain kind of elder who specializes in preaching and teaching. All elders rule, but some are given the special task and privilege of public teaching. (3) In Acts 20:17, Paul calls for the elders (*presbyteroi*) of the church to come before he leaves Ephesus. Then in Acts 20:28, while Paul is addressing the elders, he commands them to keep watch over the flock as overseers (*episkopos*) and to pastor (*poimainein*) the church of God. Elder, pastor, and overseer are used as overlapping words for the same office. (4) The New Testament sometimes refers to overseers and deacons (Phil. 1:1–2; 1 Tim. 3), sometimes to apostles and elders (Acts 15:2), and sometimes just to elders (James 5:14; 1 Pet. 5:1), but the New Testament never speaks of pastors, elders, and deacons of a given church. If pastor were a third office, we would expect to see it listed at times in place of overseer or elder.

In the end, I find the two-office view more convincing, though having served for many years in a denomination with elders, deacons, and pastors (and professors of theology), and now serving in a denomination with teaching elders and ruling elders (as one office) and deacons, I can testify that the day-to-day functioning is not terribly different. Both sides can probably agree that the pastor/teaching elder serves as a first among equals. On the other hand, both sides should also desire to honor the office of elder/ruling elder and grant to these men the authority their office demands.

DAY 233

Elders

Eldership began in the Old Testament. The word *elders* occurs almost two hundred times in the Bible, over half from the Old Testament. The phrase "elders of Israel" appears over thirty times. To be an elder of Israel was probably not a well-defined office as much as it was a group of men who formed the nucleus of leadership for God's people. There were elders from the early days of Israel's history (Num. 11:16; Deut. 27:1; 31:28). There were elders in Moses's day, elders during Joshua's rule, during the united monarchy, during the kings, after the exile, and during the prophets (Joel 1:14). There were still elders ruling the Jewish people at the time of the New Testament (Matt. 27:1).

Growing out of Jewish soil, the early church appointed elders to rule in each congregation. The leaders in the early church were initially the apostles and elders (Acts 15:2), but as the apostolic ministry literally died off, the elders became the body responsible for leadership and pastoral oversight in the church (Acts 20:17, 28). Eldership is a constant theme throughout the history of God's people. Even now in heaven, there are twenty-four elders around the throne, representative of the twelve sons of Israel from the old covenant and the twelve apostles from the new covenant (Rev. 4:4, 10).

We don't know how elders were chosen in the Old Testament, but specific requirements and qualifications are listed in the New Testament. The *presbyteroi* did not have to be old in age (1 Tim. 4:12) as much as they had to be mature in character (1 Tim. 3:1–7). The shepherds of the church were responsible for feeding, leading, guiding, and protecting the flock (cf. Ps. 23:1–3). Most basically, elder responsibilities fall in two general categories: governing and teaching (1 Tim. 5:17). Surely it is significant that many of the passages associated with eldership emphasize spiritual authority (1 Thess. 5:12–13; 1 Pet. 5:2–3) and that the one skill required of elders is being able to teach (1 Tim. 3:2; see Titus 1:9).

The qualifications for elder and deacon are similar, but two of the unique requirements for elders have to do with teaching and governing. A deacon must keep hold of the deep truths of the faith, but a deacon is not required to be able to teach (1 Tim. 3:2). The elder doesn't need to be a preacher, but he must be able to effectively communicate the truths of Scripture, whether publicly or privately. Similarly, both elders and deacons must manage their own household well, but 1 Timothy 3:5 adds for the elder that he will "care for God's church." In short, an elder teaches and governs.

This is why elders are to be men. The consistent pattern from creation in the garden to eldership in Israel to the apostolate in the New Testament reinforces the principle of male leadership. Moreover, the main responsibilities of an elder—teaching and governing—are the two things Paul explicitly forbids women from doing in the church (1 Tim. 2:12). A woman can teach and have authority in certain contexts, but in the church, she should not do so over men. Women can and should serve in ministry in hundreds of ways. At the same time, God's design from the beginning has been for men to exercise teaching and governing authority in the covenant community. May God raise up godly, helping women in service to Christ and his church, and may God raise up caring and capable men to lead Christ's church with wisdom, courage, and love.

DAY 234

Deacons

The deacon (*diakonos*) is a servant who labors alongside the elders in caring for the tangible needs of the body (Acts 6:1–6; 1 Tim. 3:8–13). The Greek word *diakonos* has the broad meaning of servant. The verb *diakoneo* means "to serve," with an emphasis on practical, hands-on assistance (Matt. 8:15; 25:44; Luke 10:40).

Like the elders, deacons must be an example of Christian virtue (1 Tim. 3:8–13). Deacons are not junior elders. They have different gifts and minister in different ways, with different emphases. All of us need to be concerned about the needy, but deacons in particular should lead the way in serving those in the church who are in need, unemployed, ill, imprisoned, abused, poor, frightened, anxious, lonely, without friends, without money, or without support.

While the question of women serving as elder is relatively straightforward, the question about women and the diaconate is more complicated. The understating of *gynaikas* in 1 Timothy 3:11 is open to two interpretations. Some exegetes have argued that the women in view are female deacons or deaconesses. In support of this position we can observe: (1) The wording in the first half of verse 8 is the same as in the first half of verse 11, suggesting that another kind of formal diaconal position is being introduced. (2) If *gynaikas* means the wives of deacons, Paul could have made his point clearer by saying "their women" instead of just "women." (3) If the women in view are the wives of deacons, why doesn't Paul include similar qualifications for the elders' wives? Isn't it important that they be spiritually mature as well?

There are, however, good reasons to think that Paul is speaking about the wives of deacons and not deaconesses per se. (1) It would be strange to introduce a new office, or subset of an office, in verse 11 and then go back to deacons in verse 12. (2) The discussion of wives in verse 11 leads naturally to the requirement in the next verse of being a one-woman man. (3) There is no requirement in verse 11 for these women to be tested first (like the deacons). (4) Paul did not include qualifications for the elders' wives because the work of teaching and governing, unlike the work of hands-on service, would not include women in the same way. (5) The office of deacon, though not involved in governing like the elder, is still an office tied to authority in the church. Deacons are mentioned side by side with elders in Philippians 1 and 1 Timothy 3. Deacons must exhibit leadership in the home. The work of deacons is tied to the church's ministry as a pillar and buttress of the truth (1 Tim. 3:15).

While my understanding of church office and ordination leads me to restrict the diaconate to qualified men, there is nothing in the scope of diaconal work as such that precludes the ministry of women. Indeed, Phoebe was a servant (*diakonos*) of the church in Cenchrea (Rom. 16:1). The New Testament includes many examples of women serving Christ and serving the church (Mark 15:40–41; Luke 8:2–3; Acts 9:36). Only some (men) will be elders and deacons. But all are called to serve and speak the word of God in other ways.

DAY 235

Divine Appointment for Church Government

Most Christians don't think a lot about church government, and when they do, they don't think the Bible has a whole lot to say about it. Sure, maybe the Bible says something about the sacraments, and maybe there are a few verses about elders and deacons in the New Testament, but can we really expect the Bible to mandate a specific form of church government?

This is an old debate. In 1662 the Anglican preacher and theologian Edward Stillingfleet published *Irenicum: A weapon-salve for the churches wounds, or The divine right of particular forms of church-government: discuss'd and examin'd according to the principles of the law of nature.* As the title suggests, Stillingfleet believed churches were being needlessly divided over issues on which Scripture never meant to speak. His title for the first chapter makes this point abundantly clear: "Things necessary for the Churches Peace, must be clearly revealed. The Form of Church-Government not so, as appears by the remaining Controversie about it. An Evidence thence, that Christ never intended any one Form, as the only means to Peace in the Church." In other words, we should not expect the Bible to mandate a particular form of church polity.

By contrast, other theologians (Presbyterians in particular) have argued that church polity is *jus divinum* (by divine right). Of course, the Bible doesn't tell us everything we might want to know. And yet once the caveats are in place, many Presbyterians insist that the word of God does "afford a model, more or less detailed, of ecclesiastical polity and organization, which it is the duty of Christians at all times and in all circumstances to imitate."[1]

On what grounds can such a statement be made? James Bannerman gives four reasons to expect church government by positive and explicit warrant.

1. The church is founded by divine warrant. The source of its authority is from without, not from within. We ought to expect that the ordering of this society would come from God, not merely from the shared opinions of its members.

2. The church is not a society founded in nature. The church exists by positive divine appointment. As such, we should not think that the principles of nature are sufficient for organizing a proper government for this society.

3. The effects of sin mitigate against any notion that man is competent by the light of reason to devise and regulate a government for the church. If the church is an institution—in its mission, in its membership, and in nature—of divine origin, it would be strange for God to let man determine its constitution and design.

4. The church is represented as an expression of the kingdom of God, as a kind of embassy of the kingdom. As founder and administrator of this visual outpost of the kingdom, why would Christ leave the establishment of the government of this institution to man?

I believe in *jure divino* Presbyterianism, but I also believe we must be honest about all the things Scripture does not tell us. We aren't told the size of the session, how often it should meet, what shepherding model to employ, whether there should be committees and commissions, or anything whatsoever about Robert's Rules of Order (surely an oversight!). Church polity is not a free-for-all.

There is a general model provided for all times and all places. But Bannerman is right: "We are not to look for a systematic delineation of Church government, or a scientific compendium of ecclesiastical law, in Scripture."[2]

1 Bannerman, *Church of Christ*, 723.
2 Bannerman, *Church of Christ*, 728.

DAY 236

Who Governs the Church: The Pope?

Church polity may not strike us as terribly interesting, but the subject is crucially important. In looking at church polity we are trying to answer the question, "Who has been given the right, under Christ, to exercise power within, for, and over the church?" To put it colloquially, we are trying to determine who has the "buck stops here" final say and authority in the church. Historically, four answers have been given: the pope, the bishops, the congregation, or the elders. We can think of these four systems as Roman Catholic, episcopalian, congregational, and presbyterian.

The Roman Catholic system of polity depends upon the assertion that a superior title was given to Peter, that this title was not personal but official, and that this official position is passed down from Peter to his successors. This supreme pontiff is the pope, the Bishop of Rome, the head of the Roman Catholic Church around the world, and sovereign of the independent state known as Vatican City.

Arguments in favor of papal authority are not convincing. Historically, there is no evidence Peter was ever in Rome, much less its bishop. More significantly, Jesus's pronouncement "on this rock I will build my church" (Matt. 16:18) did not establish Peter as the soon-to-be head of the church. For starters, even if the rock is Peter, it is anachronistic to think that Jesus meant to confer upon Peter a unique role that wasn't true of all the apostles and prophets as foundational offices in the church (Eph. 2:20). Moreover, it is very unlikely Jesus was speaking about Peter directly. (1) Peter is about to deny Christ, so he was hardly a rock. (2) The Greek words *petros* (Peter) and *petra* (rock) are distinguished both in person and in gender. (3) Why would Jesus say "this rock" instead of "you, the rock" when he so often addresses Peter as "you" in verses 17–19?

Other scriptural considerations disallow the notion of official Petrine superiority (even if he may have been an unofficial leader among the apostles). (1) The new Jerusalem has twelve foundations with the names of the twelve apostles, not just Peter (Rev. 21:14). (2) The power given to Peter to bind and loose (Matt 16:19) is later given to all the disciples (Matt. 18:18). (3) Peter refers to himself as nothing more than a fellow elder (1 Pet. 5:1).

So what is "this rock" in Matthew 16? Many Protestant interpreters take the phrase to be a reference to Peter's confession that Jesus is the Christ. While this is certainly possible, I understand the rock to be Christ himself. The word *rock* is used twelve times in the New Testament, and it is never used of anyone but Christ. He is the stone of stumbling and rock of offense (Rom. 9:33; 1 Pet. 2:8). He is the stone that Isaiah and Daniel predicted (Isa. 28:16; Dan. 2:34–35, 45). Quite simply, "the Rock was Christ" (1 Cor. 10:4). As Turretin puts it, quoting Augustine, "Therefore, thou art Peter and upon this rock, which thou hast confessed, upon this rock, which thou hast acknowledged, saying, thou art the Christ, the Son of the living God, I will build my church, upon myself, who am the Son of the living God, I will build my church, upon myself I will build, not upon thee."[1] There is only one king and head of the church: the Lord Jesus Christ. There is no other rock (Isa. 44:8).

1 Turretin, *Elenctic Theology*, 3:164.

Who Governs the Church: The Bishops?

The distinguishing feature of episcopalian polity is the presence of bishops as overseers in the church. The system is sometimes called prelacy because of high-ranking clergy members (i.e., bishops) called prelates (prelate meaning "to carry before or be set above"). The New Testament speaks of *episkopoi* ("overseers" in the ESV) in several places (Phil. 1:1; 1 Tim. 3:1; Titus 1:7). The question is whether this term refers to another ordinary and permanent office above elders and deacons.

In episcopalian polity the bishop has two unique powers: the power of ordination (*potestas ordinis*) and the power of jurisdiction (*potestas jurisdictionis*). In short, the bishop has authority over his diocese—a power not afforded to other office holders.

The best argument in favor of bishops relies on the example of the apostles and their broad authority. And yet the superior functions given to, and exercised by, the apostles were in connection with that extraordinary and temporary office. The office of bishop cannot be assumed from or read back into that unique office. We know of the apostles and the elders exercising authority over the broader church (Acts 15:2), but there is no record of another office—the office of bishop—existing in continuity with the apostles or over the elders.

The distinctive peculiarity of an episcopacy is that there exists a third order of officers (*episkopoi*) that exercises powers of ordination and jurisdiction not granted to the elders (*presbyteroi*). This is not the pattern we see in the New Testament. We know that the elders participated in ordination (1 Tim. 4:14; cf. Acts 13:1–3) and that ruling was the normal function of the elder (1 Tim. 5:17; 1 Pet. 5:1–2). We also see from Acts 15 that the elders came together (with the apostles) to exercise authority over more than one local church. In fact, the frequent pairing of "elders" with "apostles" shows that elders—not bishops—were going to carry on the apostolic mantle of authority (see Acts 15:2, 4, 6, 22–23; 16:4).

Most critically, we simply cannot make the two Greek terms—*presbyteros* and *episkopos*—bear the theological weight that the episcopalian system demands. The word *presbyteros* was used in the Jewish synagogue for elders, while the word *episkopos* was common among the Greeks for various kinds of overseers. It is little wonder, then, that the two words are used interchangeably in the New Testament. We see this most plainly in Acts 20:17 and 28 where the *presbyteroi* are later called *episkopoi*, and in Titus 1:5 and 7 where "an overseer" (*episkopos*) is another way of referring to the elders (*presbyteroi*). It is also significant that 1 Timothy 3 details qualification for two offices, not three, and that Philippians 1:1 speaks of more than one overseer (*episkopos*) in Philippi.

Finally, there is a wider theological argument to consider. The authority to preach the gospel and administer the sacraments is the chief power granted to the undershepherds. It would be strange logic to give the presbyters the *greater* power to preach and administer the sacraments but not the *lesser* power to ordain and govern. As we've seen from Acts 20, the elder-pastor-overseer is given authority to teach the word and to care for the church of God. The two responsibilities cannot be separated.

Who Governs the Church:
The Congregation?

At the heart of congregationalism lies two interlocking principles.

1. According to the congregational principle, the government of the church is administered with the authoritative concurrence of the whole church. While the elders may advise the congregation in important matters and execute the decisions of the congregation, the final authority—especially when it comes to membership and discipline—rests with the members of the church.

2. According to the independency principle, the government of the church is administered independent of every other congregation. While churches may partner together in ministry and may even agree together to affirm certain doctrinal parameters, the local congregation alone exercises power over its own affairs.

As a Presbyterian, I certainly appreciate the congregational emphasis upon the centrality of the local church and the key role its members are to play in the life and ministry of the church. And yet, as a Presbyterian, I believe biblical precedent and precepts point away from the two principles mentioned above. I'll evaluate the congregational principle here in talking about congregationalism. In the next chapter I'll look at the independency principle as I make the case for presbyterian polity.

The main difficulty with the congregational principle is the unique authority granted to the elders. The titles—rulers, overseers, shepherds—suggest a governing authority not possessed by the other members of the congregation. It is hard to see how the elders can actually be said to rule and oversee if their decisions are, in the most important matters, subject to the majority vote of the congregation. The role of the elders in Israel (more informally) and later in the synagogue (more formally) was not one in which they merely advised the congregation or executed the plans the congregation decided upon collectively. Moreover, the instructions regarding binding and loosing are given to Peter and then to the Twelve, not to every disciple. We do not see private members of the church preaching, and we do not see them ordaining those who will preach. Christ has entrusted the keys of the kingdom to the elders, not to the entire membership of the church more broadly.

One might object to this claim on two exegetical grounds: Paul mentioning "this punishment by the majority" in 2 Corinthians 2, and Jesus saying, "Tell it to the church," as the last step of discipline in Matthew 18. On the first point, there is no indication that the majority in Corinth *voted* on the punishment. Rather, given the entreaty to reaffirm their love, it seems that Paul is speaking of the punishment they have *enacted* together in treating the offending party as an outsider.

As for the second passage, we must consider the immediate context. The exercise of discipline in the synagogue was practiced by designated officers, not by the whole congregation. See, for example, how the *council* handled (badly, though it may have been) the disciplinary proceedings with Jesus in the Gospels and with Peter and John in Acts. When Jesus says, "Tell it to the church," no one in his Jewish audience would have thought of every-member congregationalism. They would have thought of the authority given to the officers to rule on behalf of God for the sake of his people.

DAY 239

Who Governs the Church: The Elders?

If Roman Catholic polity believes in a pope, episcopalian polity believes in bishops, congregational polity believes in the authority of the congregation, then presbyterianism believes in the unique authority granted to the elders. Moreover, presbyterians insist that this elder authority is exercised not just at a local session level but in presbyteries. Recall from the last chapter that congregationalism holds to the independency principle, the idea that the government of each local church is exercised independent of other churches. By contrast, presbyterians believe there is warrant for the governing body of one congregation to unite with the governing body of another congregation (or many others) for the purpose of joint authority in the exercise of a common rule over all.[1]

Let me make two exegetical observations in support of this contention.

1. The work *ekklesia* can be used to mean more than one congregation. "So the church throughout all Judea and Galilee and Samaria had peace and was being built up. And walking in the fear of the Lord and in the comfort of the Holy Spirit, it multiplied" (Acts 9:31; cf. 1 Cor. 12:28; 10:32). The church in Jerusalem, in particular, must have consisted of various congregations. With thousands being added to the church (Acts 2:41, 47; 4:4; 5:14) and with such a large number of apostles, prophets, elders, and proto-deacons ministering in the city, surely there was more than one assembly and more than one worship service. And yet we still hear of the "church in Jerusalem" (Acts 11:22). Moreover, these officers are

spoken of as belonging to the whole church in Jerusalem, implying one church under a shared system of government. No wonder, then, that when relief came from Antioch for the church in Jerusalem, they sent the collection "to the elders by the hand of Barnabas and Saul" (11:30).

2. The Council of Jerusalem provides an example of a regional church assembly exercising authority over local congregations. In Acts 15, the apostles and elders come together to determine the appropriate policy for welcoming Gentiles into the church. True, the "whole church" is mentioned in verse 22, but that is for the purpose of choosing men to deliver the message. The theological matter at hand was adjudicated by the apostles and elders (15:6). And what they decided was not mere advice but an authoritative determination meant to be followed in Antioch, Syria, and Cilicia (15:23, 28). Here we have the officers from one region of the church exercising authority over the various churches of that region (for similar examples see Acts 6:2–6; 13:1–3; 21:18–26).

In closing, it should be noted that church power in presbyterianism flows "up," not "down." Every local church is a complete church of Christ. The so-called higher judicatories cannot lord it over the lower assemblies. In fact, Berkhof argues that we normally call them major or general assemblies, not higher assemblies, because they represent the very same power, not a higher power.[2] The authority is broader, but it is not higher or truer or better. The power of the church, derived from Christ's authority, resides first of all in the local session and then is transferred to major assemblies, not the other way around.

1   Bannerman, *Church of Christ*, 839.
2   Berkhof, *Systematic Theology*, 589–90.

Decently and in Order

It has often been said—sometimes with a sense of humor and sometimes in annoyance—that Presbyterian and Reformed churches love to do things "decently and in order." I can understand both the humor and the frustration. We love our plans, our minutes, our courts, and our committees. Presbyterian and Reformed folks have been known to appoint committees just to oversee other committees (reminding me of the old *Onion* headline that announced "New Starbucks Opens in Rest Room of Existing Starbucks"). We like doing things so decently that we expect our church officers to know three things: the Bible, our confessions, and a book with "order" in the title.

But before we shake our heads in disbelief at those uber-Reformed types (physician, heal thyself!), we should recall that before "decently and in order" was a Presbyterian predilection, it was a biblical command (1 Cor. 14:40). Paul's injunction for the church to be marked by propriety and decorum, to be well-ordered like troops drawn up in ranks, is a fitting conclusion to a portion of Scripture that deals with confusion regarding gender, confusion at the Lord's Table, confusion about spiritual gifts, confusion in the body of Christ, and confusion in public worship. "Decently and in order" sounds pretty good compared to the mess that prevailed in Corinth.

The knock on Presbyterian and Reformed Christians has typically been that, though supreme in head, they are deficient in heart. We are the emotionless stoics, the changeless wonders, God's frozen chosen. But such veiled insults would not have impressed the apostle Paul, for he knew better than anyone that the opposite of order in the church is not free-flowing spontaneity; it is self-exalting chaos. God never favors confusion over peace (14:33). He never pits theology against doxology, or head against heart. As David Garland put it memorably: "The Spirit of ardor is also the Spirit of order."[1]

The reality is that every church will worship in some way, pray in some way, be led in some way, be structured in some way, and do baptism and the Lord's Supper in some way. Every church is living out some form of theology, even if that theology is based on pragmatism instead of biblical principles.

Why wouldn't we want our life together in the church to be shaped by the best exegetical, theological, and historical reflections?

Why wouldn't we want to be thoughtful instead of thoughtless?

Why wouldn't we want all things in our life together as a church to be done decently and in order? That's not the Presbyterian and Reformed way. That's God's way, and—with all appropriate zeal and passion for Christ and his kingdom—we would do well not to forget it.[2]

---

1 Garland, *1 Corinthians*, 674.

2 This section was adapted, with permission, from my foreword to the Blessings of the Faith series.

ESCHATOLOGY

Last Things

DAY 241

Death and Hell

Although death results in good things for the Christian—being at home with the Lord (2 Cor. 5:8), living with Christ (Phil. 1:21)—death is still our great and last enemy (1 Cor. 15:26). Death is the consequence of the fall (Gen. 2:15–17; Rom. 5:12–21), the wages of sin (Rom. 6:23), and the devil's chosen instrument of fear (Heb. 2:14–15). The believer's confident hope is that though we die, in Christ we shall live forever (John 11:25–26).

There are three main words for death and hell in the Bible: *sheol, hades,* and *gehenna.*

The Hebrew word *sheol,* often left untranslated in newer English versions, has the basic meaning of death or the grave (Isa. 38:10). It can refer to the place every human being goes upon death (Ps. 89:48), but it can also refer more specifically to a place of punishment for the wicked (Deut. 32:22). Even in the Old Testament, there was the promise of deliverance from Sheol for God's people. "But God will ransom my soul from the power of Sheol, for he will receive me" (Ps. 49:15). Later the psalmist expresses his confidence that God will lead him into glory: "You guide me with your counsel, and afterward you will receive me to glory" (73:24).

The Greek word *hades* occurs ten times in the New Testament. Given its coupling with death (i.e., "Death and Hades"), the concept seems to refer to the intermediate state for the wicked (Rev. 20:14). Hades is the place of torment (prior to the resurrection) opposite Abraham's bosom (Luke 16:19–31).

The Greek word *gehenna* occurs twelve times in the New Testament. Rabbi David Kimhi (c. AD 1200) claimed that the Valley of Hinnom was a garbage dump filled with trash and cadavers to burn. This has led many pastors and commentators to say that Gehenna was a smoldering rubbish heap, but there doesn't seem to be any ancient or archaeological evidence to support this claim. The word comes from the Hebrew *ge-hinnom,* meaning "Valley of Hinnom," a steep ravine to the southwest of Jerusalem. In the Old Testament this is where the Israelites would sometimes sacrifice their children to the Ammonite god Molech (2 Kings 23:10; Jer. 32:35). Eleven of the twelve uses of *gehenna* in the

New Testament come from Jesus (Matt. 5:22, 29, 30; 10:28; 18:9; 23:15, 33; Mark 9:43, 45, 47; Luke 12:5; cf. James 3:6). The word is translated as "hell" and signifies a place of eternal judgment, often associated with fire (cf. Matt. 13:41–42; 18:8; 25:46).

God's final judgment on the wicked is described in various ways in the New Testament: as destruction (Phil. 3:19; 2 Pet. 2:1; 3:16), as perishing (Matt. 18:14; Luke 13:3; John 3:16; 10:28; 1 Cor. 1:18), as a punishment of eternal fire (Jude 7), as the gloom of utter darkness (Jude 13), as a place for weeping and gnashing of teeth (Luke 13:28), and as a lake that burns with fire and sulfur (Rev. 21:8). Whether those descriptions are meant to be taken literally or not, they speak of literal pain and torment. Hell is unspeakably horrible, and it is described in bracing terms so that we might avoid it at all costs and run to Christ for refuge.

DAY 242

Hell as Divine Punishment

It has become common for Christians to describe hell as our freely chosen identity apart from God. Hell, it is said, is not so much where God sends the wicked as much as it is what the wicked choose or create for themselves. This is the view famously espoused by C. S. Lewis in *The Great Divorce*. Lewis argues that hell is our own freely chosen self-absorption and idolatry let loose for all eternity. The gates of hell may be locked for eternity, but they are locked from the inside.

There is an element of truth in all this. No one in hell is truly penitent. God doesn't punish people for a few sins in this life and then keep them locked up forever as they pour out their hearts in genuine faith and repentance. They may regret their choices like the rich man in Luke 16, but they never genuinely repent. Lewis's description of hell is also a good reminder that God does at times give us over to our sinful desire. Part of our punishment is that God says, "Alright, pursue your sinful ways." Hell is, in that limited sense, God giving us what we want.

But if that's all we say about hell, we are giving people a distorted view of divine punishment. After the first sin, God decisively sent the couple away and drove them out of the garden (Gen. 3:23–24). At the time of the flood, God responded to the rampant wickedness on the earth by declaring, "I will blot out man whom

I have created" (Gen. 6:7). In Deuteronomy 28, God promises covenantal blessing for obedience and cursing for disobedience. Both are actively sent by God. When Joshua led the Israelites in covenantal renewal, he warned them: "If you forsake the LORD and serve foreign gods, then he will turn and do you harm and consume you, after having done you good" (Josh. 24:20).

The New Testament tells the same story. Jesus exhorts us to fear God, who can destroy body and soul in hell (Matt. 10:28). Romans 1 may speak of God giving the ungodly over to their sinful desires, but Romans 2 speaks clearly of wrath stored up for "the day of wrath when God's righteous judgment will be revealed" (Rom. 2:5). Likewise, 2 Peter 3:7 warns that "the heavens and earth that now exist are stored up for fire, being kept until the day of judgment and destruction of the ungodly." Our bad choices have bad consequences, but more than that, our God is a consuming fire (Heb. 12:29).

It is not wrong to describe hell as eternal separation from God or a Christless eternity. Hell is both these things. But these euphemisms must not swallow up the unpopular notion that God's judgment is more than a lack of something or someone; it is a divine curse upon the ungodly. The one passage that describes judgment as being "away from the presence of the Lord" says in the preceding half of the sentence: "They will suffer the punishment of eternal destruction" (2 Thess. 1:9). If we always speak of eternal punishment as a "Christless eternity" or "being separated from God" or a "hell that we choose for ourselves," we are not being true to the language of Scripture. We are softening a blow that God—in his gracious, warning mercy—does not mean to soften. Wrath is not only a result. It is a recompense.

Universalism

Beginning with Origen in the third century, there have been at times in church history a small number of Christian theologians who have argued for the final salvation of all people. Despite being resoundingly rejected for almost two millennia, universalism has become more accepted in recent years. The increase in support has been owing to modern notions of fairness, lost confidence in biblical authority, a weakened notion of sin and depravity, and a reimagining of God's character.

On a popular level, some are drawn to universalism based on the promise in Ephesians 1 and in Colossians 1 that God is reconciling all things together in Christ. With their emphasis on cosmic renewal, these passages are used by some to argue against eternal punishment, but they cannot carry the theological freight universalists want them to.

Take Ephesians 1, for example. Paul says that God's plan in the fullness of time is to unite all things in Christ, things in heaven and things on earth (1:10). The Greek word for "unite" means to sum up, to bring together to a main point, or to gather together. Think of an author finishing the last chapter of his book, or a conductor bringing the symphony from cacophony to harmony. The promise of "uniting" or "bringing together" is a wonderful promise already begun in Christ. But we know from the rest of Ephesians that Paul does not expect all peoples to be reconciled to God. In chapter 2, Paul speaks of sons of disobedience and children of wrath. In chapter 5, he makes clear that the sexually immoral and the covetous have no inheritance in the kingdom of Christ. The uniting of all things does not entail the salvation of all people. It means that everything in the universe will finally be brought to its appointed end and all peoples will be given their due.

If the Bible does not teach that all are on their way to heaven now, neither does it teach that the condemned have any chance of postmortem salvation later. There is no indication that people will grow or mature or repent in the afterlife. Why would the Bible make such a big deal about repenting "today" (Heb. 3:13), about being found blameless on the day of Christ (2 Pet. 3:14), and about not neglecting such a great salvation (Heb. 2:3) if there were still opportunities to get right with God after death? Why warn about not inheriting the kingdom (1 Cor. 6:9–10), about what a fearful thing it is to fall into the hands of the living God (Heb. 10:31), or about the vengeance of our coming King (2 Thess. 1:5–12) if these warnings, ultimately, don't apply to anyone for all time?

In the end, there is a reason, as Richard Bauckham puts it, that "until the nineteenth century almost all Christian theologians taught the reality of eternal torment in hell."[1] The reason is that the Bible speaks so graphically and in so many places about eternal punishment. And no one speaks more frequently or more forcefully on the subject than Jesus. "The Son of Man will send his angels, and they will gather out of his kingdom all causes of sin and all law-breakers, and throw them into the fiery furnace. In that place there will be weeping and gnashing of teeth" (Matt. 13:41–42).

---

1 Bauckham, "Universalism," 47. For a comprehensive analysis and refutation of universalism see McClymond, *The Devil's Redemption*.

DAY 244

Annihilationism

Annihilationism is the belief that God's final judgment upon the wicked is not eternal conscious punishment, but rather the extinction of existence. The idea is sometimes called "conditional immortality" because it posits that only God is inherently immortal (1 Tim. 1:17; 6:16), and that for human beings, immortality is a gift only bestowed upon the righteous. Consequently, the punishment for the wicked and unbelieving is to be passed over for eternal life and to simply cease to exist. The doctrine of annihilationism was popularized in the twentieth century by evangelical Anglicans like J. W. Wenham, P. E. Hughes, and John Stott.

Despite its existential appeal (being snuffed out is an easier punishment to countenance than eternal conscious torment), the Bible does not allow for an annihilationist interpretation.

1. To be sure, only God is inherently immortal. Ours is a contingent immortality, but this does not mean immortality is only given to some. The Bible frequently depicts the wicked as experiencing ongoing torment in the afterlife. The rich man said, "I am in anguish in this flame" (Luke 16:24). The worm is said to never die, and the fire is never put out (Mark 9:48).

2. It is special pleading to suggest that only the *smoke* of their torment goes up forever and ever (Rev. 14:11) and not the torment itself. The Greek word for *torment* (*basanismos/basanizo*) is always used of conscious suffering in the New Testament, not of the removal of existence. The beast and the false prophet are tormented day and night (Rev. 20:10), just as the wicked have no rest day or night (Rev. 14:11).

3. How does "eternal life" stand opposite "second death" if the latter just speaks of oblivion? Is the good news of eternal life simply consciousness? The righteous receive the resurrection of life, while the wicked receive, not the resurrection unto the cessation of existence, but the resurrection of judgment (John 5:29).

Famously, Shedd's *Dogmatic Theology* has a chapter on heaven that is only a page and a half, while his chapter on hell is fifty-eight pages long. Lopsided perhaps, but that says more about the modern world's opposition to hell than Shedd's dislike for heaven. The reality is that the doctrine of hell needs to be defended in our day, not because we relish the thought of eternal punishment, but because it is such a clear teaching of Scripture and of Jesus himself. "Founded in ethics, in law, and in judicial reason, as well as unquestionably taught by the author of Christianity, it is no wonder that the doctrine of eternal retribution, in spite of selfish prejudices and appeals to human sentiment, has always been a belief of Christendom."[1]

Besides being unquestionably historical and biblical, the doctrine of hell is necessary for practical Christian discipleship. It should make us tremble before the holiness and wrath of God (Heb. 12:28–29). It should lead us to repent of our sins and turn to Christ (Matt. 10:26–31). It should spur us on to lives of holiness and godliness (2 Pet. 3:7, 11–12). It should prompt us to pray for and plead with the lost (Rom. 10:1; 2 Cor. 5:20). And the doctrine of hell can give us the freedom to forgive the worst crimes against us, knowing that God will execute final judgment in his own time (Rom. 12:19–21).

1   Shedd, *Dogmatic Theology*, 929.

DAY 245

Inclusivism

Recognizing that universalism (all people are saved) is unbiblical and that pluralism (many religions are saving) is unbiblical, some Christians argued that there might be salvation *through* Christ without explicit faith *in* Christ. This view is called "inclusivism."

Inclusivists believe that everyone who is saved is saved through the person and work of Christ. They do not, however, insist that conscious faith (on the part of sentient adults) is necessary to appropriate this saving work. Other religious people, or some good people in our neighborhoods, might be drawn to the true and the beautiful and be saved through Christ without knowing it. Inclusivists understand Jesus's declaration, "No one comes to the Father except through me" (John 14:6) to mean "through my saving work." Unlike *exclusivists*, they do not think conscious faith (on the part of sentient adults) is absolutely necessary for salvation.

Let's look closer at John 14:6. We have every reason to believe that the "through" in this verse means "through faith in me." Jesus begins the chapter by telling the disciples, "Believe . . . in me" (14:1). Then verse 7 talks about knowing the Father by knowing the Son. Verse 9 makes clear that whoever sees Jesus has seen the Father. Verses 12 and 13 repeat the exhortation to believe in Jesus. The point of the whole section is that if you know/see/believe in Jesus you know the Father. And, conversely, you cannot go to the Father or follow Jesus to his heavenly glory unless you know and believe in the Son.

This reading of John 14 is confirmed by the broader purpose of the Gospel, which is that John's readers might "believe that Jesus is the Christ, the Son of God, and that by believing you may have life in his name" (20:31). John's Gospel is full of promises for those who believe:

- Whoever believes in me shall never thirst (6:35).
- Whoever believes in me, "out of his heart will flow rivers of living water" (7:38).
- Whoever believes in me, though he die, yet shall he live (11:25).

Likewise, there are dire warnings for those who do not believe in Christ:

- Whoever believes in him is not condemned, but whoever does not believe is condemned already, because he has not believed in the name of the only Son of God. (3:18)
- Whoever who does not honor the Son does not honor the Father who sent him (5:23).
- If God were your Father, you would love me, for I came from God and I am here (8:42).

From start to finish, John's Gospel is an apologetic for conscious faith in Christ, faith that affirms certain propositions about Jesus, faith that believes he is the bread of life (6:35), the light of the world (8:12; 9:5), the gate for the sheep (10:7, 9), the good shepherd (10:11, 14), the resurrection and the life (11:25), and the true vine (15:1, 5). Unless we believe that Christ is "he," the long-awaited Messiah and the heaven-sent Son of God, we will die in our sins (8:24). Salvation comes through faith, faith comes from hearing, and hearing through the word of Christ (Rom. 10:14–17). Even the pious, God-fearing Cornelius needed the gospel preached to him if his sins were to be forgiven (Acts 10:33, 43). There is no other name given among men whereby we must be saved (4:12).

DAY 246

Do Believers Go to Heaven When They Die?

In recent years, some Christians have expressed concern that the evangelical church has historically been too focused on "going to heaven when we die." Much of this angst has trickled down from well-intentioned "missional" theologians who worry that traditional Christians have not allowed for a theology of God-rescuing-and-renewing-the-cosmos to really permeate our thinking. As the argument goes, we've imagined an ethereal eternity of strumming harps and floating around in the great by and by. We've neglected the promise of resurrection. We've forgotten the hope of heaven come to earth.

To be sure, salvation should not be reduced to a heavenly beam-up into the clouds. We are waiting for all things to be made new. And yet we should not be embarrassed to reference and exult in "going to heaven when we die." Dying saints may find it encouraging to know that the whole cosmos is going to be renewed at the end of the age, but they also can't help but wonder what the next moment will be like when they breathe their last breath.

Where we go when we die is one of the most important questions a pastor (or parent or friend) has to answer. Good news about promises that will be fulfilled years or centuries later will not suffice. It isn't enough to tell our people that they'll live in a new world at the renewal of all things. They want to know what tomorrow will be like. Will they be with Jesus in paradise or not? Paul talked about the heavenly dwelling waiting for him once he died (2 Cor. 5:1–10) and the joy he would have to depart and be with Christ (Phil. 1:19–26), so we ought to have no shame in glorying, as the saints for two millennia have done, that after death we live with God in heaven.

No doubt, some good Christians have an underdeveloped eschatology that rarely touches on crucial New Testament themes. But many of these same Christians have a sweet and simple longing for heaven, a commendable confidence that because of Christ they will, in fact, die and go to a better place. Correcting eschatological imbalances is good, but not if it means undermining or minimizing one of the most precious promises in all the Bible; namely, that to live is Christ and to die is gain (Phil. 1:21). Even the intermediate state is indescribably good: better to be away from the body and at home with the Lord, is how Paul put it (2 Cor. 5:8).

In trumpeting the good news of cosmic renewal, let us not lose sight of the hope that anchors the believer in hard times and is the reality awaiting us on the other side of suffering and death: we really do go to heaven when we die.

Intermediate State

The intermediate state describes the condition of blessedness afforded the righteous and the condition of punishment experienced by the wicked, prior to the resurrection and the final judgment. While the term is admittedly inelegant, the doctrine of the intermediate state is included in the historic Reformed confessions. For example, the Westminster Larger Catechism affirms the following:

> The communion in glory with Christ, which the members of the invisible church enjoy immediately after death, is, in that their souls are then made perfect in holiness, and received into the highest heavens, where they behold the face of God in light and glory, waiting for the full redemption of their bodies, which even in death continue united to Christ, and rest in their graces as in their beds, till at the last day they be again united to their souls. Whereas the souls of the wicked are at their death cast into hell where they remain in torments and utter darkness, and their bodies kept in their graves, as in their prisons, till the resurrection and judgment of the great day. (WLC 86)

Notice four things about this explanation of the intermediate state.

1. The catechism implicitly denies the doctrine of purgatory. There is no thought that the dead undergo further purification in the afterlife. This Roman Catholic doctrine, along with the selling of indulgences and offering of prayers for the dead, finds no support in the canonical Scriptures, nor is it consistent with the finality and sufficiency of Christ's atoning work.

2. The catechism also rejects any notion of "soul sleep." Although we don't hear much about the notion today, the idea that souls simply sleep in a state of unconsciousness in between death and the final resurrection was a significant issue during the Reformation, so much so that Calvin wrote an entire book called *Psychopannychia* on the topic. The examples of the rich man and Lazarus in

Luke 16—as well as the numerous passages expressing the joy that believers will experience immediately after death—rule out a belief in soul sleep.

3. The catechism still looks forward to the resurrection of the body. Modern critics have lambasted the doctrine of the intermediate state as neglecting the eschatological hope of the resurrection and a renewed creation. Earlier divines knew better than to think that "intermediate" means ignoring what is "final."

4. Finally, the catechism does not hesitate to speak about souls and bodies. As hard as it is for us to fully understand, there is some immaterial "part" of us that goes to be with Christ (and other believers) in heaven, even as our souls long to be clothed with embodied immortality.

The New Testament assumes an intermediate state between death and the final judgment where believers will have a glorious, though bodiless, existence. This understanding of life after death is supported by Jesus's statement to the thief on the cross ("Today you will be with me in paradise"), by Paul's desire to depart and be with Christ (Phil. 1:21–23), and by the language of departing the body to be at home with the Lord (2 Cor. 5:1–8). The intermediate state is not the final resting place for the believer nor the *summum bonum* of our hope, but it is an aspect of our singular expectation that on the other side of death we will enjoy a life of holiness and blessedness with Christ forever.

DAY 248

Judgment according to Works

The New Testament is clear that at the end of the age there will be a final judgment according to works. Jesus said, "An hour is coming when all who are in the tombs will hear his voice [the voice of the Son of God] and come out, those who have done good to the resurrection of life, and those who have done evil to the resurrection of judgment" (John 5:28–29). Likewise, Paul taught that we will all stand before the judgment seat and have to give an account to God (Rom. 14:10, 12). As he puts it in 2 Corinthians 5 even more explicitly: "For we must all appear before the judgment seat of Christ, so that each one may receive what is due for what he has done in the body, whether good or evil" (v. 10). What are we to make of this judgment according to works?

We know that salvation is not something we earn. Any notion of earning our way into heaven flies in the face of Jesus's consistent teaching about the role of faith as the instrument of eternal life (John 3:16–18; 11:25–26; 14:6; cf. 20:31). Similarly, Paul's theology is adamantly opposed to the idea that works might tip the scales in our eternal favor. From start to finish, salvation is by grace (Eph. 2:8–9), through faith (Rom. 3:23–25), and not on account of the works of the law (Gal. 2:16). The context surrounding 2 Corinthians 5 makes this clear. Paul is confident and courageous (2 Cor. 4:14, 17; 5:1, 6, 8), counting on God's undeserved favor to be his salvation, despite many trials and weaknesses (4:7; 5:5, 21). The judgment according to works at the end of the age is not a judgment to determine whether we've done enough to earn eternal life.

And yet there is a judgment according to works. The best explanation is to see this judgment not as *contributing* to our salvation, but as *corroborating* that we have been saved. Good works are the evidence of true faith. The final judgment will attest for the believer that the good tree has indeed borne good fruit (Matt. 7:15–20). Think again of 2 Corinthians 5. The judgment seat in verse 10 is meant to demonstrate that we have done something to please God (5:9) and that we have not received the grace of God in vain (6:1).

This is the same teaching we find in Revelation 20 and the so-called "great white throne" judgment. In this vision, there are *books*—in which are written the deeds of the dead—and there is *another book*, the book of life. The books of our deeds will be opened to see if there is corroborating evidence for our name being written in the book of life. It matters how you are living your life. There are no carnal Christians. There are weak Christians, struggling Christians, doubting Christians, less-sanctified-than-they-want-to-be Christians, but not carnal Christians wholly given over to the lusts of flesh, careless about the things of God, and disinterested-in-the-means-of-grace Christians. We don't earn our way into heaven by a weighing of our deeds, but when our name is in *the* book, there will be a record of general faithfulness in the *books* that are opened on the last day. The Christian is not a perfect person (on earth), but he is a changed person.

DAY 249

Heavenly Rewards

Does the Bible teach the doctrine of variable eternal rewards? We know there will be different degrees of punishment. It will be more bearable in the judgment for Tyre and Sidon than in the cities where Jesus performed his miracles (Luke 10:10–14). But what about eternal rewards? Will some people have more crowns? Will some of us have big mansions and others small apartments? Will some believers have a capacity for joy that is bigger than others? Though many (most?) Reformed theologians past and present disagree with me on this matter, I want to make the case that the Bible does *not* teach the doctrine of variable eternal rewards.[1] Rewards, yes; variable rewards, no. There is one reward: eternal life with Christ. This gift is described in many different ways, but the images and vocabulary describe the same reward, not different levels of reward.

Let me make the case against variable rewards by looking at the big picture, by noting a few specific passages, and by making a final argument from reason.

First, the big picture. The longest, fullest description of heaven—the glorious picture found in Revelation 21–22—contains nothing about variable rewards. There is no hint that some believers experience a better version of eternal life than others. This point is made even more explicitly in the parable of the laborers in the vineyard (Matt. 20:1–16). Grace is the operative principle in the kingdom, not merit. You are either in or you are out. And once you are in, your reward is not any more or less than anyone else who is in.

Second, a few specific passages. The promised rewards in Revelation 2–3 are not variable rewards, but the same reward of eternal life with Christ described in different ways to match the trial each church is facing. Likewise, the five different crowns mentioned in the New Testament all refer to eternal life. And the parable of the talents (or minas) is about kingdom opportunities, not about heavenly rewards. While we may have different opportunities and gifts on earth, each faithful servant receives the same commendation ("well done") and the same reward ("enter into the joy of your master"). Finally, the "loss" that the believer experiences at the judgment in 1 Corinthians 3:10–15 is not the loss of eternal rewards, but the realization that his work was not as profitable as he thought. Some of us will be pleasantly surprised when our works are judged; others will suffer loss. But this unique experience on judgment day does not entail a perpetual hierarchy in heaven.

Third, an argument from reason. Proponents of the doctrine are quick to say that we won't have regret or jealousy in heaven when we view the rewards of others. In fact, someone's greater reward will only increase our sense of happiness as we rejoice in their reward with them. But this line of thinking undermines the very incentive rewards are supposed to offer. If we are all wondrously happy, but some are more wondrously happy than others, but that just makes us happy too, then what difference did the reward really make? Either the rewards are variable and some believers—because of their works on earth—experience a better eternal life than others, or everyone in heaven is perfectly happy all the time, in which case we should think twice about whether the doctrine matters at all.

---

1 Influential in my thinking has been the article by Blomberg, "Degrees of Reward in the Kingdom of Heaven?," 159–72.

What Will Heaven Be Like?

The question is not about the intermediate state, what the next moment will be like after death, but about the final goal and our ultimate expectation—the coming down of heaven to earth.

On the one hand, some Christians overemphasize the continuity between this world and the next. The constant refrain that the earth will be violently shaken in a day of judgment and destruction, that the heavens will pass away, and that the heavenly bodies will be burned up and dissolved suggests we should not hope that the accomplishments of this life will "make it" into the new heavens and new earth (2 Pet. 3:6–7, 10, 12).

On the other hand, we should not think there is only discontinuity. If the world will be destroyed with fire in the same way the world was destroyed with water in the flood, then the day of judgment will not bring about a complete obliteration of the old world. Heaven will come down to earth so that in a meaningful sense, the planet we now inhabit will be our eternal home, cleansed, as the Belgic Confession puts is, "in fire and flame" (BC Art. 37).

There is much the Bible does not tell us about heaven (and perhaps that is for the best, lest we misconstrue what it will be like or underestimate how glorious it will be). We don't know much of what we will be doing (except for singing), nor do we know much about our relationships (expect that we won't be married). We are given glimpses of the new heavens and new earth as a place where the good things of this life—peace, prosperity, and domestic happiness—will reach a zenith of uninterrupted, uncorrupted perfection (Isa. 65:17–25).

The picture of heaven in Revelation 21–22 tells us who is in and who is out, what God is like, and what we will be like in his presence. The first part of chapter 22 gives hints of the physicality of heaven, but most of what Revelation has to say (taking up almost all of chapter 21) is an extended description of the church in her end-times beauty. The heavenly new Jerusalem is *glorious* (as lovely and pure as the whore Babylon is ugly and defiled), *safe* (with walls of strength and gates that never shut because nothing can threaten the church any longer), and *holy* (with cubic dimensions befitting a people who have become the holy of holies and have unfettered access to God).

Finally, let us not overlook the promise that the saints—for all eternity, and even now upon death—are reigning with Christ. We cannot be sure all that this entails. It may mean that believers affirm the judgments of Christ, or that they (along with the angels) form a heavenly counsel, or that the imagery is meant to convey that those who were trampled in this life will be vindicated in the next. At the heart of the promise is the restoration of the sons of Adam and daughters of Eve to their rightful place as image bearers who exercise dominion on the earth. We were made to be creation-kings over God's creation-kingdom. If we are called by Christ to accomplish his work here on earth, how much more can we expect, as glorified saints, to participate with his work in heaven?

WEEK 51

DAY 251

Partial Preterism

The prefix *preter* is of Latin orgin, meaning "beyond," "more than," "by," or "past." In eschatology, full preterism is the belief that all biblical prophecy has been fulfilled (i.e., is in the past), including the second coming of Christ, the final resurrection, and the complete arrival of God's kingdom.

Preterists are right to take seriously the "coming soon" language of the New Testament and cataclysmic events surrounding the destruction of the temple in AD 70. Nevertheless, there are several problems with full preterism. For starters, Jesus taught many times that his return would be personal and visible (Acts 1:9–11). Moreover, we are told repeatedly that there is a bodily resurrection yet to come (John 5:28–29; 1 Thess. 4:13–18) and that this future resurrection cannot be separated from the gospel itself (1 Cor. 15). There is also the testimony of the history of the church: neither the Christians after AD 70 nor the creeds of the first centuries understood Jesus's return and the renewal of all things to have taken place.

While full preterism cannot be squared with the Bible nor with the orthodox tradition of the church, there are good reasons for partial preterism. As the name suggests, partial preterists believe that many of the prophecies in the New Testament were fulfilled in the lifetime of the apostles, even while Christians are still waiting for the second coming of Christ, a bodily resurrection, and the final restoration of all things at the end of the age. This understanding of New Testament prophecy is consistent with the way Old Testament prophecy worked. Normally, Old Testament prophecy contained near and far fulfillment. Predictions would be made about events close at hand, using geographic, political, and personal referents that made sense at the time. But the same predictions would often expand, using cosmic and cataclysmic language that could only pertain to events in the distance.

These two horizons are often mixed in biblical prophecy. So, for example, in the Olivet Discourse, Jesus is talking about the things that will be (i.e., the destruction of the temple) *and* "what will be the sign of [his] coming and of the end of the age" (Matt. 24:1–3). The language of leaving Judea and fleeing to the mountains puts us squarely in the first century (Mark 13:14–23). Likewise, for Jesus to say that "this generation will not pass away until all these things take place" (13:30) suggests that there is, on some level, a near fulfillment for everything Jesus has said up to that point. The word "generation" refers to those living at the time of Jesus (8:12, 38; 9:19). At the same time, the disciples are told to stay awake because the master of the house is returning, and not even the Son knows the day or hour (13:32–37). Much—perhaps, even most—of Jesus's prophecy in the Olivet Discourse was fulfilled in the first century, but there are elements clearly in the future.

This way of reading the text—with prophetic foreshortening and partial fulfillment (just like in the Old Testament)—makes the most sense of prophecy in the Gospels, in Revelation, and in the rest of the New Testament.

DAY 252

The Great Tribulation

We read in Revelation 7:14 that the great multitude in white robes has come out of the great tribulation. So what is it that they have come out of? Let's start by looking at the word *tribulation*. The Greek word for *tribulation* is *thlipsis*. It occurs over forty times in the New Testament, and from these occurrences it is clear that Christians are right now in a time of tribulation. The church from the time of Christ to the end of the world will face hardships and sufferings and afflictions (John 16:33; Acts 14:21–22; 2 Thess. 1:4; Rev. 1:9).

The Bible does not teach a secret rapture of the church prior to Christ's return. Those "left behind" in Luke 17 and Matthew 24 are the faithful ones (see Gen. 7:23), not like the ones taken (as in Noah's day) for judgment or as the ones gathered (as in Matthew 13:39–43) to be burned with fire. Both "left behind" passages are about the harvest at the close of the age, not about a secret rapture.

The promise of Scripture is not that the church will be kept safe *from* tribulation but that we will be kept safe *in* tribulation. That's what is meant in Revelation 3:10 ("I will keep you from the hour of trial that is coming on the whole world"). The only other time *tereo ek* ("keep from") is used in the New Testament is in John 17:15: "I do not ask that you take them out of the world, but that you keep them from [*tereo ek*] the evil one." The promise is not for a physical rapture or the elimination of suffering for Christians, but that in our suffering Jesus will protect us from evil and sin.

Although we are currently in a period of tribulation on the earth, there will come a time just before Christ's second coming when the sufferings and afflictions will be intensified. This time—different in scope and severity, but not different in kind—is likely what Matthew 24:21 and Revelation 7:14 mean by a "great tribulation" (*thlipsis megas*). The sign of tribulation is not restricted to the end of the age, which is why the descriptions of death, famine, war, and disease in the Olivet Discourse and in Revelation can fit any era of history. At the same time, it appears that prior to Jesus's return, there will be a more extreme form of the sufferings that God's people have always been called to endure.

In Revelation 7 we have a picture of the 144,000 sealed from the sons of Israel and a picture of a great multitude from every nation. Both groups are the same, and both groups answer the question posed at the end of chapter 6: "Who can stand?" That is, "Who will be able to face the wrath of the Lamb unafraid? Who will be able to face the end of the world with confidence?" The answer is that God will seal his chosen ones from every nation prior to the end so that they will hold fast the faith and give God glory in the midst of great tribulation.

DAY 253

144,000

The 144,000 are not an ethnic Jewish remnant, nor (as Jehovah's Witnesses teach) the literal number of people who will be resurrected to heavenly life. The 144,000 "sealed from every tribe of the sons of Israel" (Rev. 7:4) represent the entire community of the redeemed. Here are several reasons for this claim.

1. In Revelation 13 we read that Satan seals all of his followers, so it makes sense that God would seal all of his people, not just the Jewish ones.

2. The image of sealing comes from Ezekiel 9, where the seal on the forehead marks out two groups of people: idolaters and nonidolaters. The sealing of the 144,000 makes a similar distinction based on who worships God and who does not.

3. The 144,000 are called the servants of our God (Rev. 7:3). There is no reason to make the 144,000 any more restricted than that. In Revelation, the phrase "servants" of God always refers to all of God's redeemed people, not just an ethnic Jewish remnant (see 1:1; 2:20; 19:2, 5; 22:3).

4. The 144,000 mentioned later in chapter 14 are those who have been "redeemed from the earth" and those who were "purchased from among men." This is generic, "everybody" kind of language. The 144,000 is a symbolic number of redeemed drawn from all peoples, not simply the Jews. If the number is not symbolic, we have to consider Revelation 14:4, which describes the 144,000 as those "who have not defiled themselves with women." Are we to think that the 144,000 refers to a chosen group of celibate Jewish men? It makes more sense to realize that 144,000 is a symbolic number that is described as celibate men to highlight the group's moral purity and set-apartness for spiritual battle.

5. The last reason for thinking that the 144,000 is the entire community of the redeemed is the highly stylized list of tribes in Revelation 7:5–8. The number itself is stylized. It's not to be taken literally. It's 12 x 12 x 1,000: twelve being the number of completion for God's people (representing the twelve tribes of Israel and the twelve apostles of the Lamb), and one thousand being a generic number suggesting a great multitude. So 144,000 is a way of saying, all of God's people under the old and new covenants.

6. Finally, look at the list of the tribes. There are more than a dozen different arrangements of the twelve tribes in the Bible. This one is unique among all of those. Judah is listed first, because Jesus was from there as a lion of the tribe of Judah. All twelve of Jacob's sons are listed—including Levi, who usually wasn't because he didn't inherit any land—except for one. Manasseh, Joseph's son (Jacob's grandson), is listed in place of Dan. So why not Dan? Dan was probably left out in order to point to the purity of the redeemed church. From early in Israel's history, Dan was the center of idolatry for the kingdom (Judg. 18:30–31). During the days of the divided kingdom, Dan was one of two centers for idolatry (1 Kings 12:28–30). And there is recorded in some nonbiblical Jewish writings that the Jews thought the antichrist would come out of Dan, based on Genesis 49:17.

The bottom line is that the number and the list and the order of the tribes are all stylized to depict the totality of God's pure and perfectly redeemed servants from all time over all the earth. That's what Revelation means by the 144,000.

666

"This calls for wisdom: let the one who has understanding calculate the number of the beast, for it is the number of a man, and his number is 666" (Rev. 13:18). All sorts of numerical schemes have been concocted in various languages to try to decode that number, 666. All of these solutions are calculated by a process known as *gematria*. In the ancient world every letter corresponded to a number, just like A might equal 1, B equal 2, C equal 3, and so on. Every letter could also be a number, so names could be translated into numbers. This process is called "gematria," and it's true that people used it in the ancient world.

If 666 refers to a specific historical person, then the best educated guess is Emperor Nero.

If you take the Greek *Neron Kaisar* and transliterate it into Hebrew, you get 50 + 200 + 6 + 50 and then 100 + 60 + 200, all of which together equals 666. A possible corroboration for this view can be found in the Latin version of his name. *Neron Kaiser* transliterated in Latin gives you 616, which is the number of the beast in some alternative manuscripts (also the area code for Grand Rapids, Michigan!). Nero fits with the storyline of Revelation better than the other alternatives. Nero killed himself in AD 68, but it was rumored that he would come back to life or was still living, just like the beast received a fatal wound that was healed. So, according to many scholars, 666 is most logically a reference to Nero. And by putting Nero in the form of a riddle like this, it protected the Christians from charges of sedition and further persecution.

But there are also problems with the Nero hypothesis. (1) It is far from certain that most of John's audience would have known Hebrew. (2) To come up with 666, we have to spell *Neron Kaisar* without a *yodh*, which is not the normal spelling in Hebrew. (3) None of the early church fathers calculated *Neron Kaisar* from 666. (4) We are not told to solve the question of 666; we are told that 666 is the answer to the question. More on that in a moment. (5) Most importantly, finding hidden, precise meanings in numbers is not the way numbers work in Revelation. The imagery in Revelation is broader and less exact. The church is symbolized with pictures (the twenty-four elders, the two witnesses, the woman) and a number (144,000). The church age is symbolized by pictures (the measured temple, the trampled witnesses, the woman protected in the wilderness) and numbers (forty-two months, 1,260 days, three and a half years). Likewise, false religion is symbolized by a picture (the beast) and a number (666). In each case, the pictures and numbers mean something, but they refer to general truths, not to specific people or referents.

In the end, the best analysis is to see that 666 as a general reference to man's number (cf. 21:17). The second beast is a counterfeit. He leads people into false religion. If seven is the number of perfection and holy completion in the book of Revelation (seven churches, seven lampstands, seven eyes, seven seals, seven trumpets, and so on) then six would be the number of imperfection and unholy incompletion. If seven is the number for God, then six is the number that most resembles but is not quite God—namely, man.

In short, 666 is man's counterfeit to 777. Whatever or whoever appears, under the guise of true Christianity, in order to draw us away to some human counterfeit, that is the work of the beast, and his number is 666.

DAY 255

All Israel Will Be Saved

In Romans 11, Paul addressed the question: "Has God rejected his people?" (v. 1). Paul's emphatic response is "By no means!" He gives two examples to show that Israel has not been completely rejected. First is Paul himself. He is an Israelite, and he has not been cut off. Second, he mentions Elijah. The Old Testament prophet seemed to be the only one left standing in his day, but God had reserved for himself seven thousand who had not bowed the knee to Baal. Likewise, though things look bleak for national Israel now, Paul insists there is an elect remnant, chosen by grace (11:5).

As Paul's argument continues, he explains how God's plan of salvation works in a cycle (11:11–16). Israel has stumbled, allowing the Gentiles to enter into the riches of salvation, which will provoke—and is now provoking (11:14)—Israel to accept their Messiah. The natural branches (physical Israel) were broken off, and the wild olive shoot (the Gentiles) has been grafted into the original tree. The ingrafted branches only remain by faith, and if the natural branches exhibit faith, they will be grafted in again (11:23). This one olive tree has for its branches anyone who believes in Jesus Christ.

This is all background for Paul's dramatic declaration in verses 25 and 26: "Lest you be wise in your own sight, I do not want you to be unaware of this mystery, brothers: a partial hardening has come upon Israel, until the fullness of the Gentiles has come in. And in this way all Israel will be saved." The phrase "all Israel" has been variously interpreted as: (1) all the ethnic descendants of Israel who ever lived, (2) all the ethnic descendants of Israel alive at the time that God removes his hardening, (3) all the elect of ethnic Israel, or (4) all the elect of both Jews and Gentiles as the Israel of God. The first two options don't work with Paul's notion of a remnant among his countrymen. Options three and four offer the best explanation.

The salvation described in verse 25 is the way in which "all Israel" will be saved. This means one of two things (options 3 and 4). On the one hand, Paul could be saying, "Israel has been hardened in part and will be up until the end. Their hardening means salvation for the Gentiles, which then produces envy in Israel. Because of this envy ("in this way") the elect Israelites (all true Israel) will come to faith." On the other hand, Paul may be saying, "Because of Israel's hardening in part, salvation has come to the Gentiles. When the full number of Gentiles comes in together with the remnant of ethnic Israel, all true spiritual members of Israel will be saved." If I had to choose between the two, I would choose the former (option 3), for every other time "Israel" is used in chapter 11 it refers to national ethnic Israel.

In short, Paul is not predicting (neither is he precluding) a mass conversion of the Jews; he is explaining how all elect Jews will be saved. Romans 11 describes a present, ongoing situation where Jews and Gentiles are both being saved and will be saved up until the full number of the elect is brought in—Gentiles by faith as a result of the Jews' disobedience and Jews by faith as a result of envy over the Gentiles.

WEEK 52

DAY 256

Millennial Views

In systematic theology, the millennium refers to the thousand-year reign of Christ prophesied in Revelation 20. Regarding the when, what, and how of this millennial reign, there are four major interpretations.

Historic premillennialism. According to this view, Christ returns before the millennium but after the great tribulation. During the current church age, we can expect the world to get worse and worse. There will be a single return of Christ, during which believers (living and newly resurrected) will be caught up in the air with Christ and then come to earth with him. There is no secret rapture of the church in historic premillennialism. Christ's reign on earth—which could be a literal or a figurative thousand years—will see evil greatly suppressed and Christ on a literal throne. After the millennium, unbelievers will be raised and the white throne judgment will ensue, followed by the eternal state.

Dispensational premillennialism. Like its much older counterpart, dispensationalism also believes that Christ will return before the millennium. But typically, in this newer view, Christ returns before the great tribulation (though there are post-, mid-, and partial-trib versions). Dispensational premillennialism is marked by a more literal hermeneutic. Christ will reign on David's throne for a thousand years, during which time there will be a massive conversion of the Jews to Christ, and many Old Testament promises to Israel will be fulfilled. This dispensational view of the end times was popularized by the Scofield Reference Bible and (in a less serious way) by the Left Behind novels.

Amillennialism. According to this view, we are already in the "thousand years" spoken of in Revelation 20. The name amillennialism is a bit of a misnomer, because proponents don't reject the idea of millennium; they simply believe that the designation is figurative, and we are already in it. Amillennialism teaches that there will be a contemporaneous development of good and evil in the world, culminating in a time of intensified tribulation. Nevertheless, during the current church age, Satan's deception has been curtailed such that the gospel has been able to spread around the world. After the millennium, Christ will return to judge all the living and the dead, followed by a new heaven and a new earth for the believer and hell for the unbeliever.

Postmillennialism. Like amillennialism, postmillennialism takes the thousand years figuratively and teaches that Christ will return after the millennium. Most Reformed theologians have been amillennial or postmillennial, and sometimes the differences can be hard to spot. The key distinction is that postmillennialists believe that the church age will blend into the millennium, a time where the influence of evil is negligible and the world is essentially Christianized. Postmillennialism does not think everyone will become Christian, but it expects the lordship of Christ to rule more and more in the world. Today this outlook often greatly affects how the postmillennialist approaches politics and the mission of the church.

In the next few chapters I will argue for an amillennial understanding of Revelation 20. Whether my exegesis is convincing or not, I encourage Christians not to dismiss the millennium discussion as esoteric theologizing with little importance for everyday discipleship. While the millennium question is not as important as, say, the Trinity, the two natures of Christ, or justification, it will often influence (and reflect) how we look at the world and how we relate to our culture. So before we throw our hands up and come down on the side of panmillennialism ("it will all pan out in the end"), we would do well to study the issue and think carefully about the Bible texts in question.

When Does the Millennium Take Place?

The overarching chronology within Revelation 20 seems straightforward. First, Satan is bound for a thousand years (20:2), during which time Christ reigns (with the saints who experience the first resurrection) for a thousand years (20:6). After the thousand years are ended, Satan is released from his prison for a short time so that he might deceive the nations (20:3, 7). There is a final battle on the earth in which the devil is defeated (20:7–9). Then there is a judgment before the great white throne (20:11). All the dead are judged. The wicked experience the second death, and are thrown into the lake of fire (20:14). Given this timeline, the millennium must take place before the last battle, before the return of Christ, and before the final judgment.

The key to understanding the when of the millennium is to recognize that the cataclysmic scenes depicted in Revelation 20 have already been depicted in the book. There are at least four times in Revelation where a final battle and the end of the world are described: in 9:13–19 where two hundred million mounted troops gather at the Euphrates; in 16:12–15 where demonic forces assemble at Armageddon; in 19:17–21 where the beasts and the kings of the earth gather with their armies to make war against the rider on the horse; and again in 20:7–10 where the devil gathers his forces for a battle against the camp of the saints. Revelation works by recapitulation, by telling the same cycle of stories over and over in different symbols. The "ending" described in Revelation 20 has been seen before.

All this means that the binding of Satan in Revelation 20 does not take place chronologically after the events of Revelation 19. It wouldn't make sense for an angel to announce that all the bad guys have been wiped out (19:17–18), only for Satan to be bound some time later. Christ has already destroyed the evil army in chapter 19. What binding could be necessary? What battle could be left? Unless the battle in Revelation 20 is the same battle we've seen before, in which case the thousand year binding of Satan and reign of Christ is not something that happens in the future but is something that is happening right now as we await the end.

The millennium is not a literal thousand years. That's not how numbers work in Revelation. The 1,260 days, the time, times, and half a time, the two hundred million mounted troops, all of the sevens, the twelves, and the fours: the numbers are symbols. Just like the things John saw are symbols: a prostitute, a beast, a second beast, a pregnant woman, a bride, a groom, eating a scroll, seven heads, ten horns, fire coming from the mouths of the two witnesses, Christ killing people with a sword in his mouth, blood as high as a horse's bridle for 200 miles. We should expect the thousand years not to be a literal thousand years, just like there is not a literal dragon or literal chains for Satan. The millennium refers simply to a long period of time, a time in which the gospel goes forward before an intense period of tribulation, the last battle, and the final judgment. In short, the millennium is now.

DAY 258

What Is Meant by Satan Being Bound for a Thousand Years?

The binding of Satan occurred in the life, death, and resurrection of Jesus Christ. Consider three passages in the Gospels.

1. In Mark 3:27 Jesus describes himself as the one who enters a strong man's house to carry off his possessions. Jesus says you can't do that unless you first bind the strong man, who is Satan. The word "bind" (*deo*) is the same word used in Revelation 20 when Satan is bound. Jesus understood his ministry as tying up Satan in knots.

2. In Luke 10:18 Jesus tells the disciples that he's seen Satan fall in their ministry. The dragon has already been cast down.

3. In John 12:31, Jesus announces that now is the time for the ruler of this world to be cast out. The word for "cast out" (*exballo*) is related to the word used in Revelation 20:3, where it says Satan was thrown down (*ballo*). Importantly, later in John 12:32 Jesus says that he will draw all men unto himself. That is significant because the purpose of binding Satan in Revelation 20 is so that he may no longer deceive the nations. We underestimate what Jesus did on the cross and the defeat that he handed to Satan.

We see these same realities in the rest of Revelation. For example, Revelation 11 shows us a picture of the church that is both vulnerable and invincible. The two witnesses (symbolic of the church) are trampled upon, but they also breathe out fire and are brought back to life. This is a picture of the church in this age. Persecuted, attacked, and under assault, but ultimately victorious. Likewise, Revelation 12 describes a war in heaven (v. 7). Michael and his angels fight against the dragon, and the dragon and his angels fight back, but the dragon is hurled down. This is the same reality we see in Revelation 20.

The binding of Satan means two things, in particular.

First, the binding of Satan means that he cannot deceive the nations and gather them together to wipe out the church. Satan may lead the whole *world* astray, but he may no longer deceive the *nations*. Worldly persons and worldly systems are in thrall to Satan, but peoples are coming to Christ. The binding of Satan does not mean that he can't harm, or that he isn't active, or that he doesn't need to be resisted. The Satan who is bound in verse 3 is unable to do what Satan in verse 7 attempts to do: namely, gathering the nations against Christ and his church. In the end, even this final attempt to wipe out God's people proves futile.

Second, the binding of Satan means that the nations will have the opportunity to respond to the gospel and know the true God. In Acts 14 Paul tells the people in Lystra that in the past God let the nations go their own way (v. 16). In Acts 17 Paul tells the people in Athens that in the past God overlooked the times of ignorance (v. 30). But those days are gone. The Gentiles do not have to be strangers and aliens to the covenants of promise (Eph. 2:12). Jesus is now drawing all men unto himself; he commissioned the church to make disciples of all nations. Revelation 20, read in light of these passages, becomes a missions text. The ancient serpent is bound during this church age that the gospel might spread across the globe.

DAY 259

What Is Meant by the First Resurrection?

The first half of Revelation 20 depicts a heavenly scene. We know this because there are thrones (Rev. 20:4; see chaps. 4–5) and because there are disembodied souls (20:4). Narrowly, the group of people in view are martyrs ("the souls of those who had been beheaded for the testimony of Jesus"). But more broadly, we are looking at anyone who has maintained faithful testimony to Jesus, anyone "who had not worshiped the beast or its image." In short, this is a picture of faithful

Christians in heaven who did not give in, who did not compromise, who proved to be conquerors.

This brings us to the end of verse 4 and the statement, "They came to life and reigned with Christ for a thousand years." This much-debated statement is a summary of what we've already seen in the passage. It is a picture of believers who, upon death, come to life (in the intermediate state) as disembodied souls and reign with Christ in heaven. Premillennialists understand this verse to be about a first physical resurrection for believers, and then a thousand years later there will be a second physical resurrection for unbelievers. But the Bible teaches that there is only one resurrection (Dan. 12:2). The good and the evil will rise from their tombs and receive their reward at the same time (John 5:25–29). According to the logic of 1 Corinthians 15, when our bodies are clothed with immortality we will know that death has been defeated. And yet if there are two physical resurrections (and in between them is a thousand years and a gory last battle), we can hardly say death has been swallowed up in victory.

All of this means that the coming to life in Revelation 20:4 must be a spiritual resurrection. What John sees are believers who, though dead, are more alive than ever before. That's why Revelation 14:13 can say, "Blessed are the dead who die in the Lord." Though away from the body, the souls in Revelation 20 are at home with the Lord (2 Cor. 5:8). As Jesus taught, God is not the God of the dead, but of the living (Luke 20:38), which means that Abraham, Isaac, and Jacob, though not yet physically raised, are now alive (20:37). The hope offered in Revelation 20:4 is the same hope offered time and again in Revelation 20: the one who conquers will be given eternal life. "If we have died with him, we will also live with him; if we endure, we will also reign with him" (2 Tim. 2:11-12).

This raises one final issue: what does it mean in Revelation 20:5 that "the rest of the dead did not come to life until the thousand years were ended"? The key is to understand that "until" (*achri*) does not always indicate a change in situation or status, but can simply mean "all the way up to that point." This is often the sense of *achri* in the New Testament (Acts 23:1; 26:22; Rom. 5:13; 8:22). Consequently, verse 5 does not mean that the rest of the dead came to life after the thousand years were ended and then suddenly reigned with Christ. It means that during this whole church age—all the way up to the end—the unbelieving dead did not have the privilege of living and reigning with Christ. The unbelieving dead will not be made to live with Christ during this age, nor ever. Not experiencing the first resurrection in Christ, they will experience the second death later in the lake of fire (Rev. 20:15).

The Glorious Appearing

When Christ was born to a virgin, in a forgotten stable in overcrowded Bethlehem, he entered our world in humility and weaknesses. This was, though the world could not see it, a glorious appearing.

But Christ's second appearing will be glorious in an unmistakable way. When Christ comes again, his all-conquering love, his unrivaled power, and his sovereign justice will be astounding. His blood-bought salvation and his never-ending kingdom will be magnificent. His face shining like the sun will be brilliant. The appearing of our great God and Savior, Jesus Christ, will be unimaginably glorious. All those who love this appearing (2 Tim. 4:8) wait for it as their blessed hope (Titus 2:13).

Throughout the book of Revelation, Jesus Christ is described in the most exalted language and with the most stunning imagery. He is the first and the last, the living one who holds the keys of death and Hades. His head looks white like wool, his robe flowing, his sash golden, his voice like many waters, his feet like burnished bronze, his mouth like a sword, and his face like the sun. He is the Amen, the faithful and true witness. He is the root of David and the bright morning star. He is the Lion of the tribe of Judah and the Lamb who was slain. He rides on a white horse, his eyes are like blazing fire, and on his head are many crowns. His robe is dipped in blood, and his name is the Word of God. He rules the nations with an iron scepter, and on his thigh he has this name written: King of kings and Lord of lords.

No wonder the book of Revelation is filled with singing. Outside of Psalms, there is no other book with so many songs of praise to God. "Holy, holy, holy is the Lord God Almighty, who was and is and is to come!" (Rev. 4:8). "Worthy are you to take the scroll and to open its seals, for you were slain, and by your blood you ransomed people for God from every tribe and language and people and nation" (5:9). "Worthy is the Lamb who was slain, to receive power and wealth and wisdom and might and honor and glory and blessing!" (5:12). "We give thanks to you, Lord God Almighty, who is and who was, for you have taken your great power and begun to reign" (11:17). "Great and amazing are your deeds, O Lord God the Almighty! Just and true are your ways, O King of the nations!" (15:3).

We are living in the eighth month of the first creation's labor. We don't know how long the last month will be, but every day the birth of a new world gets closer. Every day the glorious appearing draws nearer. And on that day the singing will be like nothing that has ever been heard on earth and louder and fuller than anything that has been sung in heaven.

"O Lord, haste the day when the faith shall be sight, the clouds be rolled back as a scroll. The trump shall resound, and the Lord shall descend, even so, it is well with my soul."[1] That is our song today, as together with the Spirit we say, "Come" (Rev. 22:17). And he who testifies to all that is true—the one who is the way, the truth, and the life—says, "Surely I am coming soon." Amen. Come, Lord Jesus! (Rev. 22:20).

1   Horatio G. Spafford, "It Is Well with My Soul," 1873.

Appendix

Background on Frequently Cited Sources

Confessional Documents

Belgic Confession (1561). Written by Guido de Bres (1522–1567) to persuade King Philip II of Spain that Protestants should not be persecuted. A Reformed pastor in the Lowlands (modern-day Belgium) who studied under Theodore Beza and John Calvin, de Bres was publicly hanged in 1567.

Heidelberg Catechism (1563). Written primarily by Zacharias Ursinus (1534–1583) as a tool for teaching children, as a guide for pastors, and as a form for confessional unity among Protestant factions in the Palatinate (modern-day Germany).

Canons of Dort (1618–1619). Issued by the international synod that met at Dordrecht in the Netherlands. The five heads of doctrine from Dort were given in response to, and as a rejection of, five theological points first issued by the Remonstrant party (i.e., followers of Jacob Arminius, or Arminians).

The Belgic Confession, Heidelberg Catechism, and Canons of Dort are known as the **Three Forms of Unity** and have served as the confessional standards for many Reformed churches around the world, especially those with connections to the Netherlands, France, and Germany.

Westminster Confession of Faith (1646). Written by a group of pastor-theologians who convened in London in more than one thousand plenary sessions over the course of a decade. The Westminster Assembly (1643–1653) was called by Parliament to give ecclesiastical and doctrinal advice in the midst of the English Civil War.

Westminster Larger Catechism (1647) and Smaller Catechism (1647). Designed to accompany the Confession of Faith. Together the Confession of Faith and the

Larger and Smaller Catechisms are called the Westminster Standards and have served as confessional standards for many Presbyterian churches around the world, especially those with connections to the British Isles.

Authors

Augustine of Hippo (354–430). North African bishop, arguably the most important theologian in the history of the church; his most famous works include *Confessions*, *On Christian Doctrine*, *On the Trinity*, and *City of God*.

Thomas Aquinas (1225–1274). Italian Dominican friar and priest, the most influential Western theologian and philosopher of the Middle Ages, distilled and compiled the fruit of scholastic theology in his most famous work, *Summa Theologica*.

Martin Luther (1483–1546). German priest, theologian, and Reformer credited with being the seminal influence that started the Protestant Reformation; in addition to writing voluminous works of theology, Luther was also an accomplished Bible translator and hymn writer.

John Calvin (1509–1564). French pastor, theologian, and Reformer who ministered in Geneva; particularly influential among Reformed Protestants in his lifetime and ever since. Among his vast literary output, he wrote commentaries on most books of the Bible and his magnum opus, the *Institutes of the Christian Religion*.

John Owen (1616–1683). English theologian, Calvinist and Congregational in outlook, who held numerous posts and proved influential in the church, in the academy, and in politics; well-known works include *Communion with God* and *The Mortification of Sin*, along with books on temptation and a multivolume series on the book of Hebrews.

Francis Turretin (1623–1687). Italian by descent, but born and raised in Geneva; pastored a French congregation and was a professor of theology at the University of Geneva; his *Institutes of Elenctic Theology* (influential among the Puritans and in the tradition of Old Princeton) is considered by many to be the high point of Reformed scholasticism.

Wilhelmus à Brakel (1635–1711). Reformed minister and theologian in the Netherlands; representative of the Dutch Further Reformation, his magnum opus, *The Christian's Reasonable Service*, combines scholastic precision with personal, warm-hearted piety.

Charles Hodge (1797–1878). American Presbyterian theologian and churchman who taught at Princeton Theologial Seminary. In fifty-six years of teaching he trained over three thousand ministers, founded and wrote often for the *Biblical Repertory and Princeton Review*. His three-volume *Systematic Theology* replaced Turretin as the theological textbook at Princeton.

James Bannerman (1807–1868). Scottish theologian who left the Church of Scotland for the Free Church in 1843; taught apologetics and pastoral theology at New College in Edinburgh; most well known for his work on Presbyterian ecclesiology, *The Church of Christ*.

William G. T. Shedd (1820–1894). American Presbyterian theologian who taught at Union Theological Seminary in New York City; his *Dogmatic Theology*, though now largely overlooked, is an impressive example of traditional Calvinism marked by erudition and is conversant with modern concerns.

Herman Bavinck (1854–1921). Dutch theologian and churchman; taught at the Theological School in Kampen and eventually at Abraham Kuyper's Free University in Amsterdam; in life and thought was orthodox yet modern. His four-volume *Reformed Dogmatics* has proved immensely influential, especially since a full English translation was made available in 2008.

Louis Berkhof (1873–1957). Dutch-American Reformed theologian born in the Netherlands who taught at Calvin Theological Seminary (Grand Rapids, Michigan) for almost four decades; his *Systematic Theology*, largely a distillation in English of Bavinck, is a model of concision and has been a standard theological textbook for nearly a century.

Works Cited

Confessional and Ecclesiastical Documents
Nicene Creed (325)
Chalcedonian Definition (451)
Belgic Confession (1561)
Heidelberg Catechism (1563)
Second Book of Discipline (1578)　.
Canons of Dort (1619)
Westminster Confession of Faith (1646)
Westminster Larger Catechism (1647)
Westminster Shorter Catechism (1647)
Savoy Declaration (1658)
Book of Common Prayer (1662)
Formula Consensus Helvetica (1675)
London Baptist Confession of Faith (1689)
Humanae Vitae (1968)
Catechism of the Catholic Church (1992)
Presbyterian Church of America *Book of Church Order* (n.d.)

Books and Articles
Alexander, Archibald. *God, Creation, and Human Rebellion*. Grand Rapids, MI: Reformation Heritage, 2019.
Aquinas, Thomas. *Summa Theologica*. 5 vols. Translated by the Fathers of the English Dominican Province. New York: Benzinger, 1948.
Athanasius. *The Festal Letters of Athanasius of Alexandria, with the Festal Index and the Historia Acephala*. Translated by David Brakke and David M. Gwynn. Liverpool, UK: Liverpool University Press, 2023.
Athanasius. *On the Incarnation*. Translated by John Behr. Yonkers, NY: St. Vladimir's Seminary Press, 2019.
Augustine of Hippo. *Confessions*. Translated by Henry Chadwick. Oxford, UK: Oxford University Press, 2008.

Augustine of Hippo. *The Trinity*. Translated by Edmund Hill and John E. Rotelle. Hyde Park, NY: New City Press, 2012.

Aulén, Gustaf. *Christus Victor: An Historical Study of the Three Main Types of the Idea of Atonement*. Translated by A. G. Hebert. Eugene, OR: Wipf & Stock, 2003.

Bannerman, James. *The Church of Christ*. Edinburgh: Banner of Truth, 2015.

Bauckham, Richard. "Universalism: A Historical Survey." *Themelios* 4 (September 1978): 48–54.

Bavinck, Herman. *Reformed Dogmatics*. Vol. 1, *Prolegomena*. Translated by John Vriend. Edited by John Bolt. Grand Rapids, MI: Baker Academic, 2003.

Bavinck, Herman. *Reformed Dogmatics*. Vol. 3, *Sin and Salvation*. Translated by John Vriend. Edited by John Bolt. Grand Rapids, MI: Baker Academic, 2003.

Belcher, Richard P., Jr. *The Fulfillment of the Promises of God: An Explanation of Covenant Theology*. Ross-shire, UK: Mentor, 2020.

Berkhof, Louis. *Introductory Volume to Systematic Theology*. Grand Rapids, MI: Eerdmans, 1996.

Bettenson, Henry, and Chris Maunder, eds. *Documents of the Christian Church*. 4th ed. Oxford, UK: Oxford University Press, 2011.

Blaising, Craig, and Darrell Bock. *Progressive Dispensationalism*. Grand Rapids, MI: Baker Academic, 2000.

Blomberg, Craig. "Degrees of Reward in the Kingdom of Heaven?" *Journal of the Evangelical Theological Society* 35 (June 1992): 159–72.

Boston, Thomas. *Human Nature in Its Fourfold State*. Edinburgh: James McEuen, 1720.

À Brakel, Wilhelmus. *The Christian's Reasonable Service*. 4 vols. Translated by Bartel Elshout. Edited by Joel R. Beeke. Grand Rapids, MI: Reformation Heritage, 1992.

Bray, Gerald. *The Doctrine of God*. Downers Grove, IL: InterVarsity Press, 1993.

Calvin, John. *Calvin's Commentaries*. 22 vols. Grand Rapids, MI: Baker, 1974.

Calvin, John. *Institutes of the Christian Religion*. 2 vols. Translated by Ford Lewis Battles. Edited by John T. McNeil. Philadelphia: Westminster Press, 1960.

Calvin, John. *Psychopannychia*, in *Tracts Relating to the Reformation*. Vol. 3. Translated by Henry Beveridge. Edinburgh: Calvin Translation Society, 1851.

Cole, Graham A. *Against the Darkness: The Doctrine of Angels, Satan, and Demons*. Wheaton, IL: Crossway, 2019.

Cyprian of Carthage. *The Lapsed, The Unity of the Catholic Church*. Translated by Maurice Bénevot. New York: Newman Press, 1957.

DeYoung, Kevin. "Foreword. In Blessings of the Faith series. 5 vols. (Phillipsburg, NJ: P&R, 2023).

DeYoung, Kevin. *The Good News We Almost Forgot: Rediscovering the Gospel in a 16th Century Catechism*. Chicago: Moody, 2010.

DeYoung, Kevin. *Grace Defined and Defended: What a 400-Year-Old Confession Teaches Us about Sin, Salvation, and the Sovereignty of God*. Wheaton, IL: Crossway, 2019.

DeYoung, Kevin. *The Hole in Our Holiness: Filling the Gap between Gospel Passion and the Pursuit of Godliness*. Wheaton, IL: Crossway, 2012.

DeYoung, Kevin. *The Lord's Prayer*. Wheaton, IL: Crossway, 2022.

DeYoung, Kevin. "The Mission of the Church," The Gospel Coalition, accessed March 21, 2024, https://www.thegospelcoalition.org/essay/the-mission-of-the-church/.

DeYoung, Kevin. "Sin," in *NIV Zondervan Study Bible*. Edited by D. A. Carson. Grand Rapids, MI: Zondervan, 2015.

Dorrien, Gary. *Imagining Progressive Religion, 1805–1900*. Vol. 1, *The Making of American Liberal Theology*. Louisville, KY: Westminster John Knox, 2001.

Edwards, Jonathan. *Ethical Writings*. Edited by Paul Ramsey and John E. Smith. Vol. 8, *The Works of Jonathan Edwards*. New Haven, CT: Yale University Press, 1989.

Edwards, Jonathan. *Religious Affections*, revised edition. Edited by John E. Smith and Harry S. Stout. Vol. 2, *The Works of Jonathan Edwards*. New Haven, CT: Yale University Press, 2009.

Fee, Gordon. *God's Empowering Presence: The Holy Spirit in the Letters of Paul*. Peabody, MA: Hendrickson, 1994.

Fesko, J. V., and Guy M. Richard. "Natural Theology and the Westminster Confession of Faith." In vol. 3, *The Westminster Confession into the 21st Century*. Edited by J. Ligon Duncan III. Ross-shire, UK: Mentor, 2009, 223–66.

Garland, David E. *1 Corinthians*, Baker Exegetical Commentary on the New Testament. Grand Rapids, MI: Baker Academic, 2003.

Golding, Peter. *Covenant Theology: The Key of Theology in Reformed Thought and Tradition*. Ross-shire, UK: Mentor, 2008.

Grudem, Wayne. *Systematic Theology*. Grand Rapids, MI: Zondervan, 1994.

Hahn, Scott, and Kimberly Hahn. *Rome Sweet Home: Our Journey to Catholicism*. San Francisco: Ignatius Press, 1993.

Haines, David. *Natural Theology: A Biblical and Historical Introduction and Defense*. Landrum, SC: Davenant Press, 2021.

Hodge, Charles. *Systematic Theology*. 3 vols. London: James Clarke, 1960.

Hodge, Charles. "The Validity of Romish Baptism." In *Church Polity*. New York: Charles Scribner's Sons, 1878.

Irons, Charles Lee. "A Lexical Defense of the Johannine Only Begotten." In *Retrieving Eternal Generation*, edited by Fred Sanders and Scott R. Swain. Grand Rapids. MI: Zondervan Academic, 2017.

John of Damascus. *On the Orthodox Faith*. Translated by Normal Russell. Yonkers, NY: St. Vladimir's Seminary Press, 2022.

Junius, Fransiscus. *A Treatise on True Theology with the Life of Franciscus Junius*. Grand Rapids, MI: Reformation Heritage, 2014.

Kilner, John. *Dignity and Destiny: Humanity in the Image of God*. Grand Rapids, MI: Eerdmans, 2015.

Kreeft, Peter. *Catholic Christianity: A Complete Catechism of Christian Beliefs based on the Catechism of the Catholic Church*. San Francisco: Ignatius Press, 2001.

Kruger, Michael J. *Canon Revisited: Establishing the Origins and Authority of the New Testament*. Wheaton, IL: Crossway, 2012.

Kuyper, Abraham. *Calvinism: Six Lectures Delivered in the Theological Seminary at Princeton*. New York: Revell, 1899.

Letham, Robert. *The Holy Trinity: In Scripture, History, Theology, and Worship*. Phillipsburg, NJ: P&R, 2004.

Locke, John. *Two Treatises of Government and A Letter Concerning Toleration*. New York: Classic Books International, 2010.

MacLeod, Donald. *The Person of Christ*. Downers Grove, IL: IVP Academic, 1998.

McClymond, Michael J. *The Devil's Redemption: A New History and Interpretation of Christian Universalism*. Grand Rapids, MI: Baker Academic, 2020.

Muller, Richard A. *Post-Reformation Reformed Dogmatics: The Rise and Development of Reformed Orthodoxy, ca. 1520 to ca. 1725*. Grand Rapids, MI: Baker Academic, 2003.

Murray, John. *Collected Writings of John Murray*. Vol. 4, *Studies in Theology*. Edinburgh: Banner of Truth, 1982.

Murray, John. *Redemption Accomplished and Applied*. Grand Rapids, MI: Eerdmans, 1955.

Gregory of Nazianzus. *On God and Christ: The Five Theological Orations and Two Letters to Cledonius*. Translated by Frederick Williams and Lionel Wickham. Yonkers, NY: St. Vladimir's Seminary Press, 2002.

O'Collins, Gerald. *The Holy Trinity: The State of the Questions*. In *The Trinity: An Interdisciplinary Symposium on the Trinity*, edited by Stephen T. Davis, Daniel Kendall, and Gerald O'Collins. Oxford, UK: Oxford University Press, 1999.

Owen, John. *The Doctrine of Justification by Faith*. Grand Rapids, MI: Reformation Heritage, 2006.

Owen, John. *Overcoming Sin and Temptation*. Edited by Kelly M. Kapic and Justin Taylor. Wheaton, IL: Crossway, 2006.

Packer, J. I. "Introduction to Hermann Witsius." In *Economy of the Covenants between God and Man*. Grand Rapids, MI: Reformation Heritage, 2021.

Packer, J. I. *Truth and Power: The Place of Scripture in the Christian Life*. Wheaton, IL: H. Shaw, 1996.

Perkins, William. *A Golden Chain*. Cambridge, UK: John Legate, 1600.

Rahner, Karl, and Herbert Vorgrimler. *Dictionary of Theology*, 2nd ed. New York: Crossroad, 1981.

Robertson, O. Palmer. *The Christ of the Covenants*. Phillipsburg, NJ: P&R, 1987.

Ryle, J. C. *Holiness: Its Nature, Hindrances, Difficulties, and Roots*. Moscow, ID: Charles Nolan, 2011.

Sanders, E. P. *Paul and Palestinian Judaism: A Comparison of Patterns of Religion*. 40th anniversary edition. Minneapolis: Fortress, 2017.

Scofield, C. I. *Scofield Reference Bible*. New York: Oxford University Pres, 1909.

Shedd, William G. T. *Dogmatic Theology*, 3rd ed. Phillipsburg, NJ: P&R, 2003.

Stott, John. *Baptism and Fullness*. Downers Grove, IL: InterVarsity Press, 1976.

Stott, John. *The Cross of Christ*. Downers Grove, IL: InterVarsity Press, 2006, 155, 326.

Turretin, Francis. *Institutes of Elenctic Theology*. 3 vols. Translated by George Musgrave Giger. Edited by James T. Dennison Jr. Phillipsburg, NJ: P&R, 1997.

Ursinus, Zacharias. *Commentary on the Heidelberg Catechism*. Translated by G. W. Williard. Phillipsburg, NJ: P&R, 1992.

Van Mastricht, Petrus. *Theoretical-Practical Theology*. Vol. 1, *Prolegomena*. Grand Rapids, MI: Reformation Heritage, 2018.

Wellum, Stephen. *God the Son Incarnate*. Wheaton, IL: Crossway, 2016.

Williamson, Paul R. "The *Pactum Salutis*: A Scriptural Concept or Scholastic Methodology?" *Tyndale Bulletin* 69:2, 2018: 259–83.

Witsius, Hermann. *Economy of the Covenants between God and Man*. Grand Rapids, MI: Reformation Heritage, 2021.

Wright, N. T. *Justification: God's Plan and Paul's Vision*. Downers Grove, IL: IVP Academic, 2009.

General Index

Abelard, 220
abortion, 283
Abraham, 144, 255
Abrahamic covenant, 143–44, 146, 149, 314
absolute attributes, 44
accidents, 45–46
accountability, of church members, 327
acquired knowledge, 22
active obedience of Christ, 216
active temptation, 127
acts of faith, 250–51
Adam: as historical person, 91–92; sin of, 116, 117, 122, 255; transgressed the covenant, 140; in the state of innocence, 121; as type of Christ, 91
ad extra works, 70, 71, 72, 93
ad fontes, 14–15
ad intra works, 70
Adonai, 42
adoption, 235, 236, 253, 261–62
adoptionism, 65, 181, 184, 190, 194
affection of advantage, 202
affection of righteousness, 202
affections, 107–8
afflictions, 219
Agabus, 330
Alexander, Archibald, 22, 23
alien righteousness, 253
"all Israel," 365–66
Alpha and Omega, 167, 174
already and not yet, in the new covenant, 150
amillennialism, 367
Amyraldianism, 83–84
Amyraut, Möise, 83–84
Analogical approach (creation), 90
analogical language, 38
anarchy, 40
ancient Near Eastern mythology, 50
angelic rebellion, 116
angels, 93–94

anhypostasia, 176–77
annihilation, 351–52
anonymous Christians, 237
Anselm, 23, 172, 217, 220
anthropology, 2, 9
anthropomorphisms, 53
apocalypsis, 210
Apocrypha, 30
Apollinarianism, 184, 185, 190
Apollinarius, 184, 187
apophatic theology, 43
apostles, 329
Apostles' Creed, 61, 199, 204, 282
apostolic doctrine, 283–84
arche, 16
archetypal knowledge, 9–10, 56
Arianism, 65, 67, 173, 182–83, 185, 190
Aristotle, 12, 45, 46–47, 107
Arius, 164, 173, 182–83
Arminianism, 84, 229, 241, 242–43
Arminius, Jacobus, 170, 375
assensus (assent), 250
assurance, 236, 251–52; not of the essence of faith, 252
Athanasian Creed, 61
Athanasius, 31, 172–73, 180, 217
atheists, 40
atonement, 212, 216–31; extent of, 84; necessity of, 217–18; perfection of, 218–19; sufficiency and intentionality of, 229
attributes of goodness, 44
attributes of greatness, 44
attributes of intellect, 55–56
attributes of personality, 44
attributes of power, 58–59
attributes of will, 57–58
Augustine, 10, 23, 51, 60–61, 69, 76, 94, 107, 120, 121, 154, 170, 180, 210, 217, 229, 338, 376
Aulen, Gustav, 223
authenticity, 281

gender, 108, 111
general calling, 240–41
general faith, 250
general revelation, 16, 23–24
generation, of the Son. *See* eternal generation
of the Son
gifts of the Spirit. *See* spiritual gifts
glorification, 235, 236, 239, 273–74
glorified state, 122
God: absolute perfection of, 50; aseity of,
49–50; attributes of, 36, 41, 42–43, 44–45,
48–49; as creator, 87–88; emotional life
of, 53; essence and energies of, 42–43; as
eternal, 227; existence of, 35–36; as Father,
62; glory of, 81, 92; goodness of, 38, 45,
57; as gracious, 57; holiness of, 57, 60, 81;
immanence of, 51, 59–60, 89; immensity
of, 51; immutability of, 51–52, 227; impassibility of, 53–54; incomprehensibility of,
36–37, 38; as infinite, 50–51; justice of, 206,
216, 254; knowability of, 36–37; knowledge of, 56; as long-suffering, 57; love of,
48, 57, 73, 216, 231; mercy of, 57, 82–83;
names of, 41–42; not author of sin or evil,
96; omnipotence of, 58; omnipresence of,
58; omniscience of, 58; oneness of, 62, 64;
personality of, 40–41; power of, 81, 96–97;
as *principia essendi*, 16; righteousness
of, 57–58, 114; simplicity of, 46, 48–49;
sovereignty of, 58–59, 77, 79, 82, 85, 86–87,
96, 246; spirituality of, 40–41; substantiality of, 40; transcendence of, 51, 59–60, 89;
triunity of, 41; truthfulness of, 56; unity
of, 39–40; wisdom of, 56
godliness, 265, 281
God-ness, 64
"golden chain" of salvation, 235
good deposit of faith, 20
Goodwin, Thomas, 23
good works, 236, 252, 256, 257, 265; as fruit
and evidence of justifying faith, 256; and
merit, 269–70; and salvation, 266–67; as
truly good, 268–69, 270
Gottschalk, 229
governance of the world, argument from, 35
governmental theory (atonement), 221
government (providence), 96
grace: as irresistible, 242–43; state of, 122
grace of habit, 179
grace of union, 178–79
gradation, argument from, 35
Great Awakening, 86
Great Commission, 295, 319

Greek philosophy, 47, 105
Gregory of Nazianzus, 65–66, 190
Gregory of Nyssa, 106
Grotius, Hugo, 217, 221
ground, curse of, 117
gynaikas, 334–35

hades, 347
Hahn, Scott and Kimberly, 324
hardening of Pharaoh's heart, 81
heaven, 355–56, 359–60
Heidelberg Catechism, 97, 118, 128, 180, 205,
252, 263–64, 300, 308, 309, 375
hell, 347–48; as divine punishment, 348–49
Herod, 77, 79
Higher Life theology, 265
historical argument (existence of God), 36
historical faith, 249
historic premillennialism, 366–67
Hodge, A. A., 23
Hodge, Charles, 1, 12, 23, 195, 299, 320, 376–77
holiness, 57, 114, 125, 269, 281–82
"Holy One" (name), 60
Holy Spirit: and covenant of redemption, 138;
deity of, 62; gift of, 207; glorifies the Son,
237; inner testimony of, 18–19, 252; in the
life of Jesus, 193–94; proceeds from the
Father and the Son, 63, 64, 65, 67–68, 70,
71; as our sanctifier and comforter, 73; as
Spirit of ardor and order, 343; as Spirit of
Christ, 68, 237; work of, 236–38
homoousios, 47, 183, 300
homosexuality, 111–12
Hormisdas, Pope, 54
Humanae Vitae, 110
human dignity, 115
humanism, 14–15
humanity: finitude of, 51; unique among all
God's creatures, 114–15
human nature, fourfold state, 121–22
human responsibility, 59, 77, 120
humility: in the church, 301; in prayer, 99; in
theology, 7–8
Hymenaeus, 247
hyper-Calvinists, 240–41
hypostasis, 65, 175
hypostatic union, 175, 176–77, 188, 190
hypothetical universalism, 83

"I am" statements, 158, 168, 173
I AM WHO I AM, 52, 173
idolatry, 116, 123

Scripture Index

Clearly Reformed

Theology for the Everyday

Learn and grow with thousands of resources
from the ministry of Kevin DeYoung.

Browse articles, sermons, books, podcasts,
and more at **clearlyreformed.org**.

Also Available
from Kevin DeYoung

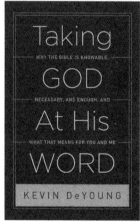

For more information, visit **crossway.org**.